*My Age of Anxiety*

ALSO BY SCOTT STOSSEL

*Sarge: The Life and Times of Sargent Shriver*

# My Age of Anxiety

*Fear, Hope, Dread and the*
*Search for Peace of Mind*

WILLIAM HEINEMANN: LONDON

Published by William Heinemann 2014

2 4 6 8 10 9 7 5 3

William Heinemann
Random House, 20 Vauxhall Bridge Road,
London SW1V 2SA

www.randomhouse.co.uk

Addresses for companies within The Random House Group Limited can be found at:
www.randomhouse.co.uk/offices.htm

The Random House Group Limited Reg. No. 954009

A CIP catalogue record for this book
is available from the British Library

ISBN 9780434019144 (Hardback)
ISBN 9780434023004 (Trade paperback)

The Random House Group Limited supports the Forest Stewardship
Council® (FSC®), the leading international forest-certification organisation.
Our books carrying the FSC label are printed on FSC®-certified paper.
FSC is the only forest-certification scheme supported by the leading
environmental organisations, including Greenpeace.
Our paper procurement policy can be found at:
www.randomhouse.co.uk/environment

Printed and bound in Great Britain by Clays Ltd, St Ives Plc

For Maren and Nathaniel—
may you be spared.

# Contents

PART V
## Redemption and Resilience

PART I

# The Riddle of Anxiety

# CHAPTER I

# The Nature of Anxiety

*And no Grand Inquisitor has in readiness such terrible tortures as has anxiety, and no spy knows how to attack more artfully the man he suspects, choosing the instant when he is weakest, nor knows how to lay traps where he will be caught and ensnared, as anxiety knows how, and no sharpwitted judge knows how to interrogate, to examine the accused as anxiety does, which never lets him escape, neither by diversion nor by noise, neither at work nor at play, neither by day nor by night.*

—SØREN KIERKEGAARD, *The Concept of Anxiety* (1844)

*There is no question that the problem of anxiety is a nodal point at which the most various and important questions converge, a riddle whose solution would be bound to throw a flood of light on our whole mental existence.*

—SIGMUND FREUD,
*Introductory Lectures on Psycho-Analysis* (1933)

I have an unfortunate tendency to falter at crucial moments.

For instance, standing at the altar in a church in Vermont, waiting for my wife-to-be to come down the aisle to marry me, I start to feel horribly ill. Not just vaguely queasy, but severely nauseated and shaky—and, most of all, sweaty. The church is hot that day—it's early July—and many people are perspiring in their summer suits and sundresses. But not like I am. As the processional plays, sweat begins to bead on my forehead and above my upper lip. In wedding photos, you can see me standing tensely at the altar, a grim half smile on my face, as I watch my fiancée come down the aisle on the arm of her father: in the photos, Susanna is glowing; I am glistening. By the time she joins me in the front of the church, rivulets of sweat are running into my eyes and dripping down my collar. We turn to face the minister. Behind him are the friends we have asked to give readings, and I see them looking at me with manifest concern. *What's wrong with him?* I imagine they are thinking. *Is he going to pass out?* Merely imagining these thoughts makes me sweat even more. My best man, standing a few feet behind me, taps me on the shoulder and hands me a tissue to mop my brow. My friend Cathy, sitting many rows back in the church, will tell me later that she had a strong urge to bring me a glass of water; it looked, she said, as if I had just run a marathon.

The wedding readers' facial expressions have gone from registering mild concern to what appears to me to be unconcealed horror: *Is he going to die?* I'm beginning to wonder that myself. For I have started to shake. I don't mean slight trembling, the sort of subtle tremor that would be evident only if I were holding a piece of paper—I feel like I'm on the verge of convulsing. I am concentrating on keeping my legs from flying out from under me like an epileptic's and am hoping that my pants are baggy enough to keep the trembling from being too visible. I'm now leaning on my almost wife—there is no hiding the trembling from her—and she is doing her best to hold me up.

The minister is droning on; I have no idea what he's saying. (I am not, as they say, present in the moment.) I'm praying for him to hurry up so I can escape this torment. He pauses and looks down at my betrothed and me. Seeing me—the sheen of flop sweat, the panic in my eyes—he is alarmed. "Are you okay?" he mouths silently. Helplessly, I nod that I am. (Because what would he do if I said that I wasn't? Clear the church? The mortification would be unbearable.)

As the minister resumes his sermon, here are three things I am actively fighting: the shaking of my limbs; the urge to vomit; and unconsciousness. And this is what I am thinking: *Get me out of here.* Why? Because there are nearly three hundred people—friends and family and colleagues—watching us get married, and I am about to collapse. I have lost control of my body. This is supposed to be one of the happiest, most significant moments of my life, and I am miserable. I worry I will not survive.

As I sweat and swoon and shake, struggling to carry out the wedding ritual (saying "I do," putting the rings on, kissing the bride), I am worrying wretchedly about what everyone (my wife's parents, her friends, my colleagues) must be thinking as they look at me: *Is he having second thoughts about getting married? Is this evidence of his essential weakness? His cowardice? His spousal unsuitability?* Any doubt that any friend of my wife's had, I fear, is being confirmed. *I knew it,* I imagine those friends thinking. *This* proves *he's not worthy of marrying her.* I look as though I've taken a shower with my clothes on. My sweat glands—my physical frailty, my weak moral fiber—have been revealed to the world. The unworthiness of my very existence has been exposed.

Mercifully, the ceremony ends. Drenched in sweat, I walk down the aisle, clinging gratefully to my new wife, and when we get outside the church, the acute physical symptoms recede. I'm not going to have convulsions. I'm not going to pass out. But as I stand in the reception line, and then drink and dance at the reception, I'm pantomiming happiness. I'm smiling for the camera, shaking hands—and wanting to die. And why not? I have failed at one of the most elemental of male jobs: getting married. How have I managed to cock this up, too? For the next seventy-two hours, I endure a brutal, self-lacerating despair.

*Anxiety kills relatively few people, but many more would welcome death as an alternative to the paralysis and suffering resulting from anxiety in its severe forms.*
—DAVID H. BARLOW, *Anxiety and Its Disorders* (2004)

My wedding was not the first time I'd broken down, nor was it the last. At the birth of our first child, the nurses had to briefly stop ministering to my wife, who was in the throes of labor, to attend to me as I turned pale and keeled over. I've frozen, mortifyingly, onstage at public lectures and presentations, and on several occasions I have been compelled to run offstage. I've abandoned dates, walked out of exams, and had breakdowns during job interviews, on plane flights, train trips, and car rides, and simply walking down the street. On ordinary days, doing ordinary things—reading a book, lying in bed, talking on the phone, sitting in a meeting, playing tennis—I have thousands of times been stricken by a pervasive sense of existential dread and been beset by nausea, vertigo, shaking, and a panoply of other physical symptoms. In these instances, I have sometimes been convinced that death, or something somehow worse, was imminent.

Even when not actively afflicted by such acute episodes, I am buffeted by worry: about my health and my family members' health; about finances; about work; about the rattle in my car and the dripping in my basement; about the encroachment of old age and the inevitability of death; about everything and nothing. Sometimes this worry gets transmuted into low-grade physical discomfort—stomachaches, headaches, dizziness, pains in my arms and legs—or a general malaise, as though I have mononucleosis or the flu. At various times, I have developed anxiety-induced difficulties breathing, swallowing, even walking; these difficulties then become obsessions, consuming all of my thinking.

I also suffer from a number of specific fears or phobias. To name a few: enclosed spaces (claustrophobia); heights (acrophobia); fainting (asthenophobia); being trapped far from home (a species of agoraphobia); germs (bacillophobia); cheese (turophobia); speaking in public (a subcategory of social phobia); flying (aerophobia); vomiting (emetophobia); and, naturally, vomiting on airplanes (aeronausiphobia).

When I was a child and my mother was attending law school at night, I spent evenings at home with a babysitter, abjectly terrified that my parents had died in a car crash or had abandoned me (the clinical term for this is "separation anxiety"); by age seven I had worn grooves in the carpet of my bedroom with my relentless pacing, trying to will my parents to come home. During first grade, I spent nearly every afternoon for months in the school nurse's office, sick with psychosomatic headaches, begging to go home; by third grade, stomachaches had replaced headaches, but my daily trudge to the infirmary remained the same. During high school, I would purposely lose tennis and squash matches to escape the agony of anxiety that competitive situations would provoke in me. On the one—the only one—date I had in high school, when the young lady leaned in for a kiss during a romantic moment (we were outside, gazing at constellations through her telescope), I was overcome by anxiety and had to pull away for fear that I would vomit. My embarrassment was such that I stopped returning her phone calls.

In short, I have since the age of about two been a twitchy bundle of phobias, fears, and neuroses. And I have, since the age of ten, when I was first taken to a mental hospital for evaluation and then referred to a psychiatrist for treatment, tried in various ways to overcome my anxiety.

Here's what I've tried: individual psychotherapy (three decades of it), family therapy, group therapy, cognitive-behavioral therapy (CBT), rational emotive therapy (RET), acceptance and commitment therapy (ACT), hypnosis, meditation, role-playing, interoceptive exposure therapy, in vivo exposure therapy, supportive-expressive therapy, eye movement desensitization and reprocessing (EMDR), self-help workbooks, massage therapy, prayer, acupuncture, yoga, Stoic philosophy, and audiotapes I ordered off a late-night TV infomercial.

And medication. Lots of medication. Thorazine. Imipramine. Desipramine. Chlorpheniramine. Nardil. BuSpar. Prozac. Zoloft. Paxil. Wellbutrin. Effexor. Celexa. Lexapro. Cymbalta. Luvox. Trazodone. Levoxyl. Propranolol. Tranxene. Serax. Centrax. St. John's wort. Zolpidem. Valium. Librium. Ativan. Xanax. Klonopin.

Also: beer, wine, gin, bourbon, vodka, and scotch.

Here's what's worked: nothing.

Actually, that's not entirely true. Some drugs have helped a little, for finite periods of time. Thorazine (an antipsychotic, which used to be classified as a major sedative) and imipramine (a tricyclic antidepressant) combined to help keep me out of the psychiatric hospital in the early 1980s, when I was in middle school and ravaged by anxiety. Desipramine, another tricyclic, got me through my early twenties. Paxil (a selective serotonin reuptake inhibitor, or SSRI) gave me about six months of significantly reduced anxiety in my late twenties before the fear broke through again. Ample quantities of Xanax, propranolol, and vodka got me (barely) through a book tour and various public lectures and TV appearances in my early thirties. A double scotch plus a Xanax and a Dramamine can sometimes, when administered before takeoff, make flying tolerable—and two double scotches, when administered in quick enough succession, can obscure existential dread, making it seem fuzzier and further away.

But none of these treatments have fundamentally reduced the underlying anxiety that seems woven into my soul and hardwired into my body and that at times makes my life a misery. As the years pass, the hope of being cured of my anxiety has faded into a resigned desire to come to terms with it, to find some redemptive quality or mitigating benefit to my being, too often, a quivering, quaking, neurotic wreck.

*Anxiety is the most prominent mental characteristic of Occidental civilization.*
    —R. R. WILLOUGHBY, *Magic and Cognate Phenomena* (1935)

Anxiety and its associated disorders represent the most common form of officially classified mental illness in the United States today, more common even than depression and other mood disorders. According to the National Institute of Mental Health, some forty million Americans, nearly one in seven of us, are suffering from some kind of anxiety disorder at any given time, accounting for 31 percent of the expenditures on mental health care in the United States. According to recent epidemiological data, the "lifetime incidence" of anxiety disorder is more than 25 percent—which, if true, means that one in four of us can expect to be stricken by debilitating anxiety at some point in our lifetimes. And it *is* debilitating: Recent academic papers have argued that the psychic and physical impairment tied to living with an anxiety disorder is equivalent to living with diabetes—usually manageable, sometimes fatal, and always a pain to deal with. A study published in *The American Journal of Psychiatry* in 2006 found that Americans lose a collective 321 million days of work because of anxiety and depression each year, costing the economy $50 billion annually; a 2001 paper published by the U.S. Bureau of Labor Statistics once estimated that the median number of days missed each year by American workers who suffer from anxiety or stress disorders is twenty-five. In 2005—three years before the recent economic crisis hit—Americans filled fifty-three million prescriptions for just two antianxiety drugs: Ativan and Xanax. (In the weeks after 9/11, Xanax prescriptions jumped 9 percent nationally—and by 22 percent in New York City.) In September 2008, the economic crash caused prescriptions in New York City to spike: as banks went belly up and the stock market went into free fall, prescriptions for antidepressant and antianxiety medications increased 9 percent over the year before, while prescriptions for sleeping pills increased 11 percent.

Though some have argued that anxiety is a particularly American affliction, it's not just Americans who suffer from it. A report published in 2009 by the Mental Health Foundation in England found that fifteen percent of people living in the United Kingdom are currently suffering from an anxiety disorder and that rates are increasing: 37 percent of British people report feeling more frightened than they used to. A recent paper in *The Journal of the American Medical Association* observed that clinical anxiety is the most common emotional disorder in many countries. A comprehensive global review of anxiety studies published in 2006 in *The Canadian Journal of Psychiatry* concluded that as many as one in six people worldwide will be afflicted with an anxiety disorder for at least a year during some point in their lifetimes; other studies have reported similar findings.

Of course, these figures refer only to people, like me, who are, according to the somewhat arbitrary diagnostic criteria established by the American Psychiatric Association, technically classifiable as *clinically* anxious. But anxiety extends far beyond the population of the officially mentally ill. Primary care physicians report that anxiety is one of the most frequent complaints driving patients to their offices—more frequent, by some accounts, than the common cold. One large-scale study from 1985 found that anxiety prompted more than 11 percent of all visits to family doctors; a study the following year reported that as many as one in three patients complained to their family physicians of "severe anxiety." (Other studies have reported that 20 percent of primary care patients in America are taking a benzodiazepine such as Valium or Xanax.) And almost everyone alive has at some point experienced the torments of anxiety—or of fear or of stress or of worry, which are distinct but related phenomena. (Those who are unable to experience anxiety are, generally speaking, more deeply pathological—and more dangerous to society—than those who experience it acutely or irrationally; they're sociopaths.)

Few people today would dispute that chronic stress is a hallmark of our times or that anxiety has become a kind of cultural condition of modernity. We live, as has been said many times since the dawn of the atomic era, in an age of anxiety—and that, cliché though it may be, seems only to have become more true in recent years as America has been assaulted in short order by terrorism, economic calamity and disruption, and widespread social transformation.

And yet, as recently as thirty years ago, anxiety per se did not exist as a clinical category. In 1950, when the psychoanalyst Rollo May published *The Meaning of Anxiety*, he observed that at that point only two others, Søren Kierkegaard and Sigmund Freud, had undertaken book-length treatments of the idea of anxiety. In 1927, according to the listing in *Psychological Abstracts*, only three academic papers on anxiety were published; in 1941, there were only fourteen; and as late as 1950, there were only thirty-seven. The first-ever academic conference dedicated solely to the topic of anxiety didn't take place until June 1949. Only in 1980—after new drugs designed to treat anxiety had been developed and brought to market—were the anxiety disorders finally introduced into the third edition of the American Psychiatric Association's *Diagnostic and Statistical Manual of Mental Disorders,* displacing the Freudian neuroses. In an important sense, the treatment predated the diagnosis—that is, the discovery of antianxiety drugs drove the creation of anxiety as a diagnostic category.

Today, thousands of papers about anxiety are published each year; several academic journals are wholly dedicated to it. Anxiety research is constantly yielding new discoveries and insights not only about the causes of and treatments for anxiety but also, more generally, about how the mind works—about the relationships between mind and body, between genes and behavior, and between molecules and emotion. Using functional magnetic resonance imaging (fMRI) technology, we can now map various subjectively experienced emotions onto specific parts of the brain and can even distinguish various types of anxiety based on their visible effect on brain function. For instance, generalized worry about future events (my concern about whether the publishing industry will survive long enough for this book to come out, say, or about whether my kids will be able to afford to go to college) tends to appear as hyperactivity in the frontal lobes of the cerebral cortex.

The severe anxiety that some people experience while speaking in public (like the sheer terror—dulled by drugs and alcohol—that I experienced while giving a lecture the other day) or that some extremely shy people experience in socializing tends to show up as excessive activity in what's called the anterior cingulate. Obsessive-compulsive anxiety, meanwhile, can manifest itself on a brain scan as a disturbance in the circuit linking the frontal lobes with the lower brain centers within the basal ganglia. We now know, thanks to pioneering research by the neuroscientist Joseph LeDoux in the 1980s, that most fearful emotions and behaviors are in one way or another produced by, or at least processed through, the amygdala, a tiny almond-shaped organ at the base of the brain that has become the target of much of the neuroscientific research on anxiety over the last fifteen years.

We also know far more than Freud or Kierkegaard did about how different neurotransmitters—such as serotonin, dopamine, gamma-aminobutyric acid, norepinephrine, and neuropeptide Y—reduce or increase anxiety. And we know there is a strong genetic component to anxiety; we are even starting to learn in some detail what that component consists of. In 2002, to cite just one example among many hundreds, researchers at Harvard University identified what the media called the "Woody Allen gene" because it activates a specific group of neurons in the amygdala and elsewhere in the crucial parts of the neural circuit governing fearful behavior. Today, researchers are homing in on numerous such "candidate genes," measuring the statistical association between certain genetic variations and certain anxiety disorders and exploring the chemical and neuroanatomical mechanisms that "mediate" this association, trying to discover precisely what it is that converts a genetic predisposition into an actual anxious emotion or disorder.

"The real excitement here, both in the study of anxiety as an emotion and in the class of disorders," says Dr. Thomas Insel, the head of the National Institute of Mental Health, "is that it's one of the places where we can begin to make the transition between understanding the molecules, the cells, and the system right to the emotion and behavior. We are now finally able to draw the lines between the genes, the cells, and the brain and brain systems."

*Fear arises from a weakness of mind and therefore does not apper-
tain to the use of reason.*
—BARUCH SPINOZA (CIRCA 1670)

And yet for all the advances brought by the study of neurochemistry and neuroanatomy, my own experience suggests that the psychological field remains riven by disputes over what causes anxiety and how to
treat it. The psychopharmacologists and psychiatrists I've consulted tell
me that drugs are a *treatment* for my anxiety; the cognitive-behavioral
therapists I've consulted sometimes tell me that drugs are partly a *cause*
of it.

The clash between cognitive-behavioral therapy and psychopharmacology is merely the latest iteration of a debate that is several millennia old. Molecular biology, biochemistry, regression analysis, and
functional magnetic resonance imaging—all of these developments
have made possible discoveries and scientific rigor, as well as courses
of treatment, that Freud and his intellectual forebears could scarcely
have dreamed of. Yet while what Thomas Insel of the NIMH says
about anxiety research being at the cutting edge of scientific inquiry
into human psychology is true, it is also true that in an important sense
there is nothing new under the sun.

The cognitive-behavioral therapists' antecedents can be traced to
the seventeenth-century Jewish-Dutch philosopher Baruch Spinoza,
who believed anxiety was a mere problem of logic. Faulty thinking
causes us to fear things we cannot control, Spinoza argued, presag-
ing by more than three hundred years the cognitive-behavioral therapists' arguments about faulty cognitions. (If we can't control something,
there's no value in fearing it, since the fear accomplishes nothing.) Spinoza's philosophy seemed to have worked for him; biographies report
him to have been a notably serene individual. Some sixteen hundred
years before Spinoza, the Stoic philosopher Epictetus anticipated the
same idea about faulty cognitions. "People are not disturbed by things
but by the view they take of them," he wrote in the first century; for
Epictetus, the roots of anxiety lay not in our biology but in how we
apprehend reality. Alleviating anxiety is a matter of "correcting errone-

ous perceptions" (as the cognitive-behavioral therapists say). The Stoics, in fact, may be the true progenitors of cognitive-behavioral therapy. When Seneca, a contemporary of Epictetus, wrote, "There are more things to alarm us than to harm us, and we suffer more in apprehension than in reality," he was prefiguring by twenty centuries what Aaron Beck, the official founder of CBT, would say in the 1950s.*

The intellectual antecedents of modern psychopharmacology lie even further in the past. Hippocrates, the ancient Greek doctor, concluded in the fourth century B.C. that pathological anxiety was a straightforward biological and medical problem. "If you cut open the head [of a mentally ill individual]," Hippocrates wrote, "you will find the brain humid, full of sweat and smelling badly." For Hippocrates, "body juices" were the cause of madness; a sudden flood of bile to the brain would produce anxiety. (Following Hippocrates, Aristotle placed great weight on the temperature of bile: warm bile generated warmth and enthusiasm; cold bile produced anxiety and cowardice.) In Hippocrates's view, anxiety and other psychiatric disorders were a medical-biological problem best treated by getting the humors back into proper equilibrium.†

But Plato and his adherents, for their part, believed that psychic life was autonomous from physiology and disagreed with the idea that anxiety or melancholy had an organic basis in the body; the biological model of mental illness was, as one ancient Greek philosopher put it, "as vain as a child's story." In Plato's view, while physicians could sometimes provide relief for minor psychological ailments (because sometimes emotional problems are refracted into the body), deep-seated emotional problems could be addressed only by philosophers. Anxiety

---

* Seneca was also in some sense anticipating FDR's famous formulation: "The only thing we have to fear is fear itself."

† Hippocrates believed that staying in good physical and mental health required maintaining the right balance of what he called the four humors, or bodily fluids: blood, phlegm, black bile, and yellow bile. A person's relative humoral balance accounted for his temperament: whereas someone with relatively more blood might have a fiery complexion and a lively or "sanguine" temperament and be given to hot-blooded explosions of temper, someone with relatively more black bile might have swarthy skin and a melancholic temperament. An optimal mixture of the humors (*eucrasia*) produced a state of health; when the humors fell into disequilibrium (*dyscrasia*), the result was disease. Though Hippocrates's humoral theory of mind is now discredited, it persisted for two thousand years, until the 1700s, and it lives on still in our use of words like "bilious" and "phlegmatic" to describe people's personalities—and in the biomedical approach to anxiety and mental illness generally.

and other mental discomfort arose not from physiological imbalances but from disharmony of the soul; recovery demanded deeper self-knowledge, more self-control, and a way of life guided by philosophy. Plato believed that (as one historian of science has put it) "if one's body and mind are in generally good shape, a doctor can come along and put minor ills to right just as one might call in a plumber; but if the general fabric is impaired, a physician is useless." Philosophy, in this view, was the only proper method for treating the soul.

Poppycock, said Hippocrates: "All that philosophers have written on natural science no more pertains to medicine than to painting," he declared.*

Is pathological anxiety a medical illness, as Hippocrates and Aristotle and modern pharmacologists would have it? Or is it a philosophical problem, as Plato and Spinoza and the cognitive-behavioral therapists would have it? Is it a psychological problem, a product of childhood trauma and sexual inhibition, as Freud and his acolytes would have it? Or is it a spiritual condition, as Søren Kierkegaard and his existentialist descendants claimed? Or, finally, is it—as W. H. Auden and David Riesman and Erich Fromm and Albert Camus and scores of modern commentators have declared—a cultural condition, a function of the times we live in and the structure of our society?

The truth is that anxiety is at once a function of biology and philosophy, body and mind, instinct and reason, personality and culture. Even as anxiety is experienced at a spiritual and psychological level, it is scientifically measurable at the molecular level and the physiological level. It is produced by nature and it is produced by nurture. It's a psychological phenomenon and a sociological phenomenon. In computer terms, it's both a hardware problem (I'm wired badly) and a software problem (I run faulty logic programs that make me think anxious thoughts). The origins of a temperament are many faceted; emotional dispositions that may seem to have a simple, single source—a bad gene, say, or a child-

---

* Or someone who followed him declared. Most historians believe that what have come down to us as the so-called Hippocratic writings were in fact produced by a number of doctors who were followers of Hippocrates. Some of the writings in the corpus seem to date from after his death and are believed to have been written by his son-in-law Polybus; Hippocrates's sons Draco and Thessalus also became famous doctors. For simplicity's sake, I treat Hippocrates's writing as the work of one man, since the mode of thinking that the writings represent derives from him.

hood trauma—may not. After all, who's to say that Spinoza's vaunted equanimity didn't derive less from his philosophy than from his biology? Mightn't a genetically programmed low level of autonomic arousal have produced his serene philosophy, rather than the other way around?

> *Neuroses are generated not only by incidental individual experiences, but also by the specific cultural conditions under which we live. . . . It is an individual fate, for example, to have a domineering or a "self-sacrificing" mother, but it is only under definite cultural conditions that we find domineering or self-sacrificing mothers.*
> —KAREN HORNEY, *The Neurotic Personality of Our Time* (1937)

I don't have to look far to find evidence of anxiety as a family trait. My great-grandfather Chester Hanford, for many years the dean of students at Harvard, was in the late 1940s admitted to McLean Hospital, the famous mental institution in Belmont, Massachusetts, suffering from acute anxiety. The last thirty years of his life were often agony. Though medication and electroshock treatments would occasionally bring about remissions in his suffering, such respites were temporary, and in his darkest moments in the 1960s he was reduced to a fetal ball in his bedroom, producing what my parents recall as an inhuman-sounding moaning. Weighed down by the responsibility of caring for him, his wife, my great-grandmother, a formidable and brilliant woman, died from an overdose of scotch and sleeping pills in 1969.

Chester Hanford's son is my maternal grandfather. Now ninety-three years old, he is an extremely accomplished and, to outward appearances, confident man. But he has a worry-prone temperament and for much of his life has been burdened by a collection of rituals typical of obsessive-compulsive disorder (OCD), which is officially classified as a species of anxiety disorder. For instance, he will never leave a building other than through the door he came in, a superstition that sometimes leads to complex logistical maneuverings. My mother, in turn, is a high-strung and inveterate worrier and suffers from many of the same phobias and neuroses that I do. She assiduously avoids heights (glass elevators, chairlifts), public speaking, and risk taking of most kinds. Like me, she is also mortally terrified of vomiting. As a young woman, she suffered from frequent and severe panic attacks. At her most anxious (or so my father, her ex-husband, insists), her fears verged on paranoia: while pregnant with me, my father says, she became convinced that a serial killer in a yellow Volkswagen was watching our apartment.* My only sibling, a younger sister, struggles with anxiety that is different from mine but nonetheless intense. She, too, has taken Celexa—and also Prozac and Wellbutrin and Nardil and Neurontin and BuSpar. None of them worked for her, and today she may be one of the few adult members of my mother's side of the family not currently taking a psychiatric medication. (Various other relatives on my mother's side have also relied on antidepressants and antianxiety medications continuously for many years.)

On the evidence of just these four generations on my mother's side (and there is a separate complement of psychopathology coming down to me on the side of my father, who drank himself into unconsciousness five nights out of every seven throughout much of my later childhood), it is not outlandish to conclude that I possess a genetic predisposition to anxiety and depression.

But these facts, by themselves, are not dispositive—because is it not possible that the bequeathing of anxiety from one generation to the next on my mother's side had nothing to do with genes and everything to do with the environment? In the 1920s, my great-grandparents had a young child who died of an infection. This was devastating to them. Perhaps this trauma, combined with the later trauma of having many of his students die in World War II, cracked something in my great-grandfather's psyche—and, for that matter, in my grandfather's. My grandfather was in elementary school at the time of his brother's death and can remember sitting alongside the tiny casket as the hearse drove to the cemetery. Perhaps my mother, in turn, acquired her own anxieties by witnessing the superstitions and obsessions of her father and the emotional anguish of her grandfather (not to mention the anxious ministrations of her worrywart mother); the psychological term for this

---

* Today, my mother and father, now divorced fifteen years, disagree about the severity of the paranoia: my father insists it was considerable; my mother says it was minor (and that, for that matter, there was actually a serial killer afoot at the time).

is "modeling." And perhaps I, observing my mother's phobias, adopted them as my own. While there is substantial evidence that specific phobias—particularly those based on fears that would have been adaptive in the state of nature, like phobias of heights or snakes or rodents—are genetically transmittable, or "evolutionarily conserved," isn't it just as plausible, if not more so, to conclude that I learned to be fearful by watching my mother be fearful? Or that the generally unsettled nature of my childhood psychological environment—my mother's constant anxious buzzing, my father's alcoholic absence, the unhappy tumult of their marriage that would end in divorce—produced in me a comparably unsettled sensibility? Or that my mother's paranoia and panic while pregnant with me produced such hormonal Sturm und Drang in the womb that I was doomed to be born nervous? Research suggests that mothers who suffer stress while pregnant are more likely to produce anxious children.* Thomas Hobbes, the political philosopher, was born prematurely when his mother, terrified by the news that the Spanish Armada was advancing toward English shores, went into labor early in April 1588. "Myself and fear were born twins," Hobbes wrote, and he attributed his own anxious temperament to his mother's terror-induced premature labor. Perhaps Hobbes's view that a powerful state needs to protect citizens from the violence and misery they naturally inflict on one another (life, he famously said, is nasty, brutish, and short) was founded on the anxious temperament imbued in him in utero by his mother's stress hormones.

Or do the roots of my anxiety lie deeper and broader than the things I've experienced and the genes I've inherited—that is, in history and in culture? My father's parents were Jews who fled the Nazis in the 1930s. My father's mother became a nastily anti-Semitic Jew—she renounced her Jewishness out of fear that she would someday be persecuted for it. My younger sister and I were raised in the Episcopal Church, our Jewish background hidden from us until I was in college. My father, for his part, has had a lifelong fascination with World War II, and spe-

---

* One study found that children whose mothers were pregnant with them on September 11, 2001, still had elevated levels of stress hormones in their blood at six months. Similar findings—showing as-yet-unborn children acquiring higher lifetime baseline levels of stressed-out physiology—have been reported during war and other chaotic times.

cifically with the Nazis; he watched the television series *The World at War* again and again. In my memory, that program, with its stentorian music accompanying the Nazi advance on Paris, is the running sound track to my early childhood.* The long-persecuted Jews, of course, have millennia of experience in having reason to be scared—which perhaps explains why some studies have shown that Jewish men suffer from depression and anxiety at rates higher than men in other ethnic groups.†

My mother's cultural heritage, on the other hand, was heavily WASP; she is a proud *Mayflower* descendant who until recently subscribed wholeheartedly to the notion that there is no emotion and no family issue that should not be suppressed.

Thus, me: a mixture of Jewish and WASP pathology—a neurotic and histrionic Jew suppressed inside a neurotic and repressed WASP. No wonder I'm anxious: I'm like Woody Allen trapped in John Calvin.

Or is my anxiety, after all, "normal"—a natural response to the times we live in? I was in middle school when *The Day After*, about the dystopian aftermath of a nuclear attack, aired on network television. As an adolescent, I regularly had dreams that ended with a missile streaking across the sky. Were these dreams evidence of anxious psychopathology? Or a reasonable reaction to the conditions I perceived—which were, after all, the same conditions that preoccupied defense policy analysts through the 1980s? The Cold War, of course, has now long since ended—but it has been replaced by the threat of hijacked airplanes, dirty bombs, underwear bombers, chemical attacks, and anthrax, not to mention SARS, swine flu, drug-resistant tuberculosis, the prospect of climate-change-induced global apocalypse, and the abiding stresses of a worldwide economic slowdown and of a global economy undergoing seemingly constant upheaval. Insofar as it's possible to measure such things, eras of social transformation seem to produce a quantum

---

* When my mother was attending law school at night, my sister and I would spend evenings moping around the house while my father played Bach fugues on the piano and then parked himself with a bowl of popcorn and a bottle of gin in front of *The World at War*.

† There's also evidence that the high IQ scores of Ashkenazi Jews are attached somehow to the high anxiety rates of that same group, and there are plausible evolutionary explanations for why both intelligence and imagination tend to be allied with anxiety. (Various studies have found that the average IQ of Ashkenazi Jews is eight points higher than that of the next highest ethnic group, Northeast Asians, and close to a full standard deviation higher than other European groups.)

increase in the anxiety of the population. In our postindustrial era of economic uncertainty, where social structures are undergoing continuous disruption and where professional and gender roles are constantly changing, is it not normal—adaptive even—to be anxious?

At some level, yes, it is—at least to the extent that it is always, or often, adaptive to be reasonably anxious. According to Charles Darwin (who himself suffered from crippling agoraphobia that left him housebound for years after his voyage on the *Beagle*), species that "fear rightly" increase their chances of survival. We anxious people are less likely to remove ourselves from the gene pool by, say, frolicking on the edge of cliffs or becoming fighter pilots.

An influential study conducted a hundred years ago by two Harvard psychologists, Robert M. Yerkes and John Dillingham Dodson, demonstrated that moderate levels of anxiety *improve* performance in humans and animals: too much anxiety, obviously, and performance is impaired, but too *little* anxiety also impairs performance. When the use of antianxiety drugs exploded in the 1950s, some psychiatrists warned about the dangers presented by a society that was not anxious enough. "We then face the prospect of developing a falsely flaccid race of people which might not be too good for our future," one wrote. Another psychiatrist averred that "Van Gogh, Isaac Newton: most of the geniuses and great creators were not tranquil. They were nervous, ego-driven men pushed on by a relentless inner force and beset by anxieties."

Is muting such genius a price society would have to pay for drastically reducing anxiety, pharmacologically or otherwise? And would that cost be worthwhile?

"Without anxiety, little would be accomplished," says David Barlow, the founder and director emeritus of the Center for Anxiety and Related Disorders at Boston University. "The performance of athletes, entertainers, executives, artisans, and students would suffer; creativity would diminish; crops might not be planted. And we would all achieve that idyllic state long sought after in our fast-paced society of whiling away our lives under a shade tree. This would be as deadly for the species as nuclear war."

*I have come to believe that anxiety accompanies intellectual activity
as its shadow and that the more we know of the nature of anxiety,
the more we will know of intellect.*
— HOWARD LIDDELL, "THE ROLE OF VIGILANCE IN THE
DEVELOPMENT OF ANIMAL NEUROSIS" (1949)

Some eighty years ago, Freud proposed that anxiety was "a riddle
whose solution would be bound to throw a flood of light on our whole
mental existence." Unlocking the mysteries of anxiety, he believed,
would go far in helping us to unravel the mysteries of the mind: consciousness, the self, identity, intellect, imagination, creativity—not to
mention pain, suffering, hope, and regret. To grapple with and understand anxiety is, in some sense, to grapple with and understand the
human condition.

The differences in how various cultures and eras have perceived and
understood anxiety can tell us a lot about those cultures and eras. Why
did the ancient Greeks of the Hippocratic school see anxiety mainly as
a medical condition, while the Enlightenment philosophers saw it as
an intellectual problem? Why did the early existentialists see anxiety
as a spiritual condition, while Gilded Age doctors saw it as a specifically
Anglo-Saxon stress response—a response that they believed spared
Catholic societies—to the Industrial Revolution? Why did the early
Freudians see anxiety as a psychological condition emanating from
sexual inhibition, whereas our own age tends to see it, once again, as
a medical and neurochemical condition, a problem of malfunctioning
biomechanics?

Do these shifting interpretations represent the forward march of
progress and science? Or simply the changing, and often cyclical, ways
in which cultures work? What does it say about the societies in question that Americans showing up in emergency rooms with panic attacks
tend to believe they're having heart attacks, whereas Japanese tend to
be afraid they're going to faint? Are the Iranians who complain of what
they call "heart distress" suffering what Western psychiatrists would call
panic attacks? Are the *ataques de nervios* experienced by South Americans simply panic attacks with a Latino inflection—or are they, as mod-

ern researchers now believe, a distinct cultural and medical syndrome? Why do drug treatments for anxiety that work so well on Americans and the French seem not to work effectively on the Chinese?

As fascinating and multifarious as these cultural idiosyncrasies are, the underlying consistency of experience across time and cultures speaks to the universality of anxiety as a human trait. Even filtered through the distinctive cultural practices and beliefs of the Greenland Inuit a hundred years ago, the syndrome the Inuit called "kayak angst" (those afflicted by it were afraid to go out seal hunting alone) appears to be little different from what we today call agoraphobia. In Hippocrates's ancient writings can be found clinical descriptions of pathological anxiety that sound quite modern. One of his patients was terrified of cats (simple phobia, which today would be coded 300.29 for insurance purposes, according to the classifications of the fifth edition of the *Diagnostic and Statistical Manual,* the *DSM-V*) and another of nightfall; a third, Hippocrates reported, was "beset by terror" whenever he heard a flute; a fourth could not walk alongside "even the shallowest ditch," though he had no problem walking *inside* the ditch—evidence of what we would today call acrophobia, the fear of heights. Hippocrates also describes a patient suffering what would likely be called, in modern diagnostic terminology, panic disorder with agoraphobia (*DSM-V* code 300.22): the condition, as Hippocrates described it, "usually attacks abroad, if a person is travelling a lonely road somewhere, and fear seizes him." The syndromes described by Hippocrates are recognizably the same clinical phenomena described in the latest issues of the *Archives of General Psychiatry* and *Bulletin of the Menninger Clinic.*

Their similarities bridge the yawning gap of millennia and circumstances that separate them, providing a sense of how, for all the differences in culture and setting, the physiologically anxious aspects of human experience may be universal.

In this book, I have set out to explore the "riddle" of anxiety. I am not a doctor, a psychologist, a sociologist, or a historian of science—any one of whom would bring more scholarly authority to a treatise on anxiety than I do. This is a work of synthesis and reportage, yoking together explorations of the idea of anxiety from history, literature, philosophy, religion, popular culture, and the latest scientific research—all of that woven through something about which I can, alas, claim extensive expertise: my own experience with anxiety. Examining the depths of my own neuroses may seem the height of narcissism (and studies do show that self-preoccupation tends to be tied to anxiety), but it's an exercise with worthy antecedents. In 1621, the Oxford scholar Robert Burton published his canonical *The Anatomy of Melancholy*, a staggering thirteen-hundred-page work of synthesis, whose torrents of scholarly exegesis only partially obscure what it really is: a massive litany of anxious, depressive complaint. In 1733, George Cheyne, a prominent London physician and one of the most influential psychological thinkers of the eighteenth century, published *The English Malady*, which includes the forty-page chapter "The Case of the Author" (dedicated to "my fellow sufferers"), in which he reports in minute detail on his neuroses (including "Fright, Anxiety, Dread, and Terror" and "a melancholy Fright and Panick, where my Reason was of no Use to me") and physical symptoms (including "a sudden violent Head-ach," "extream Sickness in my Stomach," and "a constant Colick, and an ill Taste and Savour in my Mouth") over the years. More recently, the intellectual odysseys of Charles Darwin, Sigmund Freud, and William James were powerfully driven by their curiosity about, and the desire to find relief from, their own anxious suffering. Freud used his acute train phobia and his hypochondria, among other things, to construct his theory of psychoanalysis; Darwin was effectively housebound by stress-related illnesses after the voyage of the *Beagle*—he spent years in pursuit of relief from his anxiety, visiting spas and, on the advice of one doctor, encasing himself in ice. James tried to keep his phobias hidden from the public but was often quietly terrified. "I awoke morning after morning with a horrible dread in the pit of my stomach and with a sense of insecurity of life that I never knew before," he wrote in 1902 of the onset of his anxiety. "For months, I was unable to go out in the dark alone."

Unlike Darwin, Freud, and James, I'm not out to adumbrate a whole new theory of mind or of human nature. Rather, this book is motivated by a quest to understand, and to find relief from or redemption in, anxious suffering. This quest has taken me both backward, into history, and forward, to the frontiers of modern scientific research. I have spent much of the past eight years reading through hundreds of thousands of the pages that have been written about anxiety over the last three thousand years.

My life has, thankfully, lacked great tragedy or melodrama. I haven't served any jail time. I haven't been to rehab. I haven't assaulted anyone or carried out a suicide attempt. I haven't woken up naked in the middle of a field, sojourned in a crack house, or been fired from a job for erratic behavior. As psychopathologies go, mine has been—so far, most of the time, to outward appearances—quiet. Robert Downey Jr. will not be starring in the movie of my life. I am, as they say in the clinical literature, "high functioning" for someone with an anxiety disorder or a mental illness; I'm usually quite good at hiding it. More than a few people, some of whom think they know me quite well, have remarked that they are struck that I, who can seem so even-keeled and imperturbable, would choose to write a book about anxiety. I smile gently while churning inside and thinking about what I've learned is a signature characteristic of the phobic personality: "the need and ability"—as described in the self-help book *Your Phobia*—"to present a relatively placid, untroubled appearance to others, while suffering extreme distress on the inside."*

To some people, I may seem calm. But if you could peer beneath the surface, you would see that I'm like a duck—paddling, paddling, paddling.

*The chief patient I am preoccupied with is myself.*
    —SIGMUND FREUD TO WILHELM FLIESS (AUGUST 1897)

It has occurred to me that writing this book might be a terrible idea: if it's relief from nervous suffering that I crave, then burrowing into the history and science of anxiety, and into my own psyche, is perhaps not the best way to achieve it.

---

* "For many, many people who have anxiety disorders—particularly agoraphobia and panic disorder—people would be surprised to find out that they have problems with anxiety because they seem so 'together' and in control," says Paul Foxman, a psychologist who heads the Center for Anxiety Disorders in Burlington, Vermont. "They seem to be comfortable, but there's a disconnection between the public self and the private self."

In my travels through the historical literature on anxiety, I came across a little self-help book by a British army veteran named Wilfrid Northfield, who suffered nervous prostration during the First World War and then spent ten years largely incapacitated by anxiety before successfully convalescing and writing his guide to recovery. Published in 1933, *Conquest of Nerves: The Inspiring Record of a Personal Triumph over Neurasthenia*, became a best seller; the copy I have is from the sixth printing, in 1934. In his last chapter, "A Few Final Words," Northfield writes: "There is one thing the neurasthenic must guard against very strongly, and that is talking about his troubles. He can get no comfort or assistance in so doing." Northfield goes on: "To talk of troubles in a voluble, despairing way, merely piles on the agony and 'plays-up' the emotions. Not only so, but it is selfish." Citing another author, he concludes: "'Never display a wound, except to a physician."

*Never display a wound*. Well, after more than thirty years of endeavoring—successfully much of the time—to conceal my anxiety from people, here I am putting it on protracted exhibition for acquaintances and strangers alike. If Northfield is correct (and my worried mother agrees with him), this project can hardly be auspicious for my mental health. Elements of modern research lend support to Northfield's warning: anxious people have a pathological tendency to focus their attention inward, on themselves, in a way that suggests a book-length dwelling on one's own anxiety is hardly the best way to escape it.*

Moreover, one concern I've had about writing this book is that I've subsisted professionally on my ability to project calmness and control; my anxiety makes me conscientious (I'm afraid of screwing things up), and my shame can make me seem poised (I need to hide that I'm anxious). A former colleague once described me as "human Xanax," telling me, as I chuckled inwardly, that I project such equanimity that my mere presence can be calming to others: simply to walk into a room full of

---

* David Barlow, one of the preeminent researchers in the field, notes (in the jargon-intensive terminology of the specialist) that pathological, negative self-focus "seems to be an integral part of the cognitive-affective structure of anxiety. This negative self-evaluative focus and disruption of attention is in large part responsible for decreases in performance. This attention shift in turn contributes to a vicious cycle of anxious apprehension, in which increasing anxiety leads to further attentional shifts, increased performance deficits, and subsequent spiraling of arousal."

agitated people is to administer my soothing balm; people relax in my wake. If only she knew! By revealing the fraudulence of my putative calm, am I forfeiting my ability to soothe others and thereby compromising my professional standing?

My current therapist, Dr. W., says there is always the possibility that revealing my anxiety will lift the burden of shame and reduce the isolation of solitary suffering. When I get skittish about airing my psychiatric issues in a book, Dr. W. says: "You've been keeping your anxiety a secret for years, right? How's that working out for you?"

Point taken. And there is a rich and convincing literature about how—contrary to the admonitions of Wilfrid Northfield (and my mother)—hiding or suppressing anxiety actually produces *more* anxiety.* But there is no escaping my concern that this exercise is not only self-absorbed and shameful but risky—that it will prove the Wile E. Coyote moment when I look down to discover that, instead of inner strengths or outer buttresses to support me, there is in fact nothing to stop me from falling a long way down.

> *I know how indecent and shocking Egotism is, and for an Author to make himself the Subject of his Words or Works, especially in so tedious and circumstantiated a Detail: But . . . I thought . . . perhaps it may not be quite useless to some low desponding valetudinary, over-grown Person, whose Case may have some Resemblance to mine.*
>
> —GEORGE CHEYNE, *The English Malady* (1733)

"Why," Dr. W. asks, "do you think writing about your anxiety in a book would be so shameful?"

Because stigma still attaches to mental illness. Because anxiety is seen as weakness. Because, as the signs posted on Allied gun installations in Malta during World War II so bluntly put it, "if you are a man you will not permit your self-respect to admit an anxiety neurosis or to show fear." Because I worry that this book, with its revelations of anxi-

---

* On the desk in front of me is a 1997 article from the *Journal of Abnormal Psychology* called "Hiding Feelings: The Acute Effects of Inhibiting Negative and Positive Emotions."

ety and struggle, will be a litany of Too Much Information, a violation of basic standards of restraint and decorum.*

When I explain this to Dr. W., he says that the very act of working on this book, and of publishing it, could be therapeutic. In presenting my anxiety to the world, he says, I will be "coming out." The implication is that this will be liberating, as though I were gay and coming out of the closet. But being gay—we now finally know (homosexuality was classified as a mental disorder by the American Psychiatric Association until 1973)—is not a weakness or a defect or an illness. Being excessively nervous is.

For a long time, governed by reticence and shame, I had told people who inquired about my book that it was "a cultural and intellectual history of anxiety"—true, as far as it goes—without revealing its personal aspects. But a little while ago, in an effort to test the effects of "coming out" as anxious, I began gingerly to speak more forthrightly about what the book was about: "a cultural and intellectual history of anxiety, *woven together by my own experiences with anxiety.*"

The effect was striking. When I had spoken about the book as arid history, people would nod politely, and a few would buttonhole me privately later to ask me specific questions about this or that aspect of anxiety. But as I started to acknowledge the personal parts of the book, I found myself surrounded by avid listeners, eager to tell me about their own, or their family members', anxiety.

One night I attended a dinner with a bunch of writers and artists. Someone asked what I was working on, and I delivered my new spiel ("a cultural and intellectual history of anxiety, *woven together and animated by my own experiences with anxiety*"), talking about some of my experiences with various antianxiety and antidepressant medications. To my astonishment, *each of the other nine people within earshot* responded by telling me a story about his or her own experience with

---

* As I write this, I can hear the strains of what may be my better judgment: *Even if you are so unfortunate as to be excessively anxious, at least have the dignity not to prattle on about it publicly. Keep a stiff upper lip, and keep it to yourself.*

anxiety and medication.* Around the table we went, sharing our tales of neurotic woe.†

I was struck that admitting my own anxiety over dinner had dislodged such an avalanche of personal confessions of anxiety and pharmacotherapy. Granted, I was with a bunch of writers and artists, a population ostensibly more prone, as observers since Aristotle have noted, to various forms of mental illness than other people. So maybe these stories simply provide evidence that writers are crazy. Or maybe the stories are evidence that the pharmaceutical companies have succeeded in medicalizing a normal human experience and marketing drugs to "treat" it.‡ But maybe more people than I thought are struggling with anxiety.

"Yes!" said Dr. W. when I ventured this proposition at my next session with him. Then he told me a story of his own: "My brother used to host regular salon evenings, where people would be invited in to lecture on various topics. I was asked to give a talk on phobias. After my lec-

---

* For instance, S., a nonfiction writer in her midthirties, told of taking Xanax and Klonopin for her anxiety and about how she switched from Prozac to Lexapro because Prozac had killed her libido. C., a poet in his midforties, said that he'd had to take the antidepressant Zoloft for panic attacks. (C.'s first panic attack had landed him in the emergency room, convinced he was having a heart attack. Subsequent attacks, he said, "were not so bad because you know what they are—but they're still scary because you always wonder, *Maybe this time I really* am *having a heart attack.*" Some epidemiological surveys have found that one-third of adults suffering their first panic attack end up in the emergency room.) K., a novelist, said that while she was trying to finish her last book, her anxiety got so bad that she couldn't work. Fearing she was going crazy, she went to her psychiatrist, who prescribed her Zoloft, which made her fat, and then Lexapro, which increased her anxiety so much that she could no longer even bear to pick her children up at school.

† After dinner, yet another writer approached me. The woman—let's call her E.—is a globe-trotting war correspondent and best-selling author in her late thirties who suffers, she told me, from a litany of depressive, anxious symptoms (including trichotillomania, a disorder that causes people, mainly women, to compulsively pull their hair out when under stress), for which a doctor had prescribed her the antidepressant Lexapro. I marveled that E., despite her anxiety and depression, had managed to travel all around Africa and the Middle East, filing dispatches from war-ravaged countries, often at great risk to her personal safety; for me, simply traveling more than a few miles from home can be miserably anxiety producing and bowel loosening. "I feel calmer in war zones," she said. "I know it's perverse, but I feel more calm while being shelled; it's one of the few times I *don't* feel anxiety." Waiting for an editor to make a judgment about an article she's submitted, however, can send her spiraling into anxiety and depression. (Freud observed that threats to our self-esteem or self-conception can often cause far more anxiety than threats to our physical well-being.)

‡ There is definitely some truth to that, and I will have a lot to say about the topic in part 3 of this book.

ture, every single one of the people there came up to tell me about their phobias. I think the official numbers, as high as they are, underreport."

After he told me this, I thought about Ben, my best friend from college, a rich and successful writer (he regularly graces the best-seller lists and box-office charts), whose doctor had recently prescribed him Ativan, a benzodiazepine, to combat the anxious tightness in his chest that had him convinced he was suffering a heart attack.* And I thought of Ben's neighbor M., a multimillionaire hedge fund manager, who takes Xanax constantly for his panic attacks. And of my former colleague G., an eminent political journalist, who in the years since ending up in an emergency room after a panic episode has been taking various benzodiazepines to prevent further attacks. And of another former colleague, B., whose anxiety left him stammering in meetings and unable to complete work projects until he went on Lexapro.

No, not everyone gets overwhelmed by anxiety. My wife, for one, does not. (Thank God.) Barack Obama, by all accounts, does not. Nor, evidently, does David Petraeus, the former commander of U.S. forces in Afghanistan and former director of the CIA: he once told a reporter that despite being in jobs where the day-to-day stakes are a matter of life and death, he "rarely feels stress at all."† All-Pro quarterbacks like Tom Brady and Peyton Manning manifestly do not, at least not on the field.‡ One of the things I explore in this book is why some people are preternaturally calm, exhibiting grace even under tremendous pressure, while others of us succumb to panic at the mildest hint of stress.

Yet enough of us do suffer from anxiety that perhaps writing about

---

* Even though Ben now travels the world and walks red carpets and commands tens of thousands of dollars for a speech, I can still remember the times, in the lean years before his first book came out, when he would get overwhelmed by panic attacks if we strayed too far from his apartment and when the prospect of socializing at a party would leave him so nervous he'd vomit into the bushes outside beforehand.

† Perhaps he would have been better off feeling more stress—a greater intensity of worry about consequences might have prevented the adulterous misadventure that led to his downfall.

‡ Not that coolness and toughness on the field are guarantees of equanimity off of it. Terry Bradshaw, the Steelers Hall of Fame quarterback from the late 1970s, was a fearless gladiator who went on to be debilitated by depression and panic attacks. Earl Campbell, the burly, fearsome Houston Oilers running back from the 1970s, found himself, a decade later, housebound by panic attacks.

my own ought not to be an occasion for shame but an opportunity to provide solace to some of the millions of others who share this affliction. And maybe, as Dr. W. often reminds me, the exercise will be therapeutic. "You can write yourself to health," he says.

Still, I worry. A lot. It's my nature. (Besides, as many people have said to me, how can you *not* be anxious writing a book about anxiety?)

Dr. W., for his part, says: "Put your anxiety about the book into the book."

*The planning function of the nervous system, in the course of evolution, has culminated in the appearance of ideas, values, and pleasures—the unique manifestations of man's social living. Man, alone, can plan for the distant future, and can experience the retrospective pleasures of achievement. Man, alone, can be happy. But man, alone, can be worried and anxious.*

—HOWARD LIDDELL, "THE ROLE OF VIGILANCE IN THE
DEVELOPMENT OF ANIMAL NEUROSIS" (1949)

In all the insights into history and culture that a study of anxiety might produce, is there anything that can help the individual anxiety sufferer? Can we—can I—reduce anxiety, or come to terms with it, by understanding the value and meaning of it?

I hope so. But when I have a panic attack, there is nothing interesting about it. I try to think about it analytically and I can't—it's just miserably unpleasant and I want it to stop. A panic attack is interesting the way a broken leg or a kidney stone is interesting—a pain that you want to end.

Some years ago, before embarking on the research for this project in earnest, I picked up an academic book about the physiology of anxiety to read while on a flight from San Francisco to Washington, D.C. As we flew smoothly over the West, I was immersed in the book and felt like I was gaining an intellectual understanding of the phenomenon. *So,* I thought as I read, *it's simply a flurry of activity in my amygdala that produces that acutely miserable emotion I sometimes feel? Those feelings of doom and terror are just the bubbling of neurotransmitters in my brain? That doesn't seem so intimidating.* Armed with this perspective, I continued thinking: *I can exert mind over matter and reduce the physical symptoms of anxiety to their proper place—mere routine physiology—and live more calmly in the world. Here I am, hurtling along at thirty-eight thousand feet, and I'm not even that nervous.*

Then the turbulence started. It wasn't particularly severe, but as we bumped along above the Rockies, any perspective or understanding I thought I had gained was rendered instantly useless; my fear response revved up, and despite gulping Xanax and Dramamine, I was terrified and miserable until we landed several hours later.

My anxiety is a reminder that I am governed by my physiology— that what happens in the body may do more to determine what happens in the mind than the other way around. Though thinkers from Aristotle to William James to the researchers who publish today in the journal *Psychosomatic Medicine* have recognized this fact, it runs counter to one of the basic Platonic-Cartesian tenets of Western thought—the idea that who we are, the way we think and perceive, is a product of our disembodied souls or intellects. The brute biological factness of anxiety challenges our sense of who we are: anxiety reminds us that we are, like animals, prisoners of our bodies, which will decline and die and cease to be. (No wonder we're anxious.)

And yet even as anxiety throws us back into our most primitive, fight-or-flight-driven reptilian selves, it is also what makes us more than mere animals. "If man were a beast or an angel," Kierkegaard wrote in 1844, "he would not be able to be in anxiety. Since he is both beast and angel, he can be in anxiety, and the greater the anxiety, the greater the man." The ability to worry about the future goes hand in hand with the ability to plan for the future—and planning for the future (along with remembering the past) is what gives rise to culture and separates us from other animals.

For Kierkegaard, as for Freud, the most anxiety-producing threats lay not in the world around us but rather deep inside us—in our uncertainty about the existential choices we make and in our fear of death. Confronting this fear, and risking the dissolution of one's identity, expands the soul and fulfills the self. "Learning to know anxiety is an adventure which every man has to affront if he would not go to perdition either by not having known anxiety or by sinking under it," Kierkegaard wrote. "He therefore who has learned rightly to be in anxiety has learned the most important thing."

*Learning rightly to be in anxiety.* Well, I'm trying. This book is part of that effort.

# CHAPTER 2

# What Do We Talk About
# When We Talk About Anxiety?

*Although it is widely recognized that anxiety is the most pervasive psychological phenomenon of our time . . . there has been little or no agreement on its definition, and very little, if any, progress on its measurement.*

—PAUL HOCH, PRESIDENT, AMERICAN

PSYCHOPATHOLOGICAL ASSOCIATION, IN AN ADDRESS

TO THE FIRST-EVER ACADEMIC CONFERENCE

ON ANXIETY (1949)

*For researchers as well as laymen, this is the age of anxiety. . . . [But] can we honestly claim that our understanding of anxiety has increased in proportion to the huge research effort expended or even increased perceptibility?*

   *We think not.*

—"THE NATURE OF ANXIETY: A REVIEW OF THIRTEEN

MULTIVARIATE ANALYSES COMPRISING 814 VARIABLES,"

*Psychiatric Reports* (DECEMBER 1958)

*Anxiety is not a simple thing to grasp.*

—SIGMUND FREUD, *The Problem of Anxiety* (1926)

On February 16, 1948, at 3:45 in the afternoon, my great-grandfather Chester Hanford, who had recently stepped down after twenty years as the dean of Harvard College to concentrate full-time on his academic work as a professor of government ("with a focus on local and municipal government," as he liked to say), was admitted to McLean Hospital with a provisional diagnosis of "psychoneurosis" and "reactive depression." Fifty-six years old at the time of his admission, Chester reported that his primary complaints were insomnia, "feelings of anxiety and tension," and "fears as to the future." Described by the hospital director as a "conscientious and usually very effective man," Chester had been in a state of "anxiety of a rather severe degree" for five months. The night before presenting himself at McLean, he had told his wife that he wanted to commit suicide.

Thirty-one years later, on October 3, 1979, at 8:30 in the morning, my parents—worried that I, ten years old and in the fifth grade, had of late been piling various alarming new tics and behavioral oddities on top of my already obsessive germ avoidance and acute separation anxiety and phobia of vomiting—took me to the same psychiatric hospital to be evaluated. A team of experts (a psychiatrist, a psychologist, a social worker, and several young psychiatric residents who sat hidden behind a two-way mirror and watched me get interviewed and take a Rorschach test) diagnosed me with "phobic neurosis" and "overanxious reaction disorder of childhood" and observed that I would be at significant risk of developing "anxiety neurosis" and "neurotic depression" as I got older if I wasn't treated.

Twenty-five years after *that*, on April 13, 2004, at two o'clock in the afternoon, I, now thirty-four years old and working as a senior editor at *The Atlantic* magazine and dreading the publication of my first book, presented myself at the nationally renowned Center for Anxiety and Related Disorders at Boston University. After meeting for several hours with a psychologist and two graduate students and filling out dozens of pages of questionnaires (including, I later learned, the Depression Anxiety Stress Scales and the Social Interaction Anxiety Scale and the Penn State Worry Questionnaire and the Anxiety Sensitivity Index), I was given a principal diagnosis of "panic disorder with agoraphobia" and additional diagnoses of "specific phobia" and "social phobia." The clinicians also noted in their report that my questionnaire scores indicated "mild levels of depression," "strong levels of anxiety," and "strong levels of worry."

Why so many different diagnoses? Did the nature of my anxiety change so much between 1979 and 2004? And why didn't my great-grandfather and I receive the same diagnoses? As described in his case files, the general scope of Chester Hanford's syndrome was awfully similar to mine. Were my "strong levels of anxiety" really so different from the "feelings of anxiety and tension" and "fears as to the future" that afflicted my great-grandfather? And anyway, who, aside from the most well adjusted or sociopathic among us, *doesn't* have "fears as to the future" or suffer "feelings of anxiety and tension"? What, if anything, separates the ostensibly "clinically" anxious, like my great-grandfather and me, from the "normally" anxious? Aren't we all, consumed by the getting and striving of modern capitalist society—indeed, as a consequence of being alive, subject always to the caprice and violence of nature and each other and to the inevitability of death—at some level "psychoneurotic"?

Technically, no; in fact, no one is anymore. The diagnoses that Chester Hanford received in 1948 no longer existed by 1980. And the diagnoses that I received in 1979 no longer exist today.

In 1948, "psychoneurosis" was the American Psychiatric Association's term for what that organization would, with the introduction in 1968 of the second edition of psychiatry's bible, the *Diagnostic and Statistical Manual* (*DSM-II*), officially designate as simply "neurosis" and what it has, since the introduction of the third edition (*DSM-III*) in 1980, called "anxiety disorder."*

This evolving terminology matters because the definitions—as well as the symptoms, the rates of incidence, the presumed causes, the cultural meanings, and the recommended treatments—associated with these diagnoses have changed along with their names over the years. The species of unpleasant emotion that twenty-five hundred years ago was associated with *melaina chole* (ancient Greek for "black bile") has since also been described, in sometimes overlapping succession, as "melancholy," "angst," "hypochondria," "hysteria," "vapors," "spleen," "neurasthenia," "neurosis," "psychoneurosis," "depression," "phobia," "anxiety," and "anxiety disorder"—and that's leaving aside such colloquial terms as "panic," "worry," "dread," "fright," "apprehension,"

---

* The anxiety disorders have persisted through the publication of the *DSM-III-R* (in 1987), the *DSM-IV* (in 1994), the *DSM-IV-TR* (in 2000), and the *DSM-V* (in 2013).

"nerves," "nervousness," "edginess," "wariness," "trepidation," "jitters," "willies," "obsession," "stress," and plain old "fear." And that's just in English, where the word "anxiety" was rarely found in standard psychological or medical textbooks in English before the 1930s, when translators began rendering the German *Angst* (as deployed in the works of Sigmund Freud) as "anxiety."*

Which raises the question: What are we talking about when we talk about anxiety?

The answer is not straightforward—or, rather, it depends on whom you ask. For Søren Kierkegaard, writing in the mid-nineteenth century, anxiety (*angst* in Danish) was a spiritual and philosophical problem, a vague yet inescapable uneasiness with no obvious direct cause.† For Karl Jaspers, the German philosopher and psychiatrist who wrote the influential 1913 textbook *General Psychopathology*, it was "usually linked with a strong *feeling of restlessness* . . . a feeling that one has . . . not finished something; or . . . that one has to look for something or . . . come

---

* There are long-running debates among psychologists and philologists about the differences between, say, *angoisse* and *anxiété* (not to mention *inquiétude, peur, terreur,* and *effroi*) in French and between *Angst* and *Furcht* (and *Angstpsychosen* and *Ängstlichkeit*) in German.

† Kierkegaard, the son of a Danish wool merchant, was the first nonphysician to write a serious book-length treatment of anxiety. Some fifty years before Freud, Kierkegaard distinguished anxiety from fear, defining the former as a vague, diffuse uneasiness produced by no concrete or "real" danger. Kierkegaard's father had renounced God (cursed him, in fact), and so young Søren was much preoccupied with whether to believe in or to reject Christ; the freedom to choose between these two options—and the inability to know for certain which one was correct—was what Kierkegaard believed to be the principal wellspring of anxiety. In this, Kierkegaard was arguing in the vein of Blaise Pascal, his seventeenth-century philosophical predecessor and fellow anxiety sufferer. Kierkegaard was also giving birth, more or less, to existentialism; twentieth-century successors like the psychiatrist Karl Jaspers and the philosopher-novelist Jean-Paul Sartre, among others, would take up similar questions about choice, suicide, engagement, and anxiety.

When man lost his faith in God and in reason, existentialists like Kierkegaard and Sartre believed, he found himself adrift in the universe and therefore adrift in anxiety. But for the existentialists, what generated anxiety was not the godlessness of the world, per se, but rather the freedom to choose between God and godlessness. Though freedom is something we actively seek, the freedom to choose generates anxiety. "When I behold my possibilities," Kierkegaard wrote, "I experience that dread which is the dizziness of freedom, and my choice is made in fear and trembling."

Many people try to flee anxiety by fleeing choice. This helps explain the perverse-seeming appeal of authoritarian societies—the certainties of a rigid, choiceless society can be very reassuring—and why times of upheaval so often produce extremist leaders and movements: Hitler in Weimar Germany, Father Coughlin in Depression-era America, or Jean-Marie Le Pen in France and Vladimir Putin in Russia today. But running from anxiety, Kierkegaard believed, was a mistake because anxiety was a "school" that taught people to come to terms with the human condition.

into the clear about something." Harry Stack Sullivan, one of the most prominent American psychiatrists of the first half of the twentieth century, wrote that anxiety was "that which one experiences when one's self-esteem is threatened"; Robert Jay Lifton, one of the most influential psychiatrists of the second half of the twentieth century, similarly defines anxiety as "a sense of foreboding stemming from a threat to the vitality of the self, or, more severely, from the anticipation of fragmentation of the self." For Reinhold Niebuhr, the Cold War–era theologian, anxiety was a religious concept—"the internal precondition of sin . . . the internal description of the state of temptation." For their part, many physicians—starting with Hippocrates (in the fourth century B.C.) and Galen (in the second century A.D.)—have argued that clinical anxiety is a straightforward medical condition, an organic disease with biological causes as clear, or nearly so, as those of strep throat or diabetes.

Then there are those who say that anxiety is useless as a scientific concept—that it is an imprecise metaphor straining to describe a spectrum of human experience too broad to be captured with a single word. In 1949, at the first-ever academic conference dedicated to anxiety, the president of the American Psychopathological Association opened the proceedings by conceding that although everyone knew that anxiety was "the most pervasive psychological phenomenon of our time," nobody could agree on exactly what it was or how to measure it. Fifteen years later, at the annual conference of the American Psychiatric Association, Theodore Sarbin, an eminent psychologist, suggested that "anxiety" should be retired from clinical use. "The mentalistic and multi-referenced term 'anxiety' has outlived its usefulness," he declared. (Since then, of course, the use of the term has only proliferated.) More recently, Jerome Kagan, a psychologist at Harvard who is perhaps the world's leading expert on anxiety as a temperamental trait, has argued that applying the same word—"anxiety"—"to feelings (the sensation of a racing heart or tense muscles before entering a crowd of strangers), semantic descriptions (a report of worry over meeting strangers), behaviors (tense facial expressions in a social situation), brain states (activation of the amygdala to angry faces), or a chronic mood of worry (general anxiety disorder) is retarding progress."

How can we make scientific, or therapeutic, progress if we can't agree on what anxiety is?

Even Sigmund Freud, the inventor, more or less, of the modern idea of neurosis—a man for whom anxiety was a key, if not *the* key, foundational concept of his theory of psychopathology—contradicted himself repeatedly over the course of his career. Early on, he said that anxiety arose from sublimated sexual impulses (repressed libido, he wrote, was transformed into anxiety "as wine to vinegar").* Later in his career, he argued that anxiety arose from unconscious psychic conflicts.† Late in his life, in *The Problem of Anxiety,* Freud wrote: "It is almost disgraceful that after so much labor we should still find difficulty in conceiving of the most fundamental matters."

If Freud himself, anxiety's patron saint, couldn't define the concept, how am I supposed to?

*Fear sharpens the senses. Anxiety paralyzes them.*
—KURT GOLDSTEIN, *The Organism:*
*A Holistic Approach to Biology* (1939)

Standard dictionary definitions make fear ("an unpleasant emotion caused by the belief that someone or something is dangerous, likely to cause pain, or a threat") and anxiety ("a feeling of worry, nervousness, and unease, typically about an event or something with an uncertain outcome") seem relatively synonymous. But for Freud, whereas fear (*Furcht* in German) has a concrete object—the lion that's chasing you, the enemy sniper that's got you pinned to your position in battle, or even your knowledge of the consequences of missing the crucial free

---

* Some of Freud's first writings on the subject boil anxiety down to pure biomechanics: neurotic anxiety, he theorized, was mainly the result of repressed sexual energy. Trained as a neurologist (his early research was on the nervous system of eels), Freud subscribed to the principle of constancy, which held that the human nervous system tends to try to reduce, or at least hold constant, the quantity of "excitation" it contains. Sexual activity—orgasm—was a principal means by which the body discharged excess tension.

Such beliefs about the relation between sexual tension and anxiety had ancient precedent. The Roman physician Galen describes treating a patient, whose brain he believed was affected by the rotting of her unreleased sexual fluids, "with a manual stimulation of the vagina and of the clitoris." The patient "took great pleasure from this," Galen reports, "and much liquid came out, and she was cured."

† His acolytes and would-be successors then spent a generation arguing over what those conflicts might be about: Karen Horney said "dependency needs," Erich Fromm said "security needs," and Alfred Adler said "the need for power."

throw you're about to shoot in the closing moments of an important basketball game—anxiety (*Angst*) does not. According to this view, fear, properly occasioned, is healthy; anxiety, which is often "irrational" or "free-floating," is not.*

"When a mother is afraid that her child will die when it has only a pimple or a slight cold we speak of anxiety; but if she is afraid when the child has a serious illness we call her reaction fear," Karen Horney wrote in 1937. "If someone is afraid whenever he stands on a height or when he has to discuss a topic he knows well, we call his reaction anxiety; if someone is afraid when he loses his way high up in the mountains during a heavy thunderstorm we would speak of fear." (Horney further elaborated her distinction by saying that while you always know when you are afraid, you can be anxious without knowing it.)

In Freud's later writings, he replaced his distinction between fear and anxiety with a distinction instead between "normal anxiety" (defined as anxiety about a legitimate threat, which can be productive) and "neurotic anxiety" (anxiety produced by unresolved sexual issues or internal psychic conflicts, which is pathological and counterproductive).

So am I, with my phobias and worries and general twitchiness, "neurotically" anxious? Or just "normally" so? What's the difference between "normal" anxiety and anxiety as a clinical problem? What differentiates the appropriate and even helpful nervousness that, say, a law student feels before taking the bar exam or that a Little Leaguer feels before stepping into the batters' box from the distressing cognitive and physical symptoms that attend the official anxiety disorders as defined by modern psychiatry since 1980: panic disorder, post-traumatic stress disorder (PTSD), specific phobia, obsessive-compulsive disorder (OCD), social anxiety disorder, agoraphobia, and generalized anxiety disorder?

To distinguish the "normal" from the "clinical," and the different clinical syndromes from one another, pretty much everyone in the entire wide-ranging field of mental health care relies on the American Psychiatric Association's *Diagnostic and Statistical Manual* (now in its just-published fifth edition, *DSM-V*). The *DSM* defines hundreds of

---

* This Freudian view of *Angst* has a Kierkegaardian "quality of indefiniteness and lack of object."

mental disorders, classifies them by type, and lists, in levels of detail that can seem both absurdly precise and completely random, the symptoms (how many, how often, and with what severity) a patient must display in order to receive a given psychiatric diagnosis. All of which lends the appearance of scientific validity to the diagnosing of an anxiety disorder. But the reality is that there is a large quotient of subjectivity here (both on the part of patients, in describing their symptoms, and of clinicians, in interpreting them). Studies of the *DSM-II* found that when two psychiatrists consulted the same patient, they gave the same *DSM* diagnosis only between 32 and 42 percent of the time. Rates of consistency have improved since then, but the diagnosis of many mental disorders remains, despite pretensions to the contrary, more art than science.*

Consider the relationship between clinical anxiety and clinical depression. The physiological similarities between certain forms of clinical anxiety (especially generalized anxiety disorder) and clinical depression are substantial: both depression and anxiety are associated with elevated levels of the stress hormone cortisol, and they share some neuroanatomical features, including shrinkage of the hippocampus and other parts of the brain. They share genetic roots, most notably in the genes associated with the production of certain neurotransmitters, such as serotonin and dopamine. (Some geneticists say they can find no distinction between major depression and generalized anxiety disorder.) Anxiety and depression also have a shared basis in a feeling of a lack of self-esteem or self-efficacy. (Feeling like you have no control over your life is a common route to both anxiety and depression.) Moreover, reams of studies show that stress—ranging from job worries to divorce to bereavement to combat trauma—is a huge contributor to rates of both anxiety disorders and depression, as well as to hypertension, diabetes, and other medical conditions.

If anxiety disorders and depression are so similar, why do we distinguish between them? Actually, for a few thousand years, we didn't:

---

* The bitter fights over revisions for the *DSM-V*—which have included public denunciations of it by the chairmen of the task forces that produced the *DSM-III* and *DSM-IV,* respectively—suggest that psychiatric diagnosis may be more a matter of politics and marketing than either art or science.

doctors tended to group anxiety and depression together under the umbrella terms "melancholia" or "hysteria."* The symptoms that Hippocrates attributed to *melaina chole* in the fourth century B.C. included those we would today associate with both depression ("sadness," "moral dejection," and "tendency to suicide") and anxiety ("prolonged fear"). In 1621, in *The Anatomy of Melancholy*, Robert Burton wrote, with a clinical accuracy that modern research supports, that anxiety was to sorrow "a sister, *fidus Achates* [trusty squire], and continual companion, an assistant and a principal agent in the procuring of this mischief; a cause and symptom as the other."† It is a fact—I say this from experience—that being severely anxious is depressing. Anxiety can impede your relationships, impair your performance, constrict your life, and limit your possibilities.

The dividing line between the set of disorders the American Psychiatric Association lumps under "depression" and the set of disorders it lumps under "anxiety disorders"—and, for that matter, the line between mental health and mental illness—seems to be an artifact as much of politics and culture (and marketing) as of science. Every time the scope of a given psychiatric disorder grows or shrinks in the *DSM*'s definition, it has powerfully ramifying effects on everything from insurance reimbursements to drug company profits to the career prospects of therapists in different fields and subspecialties. Quite a few psychiatrists and drug industry critics will tell you that anxiety disorders do not exist in nature but rather were invented by the pharmaceutical-industrial complex in order to extract money from patients and insurance companies. Diagnoses such as social anxiety disorder or general anxiety disorder, these critics say, turn normal human emotions into pathologies, diseases for which medication can be profitably dispensed. "Don't allow the sum total of your life to be reduced to phrases like clinical depression, bipo-

---

\* Some historians of science lump all the syndromes with this "matrix of distress symptoms"—psychological symptoms like worry and sadness and malaise, as well as physical ones like headaches, fatigue, back pain, sleeplessness, and stomach trouble—under the broad category of the "stress tradition." "Stress" can refer to both psychological stresses and physical ones, in the form of the "stress" placed on the biological nervous system that doctors since the eighteenth century believed caused "nervous disease."

† Burton wrote that in the daytime melancholics "are affrighted still by some terrible object, and torn in pieces with suspicion, fear, sorrow, discontents, cares, shames, anguish, etc., as so many wild horses, that they cannot be quiet an hour, a minute of the time."

lar disorder, or anxiety disorder," says Peter Breggin, a Harvard-trained psychiatrist who has become a fierce antagonist of the pharmaceutical industry.

As someone who has been diagnosed with some of these disorders, I can tell you the distress they cause is not invented; my anxiety, which can at times be debilitating, is real. But are my nervous symptoms necessarily constitutive of an *illness,* of a *psychiatric disorder,* as the *DSM* and the pharmaceutical companies would have it? Mightn't my anxiety be just a normal human emotional response to life, even if the response is perhaps somewhat more severe for me than for others? How do you draw the distinction between "normal" and "clinical"?

You might expect that recent scientific advances would make the distinction between normal and clinical anxiety more precise and objective—and certainly in some ways they have. Neuroscientists, working with functional magnetic resonance imaging (fMRI) technology that enables them to observe mental activity in real time by measuring oxygenated blood flow to different regions of the brain, have produced hundreds of studies demonstrating associations between specific subjectively experienced emotions and specific kinds of physiological activity that can be seen on a brain scan. For instance, acute anxiety generally appears on fMRI scans as hyperactivity in the amygdala, that tiny almond-shaped structure located deep in the medial temporal lobes near the base of the skull. Reductions in anxiety are associated with diminished activity in the amygdala and with heightened activity in the frontal cortex.*

All of which makes it sound like you should be able to identify anxiety, and gauge its intensity, on the basis of something akin to an X-ray—that you could differentiate between normal and clinical anxiety in the way X-rays can differentiate between a broken ankle and a sprained one.

Except you can't. There are people who exhibit telltale physiological signs of anxiety on a brain scan (their amygdalae light up colorfully in response to stress-inducing stimuli) but who will tell you they are not

---

* I'm oversimplifying—the full neuroscientific picture is more complex and detailed—but this is the gist of what research has found. During intensely anxious moments, the primitive effusions of the amygdala overpower the more rational thinking of the cortex.

*feeling* anxious. Moreover, the brain of a research subject who is sexually aroused by a pornographic movie will light up on an MRI scan in much the same way it does in response to a fear-inducing event; the same interconnected brain components—the amygdala, the insular cortex, and the anterior cingulate—will be activated in both cases. A researcher looking at the two brain scans without knowing their context might be unable to determine which image is a response to fear and which is to sexual arousal.

When an X-ray shows a fractured femur but the patient reports no pain, the medical diagnosis is still a broken leg. When an fMRI exhibits intense activity in the amygdala and basal ganglia and the patient reports no anxiety, the diagnosis is . . . nothing.

> *When it comes to detecting and responding to danger, the* [verte-
> brate] *brain just hasn't changed much. In some ways we are emo-*
> *tional lizards.*
>       —JOSEPH LEDOUX, *The Emotional Brain* (1996)

Researchers since Aristotle have made frequent recourse to "animal models" of emotion, and the many thousands of animal studies conducted each year are predicated on the notion that the behaviors, genetics, and neurocircuitry of a rat or a chimpanzee are similar enough to our own that we can glean relevant insight from them. Writing in *The Expression of the Emotions in Man and Animals* in 1872, Charles Darwin observed that fear reactions are fairly universal across species: all mammals, including humans, exhibit readily observable fear responses. In the presence of perceived danger, rats, like people, instinctively run, freeze, or defecate.* When threatened, the congenitally "anxious" rat trembles, avoids open spaces, prefers familiar places, stops in its tracks if encountering anything potentially threatening, and emits ultrasonic distress calls. Humans don't issue ultrasonic distress calls—but when

---

* Defecation rate—the number of pellets dropped per minute—is a standard measure of fearfulness in rodents. In the 1960s, scientists at a psychiatric hospital in London bred the famous Maudsley strain of reactive rats by pairing animals with similar poop frequencies.

we get nervous, we do tremble, shy away from unfamiliar situations, withdraw from social contact, and prefer to stay close to home. (Some agoraphobics never leave their houses.) Rats that have had their amygdalae removed (or whose genes have been altered so that their amygdalae are not working properly) are incapable of expressing fear; the same is true of humans whose amygdalae get damaged. (Researchers at the University of Iowa have for years been studying a woman, known in the literature as S.M., whose amygdala was destroyed by a rare disease—and who cannot, as a consequence, experience fear.) Moreover, if continuously exposed to stressful situations, animals will develop some of the same stress-related medical conditions that humans do: high blood pressure, heart disease, ulcers, and so forth.

"With all or almost all animals, even with birds," Darwin wrote, "terror causes the body to tremble. The skin becomes pale, sweat breaks out, and hair bristles. The secretions of the alimentary canal and of the kidneys are increased, and they are involuntarily voided, owing to the relaxation of the sphincter muscles as is known to be the case with man, and as I have seen with cattle, dogs, cats, and monkeys. The breathing is hurried. The heart beats quickly, wildly, and violently. . . . The mental faculties are much disturbed. Utter prostration soon follows, and even fainting."

Darwin pointed out that this automatic physical response to threat is evolutionarily adaptive. Organisms that respond to danger in this way—by being physiologically primed to fight or flee, or to faint—are more likely to survive and reproduce than organisms that don't. In 1915, Walter Cannon, the chair of the physiology department at Harvard Medical School, coined the term "fight or flight" to describe Darwin's idea of an "alarm reaction." As Cannon was the first to document systematically, when the fight-or-flight response is activated, peripheral blood vessels constrict, directing blood away from the extremities to the skeletal muscles, so the animal will be better prepared to fight or run. (This streaming of blood away from the skin is what makes a frightened person appear pale.) Breathing becomes faster and deeper to keep the blood supplied with oxygen. The liver secretes an increased amount of glucose, which energizes various muscles and organs. The pupils of the eyes dilate and hearing becomes more acute so that the animal can better appraise the situation. Blood flows away from the alimentary canal and digestive processes stop—saliva flow decreases (causing that anxious feeling of a dry mouth), and there is often an urge to defecate, urinate, or vomit. (Expelling waste material allows the animal's internal systems to focus on survival needs more immediate than digestion.) In his 1915 book, *Bodily Changes in Pain, Hunger, Fear and Rage,* Cannon provided a couple of simple early illustrations of the way the experience of emotion translates concretely into chemical changes in the body. In one experiment, he examined the urine of nine college students after they had taken a hard exam and after they had taken an easy one: after the hard exam, four of the nine students had sugar in their urine; after the easy exam, only one of them did. In the other experiment, Cannon examined the urine of the Harvard football team after "the final and most exciting contest" of 1913 and found that twelve of the twenty-five samples had positive traces of sugar.

The physiological response that produces fainting is different from the one that primes the organism for fighting or fleeing, but it can be equally adaptive: animals that respond to bleeding injuries with a sharp drop in blood pressure suffer less blood loss; also, fainting is an involuntary way for animals to feign death, which in certain circumstances might be protective.*

When the fight-or-flight reaction is activated appropriately, in response to a legitimate physical danger, it enhances an animal's chances of survival. But what happens when the response is activated inappropriately? The result of a physiological fear response that has no legitimate object, or that is disproportionate to the size of the threat, can be pathological anxiety—an evolutionary impulse gone awry. William

---

* Here's another way in which writing this book has been bad for me: before I started researching it, I wasn't familiar with blood-injury phobia—a condition that causes the estimated 4.5 percent of people it afflicts to get extremely anxious and sometimes, because of a drop in blood pressure, to faint when injected with needles or at the sight of blood—and was therefore able to get shots and have my blood drawn without distress, a rare area of relative noncowardice for me. Now, having learned about the physiology that produces this phenomenon, I have become phobic about fainting in these situations and have, by the power of autosuggestion, nearly done so several times.

"For God's sake, Scott," Dr. W. says when I tell him about this. "You've given yourself a new phobia." (He advises that I practice getting injected by a physician soon—a form of exposure therapy—before the phobia becomes a serious problem.)

James, the psychologist and philosopher, surmised that the cause of severe anxiety, and of what we would today call panic attacks, might be modernity itself—specifically, the fact that our primitive fight-or-flight responses are not suited to modern civilization. "The progress from brute to man is characterized by nothing so much as by the decrease in frequency of proper occasions for fear," James observed in 1884. "In civilized life, in particular, it has at last become possible for large numbers of people to pass from the cradle to the grave without ever having had a pang of genuine fear."*

In modern life, occasions for what James called "genuine" human fear of the sort occasioned in the state of nature—being chased by a saber-toothed tiger, say, or encountering members of an enemy tribe— are relatively rare, at least most of the time. The threats that today tend to activate fight-or-flight physiology—the disapproving look from the boss, the mysterious letter your wife got from her old boyfriend, the college application process, the crumbling of the economy, the abiding threat of terrorism, the plummeting of your retirement fund—are not the sorts of threats the response is designed to help with. Yet because the emergency biological response gets triggered anyway, especially in clinically anxious people, we end up marinating in a stew of stress hormones that is damaging to our health. This is because whether you are in the throes of neurotic anxiety or responding to a real threat like a mugging or a house fire, the autonomic activity of your nervous system is roughly the same. The hypothalamus, a small part of the brain located just above the brain stem, releases a hormone called corticotropin-releasing factor (CRF), which in turn induces the pituitary gland, a pea-size organ protruding from the bottom of the hypothalamus, to release adrenocorticotropin hormone (ACTH), which travels through

---

* William (along with his brother Henry and sister Alice and several other siblings) seems to have inherited his own anxious, hypochondriacal tendencies from his father, Henry James Sr., an eccentric Swedenborgian philosopher who, in an 1884 letter to William, provided a description of an experience easily recognizable to the modern clinician as a panic attack: "One day . . . toward the close of May, having eaten a comfortable dinner, I remained sitting at the table after the family had dispersed, idly gazing at the embers in the grate, thinking of nothing . . . when suddenly—in a lightning-flash as it were—'fear came upon me, and trembling, which made all my bones to shake' [he's quoting Job here]. . . . The thing had not lasted ten seconds before I felt myself a wreck; that is, reduced from a state of firm, vigorous, joyful manhood to one of almost helpless infancy."

the bloodstream to the kidneys, instructing the adrenal glands sitting atop them to release adrenaline (also known as norepinephrine) and cortisol, which cause more glucose to be released into the bloodstream, which increases heart and breathing rates and produces the state of heightened arousal that can be so useful in the case of actual danger and so misery inducing in the case of a panic attack or of chronic worrying. A large body of evidence suggests that having elevated levels of cortisol for an extended period of time produces a host of deleterious health effects, ranging from high blood pressure to a compromised immune system to the shrinking of the hippocampus, a part of the brain crucial to memory formation. An anxious physiological response deployed at the right time can help keep you alive; that same response deployed too often and at the wrong times can lead to an early death.

Like animals, humans can easily be trained to exhibit conditioned fear responses—that is, to associate objectively nonfrightening objects or situations with real threats. In 1920, the psychologist John Watson famously used classical conditioning to produce phobic anxiety in an eleven-month-old boy he called Little Albert. After Watson repeatedly paired a loud noise—which provoked crying and trembling in the boy—with the presence of a white rat (the "neutral stimulus"), he was able to elicit an acute fear response in the boy simply by presenting the rat alone, without the noise. (Before the conditioning, Little Albert had happily played with the rat on his bed.) Soon the boy had developed a full-blown phobia not only of rats and other small furry animals but also of white beards. (Santa Claus terrified Little Albert.) Watson concluded that Little Albert's phobia demonstrated the power of classical conditioning. For the early behaviorists, phobic anxiety in both animals and humans was reducible to straightforward fear conditioning; clinical anxiety, in this view, was a learned response.*

For evolutionary biologists, anxiety is merely an atavistic fear

---

* The pure behaviorist view of fear conditioning is complicated, if not largely undermined, by the fact that humans and other mammals seem genetically hardwired to develop phobias of certain things but not others. Today, evolutionary psychologists say Watson misinterpreted his Little Albert experiment: the real reason Albert developed such a profound phobia of rats was not because behavioral conditioning is so intrinsically potent but because the human brain has a natural—and evolutionarily adaptive—predisposition to fear small furry things on the basis of the diseases they carry. (I explore this at greater length in chapter 9.)

response, a hardwired animal instinct triggered at the wrong time or for the wrong reasons. For behaviorists, anxiety is a learned response acquired, like Pavlov's dogs' propensity for salivating at the sound of a bell, through simple conditioning. According to both, anxiety is as much an animal trait as a human one. "Contrary to the view of some humanists, I believe that emotions are anything but uniquely human traits," the neuroscientist Joseph LeDoux writes, "and, in fact, that some emotional systems in the brain are essentially the same in . . . mammals, reptiles, and birds, and possibly amphibians and fishes as well."

But is the sort of instinctive, mechanistic response that a mouse displays in the presence of a cat, or when it hears the bell associated with a shock—or even that Little Albert displayed after he'd been trained to fear the rat—really anxiety of the sort that I feel when boarding an airplane or obsessing about my family's finances or about the mole on my forearm?

Or consider this: Even *Aplysia californica,* a marine snail with a primitive brain and no spine, can demonstrate a physiological and behavioral response that would, if exhibited by a human, be biologically equivalent (more or less) to anxiety. Touch its gill and the snail will recoil, its blood pressure will rise, and its heart rate will increase. Is *that* anxiety?

Or what about this: Even brainless, nerveless single-celled bacteria can exhibit a learned response and display what psychiatrists call avoidant behavior. When the pond-dwelling paramecium encounters a shock by an electric buzzer—an aversive stimulus—it will retreat and thenceforth seek to avoid the buzzer by swimming away from it. Is *that* anxiety? By some definitions, it is: according to the *Diagnostic and Statistical Manual,* "avoidance" of fearful stimuli is one of the hallmarks of almost all the anxiety disorders.

Other experts say that the presumed analogies between animal and human behavioral response are risibly overextended. "It is not obvious that a rat's display of an enhanced startle reaction . . . [is a] fruitful model for all human anxiety states," says Jerome Kagan. David Barlow of Boston University's Center for Anxiety and Related Disorders asks whether "entering a seemingly involuntary state of paralysis when under attack"—the sort of animal behavior that clearly does have a strong evolutionary and physiological parallel in humans—"really [has] anything in common with the forebodings concerning the welfare of our family, our occupation, or our finances?"

"How many hippos worry about whether Social Security is going to last as long as they will," asks Robert Sapolsky, a neuroscientist at Stanford University, "or what they are going to say on a first date?"

"A rat can't worry about the stock market crashing," Joseph LeDoux concedes. "We can."

Can anxiety be reduced to a purely biological or mechanical process—the instinctive behavioral response of the rat or the marine snail retreating mindlessly from the electric shock or of Little Albert conditioned, like Pavlov's dogs, to recoil and tremble in the presence of furry things? Or does anxiety require a sense of time, an awareness of prospective threats, an anticipation of future suffering—the debilitating "fears as to the future" that brought my great-grandfather, and me, to the mental hospital?

Is anxiety an animal instinct, something we share with rats and lizards and amoebas? Is it a learned behavior, something acquirable through mechanical conditioning? Or is it, after all, a uniquely human experience, dependent on consciousness of, among other things, a sense of self and the idea of death?

> *The physician and the philosopher have different ways of defining the diseases of the soul. For instance anger for the philosopher is a sentiment born of the desire to return an offense, whereas for the physician it is a surging of blood around the heart.*
> —ARISTOTLE, *De Anima* (FOURTH CENTURY B.C.)

One morning, after months of wrestling in frustration with these questions, I dump myself on my therapist's couch in a heap of worry and self-loathing.

"What's wrong?" Dr. W. asks.

"I'm supposed to be writing a book about anxiety and I can't even work out what the basic definition of anxiety is. In all these thousands of pages I've pored through, I've come across hundreds of definitions.

Many of them are similar to one another, but many others contradict each other. I don't know which one to use."

"Use the *DSM* definitions," he suggests.

"But those aren't *definitions*, just a list of associated symptoms," I say.* "And anyway, even that's not straightforward, since the *DSM* is in the process of being revised for the *DSM-V*!"†

"I know," Dr. W. says ruefully. He laments that the mandarins of psychiatry had recently considered dropping obsessive-compulsive disorder (OCD) from the anxiety disorders category in the new *DSM*, placing it instead into a new category of "impulsive disorders," on a spectrum alongside ailments like Tourette's syndrome. He thinks this is wrong. "In all my decades of clinical work," he says, "OCD patients are *always* anxious; they worry about their obsessions."

I mention that at a conference I'd attended a few weeks earlier, one of the rationales given for why OCD might be reclassified as something other than an anxiety disorder was that its genetics and its neurocircuitry seem to be substantially different from that of the other anxiety disorders.

"Goddamned biomedical psychiatry!" he blurts. Dr. W. is ordinarily a gentle, even-keeled guy, and he is aggressively ecumenical in his approach to psychotherapy; he has tried, in his writing and in his clinical practice, to assimilate the best of all the different therapeutic modes into what he calls an "integrative approach to healing the wounded self." (He is also, I should say here, the Best Therapist Ever.) But he believes strongly that over the last several decades the claims of the biomedical model generally, and of neuroscience particularly, have become increasingly arrogant and reductionist, pushing other avenues

---

* For example, here's how the *DSM-IV* defines generalized anxiety disorder: "Excessive anxiety about a number of events or activities, occurring more days than not, for at least 6 months. The person finds it difficult to control the worry. The anxiety and worry are associated with at least three of the following six symptoms (with at least some symptoms present for more days than not, for the past 6 months): Restlessness or feeling keyed up or on edge; Being easily fatigued; Difficulty concentrating or mind going blank; Irritability; Muscle tension; Sleep disturbance." (The *DSM-IV* does in one place provide a general definition of anxiety that I think is, although both generic and technical, fairly accurate: "The apprehensive anticipation of future danger of misfortune accompanied by a feeling of dysphoria or somatic feelings of tension. The focus of anticipated danger may be internal or external.")

† I had this conversation with him before the new *DSM-V* was published in 2013.

of research inquiry to the margins and distorting the practice of psychotherapy. Some of the more hard-core neuroscientists and psychopharmacologists, he feels, would boil all mental processes down to their smallest molecular components, without any sense of the existential dimensions of human suffering or of the *meaning* of anxious or depressive symptoms. At conferences on anxiety, he laments, symposia on drugs and neurochemistry—many of them sponsored by pharmaceutical companies—have started to crowd out everything else.

I tell Dr. W. I'm on the verge of abandoning the project. "I told you I was a failure," I say.

"Look," he says. "That's your anxiety talking. It makes you excessively anxious about, among other things, finding the correct definition of anxiety. And it makes you worry relentlessly about outcomes"—about whether my definition of anxiety will be "wrong"—"instead of concentrating on the work itself. You need to focus your attention. Stay on task!"

"But I still don't know what basic definition of anxiety to use," I say.

"Use mine," he says.

*No one who has ever been tormented by prolonged bouts of anxiety doubts its power to paralyze action, promote flight, eviscerate pleasure, and skew thinking toward the catastrophic. None would deny how terribly painful the experience of anxiety can be. The experience of chronic or intense anxiety is above all else a profound and perplexing confrontation with pain.*
  —BARRY E. WOLFE, *Understanding and*
  *Treating Anxiety Disorders* (2005)

As it happens, I had chosen Dr. W. as a therapist a few years earlier precisely because I found his conception of anxiety interesting and his approach to treatment less rigid or ideological than previous therapists I'd worked with. (Also, I thought the author photo on his book jacket made him look kindly.)

I discovered Dr. W.'s work when, while in Miami attending an academic conference on anxiety, I stumbled across a book he had recently published on a display table outside a hotel ballroom. Though the book, a guide to treating anxiety disorders, was geared toward professional psychotherapists, his "integrative" conception of anxiety appealed to me. Also, after reading so many specialized books on the neuroscience of anxiety that featured sentences like "Theta activity is a rhythmic burst firing pattern of neurons in the hippocampus and related structures which, because it is synchronous across very large numbers of cells, often gives rise to a high-voltage quasi-sinusoidal electrographic slow 'theta rhythm' (approximately 5–10 Hz in the unanesthetized rat) that can be recorded from the hippocampal formation under a variety of behavioural conditions," I found his writing to be clear and nontechnical and his approach to his patients refreshingly humanistic. I recognized my own issues—the panic attacks, the dependency problems, the sublimated fear of death masked as anxiety about more trivial things—in many of the case studies in his book.

I had recently moved from Boston to Washington, D.C., and found myself for the first time in a quarter century without a regular psychotherapist. So when I read in Dr. W.'s author's note that he had a practice in the Washington area, I e-mailed him to ask if he was accepting new patients.

Dr. W. has not cured me of my anxiety. But he continues to insist that he will, and in my more hopeful moments I even sort of think he might. In the meantime, he has provided me with useful tools for trying to manage it, good and steady practical advice, and, perhaps most important, a usable definition—or a taxonomy of definitions—of anxiety.

According to Dr. W., the competing theories of and treatment approaches to anxiety can be grouped into four basic categories: the psychoanalytic, the behavioral and cognitive-behavioral, the biomedical, and the experiential.*

The psychoanalytic approach—crucial aspects of which, though

---

* This schematic overview of the different theoretical approaches to anxiety is necessarily somewhat oversimplified.

Freudianism has been widely repudiated in most scientific circles, still permeate modern talk therapy—holds that the repression of taboo thoughts and ideas (often of a sexual nature) or of inner psychic conflicts leads to anxiety. Treatment involves bringing these repressed conflicts into conscious awareness and addressing them through psychodynamic psychotherapy and the pursuit of "insight."

Behaviorists believe, like John Watson did, that anxiety is a conditioned fear response. Anxiety disorders arise when we learn—often through unconscious conditioning—to fear objectively nonthreatening things or to fear mildly threatening things too intensely. Treatment involves correcting faulty thinking through various combinations of exposure therapy (exposing yourself to the fear and acclimating to it so your fear response diminishes) and cognitive restructuring (changing your thinking) in order to "extinguish" phobias and to "decatastrophize" panic attacks and obsessional worrying. Many studies are now finding that cognitive-behavioral therapy, or CBT, is the safest and most effective treatment for many forms of depression and anxiety disorders.

The biomedical approach (where research has exploded over the last sixty years) has focused on the biological mechanisms of anxiety—on brain structures like the amygdala, hippocampus, locus coeruleus, anterior cingulate, and insula, and on neurotransmitters like serotonin, norepinephrine, dopamine, glutamate, gamma-aminobutyric acid (GABA), and neuropeptide Y (NPY)—and on the genetics that underlie that biology. Treatment often involves the use of medication.

Finally, what Dr. W. calls the experiential approach to anxiety disorders takes a more existential perspective, considering things like panic attacks and obsessional worrying to be coping mechanisms produced by the psyche in response to threats to its integrity or to self-esteem. The experiential approach, like the psychoanalytic, places great weight on the *content* and *meaning* of anxiety—rather than on the *mechanisms* of anxiety, which is where the biomedical and behavioral approaches concentrate—believing these can be clues to unlocking hidden psychic traumas or convictions about the worthlessness of one's existence. Treatment tends to involve guided relaxation to reduce anxiety symptoms and helping the patient to burrow into the anxieties to address the existential issues that lie beneath them.

The conflicts between these different perspectives—and between the psychiatrists (MDs) and the psychologists (PhDs), between the drug proponents and the drug critics, between the cognitive-behaviorists and the psychoanalysts, between Freudians and Jungians, between the molecular neuroscientists and the holistic therapists—can sometimes be bitter. The stakes are high—the future stability of large professional infrastructures rides on one theory or another predominating. And the fundamental conflict—whether anxiety is a medical disease or a spiritual problem, a problem of the body or a problem of the mind—is age-old, dating back to the clashes between Hippocrates and Plato and their followers.*

But while in many places these competing theoretical perspectives conflict with one another, they are not mutually exclusive. Often they overlap. Cutting-edge cognitive-behavioral therapy borrows from the biomedical model, using pharmacology to enhance exposure therapy. (Studies show that a drug called D-cycloserine, which was originally developed as an antibiotic, causes new memories to be more powerfully consolidated in the hippocampus and the amygdala, augmenting the potency of exposure to extinguish phobias by intensifying the power of the new, nonfearful associations to override the fearful ones.) The biomedical view, for its part, increasingly recognizes the power of things like meditation and traditional talk therapy to render concrete structural changes in brain physiology that are every bit as "real" as the changes wrought by pills or electroshock therapy. A study published

---

* Modern science has eventually shown Hippocrates to be the more correct—the mind *does* arise from the physical brain and, in fact, from the whole body—but Plato's influence on the study of psychology has nevertheless remained powerful and enduring, in part because of his influence on Freud. In the *Phaedrus*, Plato describes the soul as a team of two horses and a charioteer: one horse is powerful but obedient, the other is violent and ill behaved, and the charioteer must wrestle mightily to make them work together to move ahead. This view of the human psyche as divided into three parts—the spiritual, the libidinal, and the rational—presages the Freudian mind, with its id, ego, and superego. For Plato, even more than for Freud, successful psychological adjustment depended on the rational soul (*logistikon*) keeping the libidinal soul (*epithumetikon*) in check. This passage from Plato's *Republic* uncannily prefigures Freud's Oedipus complex: "All our desires are aroused when . . . the rational parts of our soul, all our civilized and controlling thoughts, are asleep. Then the wild animal in us rises up, perhaps encouraged by alcohol, and pushes away our rational thoughts: in such states, men will do anything, will dream of sleeping with their mothers and murdering people." (When Wilfred Trotter, an influential British neurosurgeon of the early twentieth century, came across this passage, he declared, "This remark of Plato makes Freud respectable.")

by researchers at Massachusetts General Hospital in 2011 found that subjects who practiced meditation for an average of just twenty-seven minutes a day over a period of eight weeks produced visible changes in brain structure. Meditation led to decreased density of the amygdala, a physical change that was correlated with subjects' self-reported stress levels—as their amygdalae got less dense, the subjects felt less stressed. Other studies have found that Buddhist monks who are especially good at meditating show much greater activity in their frontal cortices, and much less in their amygdalae, than normal people.* Meditation and deep-breathing exercises work for similar reasons as psychiatric medications do, exerting their effects not just on some abstract concept of mind but concretely on our bodies, on the somatic correlates of our feelings. Recent research has shown that even old-fashioned talk therapy can have tangible, physical effects on the shape of our brains. Perhaps Kierkegaard was wrong to say that the man who has learned to be in anxiety has learned the most important, or the most existentially meaningful, thing—perhaps the man has only learned the right techniques for controlling his hyperactive amygdala.†

---

* The very best meditators seem even to be able to suppress their startle response, a rudimentary physiological reaction to loud noises or other sudden stimuli that is mediated through the amygdala. (The strength of one's startle response—whether measured in infancy or adulthood—has been shown to be highly correlated with the propensity to develop anxiety disorders and depression.)

† For his part, William James, like Darwin, believed that purely physical, instinctive processes *preceded* awareness of an emotion—and, in fact, preceded the existence of a given brain state. In the 1890s, he and Carl Lange, a Danish physician, proposed that emotions were produced by automatic physical reactions in the body, rather than the other way around. According to what became known as the James-Lange theory, visceral changes generated by the autonomic nervous system, operating beneath the level of our conscious awareness, lead to such effects as changes in heart rate, respiration, adrenaline secretion, and dilation of the blood vessels to the skeletal muscles. Those purely physical effects occur first—and then it is only our subsequent *interpretation* of those effects that produces emotions like joy or anxiety. A fearful or angering situation produces a series of physiological reactions in the body—and then it is only the conscious mind's becoming aware of those reactions, and appraising and interpreting them, that produces anxiety or anger. According to James-Lange, no purely cognitive or psychological experience of anything like anxiety can be divorced from the autonomic changes in the viscera. The physical changes come first, then the emotion.

This suggests that anxiety is primarily a physical phenomenon and only secondarily a psychological one. "My theory," James wrote, "is that the bodily changes follow directly the perception of the exciting fact, and that our feeling of the same changes as they occur is the emotion. Common sense says, we lose our fortune, are sorry and weep; we meet a bear, are frightened and run; we are insulted by a rival, are angry and strike. The hypothesis here to be defended says that this order of sequence is incorrect . . . and that the more rational statement is that we feel sorry because we cry, angry because we strike, afraid because we tremble." Physical states create psychic ones and not vice-versa.

Darwin observed that the equipment that produces panic anxiety in humans derives from the same evolutionary roots as the fight-or-flight reaction of a rat or the aversive maneuvering of a marine snail. Which means that anxiety, for all the philosophizing and psychologizing we've attached to it, may be an irreducibly biological phenomenon that is not so different in humans than in animals.

What, if anything, do we lose when our anxiety is reduced to the stuff of its physiological components—to deficiencies in serotonin and dopamine or to an excess of activity in the amygdala and basal ganglia? The theologian Paul Tillich, writing in 1944, suggested that *Angst* was the natural reaction of man to "fear of death, conscience, guilt, despair, daily life, etc." For Tillich, the crucial question of life was: Are we safe in some deity's care, or are we trudging along pointlessly toward death in a cold, mechanical, and indifferent universe? Is finding serenity mainly a matter of coming to terms with that question? Or is it, rather more mundanely, a matter of properly calibrating levels of serotonin in the synapses? Or are these somehow, after all, the same thing?

---

The James-Lange theory was later undermined by research on patients with spinal cord injuries that prevented them from receiving *any* somatic information from their viscera—people who literally could not feel muscle tension or stomach discomfort; people who were, in effect, brains without bodies—yet who still reported experiencing the unpleasant psychological sensations of dread or anxiety. This suggested that the James-Lange theory was, if not wholly wrong, at least incomplete. If patients unable to receive information about the state of their bodies can still experience anxiety, then maybe anxiety *is* primarily a mental state, one that doesn't require input from the rest of the body.

But various studies conducted since the early 1960s suggest that the James-Lange theory was not, after all, completely wrong. When researchers at Columbia gave study subjects an injection of adrenaline, the heart rate and breathing rate of all the subjects increased, and they all experienced an intensification of emotion—but the researchers could manipulate what emotion the subjects felt by changing the context. Those subjects given reason to feel positive emotions felt happy, while those given reason to feel negative emotions felt angry or anxious—and in every case they felt the respective emotion (whatever it happened to be) more powerfully than those subjects who had been given a placebo injection. The injection of adrenaline increased the *intensity* of emotion, but it did not determine *what emotion that would be;* the experimental context supplied that. This suggests that the autonomic systems of the body supply the mechanics of the emotion—but the mind's interpretation of the outside environment supplies the valence.

Other recent research suggests that James and Lange were right in observing that physiological processes in the body are crucial to driving emotions and determining their intensity. For instance, a growing number of studies show that facial expressions can *produce*—rather than just reflect—the emotions associated with them. Smile and you will be happy; tremble, as James said, and you will be afraid.

*Perhaps man is one of the most fearful creatures, since added to the basic fears of predators and hostile conspecifics come intellectually based existential fears.*
—IRENÄUS EIBL-EIBESFELDT, "FEAR, DEFENCE AND AGGRESSION IN ANIMALS AND MAN: SOME ETHOLOGICAL PERSPECTIVES" (1990)

Not long ago, I e-mailed Dr. W., who has specialized in treating anxiety for forty years, to ask him to boil his definition of it down to a single sentence.

"Anxiety," he wrote, "is apprehension about future suffering—the fearful anticipation of an unbearable catastrophe one is hopeless to prevent." For Dr. W., the defining signature of anxiety, and what makes it more than a pure animal instinct, is its orientation toward the future. In this, Dr. W.'s thinking is in line with that of many leading theorists of the emotions (for instance, Robert Plutchik, a physician and psychologist who was one of the twentieth century's most influential scholars of the emotions, defined anxiety as the "combination of anticipation and fear"), and he points out that Darwin, for all his emphasis on the behavioral similarities between animals and humans, believed the same. ("If we expect to suffer, we are anxious," Darwin wrote in *The Expression of the Emotions in Man and Animals*. "If we have no hope of relief, we despair.") Animals have no abstract concept of the future; they also have no abstract concept of anxiety, no ability to worry about their fears. An animal may experience stress-induced "difficulty in breathing" or "spasms of the heart" (as Freud put it)—but no animal can *worry* about that symptom or *interpret* it in any way. An animal cannot be a hypochondriac.

Also, an animal cannot fear death. Rats and marine snails are not abstractly aware of the prospect of a car accident, or a plane crash, or a terrorist attack, or nuclear annihilation—or of social rejection, or diminishment of status, or professional humiliation, or the inevitable loss of people we love, or the finitude of corporeal existence. This, along with our capacity to be consciously aware of the sensations of fear, and to cogitate about them, gives the human experience of anxiety an existential dimension that the "alarm response" of a marine snail utterly lacks. For Dr. W., this existential dimension is crucial.

Dr. W., echoing Freud, says that while *fear* is produced by "real" threats from the world, *anxiety* is produced by threats from within our selves. Anxiety is, as Dr. W. puts it, "a signal that the usual defenses against unbearably painful views of the self are failing." Rather than confronting the reality that your marriage is failing, or that your career has not panned out, or that you are declining into geriatric decrepitude, or that you are going to die—hard existential truths to reckon with—your mind sometimes instead produces distracting and defensive anxiety symptoms, transmuting psychic distress into panic attacks or free-floating general anxiety or developing phobias onto which you project your inner turmoil. Interestingly, a number of recent studies have found that at the moment an anxious patient begins to reckon consciously with a previously hidden psychic conflict, lifting it from the murk of the unconscious into the light of awareness, a slew of physiological measurements change markedly: blood pressure and heart rate drop, skin conductance decreases, levels of stress hormones in the blood decline. Chronic physical symptoms—backaches, stomachaches, headaches—often dissipate spontaneously as emotional troubles that had previously been "somaticized," or converted into physical symptoms, get brought into conscious awareness.*

But in believing that anxiety disorders typically arise from failed efforts to resolve basic existential dilemmas, Dr. W. is, as we will see, running against the grain of modern psychopharmacology (which proffers the evidence of sixty years of drug studies to argue that anxiety and depression are based on "chemical imbalances"), neuroscience (whose emergence has demonstrated not only the brain activity associated with various emotional states but also, in some cases, the specific structural abnormalities associated with mental illness), and temperament studies and molecular genetics (which suggest, rather convincingly, a powerful role for heredity in the determination of one's baseline level of anxiety and susceptibility to psychiatric illness).

Dr. W. doesn't dispute the findings from any of those modes of

---

* Even as much of Freudianism has been substantially discredited, elements of Freud's theories have gained empirical support in the recent findings of research like this.

inquiry. He believes medication can be an effective treatment for the symptoms of anxiety. But his view, based on thirty years of clinical work with hundreds of anxious patients, is that at the root of almost all clinical anxiety is some kind of existential crisis about what he calls the "ontological givens"—that we will grow old, that we will die, that we will lose people we love, that we will likely endure identity-shaking professional failures and personal humiliations, that we must struggle to find meaning and purpose in our lives, and that we must make trade-offs between personal freedom and emotional security and between our desires and the constraints of our relationships and our communities. In this view, our phobias of rats or snakes or cheese or honey (yes, honey; the actor Richard Burton could not bear to be in a room with honey, even if it was sealed in a jar, even if the jar was closed in a drawer) are displacements of our deeper existential concerns projected onto outward things.

Early in his career, Dr. W. treated a college sophomore who had trained his entire life to become a professional concert pianist. When the patient's professors told him that he wasn't talented enough to realize his dream, he was beset by terrible panic attacks. In Dr. W.'s view, the panic was a symptom produced by the patient's inability to reckon with the underlying existential loss here: the end of his professional aspirations, the demise of his self-conception as a concert pianist. Treating the panic allowed the student to experience his despair at this loss—and then begin to construct a new identity. Another patient, a forty-three-year-old physician with a thriving medical practice, developed panic disorder when, right around the time his older son went off to college, he began getting injuries playing tennis, a sport at which he had formerly excelled. The panic, Dr. W. concluded, was precipitated by these dual losses (of his son's childhood, of his own athletic vigor), which in combination aroused existential concerns about decline into decrepitude and death. By helping the physician come to terms with these losses, and to accept the "ontological" reality of his eventual decline and mortality, Dr. W. enabled him to shake free of the anxiety and depression.*

* I should say here that I am not betraying any confidentiality in writing about these patients; Dr. W. has published (anonymous) case histories of them in various places.

In Dr. W.'s view, anxiety and panic symptoms serve as what he calls a "protective screen" (what Freud called a "neurotic defense") against the searing pain associated with confronting loss or mortality or threats to one's self-esteem (roughly what Freud called the ego). In some cases, the intense anxiety or panic symptoms patients experience are neurotic distractions from, or a way of coping with, negative self-images or feelings of inadequacy—what Dr. W. calls "self-wounds."

I find Dr. W.'s existential-meaning-based interpretations of anxiety symptoms to be in some ways more interesting than the prevailing biomedical ones. But for a long time, I found the modern research literature on anxiety—which has much more to do with "neuronal firing rates in the amygdala and locus coeruleus" (as the neuroscientists put it) and with "boosting the serotonergic system" and "inhibiting the glutamate system" (as the psychopharmacologists put it) and with identifying the specific "single-nucleotide polymorphisms" on various genes that predict an anxious temperament (as the behavioral geneticists put it) than with existential issues—to be more scientific, and more convincing, than Dr. W.'s theory of anxiety. I still do. But less so than I did before.

Not long ago in my own therapy with Dr. W., we moved gingerly into "imaginal" exposure for my phobias.* Dr. W. and I established a hierarchy of frightening situations and then did a gentle "staged deconditioning," in which I was supposed to picture certain distressing images while doing deep-breathing relaxation exercises, hoping to reduce the anxiety these images stimulated. Once I'd conjured an image and was trying to hold it in my mind without panicking, Dr. W. would ask me what I was feeling.

This proved to be surprisingly hard. Although I was sitting safely in the consulting room of Dr. W.'s suburban home and was free to stop the exercise at any time, merely imagining frightening scenarios became an agony of anxiety. The smallest, most unlikely-seeming cues—seeing myself riding on a chairlift or a turbulence-racked airplane; picturing the green bucket that would be placed by my bed when I had an upset

---

* This therapy draws on a technique called systematic desensitization, which was pioneered in the 1960s by Joseph Wolpe, an influential behavioral psychologist, whose initial research was on how to eliminate fear responses in cats.

stomach as a young boy—set me to sweating and hyperventilating. So intense was my anxious response to these purely mental images that several times I had to leave Dr. W.'s office to walk around in his backyard and calm down.

In these deconditioning sessions, Dr. W. has tried to get me to focus on what, precisely, I'm anxious about.

I have a hard time answering this question. During the imaginal exposure—let alone when I'm actually confronted with a "phobic stimulus"—I cannot focus at all on answering the question. I just feel complete, all-consuming dread, and all I want is to escape—from terror, from consciousness, from my body, from my life.*

Over the course of several sessions, something unexpected happened. When I tried to engage with the phobia, I'd get derailed by sadness. I'd sit on the couch in Dr. W.'s office, doing deep breathing and trying to picture the scene from my "deconditioning hierarchy," and my mind would start to wander.

"Tell me what you're feeling," Dr. W. would say.

"A little sad," I would say.

"Go with that," he would say.

And then seconds later I'd be racked by sobs.

I am embarrassed to recount this little tale. For one thing, how unmanly can I be? For another, I am not a believer in the magical emotional breakthrough or the cathartic release. But I confess that I did feel some kind of relief as I sat there shuddering with sobs.

This outburst of sadness occurred each time we tried the exercise.

"What's going on?" I asked Dr. W. "What does this mean?"

"It means we're onto something," he said, handing me a tissue to dry my tears.

Yes, I know, everything about this scene makes me cringe, too. But at the time, as I sobbed there on the couch, Dr. W.'s statement felt like a wonderfully supportive and authentic gesture—which touched me and made me cry even harder.

"You're in the heart of the wound now," he said.

---

* I once suggested to Dr. W. that if I had a gun and knew that I at least had the option of escaping phobic terror, then maybe my anxiety would subside, since having the *option* of escape would give me the feeling of some control.

"Perhaps," he conceded. "But it would also increase the chances of you offing yourself."

Dr. W. believes, as Freud did, that anxiety could be an adaptation meant to shield the psyche from some other source of sadness or pain. I ask him why, if that's the case, the anxiety often feels much more intense than the sadness. As hard as it's making me cry, this "wound" that I'm supposedly in feels less unpleasant than the terror I feel when I'm on a turbulent flight, or when I'm feeling nauseated, or when I was enduring separation anxiety as a child.

"That's often the case," Dr. W. says.

I'm not sure what to make of this. Why do I feel so much better—happier and relatively less anxious—after swimming around in my putative "wound"?*

"We don't know yet," Dr. W. says. "But we're getting somewhere."

---

* In their early work developing psychoanalytic techniques together during the 1890s, Sigmund Freud and his mentor Josef Breuer called this cathartic dredging up of suppressed thoughts and emotions "chimney sweeping."

PART II

# A History of My Nervous Stomach

# CHAPTER 3

# A Rumbling in the Belly

*Anxiousness—a difficult disease. The patient thinks he has some-thing like a thorn, something pricking him in his viscera, and nau-sea torments him.*
　　　*—*HIPPOCRATES, *On Diseases* (FOURTH CENTURY B.C.)

*I have this recurring nightmare of being ill as a bride, running out of the church and abandoning my husband at the altar.*
　　　*—*EMMA PELLING, QUOTED IN THE JUNE 5, 2008,
　　UNITED PRESS INTERNATIONAL ARTICLE "BRIDE'S VOMIT
　　　　　FEAR DELAYS WEDDING"

I struggle with emetophobia, a pathological fear of vomiting, but it's been a little while since I last vomited. More than a little while, actu-ally: as I type this, it's been, to be precise, thirty-five years, two months, four days, twenty-two hours, and forty-nine minutes. Meaning that more than 83 percent of my days on earth have transpired in the time since I last threw up, during the early evening of March 17, 1977. I didn't vomit in the 1980s. I didn't vomit in the 1990s. I haven't vomited in the new millennium. And needless to say, I hope to make it through the balance of my life without having that streak disrupted. (Naturally, I was reluctant even to type this paragraph, and particularly that last sentence, for fear of jinxing myself or inviting cosmic rebuke, and I am knocking wood and offering up prayers to various gods and Fates as I write this.)

What this means is that I have spent, by rough calculation, at least 60 percent of my waking life thinking about and worrying about something that I have spent 0 percent of the last three-plus decades doing. This is irrational.

A part of me protests instantly: *But wait, what if it's not irrational? What if, in fact, there's a causal relationship between my worrying about vomiting and my not doing it? What if my eternal vigilance is what protects me—through magic or through neurotic enhancement of my immune system or through sheer obsessive germ avoidance—from food poisoning and stomach viruses?*

When I've made this argument to various psychotherapists over the years, they respond: "Let's say you're right about the causal relation—your behavior is still irrational. Look how much time you waste, and what you've done to your quality of life, worrying about something that, while unpleasant, is generally rare and almost always medically insignificant." Even if the cost of relaxing my vigilance was a stomach virus or bout of food poisoning every so often, the therapists say, wouldn't that be worthwhile for what I'd gain in getting so much of my life back?

I suppose a rational, nonphobic person would answer yes. And they'd surely be right. But for me the answer remains, emphatically, no.

An astonishing portion of my life is built around trying to evade vomiting and preparing for the eventuality that I might. Some of my behavior is standard germophobic stuff: avoiding hospitals and public restrooms, giving wide berth to sick people, obsessively washing my hands, paying careful attention to the provenance of everything I eat.

But other behavior is more extreme, given the statistical unlikelihood of my vomiting at any given moment. I stash motion sickness bags, purloined from airplanes, all over my home and office and car in case I'm suddenly overtaken by the need to vomit. I carry Pepto-Bismol and Dramamine and other antiemetic medications with me at all times. Like a general monitoring the enemy's advance, I keep a detailed mental map of recorded incidences of norovirus (the most common strain of stomach virus) and other forms of gastroenteritis, using the Internet to track outbreaks in the United States and around the world. Such is the nature of my obsession that I can tell you at any given moment exactly which nursing homes in New Zealand, cruise ships in the Mediterranean, and elementary schools in Virginia are contending with outbreaks. Once, when I was lamenting to my father that there is no central clearinghouse for information about norovirus outbreaks the way there is for influenza, my wife interjected. "Yes, there is," she said. We looked at her quizzically. "You," she said, and she had a point.

Emetophobia has governed my life, with a fluctuating intensity of tyranny, for some thirty-five years. Nothing—not the thousands of psychotherapy appointments I've sat through, not the dozens of medications I've taken, not the hypnosis I underwent when I was eighteen, not the stomach viruses I've contracted and withstood without vomiting— has succeeded in stamping it out.

For several years, I worked with a therapist named Dr. M., a young psychologist who had a practice at Boston University's Center for Anxiety and Related Disorders. I had originally sought treatment for my public speaking anxiety, but after several months of consultations Dr. M. proposed that we also try applying the principles of what's known as exposure therapy toward extinguishing my emetophobia.

Which is how I came to find myself not long ago at the center of an absurdist tableau.

I'm giving a speech about the founding of the Peace Corps—which feels a little artificial and awkward to begin with, because the venue is a small conference room off a hallway in the Center for Anxiety and Related Disorders. My audience consists of Dr. M. and three graduate students she's corralled at a moment's notice from around the building. Meanwhile, in the corner of the room, a large television is showing a video loop of a series of people throwing up.

"Originally, President Kennedy's plan was to house the Peace Corps inside the Agency for International Development," I'm saying as a man on the screen to my right retches loudly. "But Lyndon Johnson had been convinced by Kennedy's brother-in-law Sargent Shriver that stuffing the Peace Corps inside an existing government bureaucracy would stifle its effectiveness and end up neutering it." On the screen, vomit spatters onto the floor.

A device attached to my finger is monitoring my heart rate and levels of blood oxygen. Every few minutes, Dr. M. interrupts my speech to say: "Give me your anxiety rating now." I'm to respond by giving her an assessment of my anxiety at that moment on a scale of 1 to 10, with 1 being completely calm and 10 being unalloyed terror. "About a six," I say truthfully. I'm less anxious than embarrassed and grossed out.

"Go on," she says, and I resume my lecture as the cacophony of puking continues on the screen. When I glance up, I can see that the graduate students, two young women and a young man, are trying to pay attention to what I'm saying, but they're clearly distracted by all the literal upheaval in the background. The male student is looking green; his Adam's apple is twitching. I can tell he's fighting his gag reflex.

I'm feeling a little anxious, yes, but also frankly ridiculous. How is giving a fake speech to a fake audience amid cascading images of vomiting going to cure me of my phobia of public speaking or of throwing up?

As bizarre as this scene was, the therapeutic principles underlying it are well established. Exposure therapy—in essence, exposure to whatever's causing the pathological fear, whether that's rats or snakes or airplanes or heights or throwing up—has for dozens of years been a standard treatment for phobias, and it is now an important component of cognitive-behavioral therapy. The logic of this approach—which has lately been undergirded by neuroscience research—is that extended exposure to the object of fear, under the guidance of a therapist, makes that object less frightening. Someone with fear of heights would, accompanied by a therapist, walk farther and farther out onto the balconies of higher and higher buildings. Someone with siderodromophobia (train phobia) would take a short subway ride, and then a longer one, and then a still-longer one, until the fear diminished and was gradually extinguished completely. A more aggressive form of exposure, known as flooding, calls for a more intense experience. To treat, say, airplane phobia using the standard exposure technique, a fearful flier might be started off with visits to the airport to watch airplanes take off and land until his anxiety level comes down. He would progress to actually walking onto an airplane and getting acclimated to being on it, allowing the intensity of physical responses and fearful emotions to crest and fall, and then advance to taking a short commercial flight in the company of a therapist. Ultimately, he would graduate to taking longer flights alone. Applying flooding to aerophobia might entail, instead, starting the patient out on a tiny twin-engine plane, flying him up into the sky, and subjecting him to stomach-churning aeronautical gymnastics. According to the theory, the patient's anxiety will spike initially but will then subside as he learns quickly that he can survive both the flying and the experience of his own anxiety. Some therapists maintain relationships with local pilots so they can offer this sort of therapy. (Dr. M. offered it to me; I declined.)

David Barlow, the former head of the Center for Anxiety and Related Disorders, says the goal of exposure therapy is to "scare the hell out of the patient" in order to teach him that he can handle the fear. Barlow's exposure techniques may sound cruel and unusual, but he claims a phobia cure rate of up to 85 percent (often within a week or less), and an ample number of studies support this claim.*

The idea behind Dr. M.'s notion of trying to combine my exposures to public speaking and to vomiting was to ratchet up my anxiety as high as possible—the better to "expose" me to it, and to the things that I feared, so that I could begin the process of "extinguishing" those fears. The problem was that these simulations were too artificial to generate the requisite level of anxiety in me. Speaking to a few graduate students in Dr. M.'s office made me nervous and uncomfortable, but it never generated anything like the all-consuming dread that a real public speaking engagement does—especially since I knew that the graduate students were all studying anxiety disorders. I didn't feel compelled, as I usually do, to try to hide my anxiety; I already assumed Dr. M.'s colleagues saw me as damaged, and therefore I didn't have to go to such anxiety-producing lengths to hide my damagedness. So although even small meetings at work could still throw me into an agony of panic— to say nothing of the large-scale public speaking engagements that I would dread for months in advance—the faux presentations I'd make in my weekly sessions with Dr. M. felt like clammy facsimiles of the real thing. Awkward and unpleasant, yes, but not sufficiently anxiety provoking to be effective exposure therapy.

Similarly, while the experience of watching the vomit videos was discomfiting and unpleasant, it produced nothing close to the level of limb-trembling, soul-shaking horror that feeling about to vomit does; I knew the videos couldn't infect me, and I knew I could always sim-

---

* On the other hand, a lot of the evidence suggests that phobic anxiety is much more easily formed than extinguished. Barlow himself has a phobia of heights that he admits he has been unable to cure himself of.

ply look away, or turn them off, if my anxiety became too much to bear. Crucially—and fatally, as far as effective exposure therapy went— escape was always possible.*

Determining—as a number of other therapists, before and since, also have—that my fear of vomiting lay at the core of my other fears (for instance, I'm afraid of airplanes partly because I might get airsick), Dr. M. proposed that we concentrate on that.

"Makes sense to me," I concurred.

"There's only one way to do that properly," she said. "You need to confront the phobia head-on, to expose yourself to that which you fear the most."

*Uh-oh.*

"We have to make you throw up."

*No. No way. Absolutely not.*

She explained that a colleague had just successfully treated an emetophobe by giving her ipecac syrup, which induces vomiting. The patient, a female executive who had flown in from New York to be treated, had spent a week visiting the Center for Anxiety and Related Disorders. Each day she'd take ipecac administered by a nurse, vomit, and then process the experience with the therapist—"decatastrophizing" it, as the cognitive-behavioral therapists say. After a week, she flew back to New York—cured, Dr. M. reported, of her phobia.

I remained skeptical. Dr. M. gave me an academic journal article reporting on a clinical case of emetophobia successfully treated with the ipecac exposure method.

"This is just a single case," I said. "It's from 1979."

"There have been lots of others," she said, and reminded me again of her colleague's patient.

"I can't do it."

---

* Incidentally, the very existence of these vomit videos—and I've now seen several—is evidence of how common emetophobia is; using them has become common practice in treating phobics. Some therapists also try to gradually decondition their emetophobic patients by exposing them to fake vomit. (In case you're interested, here's a recipe recommended by two Emory University psychologists I met at a conference in 2008: Mix one can of beef and barley soup with one can of cream of mushroom soup. Add small quantities of sweet relish and vinegar. Pour into a glass jar, seal, and leave on a windowsill for one week.)

"You don't have to do anything you don't want to do," Dr. M. said. "I'll never force you to do anything. But the only way to overcome this phobia is to confront it. And the only way to confront it is to throw up."

We had many versions of this conversation over the course of several months. I trusted Dr. M. despite the inane-seeming exposures she cooked up for me. (She was kind and pretty and smart.) So one autumn day I surprised her by saying I was open to thinking about the idea. Gently, reassuringly, she talked me through how the process would work. She and the staff nurse would reserve a lab upstairs for my privacy and would be with me the whole time. I'd eat something, take the ipecac, and vomit in short order (and I would survive just fine, she said). Then we would work on "reframing my cognitions" about throwing up. I'd learn that it wasn't something to be terrified of, and I'd be liberated.

She took me upstairs to meet the nurse. Nurse R. showed me the lab and told me that taking ipecac was a standard form of exposure therapy; she said she'd helped preside over a number of exposures for erstwhile emetophobes. "Just the other week, we had a guy in here," she said. "He was very nervous, but it worked out just fine."

We went back downstairs to Dr. M.'s office.

"Okay," I said. "I'll do it. Maybe."

Over the next few weeks, we'd keep scheduling the exposure—and then I'd show up on the appointed day and demur, saying I couldn't go through with it. I did this enough times that I shocked Dr. M. when, on an unseasonably warm Thursday in early December, I presented myself at her office for my regular appointment and said, "Okay. I'm ready."

The exercise was star-crossed from the beginning. Nurse R. was out of ipecac, so she had to run to the pharmacy to get some more while I waited for an hour in Dr. M.'s office. Then it turned out that the upstairs lab was booked, so the exposure would have to take place in a small public restroom in the basement. I was constantly on the verge of backing out; probably the only reason I didn't was that I knew I could.

What follows is an edited excerpt drawn from the dispassionate-as-possible account I wrote up afterward on Dr. M.'s recommendation. (Writing an emotionally neutral account is a commonly prescribed way of trying to forestall post-traumatic stress disorder after a traumatic experience.) If you're emetophobic yourself, or even just a little squea-mish, you might want to skip over it.

We met up with Nurse R. in the basement restroom. After some discussion, I took the ipecac.

Having passed the point of no return, I felt my anxiety surge considerably. I began to shake a little. Still, I was hopeful that sickness would strike quickly and be over fast and that I would discover the experience was not as bad as I'd feared.

Dr. M. had attached a pulse and oxygen-level monitor to my finger. As we waited for the nausea to hit, she asked me to state my anxiety level on a scale of 1 to 10. "About a nine," I said.

By now I was starting to feel a little nauseated. Suddenly I was struck by heaving and I turned to the toilet. I retched twice—but nothing felt like it was coming up. I knelt on the floor and waited, still hoping the event would come quickly and then be over with. The monitor on my finger felt like an encumbrance, so I took it off.

After a time, I heaved again, my diaphragm convulsing. Nurse R. explained that dry-heaving precedes the main event. I was now desperate for this to be over.

The nausea began coming in intense waves, crashing over me and then receding. I kept feeling like I was going to vomit, but then I would heave noisily again and nothing would come up. Several times I could actually feel my stomach convulse. But I would heave and . . . nothing would happen.

My sense of time at this point gets blurry. During each bout of retching, I would begin perspiring profusely, and when the nausea would pass, I would be dripping with sweat. I felt faint, and I worried that I would pass out and vomit and aspi-rate and die. When I mentioned feeling light-headed, Nurse R. said that my color looked good. But I thought she and Dr. M. seemed slightly alarmed. This increased my anxiety—because if *they* were worried, then I should really be scared, I thought. (On the other hand, at some level I *wanted* to pass out, even if that meant dying.)

After about forty minutes and several more bouts of retching, Dr. M. and Nurse R. suggested I take more ipecac. But I feared a second dose would subject me to worse nausea for a longer period of time. I worried I might just keep dry-heaving for hours or days. At some point, I switched from hoping that I would vomit quickly and have the ordeal over with to thinking that maybe I could fight the ipecac and simply wait for the nausea to wear off. I was exhausted, horribly nauseated, and utterly miserable. In between bouts of retching, I lay on the bathroom tiles, shaking.

A long period passed. Nurse R. and Dr. M. kept trying to convince me to take more ipecac, but by now I just wanted to avoid vomiting. I hadn't retched for a while, so I was surprised to be stricken by another bout of violent heaving. I could feel my stomach turning over, and I thought for sure that this time something would happen. It didn't. I choked down some secondary waves, and then the nausea eased significantly. This was the point when I began to feel hopeful that I would manage to escape the ordeal without throwing up.

Nurse R. seemed angry. "Man, you have more control than anyone I've ever seen," she said. (At one point, she asked peevishly if I was resisting because I wasn't prepared to terminate treatment yet. Dr. M. interjected that this was clearly not the case—I'd taken the ipecac, for God's sake.) Eventually—several hours had now elapsed since I ingested the ipecac—Nurse R. left, saying she had never seen someone take ipecac and not vomit.*

After some more time passed, and some more encouragement from Dr. M. to try to "complete the exposure," we decided to "end the attempt." I still felt nauseated, but less so than before. We talked briefly in her office, and then I left.

Driving home, I became extremely anxious that I would vomit and crash. I waited at red lights in terror.

When I got home, I crawled into bed and slept for several hours. I felt better when I woke up; the nausea was gone. But

---

* I've since read that up to 15 percent of people—a disproportionate number of them emetophobes—don't vomit from a single dose of ipecac.

that night I had recurring nightmares of retching in the bathroom in the basement of the center.

The next morning I managed to get to work for a meeting—but then panic surged and I had to go home. For the next several days, I was too anxious to leave the house.

Dr. M. called the next day to make sure I was okay. She clearly felt bad about having subjected me to such a miserable experience. Though I was traumatized by the whole episode, her sense of guilt was so palpable that I felt sympathetic toward her. At the end of the account I composed at her request, which was accurate as far as it went, I masked the emotional reality of what I thought (which was that the exposure had been an abject disaster and that Nurse R. was a fatuous bitch) with an antiseptic clinical tone. "Given my history, I was brave to take the ipecac," I wrote. "I wish that I had vomited quickly. But the whole experience was traumatic, and my general anxiety levels—and my phobia of vomiting—are more intense than they were before the exposure. I also, however, recognize that, based on this experience in resisting the effects of the ipecac, my power to prevent myself from vomiting is quite strong."

Stronger, it seems, than Dr. M.'s. She told me she had to cancel all of her afternoon appointments on the day of the exposure—watching me gagging and fighting with the ipecac evidently had made her so nauseated that she spent the afternoon at home, throwing up. I confess I took some perverse pleasure from the irony here—the ipecac *I* took made *someone else* vomit—but mainly I felt traumatized and intensely anxious. It seems I'm not very good at getting over my phobias but quite good at making my therapists and their associates sick.

I continued seeing Dr. M. for a few more months—we "processed" the botched exposure and then, both of us wanting to forget the whole thing, turned from emetophobia to various other phobias and neuroses—but the sessions now had an elegiac, desultory feel. We both knew it was over.*

---

* Eventually, she moved away, accepting a tenure-track faculty position at a university in the Southwest. I run into her occasionally at academic conferences on anxiety. Despite everything, I like her. But I always wonder: does it feel weird to her to be talking to a former patient who's now at these conferences with a notebook, posing as a journalist and a kind of lay expert on anxiety? How often does she

*That sphincter which serves to discharge our stomachs has dilations*
*and contractions proper to itself, independent of our wishes, and*
*even opposed to them.*

—MICHEL DE MONTAIGNE,

"ON THE POWER OF THE IMAGINATION" (1574)

The mind, as the neurophilosophers say, is fully embodied; it is, as Aristotle put it, "enmattered." The bodily clichés of nervous excitement ("butterflies in the stomach"), anxious anticipation ("a loosening of the bowels," "scared shitless"), or dread (felt "in the pit of the stomach") are not in fact clichés or even metaphors but truisms—accurate descriptions of the physiological correlates of anxious emotion. Doctors and philosophers have observed for millennia the potency of what the medical journals call the brain-gut axis. "There may even be some connection between a phobia and a beef-steak, so intimately related are the stomach and the brain," Wilfred Northfield wrote in 1934.

Nerve-disordered bellies are a bane of modern existence. According to a Harvard Medical School report, as many as 12 percent of all patient visits to primary care physicians in the United States are for irritable bowel syndrome, or IBS, a condition characterized by stomach pain and alternating bouts of constipation and diarrhea that most experts believe to be wholly or partly caused by stress or anxiety. First identified in 1830 by the British physician John Howship, IBS has since then been referred to as "spastic colon," "spastic bowel," "colitis," and "functional bowel disease," among other names. (Physicians in the Middle Ages and Renaissance referred to it as "windy melancholy" and "hypochondriache flatulence.") Because no one has ever definitively identified an organic cause of IBS, most doctors attribute its appearance to stress, emotional conflict, or some other psychological source. In the absence of a clear malfunction in the nerves and muscles of the gut, doctors tend to assume a malfunction in the brain—perhaps a hypersensitized awareness of sensations in the intestine. In one well-known set

think, *That's the guy I gave ipecac to, the guy I watched retching and weeping and shaking on the floor of a public restroom for hours?*

of experiments, when balloons were inflated in the colons of both IBS patients and healthy control subjects, the IBS patients reported a much lower threshold for pain, suggesting that the viscera–brain connection may be more sensitive in patients with irritable bowels.

This is consistent with a trait called anxiety sensitivity, which research has shown to be strongly correlated with panic disorder. Individuals who rate high on the so-called Anxiety Sensitivity Index, or ASI, have a high degree of what's known as interoceptive awareness, meaning they are highly attuned to the inner workings of their bodies, to the beepings and bleatings, the blips and burps, of their physiologies; they are more conscious of their heart rate, blood pressure, body temperature, breathing rates, digestive burblings, and so forth than other people are. This hyperawareness of physiological activity makes such people more prone to "internally cued panic attacks": the individual with a high ASI rating picks up on a subtle increase in heart rate or a slight sensation of dizziness or a vague, unidentifiable fluttering in the chest; this perception, in turn, produces a frisson of conscious anxiety (*Am I having a heart attack?*), which causes those physical sensations to intensify. The individual immediately perceives this intensification of sensation—which in turn generates more anxiety, which produces still more intensified sensations, and before long the individual is in the throes of panic. A number of recent studies published in periodicals like the *Journal of Psychosomatic Research* have found a powerful interrelationship among anxiety sensitivity, irritable bowel syndrome, worry, and a personality trait known as neuroticism, which psychologists define as you would expect—a tendency to dwell on the negative; a high susceptibility to excessive feelings of anxiety, guilt, and depression; and a predisposition to overreact to minor stress. Unsurprisingly, people who score high on cognitive measures of neuroticism are disproportionately prone to developing phobias, panic disorder, and depression. (People who score low on the neuroticism scale are disproportionately resistant to those disorders.)

Evidence suggests that people with irritable bowels have bodies that are more physically reactive to stress. I recently came across an article in the medical journal *Gut* that explained the circular relationship between cognition (your conscious thought) and physiological correlates (what your body does in response to that thought): people who are less anxious tend to have minds that don't overreact to stress and bodies that don't overreact to stress when their minds experience it, while clinically anxious people tend to have sensitive minds in sensitive bodies—small amounts of stress set them to worrying, and small amounts of worrying set their bodies to malfunctioning. People with nervous stomachs are also more likely than people with settled stomachs to complain of headaches, palpitations, shortness of breath, and general fatigue. Some evidence suggests that people with irritable bowel syndrome have greater sensitivity to pain, are more likely to complain about minor ailments like colds, and are more likely to consider themselves sick than other people.

Most cases of stomach upset, the physiologist Walter Cannon wrote back in 1909, are "nervous in origin." In his article "The Influence of Emotional States on the Functions of the Alimentary Canal," Cannon concluded that anxious thoughts had direct effects—through the nerves of the sympathetic nervous system—on both the physical movements of the stomach (that is, on peristalsis, the process by which the digestive system moves food through the alimentary canal) and gastric secretions. Cannon's theory has been borne out by modern surveys conducted at primary care centers, which find that most routine stomach trouble emanates from mental distress: between 42 and 61 percent of all patients with functional bowel disorders have also been given an official psychiatric diagnosis, most often anxiety or depression; one study has found a 40 percent overlap between patients with panic disorder and functional GI disease.*

---

* As further evidence that a great deal of stomach trouble starts in the brain, not in the gut, no stomach medication has yet been proved consistently effective against the symptoms of irritable bowel syndrome—but substantial evidence suggests that certain antidepressant medications can be effective. (Before the 1960s, one of the most frequent prescriptions for IBS was a cocktail of morphine and barbiturates.) In a recent study, IBS patients injected with the SSRI antidepressant Celexa reported reduced "visceral hypersensitivity."

Michael Gershon, a professor of pathology and cell biology at Columbia University, says that the reason antidepressants reduce IBS symptoms is not that they affect neurotransmitters in the brain but that they affect neurotransmitters in the stomach. Some 95 percent of the serotonin in our bodies can be found in our stomachs. (When serotonin was discovered in the 1930s, it was originally called enteramine because of its high concentration in the gut.) Gershon calls the stomach "the second brain" and observes that stomach trouble is as likely to beget anxiety as the other way around. "The brain in

"Fear brings about diarrhea," Aristotle wrote, "because the emotion causes an augmenting of heat in the belly." Hippocrates attributed both bowel trouble and anxiety (not to mention hemorrhoids and acne) to a surplus of black bile. Galen, the ancient Roman physician, blamed yellow bile. "People attacked by fear experience no slight inflow of yellow bile into the stomach," he observed, "which makes them feel a gnawing sensation, and they do not cease feeling both distress of mind and the gnawing until they have vomited up the bile."

But it was only in 1833, with the publication of a monograph called *Experiments and Observations on the Gastric Juice and the Physiology of Digestion,* that the link between emotional states and indigestion began to be understood with any kind of scientific precision. On June 6, 1822, Alexis St. Martin, a hunter employed by the American Fur Company, was accidentally shot in the stomach at close range by a musket loaded with buck shot. He was expected to die—but under the care of William Beaumont, a physician in upstate New York, he survived, albeit with an unusual condition: an unhealed open hole, or fistula, in his stomach. Beaumont realized that the hunter's fistula provided a remarkable opportunity for scientific observation: he could literally see into St. Martin's stomach. Over the next decade, Beaumont conducted many experiments using the hunter's fistula as a window into his digestive workings.

Beaumont noticed that St. Martin's emotional states had a powerful effect on his stomach, one readily observable to the naked eye: the mucosal lining of the hunter's stomach would change color dramatically, like a mood ring, in tandem with his emotional states. Sometimes the stomach lining was bright red; at other times, such as when St. Martin was anxious, it turned pale.

"I have availed myself of the opportunity afforded by an occurrence of circumstances which can probably never occur again," Beaumont wrote. But he was wrong. Medical literature records at least two subsequent instances of digestion research conducted on patients with holes in their stomachs over the course of the next century. And then, in 1941,

---

the bowel has got to work right or no one will have the luxury to think at all," he says. "No one thinks straight when his mind is focused on the toilet."

Stewart Wolf and Harold Wolff, physicians at New York Hospital in Manhattan, discovered Tom.

One day in 1904, when Tom was nine years old, he took a swig of what he thought was beer (it was in his father's beer pail) but turned out to be boiling hot clam chowder. The chowder seared his upper digestive tract and knocked him unconscious. By the time his mother delivered him to the hospital, his esophagus had fused shut. For the rest of his life, the only way for him to receive nourishment was through a surgically opened hole in the stomach wall. The hole was ringed on the outside by a segment of his stomach lining. He fed himself by chewing his food and then inserting it directly into his stomach through a funnel placed in the hole in his abdomen.

Tom came to the attention of Drs. Wolf and Wolff in 1941, when, while working as a sewer laborer, he was compelled to seek medical assistance after his wound became irritated. Recognizing the unusual research opportunity represented by Tom's condition, the doctors hired him as a lab assistant and conducted multiple experiments on him over the course of seven months. The results were published in their 1943 book, *Human Gastric Function,* a landmark of psychosomatic research.

Building on Beaumont's findings, the doctors observed that the lining of Tom's stomach varied significantly in color based on its level of activity—from "faint yellowish red to a deep cardinal shade." Greater levels of digestive activity tended to correlate with deeper shades of red (suggesting increased blood flow to the stomach), while lesser levels, including those induced by anxiety, correlated with paler colors (suggesting the flow of blood away from the stomach).

The doctors were able to chart correlations that had long been assumed but were never scientifically proved. One afternoon another doctor barged into the lab, swearing to himself and rapidly opening and closing drawers, looking for documents that had been mislaid. Tom, whose job it was to keep the lab tidy, became alarmed—he feared he would lose his job. The lining of his stomach went instantly pale, dropping from "90 percent redness" on the color scale to 20 percent. Acid secretion nearly stopped. When the doctor found the missing papers a few minutes later, acid secretion resumed and the color gradually returned to Tom's stomach.

At some level, all this is unsurprising; everyone knows that anxiety can cause gastrointestinal distress. (My friend Anne says that the most effective weight-loss program she ever tried was the Stressful Divorce Diet.) But *Human Gastric Function* represented the first time that the connections had been charted in such precise and systematic detail. The relationship between Tom's mental state and his digestion was not vague and diffuse; his stomach was a concrete and direct register of his psychology. Summing up their observations, Wolf and Wolff concluded that there was a strong inverse correlation between what they called "emotional security" and stomach discomfort.

That's certainly true in my case. Being anxious makes my stomach hurt and my bowels loosen. My stomach hurting and my bowels loosening makes me *more* anxious, which makes my stomach hurt more and my bowels even looser, and so nearly every trip of any significant distance from home ends up the same way: with me scurrying frantically from restroom to restroom on a kind of grand tour of the local latrines. For instance, I don't have terribly vivid recollections of the Vatican or the Colosseum or the Italian rail system. I do, however, have searing memories of the public restrooms in the Vatican and at the Colosseum and in various Italian train stations. One day, I visited the Trevi Fountain—or, rather, my wife and her family visited the Trevi Fountain. I visited the restroom of a nearby *gelateria,* where a series of impatient Italians banged on the door while I bivouacked there. The next day, when the family drove to Pompeii, I gave up and stayed in bed, a reassuringly short distance from the bathroom.

Some years earlier, following the fall of the Berlin Wall and the dissolution of the Warsaw Pact, I traveled to Eastern Europe to visit a girlfriend, Ann, who was studying in Poland. She had been there for six months by the time I visited; I had planned and aborted (because of anxiety) several previous trips, and only the fear that Ann would finally break up with me if I didn't visit her impelled me to fight through my tremendous dread of a transatlantic flight to meet her in Warsaw. Drugged to near unconsciousness, I flew from Boston to London and then to Warsaw. Befogged by sedatives, antiemetic medications, and jet lag, I stumbled through our first day and a half together. My bowels percolated to life about the time the rest of me did, when the Dramamine and Xanax wore off. We ended up traipsing around Eastern Europe from restroom to restroom. This was frustrating for her and harrowing for me—because, among other reasons, many Eastern European public commodes were at that time rather primitive; you often had to pay an attendant in advance on a per sheet basis for scratchy, ill-constructed toilet paper. By the end of the trip, I'd given up; Ann went sightseeing while I retreated to our hotel room, where at least I didn't have to gauge my toilet tissue use in advance.

Ann, understandably, grew peevish about this. After visiting the home of Franz Kafka (who, I note, suffered from chronic bowel trouble), we walked across Wenceslas Square in Prague while I griped about my aching belly. Ann could no longer contain her exasperation. "Maybe you should write a dissertation about your stomach," she said, mocking my preoccupation. A preoccupation, you may have noticed, that I have yet to overcome.

But when your stomach governs your existence, it's hard not to be preoccupied with it. A few searing experiences—soiling yourself on an airplane, say, or on a date—will focus you passionately on your gastrointestinal tract. You need to devote effort to planning around it—because it will not always plan around you.

Case in point: Fifteen years ago, while researching my first book, I spent part of the summer living with the extended Kennedy family on Cape Cod. One weekend, then-president Bill Clinton, who was vacationing on Martha's Vineyard, came across Nantucket Sound to go sailing with Ted Kennedy. Hyannis Port, where the Kennedys have their vacation homes, was crawling with presidential aides and Secret Service agents. With some time to kill before dinner, I decided to walk around town to take in the scene.

Bad idea. As is so often the case with irritable bowel syndrome, it was at precisely the moment I passed beyond Easily Accessible Bathroom Range that my clogged plumbing came unglued. Sprinting back to the house where I was staying, I was several times convinced I would not make it and—teeth gritted, sweating voluminously—was reduced to evaluating various bushes and storage sheds along the way for their potential as ersatz outhouses. Imagining what might ensue if a Secret Service agent were to happen upon me crouched in the shrubbery lent a kind of panicked, otherworldly strength to my efforts at self-possession.

As I approached the entrance, I was simultaneously reviewing the floor plan in my head (*Which of the many bathrooms in the mansion is closest to the front door? Can I make it all the way upstairs to my room?*) and praying that I wouldn't be fatally waylaid by a stray Kennedy or celebrity (Arnold Schwarzenegger, Liza Minnelli, and the secretary of the navy, among others, were visiting that weekend).

Fortunately, I made it into the house unaccosted. Then a quick calculation: *Can I make it all the way upstairs and down the hall to my suite in time? Or should I duck into the bathroom in the front hall?* Hearing footsteps above and fearing a protracted encounter, I opted for the latter and slipped into the bathroom, which was separated from the front hall by an anteroom and two separate doors. I scampered through the anteroom and flung myself onto the toilet.

My relief was extravagant and almost metaphysical.

But then I flushed and . . . something happened. My feet were getting wet. I looked down and saw to my horror that water was flowing out from the base of the toilet. Something seemed to have exploded. The floor—along with my shoes and pants and underwear—was covered in sewage. The water level was rising.

Instinctively, I stood up and turned around. Could the flooding be stopped? I removed the porcelain top of the toilet tank, scattering the flowers and potpourri that sat atop it, and frantically began fiddling with its innards. I tried things blindly, raising this and lowering that, jiggling this and wiggling that, fishing around in the water for something that might stem the swelling tide.

Somehow, whether of its own accord or as a result of my haphazard fiddling, the flooding slowed and then stopped. I surveyed the scene. My clothes were drenched and soiled. So was the bathroom rug. Without thinking, I slipped out of my pants and boxer shorts, wrapped them in the waterlogged rug, and jammed the whole mess into the wastebasket, which I stashed in the cupboard under the sink. *Have to deal with this later,* I thought to myself.

It was at this unpropitious moment that the dinner bell rang, signaling that it was time to muster for cocktails in the living room.

Which was right across the hall from the bathroom.

Where I was standing ankle-deep in sewage.

I pulled all the hand towels off the wall and dropped them on the ground to start sopping up some of the toilet water. I got down on my hands and knees and, unraveling the whole roll of toilet paper, began dabbing frenziedly at the water around me. It was like trying to dry a lake with a kitchen sponge.

What I was feeling at that point was not, strictly speaking, anxiety; rather, it was a resigned sense that the jig was up, that my humiliation would be complete and total. I'd soiled myself, destroyed the estate's septic system, and might soon be standing half naked before God knows how many members of the political and Hollywood elite.

In the distance, voices were moving closer. It occurred to me that I had two choices. I could hunker down in the bathroom, hiding and waiting out the cocktail party and dinner—at the risk of having to fend off anyone who might start banging on the door—and use the time to try to clean up the wreckage before slipping up to my bedroom after everyone had gone to bed. Or I could try to make a break for it.

I took all of the soiled towels and toilet paper and shoved them into the cupboard, then set about preparing my escape. I retrieved the least soiled towel (which was nonetheless dirty and sodden) and wrapped it gingerly around my waist. I crept to the door and listened for voices and footsteps, trying to gauge distance and speed of approach. Knowing I had scarcely any time before everyone converged on the center of the house, I slipped out the bathroom door and through the anteroom, sprint-walked across the hallway, and darted up the stairs. I hit the first landing, made a hairpin turn, and headed up the next flight to the second floor—where I nearly ran headlong into John F. Kennedy Jr. and another man.

"Hi, Scott," Kennedy said.*

"Uh, hi," I said, racking my brain for a plausible explanation for why I might be running through the house at cocktail hour with no pants on, drenched in sweat, swaddled in a soiled and reeking towel. But he and his friend appeared utterly unfazed—as though half-naked

---

* I'd just met him for the first time the day before. "I'm John Kennedy," he had said when he extended his hand in introduction. *I know*, I had thought as I extended mine, thinking it funny that he had to pretend courteously that people might not know his name, when in fact only a hermit or a Martian wouldn't have known who he was, so ubiquitous was his face on the cover of checkout counter magazines.

houseguests covered in their own excrement were frequent occurrences here—and walked past me down the stairs.

I scrambled down the hallway to my room, where I showered vigorously, changed, and generally tried to compose myself as best I could—which was not easy because I was continuing to sweat terribly, right through my blazer, the result of anxiety, exertion, and summer humidity.

If someone had snapped a photo of the scene at cocktails that evening, here's what it would show: various celebrities and politicians and priests all glowing with grace and easy bonhomie as they mingle effortlessly on the veranda overlooking the Atlantic—while, just off to the side, a sweaty young writer stands awkwardly gulping gin and tonics and thinking about how far he is from fitting in with this illustrious crowd and about how not only is he not rich or famous or accomplished or particularly good-looking but he cannot even control his own bowels and therefore is better suited for the company of animals or infants than of adults, let alone adults as luminous and significant as these.

The sweaty young writer is also worrying about what will happen when someone tries to use the hallway bathroom.

Late that night, after everyone had gone off to bed, I sneaked back down to the bathroom with a garbage bag and paper towels and cleaning detergent I'd purloined from the pantry. I couldn't tell whether anyone had been there since I left, but I tried not to worry about that and concentrated on stuffing the soiled rug and towels and clothes and toilet paper I'd stashed under the sink into the trash bag. Then I used the paper towels to scrub the floors, and I put those into the trash bag as well.

Outside the kitchen, between the main house and an outbuilding, was a Dumpster. My plan was to dispose of everything there. Naturally, I was terrified of getting caught. What, exactly, would a houseguest be doing disposing of a large trash bag outside in the middle of the night? (I worried that there might still be Secret Service afoot, who might shoot me before allowing me to plant what looked like a bomb or a body in the Dumpster.) But what choice did I have? I slunk through the house and out to the Dumpster, where I deposited the trash bag. Then I went back upstairs to bed.

No one ever said anything to me about the hallway bathroom or about the missing rug and towels. But for the rest of the weekend, and on my subsequent visits there, I was convinced that the household staff were glaring at me and whispering. "That's him," I imagined they were saying in disgust. "The one who broke the toilet and ruined our towels. The one who can't control his own bodily functions."*

> *Most persons with a sore colon are of a tense, sensitive, nervous*
> *temperament. They may be calm externally, but they usually seethe*
> *internally.*
> —WALTER C. ALVAREZ, *Nervousness, Indigestion, and Pain* (1943)

Of course, I know that such shame should not attach to what is, officially, a medical condition. Irritable bowel syndrome is a common gastrointestinal complaint frequently associated with mood and anxiety disorders, as has been observed since ancient times. In 1943, the eminent gastroenterologist Walter Alvarez noted in his delightfully titled *Nervousness, Indigestion, and Pain* that there is no more reason a person should feel ashamed about a nervous stomach than someone should feel ashamed at blushing at a compliment or weeping at a sad play. The nervousness and hypersensitivity that such physical reactions produce, Alvarez wrote, are associated with personality traits that, if "properly used and controlled," can "do much to help a man succeed."†

---

* As bad as my own agoraphobic belly sometimes seems to me, others have it worse. One of the more alarming case studies I've come across was of a forty-five-year-old man who showed up at a mental health clinic in Kalamazoo, Michigan, in 2007. He had been suffering from acute travel anxiety for twenty years, ever since the time a panic attack caused him to vomit and lose control of his bowels. Since then, the man had not been able to travel more than ten miles from home without experiencing uncontrollable vomiting and diarrhea. Clinicians later mapped his comfort zone by his symptoms: the farther from home he went, the more dramatic his eruptions. So violent were his gastrointestinal reactions that on several occasions he had to be rushed to emergency rooms because he was vomiting blood. After physicians ruled out ulcers and stomach cancer, he was finally referred to the psychology clinic, and he was, his therapist told me when I met him at a conference in 2008, successfully treated with a combination of exposure therapy and cognitive-behavioral therapy.

† Alvarez observed that the most common source of his patients' chronic stomach discomfort was the "challenges of modern living": "The stomach specialist has to be a psychiatrist of sorts," he wrote. "He must spend hours each week trying to teach neurotic persons to live more sensibly."
    One young woman was referred to Alvarez after vomiting "day and night for a week." When he learned that she had recently received an ominous letter from the Internal Revenue Service, he

But a nervous stomach is bad enough—what's most disabling to me is that my nervous stomach itself makes me nervous. That's the infernal thing about being an anxious emetophobe: the very fact of one's stomach hurting is itself often the most acute source of fear. Any time your stomach hurts, you worry you might vomit. Thus being anxious makes your stomach hurt, and your stomach hurting makes you anxious—which in turn makes your stomach hurt more, which makes you more anxious, and so on and so forth in a vicious cycle that hurtles rapidly toward panic. The lives of emetophobes are largely built around their phobia—some have not worked or left their houses for years because of their fears and cannot bear even to say or write "vomit" or related words. (Online emetophobia communities usually have rules requiring that such words be rendered as, for instance, "v**.")

Until recent years, emetophobia rarely appeared in the clinical literature. But the arrival of the Internet provided a means for emetophobes, many of whom had previously believed they were alone in their affliction, to find one other.* Online communities and support groups sprouted. The appearance of these virtual communities, some of which are quite large (by one estimate, the forum of the International Emetophobia Society has five times as many members as the largest flying phobia forum), came to the attention of anxiety researchers, who have started to study this phobia more systematically.

Like all anxiety disorders, emetophobia presents with elevated levels of physiological arousal, avoidance behavior (and also what experts call safety, or neutralizing, behavior, by which they mean doing what I

---

treated her by paying her back taxes—it turned out she owed only $3.85—and she was instantly cured. Another patient, whom Alvarez described as "a tense, high-pressure type of sales manager," came to him because he loved poker but couldn't play it: If he got a good hand, he would become "nauseated and chilly" and his face would turn red. Bluffing was impossible because any time he was dealt a full house or better, he would immediately have to get up and vomit. But "the cruelest prank of nature" Alvarez ever saw was the way nervous stomachs could destroy the love lives of the anxious. He treated one woman who would get stomach cramps and have to move her bowels whenever she was touched by a man, another who belched uncontrollably whenever a date became intimate, and numerous others who would break wind or vomit in romantic moments. (In his memoirs, the legendary lover Casanova reported on his escapades with a woman who, whenever she became sexually excited, would pass large quantities of gas.) Alvarez also treated "several men who were divorced by outraged wives because of their having to stop and run to the toilet whenever they became sexually excited."

* Among celebrities who have reported themselves to be emetophobic are the actress Nicole Kidman, the musician Joan Baez, and Matt Lauer, the host of the *Today* show.

do: carrying stomach remedies and antianxiety medications in case of emergency), attention disruption (meaning that in the presence of a phobic stimulus, such as a virus going around the office or through the family, we can concentrate on little else), and, typically, problems with self-esteem and self-efficacy. We emetophobes tend to think poorly of ourselves and to believe we have trouble coping with the world, and especially with something as catastrophic-seeming as vomiting.*

As we've seen, both patients with panic disorder and patients with irritable bowel syndrome (who much of the time are the *same* patients) have what mental health experts call "high somatization vulnerability" (that is, a tendency to convert emotional distress into physical symptoms) and "cognitive biases in the discrimination and interpretation of bodily symptoms" (that is, they are especially conscious of even minor changes in physiology and have an attendant predisposition to interpret those symptoms in a catastrophic, worst-case-scenario way). But whereas the primary concern for most panic patients tends to be that anxious bodily symptoms augur a heart attack or suffocation or insanity or death, emetophobes are afraid that the symptoms foretell imminent vomiting (and also insanity and death). And whereas the fears of the panic patients are, except in rare cases of anxiety-induced sudden cardiac death, extremely unlikely to be realized, emetophobes are quite capable of bringing on, through their anxious symptoms, the very thing they fear most. Which, of course, is another reason to be constantly afraid of being constantly afraid. Is it any wonder that sometimes I feel like my brain is turning inside out?

Psychologists have developed several standardized scales for measuring control-freakiness—there is, for instance, Rotter's Locus of Control Scale and also the Health Locus of Control Scale. That anxiety and depression are bound up tightly not only with self-esteem issues but with control issues (anxiety disorder patients tend both to feel like they don't have much control over their lives and to be afraid of losing control of their bodies or their minds) has been thoroughly established by generations of researchers—but that connection seems to be especially pronounced in people with emetophobia. A study published in

---

* According to emerging research data, emetophobes also tend to demonstrate "a heightened sensitivity to the opinions of others."

the *Journal of Clinical Psychology* observed that "emetophobics appear completely unable to negate their insatiable desire for the maintenance of control."*

Dr. W. has pointed out what he believes is the obvious multilayered symbolism of my emetophobia. Vomiting represents a loss of control and also my fear of letting my insides out, of revealing what's inside me. Most of all, he says, it represents my fear of death. Vomiting, and my unruly nervous stomach generally, are inarguable evidence of my embodiedness—and consequently of my mortality.†

Someday I'm going to vomit; someday I'm going to die.

Am I wrong to live in quivering terror of both?

---

* I once dated a woman whose aunt had for decades been a full-blown bulimic. From her teens into sometime in her thirties, my girlfriend's aunt had made herself vomit after most meals. To me, this was as fascinating as it was unfathomable. *Someone would actually choose to make herself vomit?* I had known about anorexia and bulimia since junior high, when I'd watched after-school specials about them on TV, but hadn't to my knowledge ever met anyone who voluntarily regurgitated on a regular basis. My whole life was built around trying *not* to vomit—and here was someone who vomited, all the time, by *choice?* True, this person was mentally ill, easily diagnosable according to the *DSM:* "Bulimia: Eating, in a discrete period of time, an amount of food that is definitely larger than most people would eat during a similar period of time and under similar circumstances [combined with] recurrent inappropriate compensatory behavior to prevent weight gain [such as] 1. Self-induced vomiting." But wasn't I also, according to the very same authority, ill? "Phobia: A. Marked and persistent fear that is excessive or unreasonable, cued by the presence or anticipation of a specific object or situation. B. Exposure to the phobic stimulus almost invariably provokes an immediate anxiety response, which may take the form of a situationally bound or situationally predisposed panic attack."

Even at the time, it struck me that our disorders were oddly self-canceling. If I could get my mind to embrace the idea that some people vomited by choice to make themselves feel *better,* could that maybe lead me to accept that vomiting was not so catastrophic? And if bulimics could assimilate some of my horrified aversion to vomiting, mightn't that help to decondition them away from the practice?

A modest proposal: Why not fill a group home with bulimics and emetophobes and hope that they model themselves out of their pathologies? The emetophobes, watching the bulimics make themselves vomit routinely, will learn that throwing up is not that big a deal; the bulimics, seeing the terror and disgust of the emetophobes, might be conditioned against such casual regurgitation.

And anyway, aren't we fundamentally both, bulimics and emetophobes alike, afraid of the same thing: the loss of control? It's not so much being fat that anorexics fear—it's feeling out of control, a feeling that purging helps them perversely to combat. They binge and then, not feeling in control of their own appetites, seek to exert dominion over their bodies by purging. But locked into this cycle of binge and purge, they are not really in control at all.

† As the British physician and philosopher Raymond Tallis has put it, "One sure-fire cure for . . . any whimsical or philosophical stance on one's own body . . . is vomiting. . . . Your body has you in its entire grip. . . . There is a kind of terror in vomiting: it is a shouted reminder that we are embodied in an organism that has its own agenda."

*I find the noodle and the stomach are antagonistic powers. What thought has to do with digesting roast beef, I cannot say, but they are brother faculties.*
—CHARLES DARWIN TO HIS SISTER CAROLINE (1838)

I try to draw solace from the knowledge that I am hardly alone in having both a mind and a belly so easily perturbed by anxiety. Observers going back to Aristotle have noted that nervous dyspepsia and intellectual accomplishment often go hand in hand. Sigmund Freud's trip to the United States in 1909, which introduced psychoanalysis to this country, was marred (as he would later frequently complain) by his nervous stomach and bouts of diarrhea. Many of the letters between William and Henry James, first-class neurotics both, consist mainly of the exchange of various remedies for their stomach trouble.

But for debilitating nervous stomach complaints, nothing compares to that which afflicted poor Charles Darwin, who spent decades of his life prostrated by his upset stomach.

In 1865, he wrote a desperate letter to a physician named John Chapman, listing the array of symptoms that had plagued him for nearly thirty years:

Age 56–57.—For 25 years extreme spasmodic daily & nightly flatulence: occasional vomiting, on two occasions prolonged during months. Vomiting preceded by shivering, hysterical crying[,] dying sensations or half-faint. & copious very palid urine. Now vomiting & every passage of flatulence preceded by ringing of ears, treading on air & vision. . . . Nervousness when E[mma Darwin, his wife] leaves me.

Even this list of symptoms is incomplete. At the urging of another doctor, Darwin had from July 1, 1849, to January 16, 1855, kept a "Diary of Health," which eventually ran to dozens of pages and listed such complaints as chronic fatigue, severe stomach pain and flatulence, frequent vomiting, dizziness ("swimming head," as Darwin described it), trembling, insomnia, rashes, eczema, boils, heart palpitations and pain, and melancholy.

Darwin was frustrated that dozens of physicians, beginning with his own father, had failed to cure him. By the time he wrote to Dr. Chapman, Darwin had spent most of the past three decades—during which time he'd struggled heroically to write *On the Origin of Species*—housebound by general invalidism. Based on his diaries and letters, it's fair to say he spent a full third of his daytime hours since the age of twenty-eight either vomiting or lying in bed.

Chapman had treated many prominent Victorian intellectuals who were "knocked up" with anxiety at one time or another; he specialized in, as he put it, those high-strung neurotics "whose minds are highly cultivated and developed, and often complicated, modified, and dominated by subtle psychical influences, whose intensity and bearing on the physical malady it is difficult to apprehend." He prescribed the application of ice to the spinal cord for almost all diseases of nervous origin.

Chapman came out to Darwin's country estate in late May 1865, and Darwin spent several hours each day over the next several months encased in ice; he composed crucial sections of *The Variation of Animals and Plants Under Domestication* with ice bags packed around his spine.

The treatment didn't work. The "incessant vomiting" continued. So while Darwin and his family enjoyed Chapman's company ("We liked Dr. Chapman so very much we were quite sorry the ice failed for his sake as well as ours," Darwin's wife wrote), by July they had abandoned the treatment and sent the doctor back to London.

Chapman was not the first doctor to fail to cure Darwin, and he would not be the last. To read Darwin's diaries and correspondence is to marvel at the more or less constant debilitation he endured after he returned from the famous voyage of the *Beagle* in 1836. The medical debate about what, exactly, was wrong with Darwin has raged for 150 years. The list proposed during his life and after his death is long: amoebic infection, appendicitis, duodenal ulcer, peptic ulcer, migraines, chronic cholecystitis, "smouldering hepatitis," malaria, catarrhal dyspepsia, arsenic poisoning, porphyria, narcolepsy, "diabetogenic hyperinsulism," gout, "suppressed gout,"* chronic brucellosis (endemic to Argentina, which the *Beagle* had visited), Chagas' disease (possibly contracted from a bug bite in Argentina), allergic reactions to the pigeons he worked with, complications from the protracted seasickness he experienced on the *Beagle,* and "refractive anomaly of the eyes." I've just read an article, "Darwin's Illness Revealed," published in a British academic journal in 2005, that attributes Darwin's ailments to lactose intolerance.[†]

But a careful reading of Darwin's life suggests that the precipitating factor in every one of his most acute attacks of illness was anxiety. According to Ralph Colp, a psychiatrist and historian who in the 1970s combed through all the available Darwin journals, letters, and medical accounts, the worst periods of illness corresponded with stress either about his work on the theory of evolution or about his family. (The anticipation of his wedding produced a "bad headache, which continues two days and two nights, so that I doubted whether it ever meant to allow me to be married.") In a 1997 article from *The Journal of the American Medical Association* called "Charles Darwin and Panic Disorder," two doctors argue that, according to his own account of his symptoms, Darwin would easily qualify for the *DSM-IV*'s diagnosis of panic disorder with agoraphobia since he demonstrated nine of the thirteen symptoms associated with it. (Only four symptoms are required to receive the diagnosis.)[‡]

The voyage of the *Beagle,* four years and nine months long, was

---

* "What the devil is this 'suppressed gout' upon which doctors fasten every ill they cannot name," Darwin's friend Joseph Hooker wrote to him when informed of this diagnosis. "If it is *suppressed* how do they know it is gout? If it is apparent, why the devil do they call it *suppressed?*"

† The authors, two Welsh biochemists, studied Darwin's journals and health diary to draw correlations between his diet and his bouts of upset stomach.

‡ In 1918, Edward J. Kempf, an early American psychoanalyst, suggested in *The Psychoanalytic Review* that the trembling and eczema that afflicted Darwin's hands were evidence of "neurotic hands"—which would, Kempf concluded, "lead one strongly to suspect an auto-erotic difficulty that had not been completely mastered." Less outlandish psychological explanations ventured in the years since include hypochondriasis, depression, repressed feelings of guilt about his hostility toward his father, "severe anxiety neurosis in an obsessional character, certainly much complicated by genius," and "bereavement syndrome" produced by the loss of his mother at a very young age. (Creationists have seized upon all this with zealous aplomb, implying in one pseudoscholarly paper I came across that the evidence of mental illness suggests Darwin was "psychotic" and that therefore his theory of evolution was the product of delusion.)

a pivotal experience, enabling Darwin to develop his scientific work.* The months in port prior to the launch of the *Beagle* were, as Darwin would write in his old age, "the most miserable which I ever spent"— and that's saying something, given the terrible physical suffering he would later endure.

"I was out of spirits at the thought of leaving all my family and friends for so long a time, and the weather seemed to me inexpressibly gloomy," he recalled. "I was also troubled with palpitations and pain about the heart, and like many a young ignorant man, especially one with a smattering of medical knowledge, was convinced I had heart disease." He also suffered from faintness and tingling in his fingers. These are all symptoms of anxiety—and in particular of the hyperventilation associated with panic disorder.

Darwin forced himself to overcome his low spirits and embark on the voyage, and though he was beset by both claustrophobia (which put him in "continual fear") and grievous seasickness, he was mostly healthy on the trip, gathering the evidence on which he would make his name and build his life's work. But after the *Beagle* docked in Falmouth, England, on October 2, 1836, Darwin would never again set foot outside England. After nearly five years of traveling, Darwin found his geographical ambit increasingly circumscribed. "I dread going anywhere, on account of my stomach so easily failing under any excitement," he told his cousin.

It's remarkable that *On the Origin of Species* ever got written. Soon after his marriage, when Darwin was beginning in earnest his work on evolution, he suffered the first of his many episodes of "periodic vomiting," stretches where he would vomit multiple times daily and be bedridden for weeks—or, in several cases, years—on end. Excitement or socializing of any kind could throw him into great physical upheaval. Parties or meetings would leave him "knocked up" with anxiety, bringing on "violent shivering and vomiting attacks." ("I have therefore been compelled for many years to give up all dinner-parties," he wrote.) He

---

* Darwin's discovery of variant species of finches in the Galápagos Islands would eventually prompt his realization that species were not fixed for all time but rather transmuted—or, as he would later say, evolved—over time.

installed a mirror outside his study window so he could see guests coming up the drive before they saw him, allowing him time to brace himself or to hide.

In addition to Dr. Chapman's ice treatment, Darwin tried the "water cure" of the famous Dr. James Gully (who also treated Alfred Tennyson, Thomas Carlyle, and Charles Dickens around this time), exercise, a sugar-free diet, brandy and "Indian ale," chemical concoctions (scores of them), metal plates strapped to his torso meant to galvanize his insides and "electric chains" (made of brass and zinc wires) meant to electrify him, and drenching his skin with vinegar. Whether the result of the placebo effect, distraction, or actual efficacy, some of these sort of worked some of the time. But always the illness returned. A day trip to London or any mild disturbance in his well-ordered routine would bring on "a very bad form of vomiting" that would send him to bed for days or weeks. Any work, especially on *Origin*—"my abominable volume," as Darwin called it—could lay him low for months. "I have been bad, having two days of bad vomiting owing to the accursed Proofs," he wrote to a friend in early 1859 while going over printer's corrections. He installed a special lavatory in his study where he could vomit behind a curtain. He finished with the proofs amid fits of vomiting on October 1, 1859, ending a fifteen-month period during which he had rarely been able to work free of stomach discomfort for more than twenty minutes at a time.

When *On the Origin of Species,* more than twenty years in gestation, was finally published in November 1859, Darwin was laid up in bed at a hydropathy spa in Yorkshire, his stomach in as much tumult as ever, his skin aflame. "I have been very bad lately," he wrote. "Had an awful 'crisis'—one leg swelled up like elephantiasis—eyes almost closed up— covered with a rash and fiery Boils . . . it was like living in Hell."*

Darwin continued in poor health even after the book's publication. "I shall go to my grave, I suppose, grumbling and growling with daily,

---

* One of Darwin's biographers, the British psychoanalyst John Bowlby, noted in the 1980s that the sorts of eruptions of boils and rashes that Darwin endured were thought by dermatologists to be associated with people who "strive to suppress their feelings and who are given to low self-esteem and overwork." Bowlby, like other biographers, also observed that any stress or "increase in arousal, however trivial," would produce physical symptoms in Darwin.

almost hourly, discomfort," he wrote in 1860. Those who argue that Darwin suffered from some germ-based or structural disease point to the severity and duration of his symptoms. ("I must tell you how ill Charles has been," his wife wrote to a family friend in May 1864. "He has had almost daily vomiting for 6 months.") But in rebuttal there is this: When Darwin would stop working and go riding or walking in the Scottish Highlands or North Wales, his health would be restored.

*Charles is too much given to anxiety, as you know.*
—EMMA DARWIN TO A FRIEND (1851)

If I seem unduly preoccupied with Darwin's stomach, perhaps you can understand why. It seems both apt and ironic that the man responsible for launching the modern study of fear—and for identifying it as an emotion with concrete physiological, and especially gastrointestinal, effects—was himself so miserably afflicted by a nervous stomach.

Then there is the matter of his excessive dependence on his wife, Emma. "Without you, when I feel sick I feel most desolate," he wrote to her at one point. "O Mammy I do long to be with you & under your protection and then I feel safe," he wrote at another.

*Mammy?* No wonder some Freudians would later argue that Darwin had dependency issues, as well as Oedipal ones. I suppose this is the place to say that—based on my burdensome overreliance on my wife and, before that, on my parents—Dr. W. has diagnosed me with dependent personality disorder, which is, according to the *DSM-V,* characterized by excessive psychological dependence on other people (most often a loved one or caretaker) and the belief that one is inadequate and helpless to cope on one's own.

Finally, of course, there is the matter of Darwin's decades of constant vomiting. For an emetophobe like me, this holds a morbid fascination. His anxiety produced vomiting, yet his vomiting did not (or so it seems) produce additional anxiety. Moreover, Darwin lived, despite his years of vomiting, to the old-for-the-time age of seventy-three. Shouldn't Darwin's accomplishments in defiance of such a debilitating gastrointestinal affliction provide reassurance that if, say, I were to throw up just once, or even five times, or even five times in a day—or even, like Darwin, five times a day for years on end—I might not only survive but perhaps even remain productive?

If you're not an emetophobe, this question surely seems impossibly strange—patent evidence of the irrational obsession at the core of my mental illness. And you're right. But if you *are* an emetophobe—well, then, you know exactly what I'm talking about.

# CHAPTER 4

# Performance Anxiety

*Many lamentable effects this fear causeth in men, as to be red, pale, tremble, sweat; it makes sudden cold and heat to come over all the body, palpitation of the heart, syncope, etc. It amazeth many men that are to speak or show themselves in public assemblies, or before some great personages; as Tully confessed of himself, that he trembled still at the beginning of his speech; and Demosthenes, that great orator of Greece, before Philippus.*
    —ROBERT BURTON, *The Anatomy of Melancholy* (1621)

*All public speaking of merit is characterized by nervousness.*
    —CICERO (FIRST CENTURY A.D.)

I've finally settled on a pretalk regimen that enables me to avoid the weeks of anticipatory misery that the approach of a public speaking engagement would otherwise produce.

Let's say I'm speaking to you at some sort of public event. Here's what I've likely done to prepare. Four hours or so ago, I took my first half milligram of Xanax. (I've learned that if I wait too long to take it, my sympathetic nervous system goes so far into overdrive that medication is not enough to yank it back.) Then, about an hour ago, I took my second half milligram of Xanax and perhaps twenty milligrams of Inderal. (I need the whole milligram of Xanax plus the Inderal, which is a blood pressure medication, or beta-blocker, that dampens the response of the sympathetic nervous system, to keep my physiological responses to the anxious stimulus of standing in front of you—the sweating, trembling, nausea, burping, stomach cramps, and constriction in my throat and chest—from overwhelming me.) I likely washed those pills down with a shot of scotch or, more likely, of vodka. Even two Xanax and an Inderal are not enough to calm my racing thoughts and to keep my chest and throat from constricting to the point where I cannot speak; I need the alcohol to slow things down and to dampen the residual physiological eruptions that the drugs are inadequate to contain. In fact, I probably drank my second shot—yes, even though I might be speaking to you at, say, nine in the morning—between fifteen and thirty minutes ago, assuming the pretalk proceedings allowed me a moment to sneak away for a quaff. And depending on how intimidating an audience I anticipated you would be, I might have made that second shot a double or a triple. If the usual pattern has held, as I stand up here talking to you now, I've got some Xanax in one pocket (in case I felt the need to pop another one before being introduced) and a minibar-size bottle or two of vodka in the other. I have been known to take a discreet last-second swig while walking onstage—because even as I'm still experiencing the anxiety that makes me want to drink more, my inhibition has been lowered, and my judgment impaired, by the liquor and benzodiazepines I've already consumed. If I've managed to hit the sweet spot—that perfect combination of timing and dosage where the cognitive and psychomotor sedating effect of the drugs and alcohol balances out the physiological hyperarousal of the anxiety—then I'm probably doing okay up here: nervous but not miserable; a little fuzzy but still able to convey clarity; the anxiogenic effects of this situation (me, speaking in front of people) counteracted by the anxiolytic effects of what I've consumed.* But if I've overshot on the medication—too much Xanax or liquor—I may seem loopy or slurring or otherwise impaired. And if I didn't self-medicate enough? Well, then, either I'm miserable and probably sweating profusely, with my voice quavering weakly and my attention folding in upon itself, or, more likely, I ran offstage before I got this far.

I know. My method of dealing with my public speaking anxiety is not healthy. It's evidence of alcoholism; it's dangerous. But it works.

---

* Together, the alcohol and the benzodiazepines slow the firing of neurons in my amygdala, increase transmission of dopamine and gamma-aminobutyric acid, boost production of beta-endorphins in my hypothalamus, and decrease transmission of acetylcholine.

Only when I am sedated to near stupefaction by a combination of benzodiazepines and alcohol do I feel (relatively) confident in my ability to speak in public effectively and without misery. As long as I know that I'll have access to my Xanax and liquor, I'll suffer only moderate anxiety for days before a speech, rather than miserable, sleepless dread for months.

Self-medicating, sometimes dangerously so, is a time-honored way of warding off performance anxiety. Starting when he was thirty, William Gladstone, the long-serving British prime minister, would drink laudanum—opium dissolved in alcohol—with his coffee before speeches in Parliament. (Once, he accidentally overdosed and had to go to a sanatorium to recover.) William Wilberforce, the famous eighteenth-century British antislavery politician, took opium as a "calmer of nerves" before all his speeches in Parliament. "To that," Wilberforce said of his prespeech opium regimen, "I owe my success as a public speaker."* Laurence Olivier, convinced that he was about to be driven to what he was sure would be reported as a "mystifying and scandalously sudden retirement" by his stage fright, finally confided his distress to the actress Dame Sybil Thorndike and her husband.

"Take drugs, darling," Thorndike told him. "We do."†

I try to draw solace from what I have learned about Gladstone, Olivier, and other successful and exalted people who have been debilitated by their stage fright.

Demosthenes, a Greek statesman renowned for his oratorical skills, was, early in his career, jeered for his anxious, stammering performances. Cicero, the great Roman statesman and philosopher, once froze while speaking during an important trial in the Forum and ran offstage. "I turn pale at the outset of a speech and quake in every limb and in all my soul," he wrote. Moses, according to various interpretations of Exodus

---

* Of course, to opium Wilberforce likely owed many other things, too, among them his horrible depression and a host of physical problems. After initially being prescribed the drug for bowel troubles, he became addicted, taking it every day for forty-five years straight.

† Actually, Olivier seems not to have resorted to drugs. "There was no other treatment than the well-worn practice of wearing *it*—the terror—out," he wrote in his autobiography, "and it was in that determined spirit that I got on with the job." But he did quit the stage for five years to escape his anxiety.

4:10, had a fear of public speaking or was a stutterer; he overcame this to become the voice of his people.

Every era of history seems to offer up examples of prominent, accomplished figures who managed—or didn't manage—to overcome crippling public speaking anxiety. On the morning before William Cowper, the eighteenth-century British poet, was to appear before the House of Lords to discuss his qualifications for a government position, he tried to hang himself, preferring to die rather than endure a public appearance. (The suicide attempt failed, and the interview was postponed.) "They . . . to whom a public examination of themselves on any occasion is mortal poison may have some idea of the horrors of my situation," Cowper wrote. "Others can have none."

In 1889, a young Indian lawyer froze during his first case before a judge and ran from the courtroom in humiliation. "My head was reeling and I felt as though the whole court was doing likewise," the lawyer would write later, after he had become known as Mahatma Gandhi. "I could think of no question to ask." Another time, when Gandhi stood up to read remarks he had prepared for a small gathering of a local vegetarian society, he found he could not speak. "My vision became blurred and I trembled, though the speech hardly covered a sheet of foolscap," he recounted. What Gandhi called "the awful strain of public speaking" prevented him for years from speaking up even at friendly dinner parties and nearly deterred him from developing into the spiritual leader he ultimately became. Thomas Jefferson, too, had his law career disrupted by a fear of public speaking. One of his biographers notes that if he tried to declaim loudly, his voice would "sink in his throat." He never spoke during the deliberations of the Second Continental Congress and, remarkably, he gave only two public speeches—his inaugural addresses—during his years as President. After reviewing Jefferson's biographies, psychiatrists at Duke University, writing in the *Journal of Nervous and Mental Disease,* diagnosed him posthumously with social phobia.

The novelist Henry James dropped out of law school after giving what he felt was an embarrassing performance in a moot court competition in which he "quavered and collapsed into silence"; thereafter, he avoided making formal public presentations, despite being known for his witty dinner party repartee. Vladimir Horowitz, perhaps the most talented concert pianist of the twentieth century, developed stage fright so acute that for fifteen years he refused to perform in public. When he finally returned to the stage, he did so only on the condition that he could clearly see his personal physician sitting in the front row of the audience at all times.

Barbra Streisand developed overwhelming performance anxiety at the height of her career; for twenty-seven years she refused to perform for money, appearing live only at charity events, where she believed the pressure on her was less intense. Carly Simon abandoned the stage for seven years after collapsing from nerves before a concert in front of ten thousand people in Pittsburgh in 1981. When she resumed performing, she would sometimes drive needles into her skin or ask her band to spank her before going onstage to distract her from her anxiety. The singer Donny Osmond quit performing for a number of years because of panic attacks. (He is now a spokesman for the Anxiety and Depression Association of America.) The comedian Jay Mohr tells a story about frantically trying to pop a Klonopin on live television to stave off what he feared would be a career-ending panic attack while performing a skit on *Saturday Night Live*. (What saved Mohr on that occasion was not the Klonopin but the distracting hilarity of his sketch mate Chris Farley.) A few years ago, Hugh Grant announced his semiretirement from acting because of the panic attacks he'd get when the cameras started rolling. He survived one film only by filling himself "full of lorazepam," the short-acting benzodiazepine with the trade name Ativan. "I had all these panic attacks," he said. "They're awful. I freeze like a rabbit. Can't speak, can't think, sweating like a bull. When I got home from doing that job, I said to myself, 'No more acting. End of films.'" Ricky Williams, who won the Heisman Trophy in 1998, retired from the National Football League for several years because of his anxiety; social interactions made him so nervous that he would give interviews only while wearing his football helmet.* Elfriede Jelinek, the Austrian novelist who won the Nobel Prize in Literature in 2004, refused to

---

* For a time, Williams took Paxil for his anxiety, and he briefly became a pitchman for SmithKline Beechman—though he later told *The Miami Herald* that marijuana "worked 10 times better for me than Paxil."

accept her award in person because her acute social phobia made it impossible to bear being looked at in public.

Cicero, Demosthenes, Gladstone. Olivier, Streisand, Wilberforce. Physicians and scientists and statesmen. Oscar winners and Heisman winners and Nobel laureates. Gandhi and Jefferson and Moses. Shouldn't I draw consolation from the knowledge that so many people so much greater than I am have been, at times, undone by their stage fright? And shouldn't their ability to persevere and, in some cases, to overcome their anxiety give me hope and inspiration?

*Why should the thought that others are thinking about us affect our capillary circulation?*
—CHARLES DARWIN, *The Expression of the Emotions in Man and Animals* (1872)

*The symptoms of performance anxiety can sometimes take the form of what seems to be a terrible joke custom-designed to humiliate.*
—JOHN MARSHALL, *Social Phobia* (1994)

The *DSM* officially divides social anxiety disorder into two subtypes: specific and general. Those patients diagnosed with specific social anxiety disorder have anxiety attached to very particular circumstances, almost always relating to some form of public performance. By far the most common specific social phobia is the fear of public speaking, but others include the fear of eating in public, the fear of writing in public, and the fear of urinating in a public restroom. A startlingly large number of people arrange their lives around not eating in front of people, or are filled with dread at the prospect of having to sign a check in front of other people, or suffer what's known as paruresis when standing at a urinal.

Patients suffering from the general subtype of social anxiety disorder feel distress in any social context. Routine events such as cocktail parties, business meetings, job interviews, and dinner dates can be occasion for significant emotional anguish and physical symptoms. For the more severely afflicted, life can be an unremitting misery. The most mundane social interaction—talking to a store clerk or engaging in watercooler chitchat—induces a kind of terror. Many social phobics endure lives of terrible loneliness and professional impairment. Studies find strong links between social phobia and both depression and suicide. Social phobics are also, unsurprisingly, highly prone to alcoholism and drug abuse.*

The terrible irony of social phobia is that one of the things people suffering from it fear most is having their anxiety exposed—which is precisely what the symptoms of this anxiety serve to do. Social phobics worry that their interpersonal awkwardness or the physical manifestations of anxiety—their blushing and shaking and stammering and sweating—will somehow reveal them to be weak or incompetent. So they get nervous, and then they stammer or blush, which makes them more nervous, which makes them stammer and blush more, which propels them into a vicious cycle of increasing anxiety and deteriorating performance.

Blushing is infernal in this regard. The first case study of erythrophobia (the fear of blushing in public) was published in 1846 by a German physician who described a twenty-one-year-old medical student driven to suicide by shame over his uncontrolled blushing. A few years later, Darwin would dedicate a full chapter of *The Expression of the Emotions in Man and Animals* to his theory of blushing, observing how at the moment of most wanting to hide one's anxiety, blushing betrays it. "It is not a simple act of reflecting on our own appearance but the thinking of others thinking of us which excites a blush," Darwin wrote. "It is notorious that nothing makes a shy person blush so much as any remark, however slight, on his personal appearance."

Darwin was right: I've had colleagues prone to nervous blushing, and nothing makes them glow redder than to have their blushing publicly remarked upon. Before her wedding, one such colleague tried multiple combinations of drug treatments, and even contemplated surgery, in hopes of sparing herself what she believed would be intolerable humiliation. (Every year thousands of nervous blushers undergo an endoscopic transthoracic sympathectomy, which involves destroying the ganglion of a sympathetic nerve located near the rib cage.)

---

* Early in his career, Sigmund Freud took cocaine to medicate his social anxiety before salons at the home of one of his mentors.

I, who am fortunate not to count blushing among one of my regular nervous symptoms, observe her and think how silly she is to believe that blushing at her wedding would be humiliating. And then I think how ashamed I was of sweating and trembling at my own wedding and wonder if I am not any less silly than she.

Shame, perhaps, is the operative emotion here—the engine that underlies both the anxiety and the blushing. In 1839, Thomas Burgess, a British physician, argued in *The Physiology or Mechanism of Blushing* that God had designed blushing so that "the soul might have sovereign power of displaying in the cheeks the various internal emotions of the moral feelings." Blushing, he wrote, can "serve as a check on ourselves, and as a sign to others that [we're] violating rules which ought to be held sacred." For Burgess as for Darwin, blushing is physiological evidence of both our self-consciousness and our sociability—a manifestation of not only our awareness of ourselves but our sensitivity to how others perceive us.

Later work by Darwin, as well as by modern evolutionary biologists, posits that blushing is not only a signal from our bodies to ourselves that we're committing some kind of shameful social transgression (you can feel yourself blush by the warming of your skin) but also a signal to others that we are feeling modest and self-conscious. It's a way of showing social deference to higher-ranking members of the species—and it is, as Burgess would have it, a check on our antisocial impulses, keeping us from deviating from prevailing social norms. Social anxiety and the blushing it produces can be evolutionarily adaptive—the behavior it promotes can preserve social comity and can keep us from being ostracized from the tribe.

Though social anxiety disorder as an official diagnosis is relatively new in the history of psychiatry—it was born in 1980, when the disease was one of the new anxiety disorders carved out of the old Freudian neuroses by the third edition of the *DSM*—the syndrome it describes is age-old, and the symptoms are consistent from age to age.* Writing in 1901, Paul Hartenberg, a French novelist and psychiatrist, described a

---

* The term "social phobia" first appeared in 1903, when Pierre Janet, an influential French psychiatrist who was a contemporary and rival of Freud, published a taxonomy of mental illnesses that classified erythrophobia among what he called *phobies sociales* or *phobies de la société*.

syndrome whose constellation of physical and emotional symptoms corresponds remarkably to the *DSM-V* definition of social anxiety disorder. The social phobic (*timide*) fears other people, lacks self-confidence, and eschews social interactions, Hartenberg wrote in *Les timides et la timidité*. In anticipation of social situations, Hartenberg's social phobic experiences physical symptoms such as a racing heart, chills, hyperventilation, sweating, nausea, vomiting, diarrhea, trembling, difficulty speaking, choking, and shortness of breath, plus a dulling of the senses and "mental confusion." The social phobic also always feels ashamed. Hartenberg even anticipates the modern distinction between people who feel anxious in all social situations and those who experience anxiety only before public performances—a particularized emotional experience he called *trac*, which he described as afflicting many academics, musicians, and actors before a lecture or performance. (This experience, Hartenberg writes, is like vertigo or seasickness—it descends suddenly, often without warning.)

Yet despite what seems to be the consistency in descriptions of social anxiety across the millennia, the diagnosis of social anxiety disorder remains controversial in some quarters. Even after the syndrome was formally inscribed in the *DSM* in 1980, diagnoses of social phobia remained rare for a number of years. Western psychotherapists tended to see it as a predominantly "Asian disorder"—a condition that flourished in the "shame-based cultures" (as anthropologists describe them) of Japan and South Korea, where correct social behavior is highly valued. (In Japanese psychiatry, a condition called *Taijin-Kyofu-Sho*, roughly comparable to what we call social anxiety disorder, has long been one of the most frequent diagnoses.) A cross-cultural comparison conducted in 1994 suggested that the relative prevalence of social phobia symptoms in Japan could be related to "the socially promoted show of shame among Japanese people." Japanese society itself, the lead researcher of the survey argued, could be considered "pseudo-sociophobic" because feelings and behaviors that in the West would be considered psychiatric symptoms—excessive shame, avoidance of eye contact, elaborate displays of deference—are cultural norms in Japan.*

---

* If nothing else, this demonstrates the complex ways in which culture and medicine interact: what's normal, even valorized, in one culture is considered pathological in another.

In the United States, social anxiety disorder found an early champion in Michael Liebowitz, a psychiatrist at Columbia University who had served on the *DSM* subcommittee that brought the disease into official existence. In 1985, Liebowitz published an article in the *Archives of General Psychiatry* called "Social Anxiety—the Neglected Disorder," in which he argued that the disease was woefully underdiagnosed and undertreated.* After the article appeared, research on social phobia began to accrete slowly. As recently as 1994, the term "social anxiety disorder" had appeared only fifty times in the popular press; five years later, it had appeared hundreds of thousands of times. What accounts for the disorder's colonization of the popular imagination? Largely this single event: the Food and Drug Administration's approval of Paxil for the treatment of social anxiety disorder in 1999.† SmithKline Beecham quickly launched a multimillion-dollar advertising campaign aimed at both psychiatrists and the general public.

"Imagine you were allergic to people," went the text of one widely distributed Paxil ad. "You blush, sweat, shake—even find it hard to breathe. That's what social anxiety disorder feels like." Propelled by the sudden cultural currency of the disease—that same ad claimed that "over ten million Americans" were suffering from social anxiety disorder—prescriptions of Paxil exploded. The drug passed Prozac and Zoloft to become the nation's best-selling SSRI antidepressant medication.

Before 1980, no one had ever been diagnosed with social anxiety disorder; twenty years later, studies were estimating that some ten million to twenty million Americans qualified for the diagnosis. Today, the official statistics from the National Institute of Mental Health say that more than 10 percent of Americans will suffer from social anxiety disorder at some point in their lifetimes—and that some 30 percent of these people will suffer acute forms of it. (Studies in reputable medical journals present similar statistics.)

No wonder there's controversy: from zero patients to tens of millions of them in the course of less than twenty years. It's easy to lay out the cynical plot: A squishy new psychiatric diagnosis is invented;

---

* Liebowitz also developed what became the standard psychological rating scale for measuring a patient's degree of social anxiety.

† Paxil had earlier been approved for the treatment of depression, obsessive-compulsive disorder, and generalized anxiety disorder.

initially very few patients are deemed to be ill with it. Then a drug is approved to treat it. Suddenly diagnoses explode. The pharmaceutical industry reaps billions of dollars in profit.

Moreover, these critics say, there's another name for the syndrome ostensibly afflicting those with social anxiety disorder. It's called shyness, a common temperamental disposition that should hardly be considered a mental illness. In 2007, Christopher Lane, a professor of English at Northwestern University, published a book-length version of this argument, *Shyness: How Normal Behavior Became a Sickness*, claiming that psychiatrists, in cahoots with the pharmaceutical industry, had succeeded in pathologizing an ordinary character trait.*

On the one hand, the sudden explosion in diagnoses of social anxiety disorder surely does speak to the power of the pharmaceutical industry's marketing efforts to manufacture demand for a product. Besides, some quotient of nervousness about social interactions is normal. How many of us *don't* feel some discomfort at the prospect of having to make small talk with strangers at a party? Who *doesn't* feel some measure of anxiety at having to perform in public or to be judged by an audience? Such anxiety is healthy, even adaptive. To define such discomfort as something that needs to be treated with pills is to medicalize what is merely human. All of which lends weight to the idea of social anxiety disorder as nothing more than a profit-seeking concoction of the pharmaceutical industry.

On the other hand, I can tell you, both from extensive research and from firsthand experience, that as convincing as the case made by Lane and his fellow antipharma critics can be, the distress felt by some social phobics is real and intense. Are there some "normally" shy people, not mentally ill or in need of psychiatric attention, who get swept up in the broad diagnostic category of social anxiety disorder, which has been swollen by the profit-seeking imperatives of the drug companies? Surely. But are there also socially anxious people who can legitimately benefit from medication and other forms of psychiatric treatment—

---

* Lane's book is representative of a substantial and ever-growing literature that accuses the pharmaceutical-industrial complex of creating new disease categories for profit. I will have more to say about this in part 3.

who in some cases are saved by medication from alcoholism, despair, and suicide? I think there are.

A few years ago, the magazine I work for published an essay about the challenges of being an introvert. Not long after that, this letter arrived at my office:

> I just read your article on introversion. A year ago my 26-year-old son bemoaned the fact he was an introvert. I assured him he was fine, we are all quiet introverts in our family. Three months ago he left us a note, bought a shotgun, and killed himself. In his note he said he wasn't wired right. . . . He felt anxious and awkward around people and he couldn't go on. . . . He was smart, gentle and very educated. He had just started an internship dealing with the public and I think it pushed him over the edge. I wish he had said something before he bought the gun. It seems he thought it was his only option. This was a guy who got nervous before getting his blood drawn. You can't imagine how horrible it has been.

One study has found that up to 23 percent of patients diagnosed with social anxiety disorder attempt suicide at some point. Who wants to argue that they are just shy or that a drug that might have mitigated their suffering was purely a play for profit?

*No passion so effectively robs the mind of acting and reasoning as fear.*
    —EDMUND BURKE, *A Philosophical Inquiry into the Origin of Our Ideas of the Sublime and Beautiful* (1756)

As best I can recall, my performance anxiety blossomed when I was eleven. Before then, I had made presentations in class and in front of school assemblies and had experienced only nervous excitement. So I was blindsided when, standing onstage in the starring role in my sixth-grade class's holiday performance of *Saint George and the Dragon,* I suddenly found I could not speak.

It was an evening in mid-December, and the auditorium was filled with a few dozen parents, siblings, and teachers. I remember standing backstage beforehand, awaiting my cue to enter stage left, and feeling only mildly nervous. Though it's hard for me to imagine now, I think I was even enjoying myself, looking forward to the attention I would receive as star of the play. But when I walked to center stage and looked out into the auditorium to see all those eyes upon me, my chest constricted.* After a few seconds, I found myself in the grip of both physical and emotional panic, and I could barely speak. I eked out a few quavering lines with a diminishing voice—and then arrived at a point where I could make no more words emerge. I stopped, midsentence, feeling that I was about to vomit. A few agonizing seconds of silence ticked by until my friend Peter, who was playing my valet, bailed me out by saying his next line.† This surely seemed to the audience like a non sequitur, but it moved the scene to its conclusion and mercifully got me off the stage. By my next scene, the physical symptoms of my anxiety had abated a little; at the end of the play I slew the dragon as directed. Afterward, people said they had liked my fight scene, and (out of politeness, I was sure) nobody remarked on my first scene, where it must have looked, at best, like I had forgotten my line or, at worst, like I had frozen in terror.

A trapdoor opened beneath me that night. After that, public performances were never the same. At the time, I was singing in a professional boys' choir that appeared in churches and auditoriums all over New England. Concerts were torture. I was not one of the better singers, so I never had solos; I was just one of twenty-four prepubescent boys standing anonymously onstage. But every moment was misery. I'd hold my score in front of my face so the audience couldn't see me and mouth the words silently. I'd have that horrible choking feeling, and

---

* Research has shown that being the object of another's direct gaze is highly emotionally and physiologically arousing. One of the surest ways to cause the neurons in the amygdala of a human test subject to fire is simply to have someone stare at the subject. Many studies have demonstrated that the amygdalae of those diagnosed with social anxiety disorder tend to be consistently more reactive to the human gaze than those of healthy control subjects.

† Peter, I can only assume, felt no such anxiety. He went on to become a member of President Barack Obama's first-term cabinet.

my stomach would hurt, and I would fear that if I made any sound, I'd vomit.*

I quit the choir, but I couldn't completely avoid public performances—especially as my anxieties worsened and my definition of public got broader. The next year, I was making a presentation in Mr. Hunt's seventh-grade science class. True to my phobic preoccupations, I had chosen to do a report on the biology of food poisoning. Standing at the front of the class, I became overwhelmed by dizziness and nausea. I made it only a few halting sentences into my presentation before pausing and then squeaking plaintively, "I don't feel well." Mr. Hunt told me to go sit down. "Maybe he's got food poisoning!" a classmate joked. Everyone laughed while I burned with humiliation.

A couple of years later, I won a junior tennis tournament at a local club. Afterward, there was a luncheon banquet, where trophies were to be given out. All that was required of me was to walk onto the dais when my name was called, shake the hand of the tournament director, smile for the camera, and walk off the dais again. I wouldn't even have to speak.

But as the tournament organizers proceeded down through the different age groups, I started to tremble and sweat. The prospect of having all those eyes upon me was terrifying—I was sure I would humiliate myself in some indeterminate way. Several minutes before my name was announced, I slipped out the back door and ran down to a basement restroom to hide, emerging only several hours later, when I was sure the luncheon had ended. (This sort of extreme avoidant behavior is common among social phobics. I once came across a report in the clinical literature of a woman who, feigning illness, skipped a company banquet where she was to be given an award for outstanding performance, because the prospect of being the center of attention made her so nervous. After she missed the dinner, a small group of colleagues planned a more intimate reception in her honor. She quit her job rather than attend.)

---

* It didn't help that the choir director was a strange and tyrannical man who lived with his parents and had a horrific stutter. He'd start screaming at you during choir practice and would get stuck on a word, his face contorted into a paroxysm of anger and frustration, and you would have to wait many seconds for whatever expletive he was trying to direct at you to finally burst out.

Once, in college, I applied for a fellowship that required me to sit for an interview with a committee of half a dozen faculty members, most of whom I was already friendly with. We bantered easily before the official proceedings began. But when the interview started and they asked me the first formal question, my chest constricted and I could make no sound emerge from my trachea. I sat there, mouth silently gaping open and then shutting like some kind of fish or suckling mammal. When finally I was able to get my voice to work, I excused myself and scurried out, feeling the committee's befuddled eyes on my back, and that was that.

The problem, alas, has persisted into adulthood. There have been humiliating minor catastrophes (walking offstage midsentence during public presentations) and scores of near misses (television shows where I've felt the chest constriction begin; lectures and interviews where the room started to swim, nausea rose in my gullet, and my voice diminished to a sickly warble). Somehow, in many of those near-miss instances, I've managed to fight through and continue. But in all these situations, even when they're apparently going well, I feel I am living on the razor's edge between success and failure, adulation and humiliation—between justifying my existence and revealing my unworthiness to be alive.

*People are not disturbed by things but by the view they take of them.*
—EPICTETUS, "ON ANXIETY" (FIRST CENTURY A.D.)

Why does my body betray me in these situations?

Performance anxiety is not some ethereal feeling but rather a vivid mental state with concrete physical aspects that are measurable in a laboratory: accelerated heart rate, heart palpitations, increased levels of epinephrine and norepinephrine in the bloodstream, decreased gastric motility, and elevated blood pressure. Almost everyone experiences a measurable autonomic nervous response while performing in public: most people register a two- to threefold increase in the level of norepinephrine in their bloodstream at the beginning of a lecture, a rush of adrenaline that can improve performance—but in social phobics this autonomic response tends to be more acute, and it translates into debilitating physical symptoms and emotional distress. Studies at the University of Wisconsin have found that in the run-up to a speech, socially anxious individuals show high activation of their right cerebral hemispheres, which seems to interfere with both their logical processing and their verbal abilities—the sort of brain freeze that young Gandhi experienced in the courtroom. The experience of struggling to think or speak clearly in moments of social stress has clear biological substrates.

Cognitive-behavioral therapists argue that social anxiety disorder is a problem of disordered logic, or faulty thinking. If we can correct our false beliefs and maladaptive attitudes—our "cognitions" or "schema," as they say—we can cure the anxiety. Epictetus, a Greek slave and Stoic philosopher living in Rome in the first century A.D., was the prototype of the cognitive-behavioral therapist. His essay "On Anxiety," in addition to being one of the earliest contributions to the literature of self-help, seems to be the first attempt to connect performance anxiety to what we would today call issues of self-esteem.

"When I see anyone anxious, I say, 'what does this man want?'" Epictetus writes. "Unless he wanted something or other not in his own power, how could he still be anxious? A musician, for instance, feels no anxiety while he is singing by himself; but when he appears upon the stage he does, even if his voice be ever so good, or he plays ever so well. For what he wishes is not only to sing well but likewise to gain applause. But this is not in his own power. In short, where his skill lies, there is his courage." In other words, you can't ultimately control whether the audience applauds or not, so what use is there in worrying about it? For Epictetus, anxiety was a disorder of desire and emotion to be overcome by logic. If you can train your mind to perform the same way whether you're alone or being observed, you'll not get derailed by stage fright.

Two influential twentieth-century psychotherapists, Albert Ellis and Aaron Beck, the founders of rational emotive behavioral therapy (REBT) and cognitive-behavioral therapy (CBT) respectively, each argued that the treatment of social anxiety boils down to overcoming fear of disapproval. To overcome social anxiety, they say, you need to inure yourself to needless shame.

To this end, when Dr. M., a practitioner in the CBT mold, was treating me at Boston University's Center for Anxiety and Related Disorders, she aimed, as a therapeutic exercise, to intentionally embarrass me. She would escort me to the university bookstore next door to the Center and lurk discreetly nearby while I asked purposely dumb questions of the clerks or told them I needed a bathroom because I was going to throw up. I found this excruciatingly awkward and embarrassing (which was the whole point), and it didn't really help. But this is standard exposure therapy for social phobics; a growing body of controlled studies support its effectiveness. The idea, in part, is to demonstrate to the patient that revealing imperfection, or doing something stupid, need not mean the end of the world or the unraveling of the self.*

Therapists of a more psychoanalytic bent tend to focus on the social phobic's firmly held view of himself as a deeply flawed or disgusting human being devoid of intrinsic value. Kathryn Zerbe, a psychiatrist in Portland, Oregon, has written that the social phobic's biggest fear is that other people will perceive his true—and inadequate—self. For the social phobic, any kind of performance—musical, sporting, public speaking—can be terrifying because failure will reveal the weakness and inadequacy within. This in turn means constantly projecting an image that feels false—an image of confidence, competence, even perfection. Dr. W. calls this impression management, and he observes that while it can be a *symptom* of social anxiety, it's an even bigger *cause*. Once you've invested in the perpetuation of a public image that feels untrue to your core self, you feel always in danger of being exposed as a fraud: one mistake, one revelation of anxiety or weakness, and the façade of competence and accomplishment is exposed for what it is—an artificial persona designed to hide the vulnerable self that lies within. Thus the stakes for any given performance become excruciatingly high: success means preserving the perception of value and esteem; failure means exposure of the shameful self one is trying so hard to hide. Impression management is exhausting and stressful—you live in constant fear that, as Dr. W. puts it, the house of cards that is your projected self will come crashing down around you.

---

* On a number of occasions, I saw other therapists from the center putting their patients through similar exposures at the same store, forcing them to ask strange questions or to make obvious and embarrassing mistakes. The store employees must have wondered why they had so many weird interactions with apparently deranged customers every day.

*A stammering man is never a worthless one. Physiology can tell you why. It is an excess of sensibility to the presence of his fellow creature, that makes him stammer.*

—THOMAS CARLYLE, FROM A LETTER TO
RALPH WALDO EMERSON (NOVEMBER 17, 1843)

As early as 1901, Paul Hartenberg anticipated one of the key findings of modern research on social phobics. While social phobics are unusually attentive to other people's feelings, he wrote in *Les timides et la timidité,* scrutinizing the verbal intonations, facial expressions, and body language of their interlocutors for signs of how people are reacting to them, they are also unduly confident about the conclusions they draw based on those observations—and specifically about the *negative* conclusions they draw. That is, social phobics are better at picking up on subtle social cues than other people are—but they tend to overinterpret anything that could be construed as a negative reaction. Since they are predisposed to believe that people won't like them or will react badly to them (they tend to have obsessive thoughts like *I'm boring* or *I'm going to make a fool of myself by saying something stupid*), they're always seeking confirmation of this belief by interpreting, say, a suppressed yawn or a slight twitch of the mouth as disapproval. "Highly anxious people read facial expressions faster than less anxious people," says R. Chris Fraley, a professor of psychology at the University of Illinois, Urbana-Champaign, "but they are also more likely to misread them." Alexander Bystritsky, the director of the Anxiety Disorders Program at UCLA, says that while anxious people do have "a sensitive emotional barometer" that allows them to detect subtle changes in emotion, "this barometer can cause them to read too much into an expression."

Social phobics are, in at least this one respect, gifted—faster and better at picking up behavioral cues from other people, with social antennae so sensitive that they receive transmissions that "normal" people can't. Put the other way around, the perception of healthy people may be adaptively blunted; they may not pick up on the negative cues— that yawn of boredom or twitch of disdain—that are in fact present.

Arne Öhman, a Swedish neuroscientist at Uppsala University who has written extensively about the evolutionary biology of phobic behavior, believes that oversensitive emotional barometers are genetically hardwired into social phobics, causing them to be acutely aware of social status in interpersonal interactions. Consider the case of Ned, a fifty-six-year-old dentist who had been in practice for three decades. To outward appearances, Ned was successful. But when he showed up in a psychiatrist's office, Ned said his career had been destroyed by his fear of "doing something foolish."* Anxiety about doing something wrong that will lead to social humiliation is quite common. But Ned's fear was interestingly specific: his performance anxiety was only acute when working on patients whom he perceived—based on the kind of insurance they carried—to have social status greater than he did. While he worked on Medicaid patients or those without insurance, his anxiety was negligible. But while treating patients with fancy insurance indicative of a high-status job, Ned was terrified that his hands would shake visibly or that he would sweat excessively, revealing his anxiety to his patients, who he believed were immune to anxiety and (as he put it) "completely at home in the world" and therefore prone to judge and even to ridicule him for his weakness.

Symptoms of this kind of status-based social anxiety—and particularly the fear of being exposed as "weak" relative to one's peers—appear regularly in the psychiatric literature going back a century. And lots of evidence supports Öhman's proposition that people like Ned have an awareness of social status, and of social slights, that is too finely calibrated. A National Institute of Mental Health study published in 2008 found that the brains of people with generalized social phobia responded differently to criticism than the brains of other people. When social phobics and healthy control subjects read neutral comments about themselves, their brain activity looked the same. But when the two groups read *negative* comments about themselves, those diagnosed with social anxiety disorder had markedly increased blood flow to the amygdala and the medial prefrontal cortex—two parts of the brain associated with anxiety and the stress response. The brains of

* Ned's case is drawn from John Marshall's book, *Social Phobia*.

social phobics appear physiologically primed to be hyperresponsive to negative comments.

This finding aligns with the many studies showing that social phobics demonstrate a more hyperreactive amygdala response to negative facial expressions. When social phobics see faces that appear angry, frightened, or disapproving, the neurons in their amygdalae fire faster and more intensively than those of healthy control subjects. As the NIMH researchers put it, "Generalized-social-phobia-related dysfunction may at least partly reflect a negative attitude toward the self, particularly in response to social stimuli, as instantiated in the medial prefrontal cortex." What this means, in plain English, is that shame and low self-esteem have a biological address: they reside, evidently, in the interconnections between the amygdala and the medial prefrontal cortex.

There's now a whole subgenre of fMRI studies that demonstrate that the amygdala reacts vividly to social stimuli not perceived by the conscious mind. When individuals are placed in an fMRI machine and shown images of faces displaying fear or anger, their amygdalae flare with activity. This is not surprising: we know that the amygdala is the seat of the fear response. It's also not surprising that neurons in the amygdalae of diagnosed social phobics tend to fire more frequently and intensively than those of other people in response to frightened or angry faces. What is surprising is that all people—social phobics and healthy control subjects alike—show a marked amygdala response to photos they are not consciously aware of seeing. That is, if you watch a slide show of innocuous images of flowers interspersed with pictures of scared or angry faces flashed so quickly you are not consciously aware of seeing them, your amygdala will flare in response to the emotional faces—even though you don't know you saw them. Ask the test subjects in these experiments whether they saw the scared or angry faces and they will say they did not; the images flashed by too quickly for the conscious brain to register them. But the amygdala, operating with lightning-fast acuity beneath the level of conscious awareness, perceives the distressing faces and flares in the fMRI. Some subjects report feeling anxiety at these moments—but they can't identify its source. This would seem to be neuroscientific evidence that Freud was right about the existence of the unconscious: the brain reacts powerfully to stimuli that we are not explicitly aware of.

Hundreds of studies reveal an unconscious neurobiological stress response to social stimuli. To cite just one, a 2008 study published in the *Journal of Cognitive Neuroscience* found that people shown images of emotional faces for thirty milliseconds—faster than the conscious mind can perceive them—demonstrated "marked" brain responses. (The socially anxious had the strongest brain responses.) Fascinatingly, when test subjects were asked to judge whether images of surprised faces were positive or negative, their judgments were powerfully affected by the subliminal images flashed just beforehand: when the image of the surprised face was preceded by a subliminal image of an angry or scared face, subjects were much more likely to say that the surprised face they were looking at was negative, expressing fear or anger; when the image of the same surprised face was preceded by a flashed happy face, the test subjects were more likely to say the same surprised face was expressing joy. As one of the researchers put it, "Unconsciously perceived signals of threat . . . bubble up and unwittingly influence social judgments."

What's the point of having such finely tuned social perception equipment? Why do our brains make judgments we're not consciously aware of?

One theory is that such "quick social judging" historically enhanced our odds of survival. In a baboon troop or a tribe of hunter-gatherers, you don't want to make social impressions that will invite attacks from your peers or cause you to be banished. For baboons, being kicked out of the troop is often tantamount to death: a lone monkey found by another group is likely to be set upon and killed. To be an early human banished from the tribe was to be both denied access to communal food supplies and rendered vulnerable to animal predators. Thus a certain social sensitivity—a keen attunement to what group norms demand, an awareness of social threats, a sense of how to signal the deference that will keep you from getting pummeled by a higher-status member of your troop or banished from your tribe—is adaptive. (This is where blushing can be helpful as an automatic signal of deference to others.) Being aware of how your social behavior—your "performance"—is being perceived by others can help you stay alive. Calling attention to yourself and being judged negatively is always risky: you're in danger of having your status challenged or of being kicked out of the tribe for making a bad impression.*

Murray Stein, a psychiatrist at the University of California, San Diego, has observed that social submissiveness in baboons and other primates has striking parallels with social phobia in humans. The stress that social phobics feel in anticipation of normal human interactions, and especially of public performances, Stein says, produces the same hypercortisolism—an elevation in the levels of stress hormones and an activation of the hypothalamic-pituitary-adrenal (HPA) axis—that subordinate status does in baboons. Hypercortisolism, in turn, kindles the amygdala, which has the effect of both intensifying anxiety in the moment and tying social interactions more deeply to a stress response in the future.†

Stein's research builds on the work of Robert Sapolsky, a neurobiologist at Stanford who has done fascinating research showing a direct correlation between a baboon's status in his troop and the quantity of stress hormones in his blood. Baboon populations have strictly ordered male hierarchies: there is the alpha male, who is usually the biggest and strongest and has the most access to food and females and is deferred to by all the other male monkeys, then there is the second-highest-ranking monkey, who is deferred to by all the other monkeys except for the alpha male—and so on, all the way down to the lowest-ranking male at the bottom of the social ladder. If a fight breaks out between two baboons and the higher-ranking one wins, the social order is preserved; if the lower-ranking one wins, there is a re-sorting, with the victorious baboon moving up the social ladder. Through careful obser-

---

* Some social phobics find even positive attention to be aversive. Think of the young child who bursts into tears when guests sing "Happy Birthday" to her at a party—or of Elfriede Jelinek afraid to pick up her Nobel Prize. Social attention—even positive, supportive attention—activates the neurocircuitry of fear. This makes sense from an evolutionary perspective. Calling positive attention to yourself can incite jealousy or generate new rivalries.

† The phobic response gets deeply consolidated in the neurons of the amygdala and the hippocampus—which is in part what makes it so hard to stamp out phobias. In this way, anxiety can be wretchedly self-reinforcing: stress activates the amygdala, which increases anxiety; increased anxiety stimulates the HPA axis, which makes the amygdala twitchier still—and all of this neural activity deepens the association of anxiety with the phobic stimulus, whether that's social interaction or a turbulent plane flight. In short, being anxious conditions you to be more anxious in the future.

vation, Sapolsky's team has been able to determine the social hierarchies of particular baboon populations. Using blood tests from these primates, Sapolsky has found that testosterone levels correlate directly with social standing: the higher ranking the baboon, the more testosterone he'll have. Moreover, when a baboon rises in the social hierarchy, the amount of testosterone he produces increases; when a baboon declines in status, his testosterone levels fall. (The causation seems to work in both directions: testosterone produces dominance, and dominance produces testosterone.)

But just as higher rank is associated with testosterone, lower rank is associated with stress hormones like cortisol: the lower a baboon's standing in the hierarchy, the greater the concentration of stress hormones in his blood. A subordinate male not only has to work harder to procure food and access to females but also has to tread carefully so as not to get beaten up by a dominant animal. It's unclear whether high levels of cortisol cause a baboon to become submissive or whether the stress of being low status causes cortisol levels to rise. Most likely it's both—the physical and psychological pressures of being a subordinate baboon lead to elevated levels of stress hormones, which produce more anxiety, which produces more stress hormones, which produce more submissiveness and general ill health.

While findings from animal studies can be applied to our understanding of human nature only indirectly (we can reason in ways other primates cannot), Ned's anxious response to practicing dentistry on "higher-status" patients may well have its roots in primitive concerns about overstepping bounds in the status hierarchy. Low-ranking baboons and orangutans that fail to lower their eyes—to signal their submissiveness—in the presence of higher-ranking ones risk inviting attack. A baboon's status in the social hierarchy—and, beyond that, his skillfulness at behaving in accord with his rank, whatever that may be— does a lot to determine his physical well-being.*

Both low-ranking baboons and humans with social anxiety dis-

---

* Interestingly, recent studies have found that the happiest-seeming and least stressed monkeys are what we might call the beta males—those monkeys near the top of the hierarchy, who tend to be easygoing and socially skillful. Being the highest-ranking male is a lot healthier and less stressful than being the lowest-ranking male—but being a *high*-ranking male who is not the *highest*-ranking male is

order resort easily to submissive behavior. Like low-ranking animals, people with the general subtype of social anxiety disorder tend
to look downward, avoid eye contact, blush, and engage in behaviors
that advertise their submissiveness, eagerly seeking to please their
peers and superiors and actively deferring to others to avoid conflict.
For low-ranking baboons, this behavior is a protective adaptation. It
can be adaptive in humans, too—but in social phobics it is more often
self-defeating.

Low-status monkeys and socially phobic humans also tend to have
notable irregularities in the processing of certain neurotransmitters.
Studies have found that monkeys with enhanced serotonergic function (in essence, higher levels of serotonin in their brain synapses) tend
to be more dominant, more friendly, and more likely than those with
normal serotonin levels to bond with their peers. In contrast, monkeys
with unusually low serotonin levels are more likely to display avoidant behavior: they keep to themselves and avoid social interactions.
Recent studies of humans have found altered serotonin function in certain brain regions of patients diagnosed with social anxiety disorder.
These findings help explain why selective serotonin reuptake inhibitors
like Prozac and Paxil can be effective in treating social anxiety. (Studies have also found that when nonanxious, nondepressed people take
SSRIs, they become more friendly.)

Dopamine has also been implicated in shaping social behavior.
When monkeys who have been housed alone are taken from their cages
and placed into a group setting, the monkeys that rise the highest in
the dominance hierarchy tend to have more dopamine in their brains—
which is interesting in light of studies finding that people diagnosed
with social anxiety disorder tend to have *lower*-than-average dopamine
levels. Some studies have found striking correlations between social
anxiety and Parkinson's disease, a neurological condition associated
with a deficit of dopamine in the brain. One 2008 study found that half
of Parkinson's patients scored high enough on the Liebowitz Social
Anxiety Scale to be diagnosed with social phobia. Multiple recent stud-

---

even more healthy and less stressful, because you're not always having to worry about the palace coup
that threatens to topple you.

ies have found "altered dopamine binding potential" in the brains of the socially anxious.* Murray Stein, among others, has hypothesized that the awkwardness and interpersonal clumsiness of social phobics are directly connected to problems in dopamine functioning; the dopamine "reinforcement/reward" pathways that help guide correct social behavior in healthy people may somehow be askew in the brains of social phobics.

My sister, who has for years suffered from social anxiety, strongly endorses this view. Without knowing anything about neurobiology, she has long insisted that her brain is "wired wrong."

"Social situations that normal people breeze through unthinkingly cause my brain to shut down," she says. "I can never think of what to say."

Though her brain otherwise functions well (she's a successful cartoonist, editor, and children's book author who graduated from Harvard), she has, ever since junior high, wrestled with what she calls her "talking problem." Neither decades of psychotherapy nor dozens of drug combinations have much alleviated it. She has been evaluated for Asperger's syndrome and other disorders on the autism spectrum, but she doesn't lack empathy the way Asperger's patients do.†

The association of dopamine and serotonin with social phobia doesn't prove that neurotransmitter deficits *cause* social anxiety—those irregularities could be the *effects* of social anxiety, the neurochemical "scars" that develop when a brain becomes overstressed from having to be so vigilant all the time, constantly scanning the environment for social threats. But emerging research suggests that the efficiency with which dopamine and serotonin get ferried across the synapses is genetically determined. Researchers have found that which variant of the serotonin transporter gene you have determines the density of serotonin receptors in your neurons—and that the relative density of your

---

* All drugs of abuse elevate dopamine levels in the basal ganglia—an area of the brain where dopamine is low in socially anxious patients. A chronic dopamine deficit may help account for why social phobics are more likely than others to struggle with addiction.

† Although Asperger's patients and social phobics in some ways suffer from a similar problem—a difficulty in managing social interactions that puts off others—they arrive at it from more or less opposite directions: whereas the Asperger's patient is no good at imagining what's in other people's minds, the social phobic is *too* good at it.

serotonin receptors helps determine where you fall on the spectrum between shy and extroverted.*

The introduction of social uncertainty into a group of baboons does interesting things to rates of anxiety. Low-ranking baboons are always stressed. But Robert Sapolsky has found that whenever a new male joins the troop, the glucocorticoid levels of *all* the baboons—not just the low-ranking ones—become elevated. With the introduction of new members into a social hierarchy, appropriate rules of conduct, such as who should defer to whom, become unclear; there are more fights and general agitation. Once the new baboon has been assimilated into the tribe, stress levels and glucocorticoid concentrations decline, and social behavior returns to normal.

This also happens in humans. In the late 1990s, Dirk Hellhammer, a German psychobiologist, coded sixty-three army recruits at boot camp according to their relative position in the social hierarchy (as determined by anthropological observation) and then measured their cortisol levels every week. During stable periods, the more dominant recruits had lower baseline levels of salivary cortisol than the subordinate ones—just like baboons. But during periods of experimentally induced psychological and physical stress, cortisol levels increased in all the soldiers—markedly in the dominant subjects and modestly in the subordinate ones. While it's always stressful being a low-ranking member of the tribe, disruptions to the social order seem to make everyone, even the high-ranking members, stressed.†

---

* I will discuss the relation between genes and anxiety in greater depth in chapter 9.

† One of the hallmarks of modernity is an abiding uncertainty about status. Hunter-gatherer societies tended not to be very socially stratified; for most of human history, people lived in fairly egalitarian groups. That changed during the Middle Ages. From the twelfth century or so all the way through the American Revolution, society was highly stratified—but also largely fixed: people didn't move between feudal castes. Modern society, in contrast, is both highly stratified (there's a high degree of income inequality in many countries) and highly fluid. The notion that anyone can, with luck and pluck, rise from poverty to the middle class, or from the middle class to great wealth, is integral to our idea of success. But not all mobility is upward. Unlike in a society with more fixed socioeconomic strata, there is always the fear of falling—a fear that is heightened in economic times like these. The many forces bearing down on the American worker—the creative destruction of free-market capitalism; the disruptions to the labor force caused by technology; the changing and uncertain relations between the sexes and the accompanying confusion about gender roles—combine to produce constant uncertainty. People naturally worry: *Am I being overtaken by other people with more relevant job skills? Will I lose my job and fall out of the middle class?* Some have argued that this chronic uncertainty is physically rewiring our brains to be more anxious.

*Many of us have strived for perfection in order to try to control our world. . . . There is generally a deep-seated feeling of not being good enough, of being deficient or defective in some way, or of being different from others in a way that will not be accepted by others. This creates a feeling of shame and a fear of embarrassment and humiliation in exposing your true self in front of others.*
—JANET ESPOSITO, *In the Spotlight* (2000)

Recently, while sifting through the records from my treatment with Dr. M. nearly a decade ago, I came across a document I'd written at her request. She had asked me to write down what the outcome of a worst-case-scenario public speaking catastrophe would be for me. The idea behind this sort of exercise is to fully imagine the worst thing that could happen (total failure, complete humiliation) and then, once you've really thought about it, to conclude that, first, the worst-case scenario was unlikely to unfold and, second, even if it did, maybe it would not be so shatteringly catastrophic. Reaching that conclusion, and assimilating it intellectually and emotionally, is supposed to lower the stakes of the performance and therefore diminish anxiety.

That's the theory anyway. But when I showed up at my lunchtime appointment one Thursday after having e-mailed her my imagined worst-case public speaking scenario (humiliation and physical collapse followed by unemployment, divorce, and ostracism from society), Dr. M. looked stricken.

"Your write-up," she said. "It's the most negative thing I've ever read." She told me she had been horrified at what I'd written and had felt compelled to show my account to her department supervisor in search of more experienced counsel. As she looked at me with sympathy, concern, and, I believe, no small alarm, I suspected she'd raised the question of whether I might be gravely depressed and possibly psychotic.

Perhaps I have an overactive imagination; perhaps I'm unduly pessimistic. But I now know that negativity and poor self-image—along with a desperate desire to conceal that poor self-image—are textbook for a social phobic. Nearly every book on the subject, both popular and academic, observes that social anxiety disorder is associated with feelings of inferiority and with extreme sensitivity to any kind of criticism or negative evaluation.*

"Jeez," Dr. W. said to me one day when I was explaining to him the high stakes I ascribed to an upcoming public event and how important I thought it was to maintain my façade of efficacy and to hide my sense of fraudulence and weakness. "Do you realize how potently your sense of shame contributes to your anxiety?"

Both Dr. M. and Dr. W.—not to mention Epictetus—would say that the best cure for this kind of social anxiety is to diminish the power of shame. The embarrassing exposures that Dr. M. subjected me to were designed to inure me somewhat to feelings of shame.

"Go ahead, put it out there," Dr. W. says, speaking of my anxiety. "You may be surprised by how people respond.

"Stop caring so much about what other people think," he says, echoing the advice of a hundred self-help books.

If only it were that easy.

*The day I'm not nervous is the day I quit. To me, nerves are great. That means you care, and I care about what I do.*
—TIGER WOODS, AT A PRESS CONFERENCE BEFORE THE 2009 WGC–ACCENTURE MATCH PLAY CHAMPIONSHIP

*I don't give a shit what you say. If I go out there and miss game winners and people say, "Kobe choked" or "Kobe is seven for whatever in pressure situations," well, fuck you. Because I don't play for your fucking approval. I play for my own love and enjoyment of the*

---

* Even, and perhaps especially, psychotherapists are not immune. Because they feel patients and peers look to them to be in control of their emotions, the pressure psychotherapists put on themselves not to appear anxious or agitated can be great—and can perversely make them feel more anxious and out of control. I have on my shelf several books by therapists who have at times felt handicapped and humiliated by their own anxiety. *The Anxiety Expert: A Psychiatrist's Story of Panic* (2004) was written by Marjorie Raskin, a psychiatrist specializing in anxiety who was tortured by panic attacks brought on by public speaking. She went to great lengths to hide her anxiety and, like me, medicated herself heavily with benzodiazepines. *Painfully Shy: How to Overcome Social Anxiety and Reclaim your Life* (2001) was cowritten by a psychologist, Barbara Markway, who concedes that she herself has not, in fact, ever fully "overcome her social anxiety or reclaimed her life."

*game. And to win. That's what I play for. Most of the time, when guys feel the pressure, they're worried about what people might say about them. I don't have that fear, and it enables me to forget bad plays and to take shots and play my game.*

—KOBE BRYANT, DURING AN INTERVIEW FOLLOWING GAME 3
OF THE 2012 NBA WESTERN CONFERENCE SEMIFINALS

One day in seventh grade, while playing my classmate Paul in a tennis match, I become overwhelmed with anxiety. My stomach is distended; I am burping uncontrollably. Before the match started, the most important thing was that I win. But now that I am in the middle of the match and my stomach hurts and I am afraid of throwing up, the most important thing is that I get off the court as quickly as possible. And the quickest way to do that is to lose. And so I hit balls out. I hit them into the net. I double-fault. I lose 6–1, 6–0, and when I shake hands and get off the court, the first thing I feel is relief. My stomach settles. My anxiety relents.

And the next thing I feel is self-loathing. Because I have lost to the overweight and oleaginous Paul, who is now strutting around proudly, crowing about how badly he has beaten me. The stakes are low: it is a challenge match for one of the lower ladder positions on the middle-school junior varsity. But to me they feel existentially high. I have lost to Paul, who is not a particularly good player—his skills, his quickness, his fitness are manifestly worse than mine—and the result is there on the score sheet and on the ladder hanging on the locker room wall and radiating from Paul's puffed-out chest, for all to see: he has won, so he is superior to me. I have lost; I am therefore, by definition, a loser.

This sort of thing—purposely losing matches to escape intolerable anxiety—happened dozens of times throughout my school sports career. Not every thrown match was as egregious as the one against Paul (whose name, by the way, I have changed here)—I often tanked matches against players who would likely have beaten me even if I hadn't suffered an anxious meltdown—but some of them were. My coaches were baffled. How could it be, they wondered, that I could look so skillful in practice and yet so rarely win a significant match?

The exception was tenth grade, when I played for the junior varsity squash team and went undefeated: 17–0 or something. What, you might ask, accounts for that?

Valium.

Squash matches, even squash practices, were making me so miserable that the child psychiatrist I was seeing then, Dr. L., prescribed a small dose of the benzodiazepine. Every day during squash season that year, I took the pill surreptitiously with my peanut butter sandwich at lunch. And I didn't lose a match. I was still unhappy during squash season: my agoraphobia and separation anxiety made me hate traveling to matches, and my competitive anxieties still made me hate playing in them. But the Valium took enough of the physical edge off my nerves that I could focus on trying to play well instead of on trying to get off the court as quickly as possible. I didn't feel compelled to lose matches on purpose anymore. Drugs got me into the zone of performance where anxiety is beneficial.

In 1908, two psychologists, Robert M. Yerkes and John Dillingham Dodson, published an article in *The Journal of Comparative Neurology and Psychology* demonstrating that animals trained to perform a task performed it slightly better if they were made "moderately anxious" beforehand. This led to what has become known as the Yerkes-Dodson law, whose principles have been experimentally demonstrated in both animals and humans many times since then. It's kind of a Goldilocks law: too little anxiety and you will not perform at your peak, whether on a test or in a squash match; too much anxiety and you will not perform well; but with just the right amount of anxiety—enough to elevate your physiological arousal and to focus your attention intensely on the task, but not so much that you are distracted by how nervous you are—you'll be more likely to deliver a peak performance. For me, evidently, getting from the too-anxious part of the curve to the optimum-performance part required a small dose of Valium.*

---

* There have been elite athletes for whom this has been the case, too. Reno Bertoia, to name just one, was a young third baseman for the Detroit Tigers who once seemed to have a bright future in the major leagues—until, in 1957, he became so overwhelmed by anxiety that, as the Tigers' trainer observed, he "couldn't hit and sometimes bobbled fielding plays that should have been easy." The more nervous Bertoia got, the worse he played; the worse he played, the more nervous he got—a

. . .

I wish I could say competitive anxiety was merely an adolescent phase. But about ten years ago, I found myself playing in the finals of a squash tournament against my friend Jay, a personable young physician. It was championship night at the squash club, and a couple of dozen people had turned out to watch. We were two just-better-than-average club players; absolutely nothing of significance (no money, hardly a trophy to speak of) was on the line.

In this tournament, matches were best of five games; to win a game you needed nine points. I jumped out confidently to an early lead in the first game, but I let it slip away. I won the second game; Jay won the third. My back against the wall, I won the fourth, and Jay sagged visibly. I could see that he was tired—more tired than I was. In the fifth and deciding game, I pulled steadily ahead and got to 7–3, two points away from victory. Jay looked defeated. Victory was mine.

Except it wasn't.

The prospect of imminent victory sent anxiety cascading through my body. My mouth went dry. My limbs grew impossibly heavy. Worst of all, my stomach betrayed me. Overwhelmed with nausea and panic, I hit weak shots, desperate shots. Jay, moments earlier disconsolate and resigned to losing, perked up. I'd given him a ray of hope. He gained momentum. My anxiety mounted, and suddenly it was like I was back in seventh grade, playing tennis against Paul: all I want is out. I withered before everyone's eyes. I began, on purpose, to lose.

Jay seized his opportunity, Lazarus from the grave, and beat me. Afterward, I tried to be gracious in defeat, but when everyone inevitably commented on how dramatically I had blown my near victory, I attributed my collapse to back trouble. My back did hurt—but it was

---

classic vicious cycle of ever-increasing anxiety and ever-decreasing performance. Soon, his play had so deteriorated that Tigers management was on the verge of dropping him from the team. Desperate and unhappy, Bertoia resorted to taking Miltown, an early, pre-Valium tranquilizer. The transformation was astounding. Bertoia "stopped holding himself in," the trainer reported. "He's a different man on the bench—talking and joking—and much more relaxed." On the field, meanwhile, he started "pounding the ball in tremendous fashion." His batting average rose a hundred points.

not why I lost. I had the championship in my clutches, and I let it slip away because I was too anxious to compete.

I choked.

Just about the worst epithet one can sling at an athlete—worse, in some ways, than "cheater"—is "choker": to choke is to wilt under pressure, to fail to perform at the moment of greatest importance. (A technical definition, as laid out by Sian Beilock, a University of Chicago cognitive psychologist who specializes in the topic, is "suboptimal performance—worse performance than expected given what a performer is capable of doing and what this performer has done in the past.") The etymological stem of "anxious"—*anx*—comes from the Latin *angere*, which means "to choke"; the Latin word *anxius* probably referred to the feeling of chest constriction experienced during a panic attack. To choke, in an athletic or any other kind of performance context, implies an absence of fortitude, a weakness of character. The most common explanation for choking in a sporting event is, in the shorthand of the sports reporter, "nerves." Choking, in other words, is produced by anxiety—and in the sporting arena, as well as on the field of battle or in the workplace, anxiety is ipso facto a sign of weakness.

Since my collapse in the club finals that year, I have learned the beneficial effects of prematch meditation and have gotten better at titrating my dosages of prophylactic antianxiety medication. My wife has also borne us two children, which should have put into perspective the existential insignificance of a recreational sporting event. And yet the problem persists.

Not long ago, I found myself in the semifinals of another squash tournament.

"Why do you play in these tournaments if they make you so miserable?" Dr. W. had asked me several years earlier. "If you can't learn to enjoy them, stop torturing yourself by playing in them!"

And so I had stopped for a while. And when I started again, I did so with a conscious lack of emotional investment. *I'm just doing it for the exercise,* I tell myself. *I can enjoy the competition without making myself anxious and miserable about the outcome.* And through the first rounds of this tournament, I do. Sure, there are tense moments; at times I feel pressure, which fatigues me and diminishes the quality of my play. But that's normal, the vicissitudes of competition; it doesn't debilitate me. And I keep winning.

So when I step out onto the court for the semifinals, I tell myself, *I still do not care.* Only five people are watching. I lose a close first game. But it's fun. *No big deal. I don't care. My opponent is good. I* should *lose this match. No expectations, no pressure.*

But then I win the next game. *Wait a minute,* I think. *I'm in this match. I could win it.* The moment my competitive impulse surges, the familiar heaviness descends and my stomach inflates with air.

*C'mon, Scott,* I tell myself. *Have fun. Who cares who wins?*

I try to relax but my breathing is getting heavier. I'm sweating more profusely. And as word spreads that the match is a close one, more people begin gathering behind the court to watch.

I try to slow everything down—my breathing, the pace of my play. As my anxiety rises, the quality of my game deteriorates. But I am still, for the moment anyway, focusing on trying to play well, on trying to win. To my surprise, my slowing-the-pace-down strategy works: I come from behind to win the third game. One more game and I will be in the championship.

At which point I find I am so enervated by my anxiety that I can no longer play. My opponent wins the next game quickly, evening the match at 2–2. Whoever wins the next game will be into the finals.

I use the allotted two-minute break between games to retreat to the men's room to try to collect myself. I am pale and shaking—and, most terrifying to me, nauseated. As I walk back out on the court, the referee asks if I am okay. (I clearly do not look well.) I mumble that I am. The fifth game begins, and I no longer care at all about winning; as in my match against Paul thirty years earlier, I care only about getting off the court without vomiting. Once again, I start trying to lose as quickly as possible: I stop running for the ball; I shank balls on purpose. My opponent is puzzled. After I fail to run for an easy drop shot, he turns and asks me if I'm okay. Mortified, I nod that I am.

But I am not okay. I am terrified that I will not be able to lose enough points quickly enough to get off the court before retching and humiliating myself. In seventh grade, at least, I had been able to stay on the court until the end of the match with Paul; this time, with so many eyes upon me and my gorge rising, I cannot do even that. Two points later, with the match many points from conclusion, I raise my hand in defeat.

"I concede," I say to my opponent. "I'm sick." And I scurry off the court in defeat.

I have not just lost. I have given up. Folded like a cheap lawn chair. I feel mortified and pathetic.

Friends in the audience murmur words of consolation in my direction. "We could tell you weren't feeling well," they say. "Something wasn't right." I shake them off ("Bad fish for lunch," I mumble) and retreat to the locker room. As ever, once I am out of the competitive moment, and out of public view, my anxiety recedes.

But I have lost to another opponent I might well have beaten. In truth, I don't really care about the losing. What bothers me is that, yet again, my anxiety has defeated me, reduced me to a helpless mass of quivering jelly and exposed me to what feels like minor public embarrassment.

I know: the reality is that no one cares. Which somehow just makes this all the more pathetic.

*Never in my career have I experienced anything like what happened. I was totally out of control. And I couldn't understand it.*
—GREG NORMAN, TO *GOLF MAGAZINE* ON BLOWING A LARGE
LEAD AT THE 1996 MASTERS

The list of elite athletes who have choked spectacularly, or who have developed bizarre and crippling performance anxieties, is extensive.

Greg Norman, the Australian golfer, came unglued at the 1996 Masters, nervously frittering away a seemingly insurmountable lead over the final few holes; he ended up sobbing in the arms of the man who beat him, Nick Faldo. Jana Novotna, the Czech tennis star, was five points away from winning Wimbledon in 1993 when she disintegrated under pressure and blew a huge lead over Steffi Graf; she ended up sobbing in the arms of the Duchess of Kent. On November 25, 1980, Roberto Durán, then the reigning world welterweight boxing champion, squared off against Sugar Ray Leonard in one of the most famous bouts ever. With sixteen seconds left in the eighth round—and millions of dollars on the line—Durán turned to the referee, raised his hands in surrender, and pleaded, "*No más, no más* [No more, no more]. No more box." He would later say his stomach hurt. Until that moment, Durán was perceived to be invincible, the epitome of Latino machismo. Since then, he has lived in infamy—considered one of the greatest quitters and cowards in sports history.

These are all classic chokes—mental and physical collapses in isolated moments of high anxiety. More puzzling are those professional athletes who, in an excruciatingly public manifestation of performance anxiety, go into a kind of chronic choke. In the mid-1990s, Nick Anderson was a guard for the Orlando Magic. He entered the 1995 NBA finals as a solid free-throw shooter, having made about 70 percent of his foul shots throughout his career. But in the first game of the championship series against the Houston Rockets that year, Anderson had four consecutive opportunities to secure a victory for Orlando with a foul shot in the final seconds of regulation time: all he had to do was hit one shot.

He missed all four. The Magic went on to lose that game in overtime, and then to lose the series in a four-game sweep. After that, Anderson's free-throw percentage plummeted; for the remainder of his career, he was a disaster at the foul line. This caused him to play less aggressively on offense because he was afraid he'd get fouled and have to shoot free throws. The missed championship free throws, Anderson recalled later, were "like a song that got in my head, playing over and over and over." He was driven to early retirement.

In 1999, Chuck Knoblauch lost the ability to throw a baseball from second to first base. This would not have been a problem had he not happened to be, at the time, the starting second baseman for the New York Yankees. Knoblauch had no physical injury that would have impeded him—he could throw to first just fine during practice. During games, however, with forty thousand fans watching him in the stadium and millions more watching him on television, he repeatedly overthrew the base, launching the ball into the stands.

Two decades earlier, just a year removed from being named the National League's rookie of the year, Steve Sax, the second baseman for the Los Angeles Dodgers, developed the same affliction as Knoblauch. He had no trouble in practice, though, even successfully throwing blindfolded in an effort to break the habit.

Most infamously there is Steve Blass, an All-Star pitcher for the Pittsburgh Pirates who, in June 1973, following a stretch when he was perhaps the best pitcher in baseball, was suddenly unable to throw the ball through the strike zone. In practice, he could throw as well as ever. But during games, he couldn't control where the ball was going. After psychotherapy, meditation, hypnotism, and all manner of cockeyed home remedies (including wearing looser underwear) failed to cure him, he retired.

Odder still are the examples of Mike Ivie and Mackey Sasser, catchers for the San Diego Padres and New York Mets, respectively. Both became so phobic about throwing the ball back to the pitcher—the sort of thing Little Leaguers do without trouble—that they ended up having to leave their positions. (The sports psychiatrist Allan Lans half jokingly coined the term "disreturnophobia" to describe this affliction.)

The explicit monitoring theory of choking, derived from recent findings in cognitive psychology and neuroscience, holds that performance falters when athletes concentrate too much attention on it. Thinking *too much* about what you are doing actually impairs performance. This would seem to run counter to all the standard bromides about how the quality of your performance is tied to the intensity of your focus. But what seems to matter is the type of focus you have. Sian Beilock, who studies the psychology of choking at her lab at the University of Chicago, says that actively worrying about screwing up makes you more likely to screw up. To achieve optimal performance—what some psychologists call flow—parts of your brain should be on automatic pilot, not actively thinking about (or "explicitly monitoring") what you are doing. By this logic, the reason Ivie's and Sasser's "disreturnophobia" became so severe was that they were thinking too much about what should have been the mindless mechanics of throwing the ball back to the pitcher. (*Am I gripping the ball right? Am I following through in the right arm position? Do I look funny? Am I going to screw this up again? What's wrong with me?*) Beilock has found that she can dramatically improve athletes' performance (at least in experimental situations) by getting them to focus on something other than the mechanics of their stroke or swing; having them recite a poem or sing a song in their head, distracting their *conscious* attention from the physical task, can rapidly improve performance.

But anxious people generally can't stop thinking about everything, all the time, in all the wrong ways. *What if this? What if that? Am I doing this right? Do I look stupid? What if I make a fool of myself? What if I throw it into the stands again? Am I blushing visibly? Can people see me trembling? Can they hear my voice quavering? Am I going to lose my job or get demoted to the minors?*

When you look at brain scans of athletes pre- or midchoke, says the sports psychologist Bradley Hatfield, you see a neural "traffic jam" of worry and self-monitoring. Brain scans of nonchokers, on the other hand—the Tom Bradys and Peyton Mannings of the world, who exude grace under pressure—reveal neural activity that is "efficient and streamlined," using only those parts of the brain relevant to efficient performance.

In a sense, the anxiety exhibited by all these choking athletes is a version of the blushing problem: their fear of embarrassing themselves in public leads them to embarrass themselves in public. Their anxiety drives them to do the very thing they most fear. The more self-conscious you are—the more susceptible to shame—the worse you will perform.

*If you are a man you will not permit your self-respect to admit an anxiety neurosis or to show fear.*
—SIGNS POSTED ON ALLIED GUN SITES IN MALTA
DURING WORLD WAR II

In 1830, Colonel R. Taylor, the British consul in Baghdad, was exploring an archaeological excavation on the site of an ancient Assyrian palace when he came across a six-sided clay prism covered with cuneiform. The Taylor prism, which today is housed in the British Museum, tells of the military campaigns of King Sennacherib, who ruled Assyria in the eighth century B.C. The prism has been of great value to historians and theologians because of the contemporaneous accounts it provides of events described in the Old Testament. To me, however, the most interesting passage on the prism describes Assyria's battle with two young kings of Elam (southwestern Iran on a modern map).

"To save their lives they trampled over the bodies of their soldiers and fled," the prism reads, recounting what happened when Sennacherib's army overwhelmed them. "Like young captured birds they lost their courage. With their urine they defiled their chariots and let fall their excrements."

Here, in one of the earliest written records ever discovered, is the damning judgment cast on the weak stomach and moral character of the anxious warrior.

Many of the sports tropes about heroism, courage, and "grace under pressure" are also applied to war. But the stakes attending a sporting performance pale beside those attending performance in war, where the difference between success and failure is often the difference between life and death.

Societies grant the highest approbation to soldiers (and athletes) who display grace under pressure—and harshly disparage those who falter under it. The anxious are inconstant and weak; the brave are stolid and strong. Cowards are governed by their fears; heroes are unperturbed by them. In his *Histories,* Herodotus tells of Aristodemus, an elite Spartan warrior whose "heart failed him" at the Battle of Thermopylae in 480 B.C.; he remained in the rear guard and did not join the fight. Thenceforth Aristodemus became known as the Trembler, and he "found himself in such disgrace that he hanged himself."

Militaries have always gone to considerable length to inure their soldiers to anxiety. The Vikings used stimulants made from deer urine to provide chemical resistance to fear. British military commanders historically girded their soldiers with rum; the Russian army used vodka (and also valerian, a mild tranquilizer). The Pentagon has been researching pharmacological means of shutting down the fight-or-flight response, with an eye toward eradicating battlefield fear. Researchers at Johns Hopkins University recently designed a system that would allow commanders to monitor their soldiers' stress levels in real time by measuring the hormone hydrocortisone—the idea being that if a soldier's stress hormones exceed a certain level, he should be removed from battle.

Militaries denigrate fearful behavior for good reason: anxiety can be devastating to the soldier and to the army he fights in. The *Anglo-Saxon Chronicle* recounts the battle between England and Denmark that took place in 1003, in which Ælfric, the English commander, became so anxious that he began to vomit and could no longer command his men, who ended up being slaughtered by the Danes.

Anxiety can spread by contagion, so armies seek aggressively to contain it. During the Civil War, the Union army tattooed or branded soldiers found guilty of cowardice. During World War I, any British soldier who developed neurosis as a result of war trauma was declared to be "at best a constitutionally inferior human being, at worst a malingerer and a coward." Medical writers of the time described anxious soldiers as "moral invalids." (Some progressive doctors—including W. H. R. Rivers, who treated the poet Siegfried Sassoon, among others—argued that combat neurosis was a medical condition that could affect even soldiers of stern moral stuff, but such doctors were in the minority.) A 1914 article in *The American Review of Reviews* argued that "panic may be checked by officers firing on their own men." Until the Second World War, the British army punished deserters with death.

The Second World War was the first conflict in which psychiatrists played a significant role, both as screeners of soldiers before combat and as healers of their psychic wounds afterward. More than a million U.S. soldiers were admitted to hospitals for psychiatric treatment of battle fatigue. But some senior officers fretted about what this more humane treatment of soldiers meant for combat effectiveness. George Marshall, the U.S. Army general who later became secretary of state, lamented that soldiers who on the front lines would be considered cowards and malingerers were considered by psychiatrists to be patients. The "hyperconsiderate professional attitude" of the psychiatrist, Marshall complained, would lead to an army of cosseted cowards. British generals stated in reputable medical journals that men who panicked during combat should be sterilized "because only such a measure would prevent men from showing fear and passing on to another generation their mental weakness." High-ranking officers on both sides of the Atlantic argued that soldiers diagnosed with "war neurosis" should not be allowed to poison the gene pool with their cowardice. "It is now time that our country stopped being soft," one British colonel declared, "and abandoned its program of mollycoddling no-goods." For his part, General George Patton of the U.S. Army denied there was such a thing as war neurosis. He preferred the term "combat exhaustion" and said it was a mere "problem of the will." In order to prevent combat exhaustion from spreading, Patton proposed to the commanding general, Dwight Eisenhower, that it be punishable by death. (Eisenhower declined to implement the suggestion.)

Modern armies still struggle with what to do about soldiers undone by their combat-shattered nerves. During the Iraq war, *The New York Times* reported on an American soldier who had been dishonorably discharged for cowardice. The soldier contested his discharge, arguing it should have been an honorable one. He was not a coward, he said, but rather a medical patient suffering from a psychiatric illness: the stress of war had given him panic disorder, which caused him debilitating anxiety attacks. He was sick, his lawyers argued, not cowardly. The military, in this instance, initially refused to recognize the distinction—though Army officials later dropped the cowardice charges, reducing them to the lesser offense of dereliction of duty.

Throughout history there have always been anxious soldiers, men whose nerve failed them and whose bodies betrayed them in crucial moments. After his first experience with combat, in 1862, William Henry, a young Union soldier of the Sixty-Eighth Pennsylvania Volunteers, suffered horrible stomach pains and diarrhea. Deemed by his doctors to be in otherwise good physical health, Henry was the first person to be formally diagnosed with "soldier's heart," a syndrome brought on by the stress of combat.* Studies of "self-soiling rates" among U.S. soldiers during World War II consistently found that 5 to 6 percent of combatants lost control of their bowels, with rates in some combat divisions exceeding 20 percent. Before landing on Iwo Jima in June 1945, American troops suffered rampant diarrhea; some soldiers used this as an excuse to avoid combat. A survey of one U.S. combat division in

---

* This diagnosis had been applied informally since the French Revolution to men who broke down during combat, but it was only in 1871, when a physician named Jacob Mendes Da Costa wrote up a case study on Henry for *The American Journal of the Medical Sciences,* that the condition was formally inscribed in the scientific literature as soldier's heart or irritable heart or Da Costa's syndrome. Historians of psychiatry often identify this article as the first in the medical literature to describe the conditions we would today call panic disorder and post-traumatic stress disorder.

France in 1944 revealed that more than half of the soldiers broke out in cold sweats, felt faint, or lost control of their bowels during battle. Another survey of World War II infantrymen found that only 7 percent said they never felt fear—whereas 75 percent said their hands trembled, 85 percent said they got sweaty palms, 12 percent said they lost bowel control, and 25 percent said they lost bladder control. (Upon hearing that a quarter of survey respondents admitted to losing control of their bladders during battle, one army colonel said, "Hell . . . all that proves is that three out of four are damned liars!") Recent findings issued by the Pentagon revealed that a high number of soldiers deployed in Iraq vomited from anxiety before going out on patrol in combat areas.

William Manchester, who would go on to become an eminent American historian, fought at Okinawa during the Second World War. "I could feel a twitching in my jaw, coming and going like a winky light signaling some disorder," he wrote, recalling his first experience of direct combat, in which he approached a Japanese sniper hiding out in a shack. "Various valves were opening and closing in my stomach. My mouth was dry, my legs quaking, and my eyes out of focus." Manchester shot and killed the sniper—and then vomited and urinated on himself. "Is this what they mean by 'conspicuous gallantry'?" he wondered.

I would argue that Manchester's anxious physiological reaction had an almost moral quality to it, a sensitivity to the existential gravity of the situation. Anxiety, as observers since Augustine have noted, can be usefully allied to morality; people who have no physiological reaction in these situations are the proverbial cold-blooded killers. As the writer Christopher Hitchens—no one's idea of a coward—once put it, "Now, those who fail to register emotion under pressure are often apparently good officer material, but that very stoicism can also conceal—as with officers who don't suffer from battle fatigue or post-traumatic stress—a psychopathic calm that sends the whole platoon into a ditch full of barbed wire and sheds no tears."

Nevertheless, there is a culturally accepted connection stretching back to ancient times between courage and manliness, as well as an approbative moral quality assigned to the ability to control one's bodily functions when in extremis. Legend has it that when Napoleon needed a man "with iron nerve" for a dangerous mission, he ordered several volunteers before a fake firing squad and chose the one who "showed no tendency to move his bowels" when fired upon with blanks.

My colleague Jeff, a journalist who has reported from war zones all over the world and has been kidnapped by terrorist organizations, says that neophyte war correspondents always wonder about what will happen the first time they find themselves pinned down by gunfire. "Until you've been under fire," he says, "the question you ask yourself is, Will I shit my pants? Some do; some don't. I didn't—and I knew from then on I would be fine. But until it happens, you just don't know."

Happily, I've never been fired upon. But I suspect I know into which category I would fall.

> *A coward changes color all the time, and cannot sit still for nervousness, but squats down, first on one heel, then on the other; his heart thumps in his breast as he thinks of death in all its forms, and one can hear the chattering of his teeth. But the brave man never changes color at all and is not unduly perturbed, from the moment when he takes his seat in ambush with the rest.*
> —HOMER, *THE ILIAD* (CIRCA EIGHTH CENTURY B.C.)

Why do some people exhibit grace under fire while others fall so readily to pieces? Studies show that almost everyone—all but the most resilient and the most sociopathic—has a breaking point, a psychic threshold beyond which he or she can bear no more combat stress without emotional and physical deterioration or collapse. But some people can withstand lots of stress before breaking down and can recover from combat exhaustion quickly; others break down easily and recover slowly and with difficulty—if they recover at all.

There seems to be remarkable consistency across human populations: a fixed percentage of individuals will crack under pressure, and another fixed percentage will remain largely immune to it. Comprehensive studies conducted during World War II found that in the typical combat unit, a fairly constant proportion of men will emotionally collapse early on, usually even before getting to the battlefield; another relatively fixed proportion (some of them sociopathic) will be able to withstand extraordinary amounts of stress without ill effect; and the majority of men will fall somewhere between these extremes.

John Leach, a British psychologist who studies cognition under extreme stress, has observed that, on average, 10 to 20 percent of people will remain cool and composed in combat situations. "These people will be able to collect their thoughts quickly," he writes in *Survival Psychology*. "Their awareness of the situation will be intact and their judgment and reasoning abilities will not be impaired to any significant extent." At the other extreme, 10 to 15 percent of people will react with "uncontrolled weeping, confusion, screaming and paralyzing anxiety." But most people, Leach says, up to 80 percent of them, will in high-stress lethal conditions become lethargic and confused, waiting for direction. (This perhaps helps account for why so many people submit so readily to authoritarianism in periods of extreme stress or disruption.)

On the other hand, British psychiatrists observed that during World War II, as the Luftwaffe rained bombs on London, civilians with pre-existing neurotic disorders found that their general levels of anxiety actually *declined*. As one historian has written, "Neurotics turned out to be remarkably calm about being threatened from the skies"—probably because they felt reassured to discover that "normal" people shared their fears during the Blitz. One psychiatrist speculated that neurotics felt reassured by the sight of other people "looking as worried as they have felt over the years." When it's acceptable to feel anxious, neurotics feel less anxious.

One fascinating study of stress during wartime was conducted by V. A. Kral, a doctor who was held in the concentration camp Theresienstadt during World War II. In 1951, he published an article in *The American Journal of Psychiatry* reporting that although thirty-three thousand people died at Theresienstadt—and another eighty-seven thousand were transferred to other Nazi concentration camps to be killed—no new cases of phobia, neurosis, or pathological anxiety developed there. In fact, Kral, who worked at the camp hospital, noted that while most detainees became depressed, few experienced clinical anxiety. He wrote that those who had before the war suffered from "severe and long-lasting psychoneuroses such as phobias and compulsive obsessive neuroses" found that their ailments had gone into remission. "[Patients'] neuroses either disappeared completely in Theresienstadt or improved to such a degree that patients would work and did not have to seek medical aid." Interestingly, those patients who survived the war relapsed into their old neurotic patterns afterward. It was as though real fear crowded out their neurotic anxiety; when the fear relented, the anxiety crept back.

Military psychiatrists have collected a lot of data on what kinds of situations cause soldiers the greatest anxiety. Many studies have shown that the amount of control a soldier feels he has strongly determines how much anxiety he experiences. As Roy Grinker and his colleagues first described in *Men Under Stress,* the classic study of combat neuroses during World War II, while fighter pilots were terrified of flak shot from the ground, they found fighting with enemy planes to be exhilarating.*

Combat trauma is a powerful psychic destroyer: many soldiers break down emotionally during war; still more break down afterward. Vietnam produced thousands of traumatized soldiers, many of whom ended up homeless and addicted to drugs. Some fifty-eight thousand U.S. soldiers died during active combat in Vietnam between 1965 and 1975—but an even greater number have committed suicide since then. Suicide is also rampant among veterans of our recent wars in Iraq and Afghanistan. According to numbers from the Army Behavioral Health Integrated Data Environment, the suicide rate among active-duty soldiers increased 80 percent between 2004 and 2008; a 2012 study published in *Injury Prevention* reported that the number of suicides is "unprecedented in over 30 years of U.S. Army records." A study in *The Journal of the American Medical Association* concluded that more than 10 percent of Afghanistan veterans and nearly 20 percent of Iraq veterans suffer from anxiety or depression. Other studies have found massive rates of antidepressant and tranquilizer consumption among Iraq veterans; ABC News reports that one in three soldiers is now taking psychiatric medication. The mortality rates for those who break down under combat stress are much higher than for those who don't: a

---

* The relationship between lack of control and anxiety has been demonstrated many times over the years in noncombat situations, too. Researchers have produced ulcers in mice simply by depriving them of control over their environment, and a raft of studies have demonstrated that people in jobs where they don't perceive themselves to have a lot of control are much more susceptible to developing clinical anxiety and depression, as well as stress-related medical conditions like ulcers and diabetes.

recent study published in the *Annals of Epidemiology* showed that army veterans diagnosed with post-traumatic stress disorder have twice the premature death rate of their unafflicted peers. The rates of postcombat suicide have become so high in recent years that the U.S. military has made providing prophylactic treatment for post-traumatic stress disorder a high priority. In 2012, the suicide rate reached a ten-year high— a staggering eighteen current and former servicemen are killing themselves every day in the United States, according to Admiral Mike Mullen, the former chairman of the Joint Chiefs of Staff.

Of course, until 1980, when the diagnosis was decreed into existence alongside the other anxiety disorders with the publication of the *DSM-III,* there was officially no such thing as PTSD.* As with social anxiety disorder, there remains some controversy over whether such a thing as post-traumatic stress disorder really exists in nature—and over whether, if it does, how broadly it should be defined. These debates inevitably get politicized because of the billions of dollars at stake in veterans' medical benefits and drug company revenues and because of abiding tensions over the distinction between moral cowardice and a medical condition. For its part, the U.S. military today views PTSD as a real and serious problem and is dedicating considerable resources to researching its causes, treatment, and prevention. The Pentagon underwrites many studies of Navy SEALs, generally the toughest, most resilient soldiers in the military, to uncover what combination of genes, neurochemistry, and—especially—training makes them so mentally formidable. Experiments have consistently found that SEALs think more clearly, and make faster and better decisions, than other soldiers in chaotic or stressful situations.

As important as the nature of the combat stress a soldier experiences is, recent findings in neuroscience and genetics suggest that the nature of the soldier may be more important in contributing to the likelihood of a nervous breakdown. Whether you are more likely to break down under modest combat stress or to remain implacable even under

---

* PTSD is the successor to soldier's heart, shell shock, battle fatigue, and war neurosis, among other diagnoses.

extreme wartime conditions may be largely attributable to the neuro-
chemicals you bring to the battle, and these are partly a product of your
genes.

Andy Morgan, a psychiatrist at the Yale School of Medicine, has
studied the Special Operations Forces trainees at Fort Bragg who
undergo the famous SERE (Survival, Evasion, Resistance, and Escape)
program. These aspiring Navy SEALs and Green Berets are exposed
to three weeks of extreme physical and psychological hardship to determine whether they could withstand the stress of being a prisoner of
war. They endure pain, sleep deprivation, isolation, and interrogation—
including "advanced techniques" such as waterboarding. The trainees
selected for the program have already made it through a couple of
years of training at places such as Fort Bragg's John F. Kennedy Special
Warfare Center and School. The physically and psychologically weak
get weeded out long before SERE. But even for the elite troops who
make it this far, SERE can be astonishingly stressful. In a 2001 paper,
Morgan and his collaborators noted that recorded changes in the stress
hormone cortisol during SERE "were some of the greatest ever docu-
mented in humans"—greater even than those associated with open-
heart surgery.

Morgan recently discovered that the Special Forces recruits who
performed most effectively during SERE had significantly higher
levels—as much as one-third higher—of a brain chemical called neuropeptide Y than the poorer-performing recruits did. Discovered in 1982,
neuropeptide Y (or NPY, as the researchers call it) is the most abundant
peptide in the brain, involved in regulating diet and balance—and the
stress response. Some individuals with high NPY levels seem *completely
immune to* developing post-traumatic stress disorder—no amount of
stress can break them. The correlation between NPY and stress resistance is so strong that Morgan has found he can predict with remarkable accuracy who will graduate from Special Forces training and who
will not simply by performing a blood test. Those with high NPY levels
will graduate; those with low levels will not. Somehow, NPY confers
psychological resistance and resilience.*

---

* Researchers are currently investigating whether administering NPY via a nasal spray could help
block the development of post-traumatic stress disorder.

It's possible that those in the Special Forces who thrive under pressure have *learned* to be resilient—that their high NPY levels are the product of their training or their upbringing. Resilience is a trait that can be taught; the Pentagon is spending millions trying to figure out how to do that better. But studies suggest that a person's allotment of NPY is relatively fixed from birth, more a function of heredity than of learning. Researchers at the University of Michigan have found correlations not only between which variation of the NPY gene you have and how much of the neurotransmitter you produce but also between how much NPY you produce and how intensely you react to negative events. People with low levels of NPY showed more hyperreactivity in the "negative emotion circuits" of the brain (such as the right amygdala) than people with high NPY levels and were much slower to return to calm brain states after a stressful event. They were also more likely to have had episodes of major depression—and that was independent of anything having to do with their serotonin systems, which is where much of the neuroscience research over the last few decades has been concentrated. Conversely, having ample quantities of NPY seems to prepare you to thrive under stress.

Other research has found that soldiers whose bodies are more reactive to stress hormones are more likely to crack under pressure. A 2010 study published in *The American Journal of Psychiatry* concluded that soldiers with more glucocorticoid receptors in their blood cells were at greater risk for developing PTSD after combat. Studies like this tend to validate the idea that how likely you are to break down under pressure is largely determined by the relative sensitivity of your hypothalamic-pituitary-adrenal axis: if you have a hypersensitive HPA axis, you're much more likely to develop PTSD or some other anxiety disorder in the aftermath of a traumatic experience; if you have a low-reactive HPA axis, you will be much more resistant, if not largely immune, to developing PTSD. And while we know that lots of things condition the sensitivity of your HPA axis—from how much affection your parents gave you to your diet to the nature of the trauma itself—your genes are a major determinant. All of which suggests a strong correlation between your genetically conferred physiology and how likely you are to crack under stress.

But if grace under pressure is largely a matter of the quantity of a certain peptide in the brain, or of your inborn level of HPA sensitivity, what kind of grace is that?

*The hero and the coward both feel the same thing, but the hero uses his fear, projects it onto his opponent, while the coward runs. It's the same thing, fear, but it's what you do with it that matters.*
—CUS D'AMATO, BOXING MANAGER WHO TRAINED
FLOYD PATTERSON AND MIKE TYSON

Are those of us with hypersensitive HPA axes, our bodies set to quivering like mice in response to the mildest perturbances, doomed to falter at the moments of greatest importance? Destined, like Aristodemus the Trembler and Roberto Durán, for shame and humiliation? Fated always to be victims of our twitchy bodies and unruly emotions?

Not necessarily. Because when you begin to untangle the relationships between anxiety and performance, and between grace and courage, they turn out to be more complicated than they at first seem. Maybe it's possible to be simultaneously anxious and effective, cowardly and strong, terrified and heroic.

Bill Russell is a Hall of Fame basketball player who won eleven championships with the Boston Celtics (the most by anyone in any major American sport, ever), was selected to the NBA All-Star team twelve times, and was voted the league's most valuable player five times. He is generally acknowledged to be the greatest defender and all-around winner of his era, if not of all time. He is the only athlete in history, in any sport, to win a national college championship, an Olympic gold medal, and a professional championship. No one would question Russell's toughness or his championship qualities or his courage. And yet, to my amazement, this is a man who vomited from anxiety before the majority of the games he played in. According to one tabulation, Russell vomited before 1,128 of his games between 1956 and 1969, which would put him nearly in Charles Darwin territory. "[Russell] used to throw up all the time before a game, or at halftime," his teammate John Havlicek told the writer George Plimpton in 1968. "It's a welcome sound, too, because it means he's keyed up for the game and around the locker room we grin and say, 'Man, we're going to be all right tonight.'"

Like someone with an anxiety disorder, Russell had to contend with nerves that wreaked havoc with his stomach. But a crucial difference between Russell and the typical anxiety patient (aside, of course, from Russell's preternatural athleticism) was that there was a positive correlation between his anxiety and his performance—and therefore between his upset stomach and his performance. Once, in 1960, when the Celtics' coach noted with concern that Russell *hadn't* vomited yet, he ordered that the pregame warm-up be suspended until Russell could regurgitate. When Russell stopped throwing up for a stretch at the end of the 1963 season, he suffered through one of the worst slumps of his career. Fortunately, when the play-offs started that year and he saw the crowd gathering before the opening game, he felt his nerves jangling, and he resumed his nervous vomiting—and then went out and gave his best performance of the season. For Russell, a nervous stomach correlated with effective, even enhanced, performance.*

Nor is cowardice always necessarily an impediment to greatness. In 1956, Floyd Patterson, at the age of twenty-one, became the youngest world heavyweight boxing champion. Then, in a series of classic bouts with Ingemar Johansson between 1959 and 1961, he became the first boxer in history to regain the title after losing it. The following year he lost the title for good in a match against Sonny Liston, but he remained an intermittent contender for another decade, fighting against Liston, Jimmy Ellis, and Muhammad Ali.

Patterson was tough and fierce and strong—for several years, by

---

* Of course, when a nervous stomach impairs performance, the complexion changes dramatically. Consider the difference between Bill Russell and Donovan McNabb, the quarterback for the Philadelphia Eagles during the 2005 Super Bowl. Like Russell, McNabb was an elite athlete. A six-time Pro Bowler and the holder of almost all the Eagles' passing records, McNabb was one of the most successful college and pro quarterbacks of his generation. Yet despite many playoff victories, McNabb, unlike Russell, never won a championship—and ever since his team lost that 2005 Super Bowl game, he has been dogged by the claims of several teammates (which McNabb denies) that he was vomiting in the huddle and couldn't call plays. (The debate over whether McNabb did or did not vomit in the huddle still continues eight years after the game, and has been called "one of the great mysteries in the history of sport.") The implication is that McNabb, for all his athletic talent, was overwhelmed by the pressure of the occasion and succumbed to nerves, that he lacked the leadership qualities, the toughness—the literal intestinal fortitude—to keep his stomach in check and lead the Eagles to victory. McNabb has never been seen the same way since. (Augmenting his reputation as a choker: McNabb's stats in crucial playoff games were markedly worse than his stats in ordinary regular-season games.)

dint of being heavyweight champion, probably among the toughest and
fiercest and strongest men in the world. Yet he was also, by his own
account, a coward. After his first defeat by Liston, he took to bringing
disguises—fake beards and mustaches, hats—to his fights, in case he
lost his nerve and wanted to slip out of the dressing room before the
bout or to hide afterward if he lost. In 1964, the writer Gay Talese, who
was profiling Patterson for *Esquire*, asked him about his penchant for
carrying disguises.

"You must wonder what makes a man do things like this," Patterson said. "Well, I wonder too. And the answer is, I don't know . . . but
I think that within me, within every human being, there is a certain
weakness. It is a weakness that exposes itself more when you're alone.
And I have figured out that part of the reason I do the things I do,
and cannot seem to conquer that one word—*myself*—is because . . . is
because . . . I am a coward."

Of course, Patterson's definition of cowardice might be different
from yours or mine; it's hardly conventional.* But it nevertheless suggests that inner anxiety can be coupled with the outer appearance of
physical bravery, that weakness is not incompatible with strength.

In rare instances, anxiety can even be the source of heroism. During
the 1940s, Giuseppe Pardo Roques was the leader of the Jewish community in Pisa, Italy. He was widely respected as a spiritual guide—but
he was also impaired by crippling anxiety, in particular by an overwhelming phobia of animals. Hoping to conquer his anxiety, he tried
everything: sedatives, "tonics" (neurophosphates meant to strengthen
the nervous system), psychoanalysis with one of Freud's protégés,
and—in an endeavor I can relate to—reading everything he could get
his hands on, from Hippocrates to Freud, about the theory and science
of phobias. Nothing worked; his phobia dominated his life. He was
unable to travel—was barely able to leave his house—because of the
irrational fear that he would be set upon by dogs. When he did muster
the courage to walk the streets, he would swing a cane wildly around

---

* "When did you first think you were a coward?" Talese asked him. "It was after the first Ingemar
fight," Patterson said. "It's in defeat that a man reveals himself. In defeat, I can't face people. I haven't
the strength to say to people, 'I did my best, I'm sorry,' and whatnot."

himself at all times to fend off the animals he feared might attack. After neighbors acquired a pet dog, he contrived a reason to get them evicted because he couldn't bear to have an animal so close by. He spent hours every day completing elaborate rituals meant to assure him there were no animals in his house. (Today, he would be diagnosed with OCD.)

Roques recognized the irrationality of his fear but was powerless to overcome it. "Its intensity is just as great as its absurdity," he once said. "I am lost. My heart beats fast; my face no doubt changes expression. I am no longer myself. The panic increases, and the fear of the fear increases the fear. A crescendo of suffering engulfs me. I believe I will not be able to hold my own. I search for help; I don't know where to find it. I am ashamed to ask for help, and yet I am afraid the fear will make me die. I do die, like a coward, a thousand deaths."

Silvano Arieti, a young man who lived in the community, was fascinated by Roques. How was it, Arieti asked himself, that a man as brilliant and wise as Roques could allow his life to be circumscribed by so irrational a fear? Roques was afraid to travel—he had never left Pisa in all his sixty years—and there were days when his anxiety was so bad that he couldn't even leave his bedroom. But—and here's what was so fascinating to Arieti—Roques showed himself in other ways "to be an utterly fearless man, courageously prepared to defend the underprivileged, the underdog, the distressed in any way. . . . His almost constant fear was accompanied by a constantly available courage." He could handle "real" fears and, in fact, would bravely help others beset by them. But his own phobias, "in their fully tragic intensity," he was helpless to do anything about. Was there a link, Arieti wondered, between Roques's moral strength and his mental illness?

Many years later, after he had moved to America and become one of the world's foremost scholars on mental illness, Arieti would publish a book, *The Parnas: A Scene from the Holocaust* (1979), in which he recounted what happened in Pisa after the Germans occupied part of Italy. Throughout 1943 and 1944, as first the Italian Fascists and then the Nazis terrorized Pisa's Jewish community, most Jews fled. But Roques, prevented by his anxiety from traveling, stayed in Pisa. "The idea of going far away from home, to another city, or to the country, increases my anxiety to the point of panic," Roques told six friends who chose for various reasons to remain in the city with him. "I know that these fears are absurd to the point of being ridiculous, but it is useless to tell myself so. I cannot overcome them." When his followers tried to attribute his willingness to brave bombs and Nazis to courage or spiritual grace, Roques demurred. His illness, he said, "has caused such a narrowing of my life, not to mention gossip and ridicule, and has shadowed my whole existence. I live, trembling, with a totally irrational fear of animals, especially of dogs. I also have a fear of the fear itself. . . . Had I not felt this sick fear constantly, I would not be here; I would be far away. What you call a special gift is illness." But the fact that his fear of dogs was greater than his fear of bombs and Nazis made him appear brave.

Early on the morning of August 1, 1944, the Nazis arrived at Roques's home and demanded that he surrender the guests who were staying with him. He refused.

"Aren't you afraid of dying?" the Nazis demanded. "We will kill you, you filthy Jew."

"I am not afraid," he told them.

And according to those who survived and were later interviewed by Arieti, Roques manifestly was not afraid, even though he knew the Nazis were about to murder him. As real danger approached, he appeared to be free of fear.*

Giuseppe Pardo Roques was not the only Pisan imprisoned by his

---

* In his book, Arieti elaborates a theory about why this should have been the case. His view was that Roques's phobia of and disgust at animals was a displacement of his disgust at the evil inherent in man. As a young boy, Roques had been happy and optimistic. But during his studies as an adolescent, he discovered the facts of the Crusades, the Inquisition, and the myriad other horrors that man has visited upon man across history. He couldn't bear this. To preserve a loving view of humankind, and a view of the world as a friendly place, Arieti theorizes, Roques projected onto animals the evil that is in man, preferring to fear animals rather than give up his view of mankind as essentially good. When Roques was confronted unavoidably with evil in the form of the Nazis, his animal phobia disappeared. This, Arieti argues, gives his phobic anxiety an almost spiritual quality, since it permitted him to displace revulsion and anxiety onto insentient creatures, allowing him to retain love for humankind.

"When the sensitive youngster has made these unpleasant realizations [about the evil in man and the danger and hardship of existence]," Arieti writes, "he has difficulties in facing life. How can he trust, how can he love or retain a loving attitude towards fellow human beings? He might then become suspicious and paranoid; he might become a detached person unable to love. But this is not the case with the phobic. The phobic is a person who retains his ability to love. As a matter of fact, in my long psychiatric career I have never seen a phobic person who was not a loving person." We are born, it seems, into a Rousseauian state of innocence, but if we accurately observe life and human nature, we must adopt a Hobbesian defensive crouch against life's depredations. Phobias sublimate our Hobbesian horror into neurotic and irrational fears, Arieti argues, allowing us to preserve a more innocent and loving stance toward the world.

anxiety during the war. When the bombs started falling, reducing parts of the city to rubble, most people left. But Pietro, a young man who lived not far from Roques, could not go more than a block from his house; his agoraphobia would not permit it. So he stayed home. Pietro would sooner have had a bomb dropped on his head than endure the terror that seized him when he walked too far from his house. "The fear caused by the neurosis was stronger than the fear of the dangers of the war," Arieti observes.

Pietro survived the war—and ended up decorated as a hero for his courage. After each bombing, he would run out into the ruins (so long as they were within a block of his house) and free people trapped in them. In this way, he saved several lives. Only because he was constrained by his phobia was he available to help the bombing victims. "His illness made him become a hero," Arieti writes.

To someone who suffers from anxiety, the stories of Roques and Pietro, and of Bill Russell and Floyd Patterson, hold obvious appeal; in their anxiety lies not just redemption but a source of moral heroism and even, perhaps, a strange sort of courage.

PART III

# Drugs

# CHAPTER 5

# "A Sack of Enzymes"

*From time immemorial, [drugs] have been making possible some degree of self-transcendence and a temporary release from tension.*
—ALDOUS HUXLEY, IN A MAY 9, 1957, PRESENTATION TO
THE NEW YORK ACADEMY OF SCIENCE

*Wine drunk with an equal quantity of water puts away anxiety and terror.*
—HIPPOCRATES, *APHORISMS* (FOURTH CENTURY B.C.)

In anticipation of the release of my first book, in the spring of 2004, my publisher arranged a modest publicity tour that entailed national television and radio appearances, as well as bookstore readings and public lectures around the country. This should have been a delightful prospect—the chance to promote my book, to travel on someone else's nickel, to connect with readers, to achieve a kind of temporary, two-bit celebrity. But I can scarcely convey what powerful dread this book tour conjured in me.

In desperation, I sought help from multiple sources. I first went to a prominent Harvard psychopharmacologist who had been recommended by my principal psychiatrist a year earlier. "You have an anxiety disorder," the psychopharmacologist had told me after taking my case history at our initial consultation. "Fortunately, this is highly treatable. We just need to get you properly medicated." When I gave him my standard objections to reliance on medication (worry about side effects, concerns about drug dependency, discomfort with the idea of taking pills that might affect my mind and change who I am), he resorted to the clichéd—but nonetheless potent—diabetes argument, which goes like this: "Your anxiety has a biological, physiological, and genetic basis; it is a medical illness, just like diabetes is. If you were a diabetic, you wouldn't have such qualms about taking insulin, would you? And you wouldn't see your diabetes as a moral failing, would you?" I'd had versions of this discussion with various psychiatrists many times over the years. I would try to resist whatever the latest drug was, feeling that this resistance was somehow noble or moral, that reliance on medication evinced weakness of character, that my anxiety was an integral and worthwhile component of who I am, and that there was redemption in suffering—until, inevitably, my anxiety would become so acute that I would be willing to try anything, including the new medication. So, as usual, I capitulated, and as the book tour loomed, I resumed a course of benzodiazepines (Xanax during the day, Klonopin at night) and increased my dosage of Celexa, the SSRI antidepressant I was already taking.

But even drugged to the gills, I remained filled with dread about the impending book tour, so I went also to a young but highly regarded Stanford-trained psychologist who specialized in cognitive behavioral therapy, or CBT. "First thing we've got to do," she said in one of my early sessions with her, "is to get you off these drugs." A few sessions later, she offered to take my Xanax from me and lock it in a drawer in her desk. She opened the drawer to show me the bottles deposited there by some of her other patients, holding one up and shaking it for effect. The drugs, she said, were a crutch that prevented me from truly experiencing and thereby confronting my anxiety; if I didn't expose myself to the raw experience of anxiety, I would never learn that I could cope with it on my own.

She was right, I knew. Exposure therapy is based on fully experiencing your anxiety, which is hard to do if you're taking antianxiety medications. But with the book tour looming, my fear was that I might *not*, in fact, be able to cope with it.

I went back to the Harvard psychopharmacologist (let's call him Dr. Harvard) and described the course of action the Stanford psychologist (let's call her Dr. Stanford) had proposed. "It's your call," he said. "You could try giving up the medication. But your anxiety is clearly so deeply rooted in your biology that even mild stress provokes it. Only medication can control your biological reaction. And it may well be that your anxiety is so acute that the only way you'll be able to get to the point where any kind of behavioral therapy can begin to be effective is by taking the edge off your physical symptoms with drugs."

"What if I get addicted to Xanax and have to be on it all my life?" I asked. Benzodiazepines are notorious for inducing dependency. Withdrawing too suddenly from them can produce horrific side effects.

"So what if you do?" he said. "I have a patient coming in this afternoon who's been taking it for twenty years. She couldn't live without it."

At my next session with Dr. Stanford, I told her I was afraid to give up my Xanax and related what Dr. Harvard had said to me. She looked betrayed. I thought for a moment that she might cry. After that, I stopped telling her about my visits to Dr. Harvard. My continued consultations with him felt illicit.

Dr. Stanford was more likable, and more pleasant to talk to, than Dr. Harvard; she tried to understand what caused my anxiety and seemed to care about me as an individual personality. Dr. Harvard, on the other hand, seemed to see me as a type—an anxiety patient—to be treated with a one-size-fits-all solution: drugs. One day I read in the newspaper that he was treating a depressed gorilla at the local zoo. Dr. Harvard's treatment of choice for the gorilla in question? Celexa, the same SSRI he was prescribing for me.

I can't say for certain whether the drug worked for the gorilla. Reportedly, it did. But could there be a more potent demonstration that Dr. Harvard's approach to treatment was resolutely biological? For him, the content of any psychic distress—and certainly the meaning of it—mattered less than the fact of it: such distress, whether in a human or some other primate, was a medical-biological malfunction that could be fixed with drugs.

What to do? Dr. Harvard was telling me that I, like the gorilla, had a medical problem in need of pharmaceutical intervention. Dr. Stanford was telling me that my problem was not principally biological but rather cognitive: if I could simply correct dysfunctions in how I thought (through force of will and cognitive retraining and direct exposure to my greatest fears), then my anxiety would be reduced. But the drugs I was on, Dr. Stanford said, were impeding my ability to address those dysfunctions in an effective way.*

I kept trying to give up my Klonopin and Xanax in order to do proper cognitive retraining, and I would sometimes even succeed at this in small ways—only to be overwhelmed with anxiety again and resort to fumbling miserably through my pockets for the Xanax. As much as I would have liked to have cured myself through fixing my thinking, or achieving spiritual peace, or simply learning to cope, I seemed always to be ending up like the depressed gorilla, in need of artificial adjustments to my neurotransmitters to fix my anxious, broken brain.

*Tranquilizers, by attenuating the disruptive influence of anxiety on the mind, open the way to a better and more coordinated use of the existing gifts. By doing this, they are adding to happiness, human achievement, and the dignity of man.*
> —FRANK BERGER, "ANXIETY AND THE DISCOVERY OF
> TRANQUILIZERS," IN *Discoveries in Biological Psychiatry* (1970)

*To what extent would Western culture be altered by widespread use of tranquilizers? Would Yankee initiative disappear? Is the chemical deadening of anxiety harmful?*
> —STANLEY YOLLES, DIRECTOR OF THE NATIONAL INSTITUTE OF
> MENTAL HEALTH, IN TESTIMONY GIVEN TO THE U.S. SENATE
> SELECT COMMITTEE ON SMALL BUSINESS, MAY 1967

Sigmund Freud, the father of psychoanalysis, relied heavily on drugs in managing his anxiety. Six of his earliest scientific papers were on the benefits of cocaine, which he used regularly for at least a decade beginning in the 1880s. "In my last serious depression I took cocaine again," he wrote to his wife in 1884, "and a small dose lifted me to the heights in a wonderful fashion. I am just now collecting the literature

---

* Actually, Dr. Stanford also conceded a strong biological component to anxiety; her view was that biology can be overcome by cognitive retraining. And research does suggest that cognitive retraining, as well as other forms of talk therapy, can *change* biology in the same way that medication does, sometimes more profoundly and enduringly—a literal manifestation of mind over matter.

for a song of praise to this magical substance." He believed his research on the drug's medicinal properties would make him famous. Deeming the drug to be no more addictive than coffee, he prescribed it, to himself and to others, as a treatment for everything from nervous tension and melancholy to indigestion and morphine addiction. Freud called cocaine a "magic drug": "I take very small doses of it regularly against depression and against indigestion, and with the most brilliant success." He also took it to alleviate his social anxiety before the evening salons he attended at the Paris home of his mentor Jean-Martin Charcot.* Only after he prescribed cocaine to a close friend who went on to become fatally addicted did Freud's enthusiasm for the drug wane. But by then Freud's own experience with cocaine had solidified his conviction that some mental illnesses have a physical basis in the brain. It is an irony of medical history that even as Freud's later work would make him the progenitor of modern psychodynamic psychotherapy, which is generally premised on the idea that mental illness arises from unconscious psychological conflicts, his papers on cocaine make him one of the fathers of biological psychiatry, which is governed by the notion that mental distress is partly caused by a physical or chemical malfunction that can be treated with drugs.

Much of the history of modern psychopharmacology has the same ad hoc quality as Freud's experimentation with cocaine. Every one of the most commercially significant classes of antianxiety and antidepressant drugs of the last sixty years was discovered by accident or was originally developed for something completely unrelated to anxiety or depression: to treat tuberculosis, surgical shock, allergies; to use as an insecticide, a penicillin preservative, an industrial dye, a disinfectant, rocket fuel.

Yet despite its haphazardness, the recent history of psychopharmacology has shaped our modern understanding of mental illness. Recall that neither "anxiety" nor "depression"—two terms that today have become part of both the medical and the popular lexicon—existed as clinical categories half a century ago. Before the 1920s, no one had ever

---

* Freud was also, by his own admission, addicted to nicotine, smoking twenty or more cigars a day for most of his life, a habit that would reward him with mouth cancer in his sixties.

been diagnosed with depression; before the 1950s, hardly anyone was diagnosed with straightforward anxiety.

So what changed? One answer is that pharmaceutical companies in effect *created* these categories. What began as targets for marketing campaigns eventually became reified as diseases.

By this I do not mean to suggest that before the 1950s people were not "anxious" or "depressed" in the senses we understand those words today. Some people, some percentage of the time, have always felt pathologically unhappy and afraid. This was the case for millennia before the terms "anxiety" and "depression" were popularized to describe emotional states or clinical disorders. ("The tears of the world are a constant quantity," as Samuel Beckett put it.) But not until the middle of the last century, when new drugs geared toward mitigating these emotional states were concocted, did these states get delimited as the "diseases" we understand them to be today.

Before 1906, when the fledgling Food and Drug Administration started requiring drugmakers to list their products' ingredients, consumers didn't realize that in taking some of the most popular antianxiety remedies of the time—such as Neurosine or Dr. Miles's Nervine (advertised as "the scientific remedy for nervous disorders") or Wheller's Nerve Vitalizers or Rexall's Americanitis Elixir—they were ingesting alcohol or marijuana or opium.* In 1897, the German drug company Bayer began marketing diacetylmorphine, a compound that had been widely used on the battlefields of the American Civil War and the Franco-Prussian War, as a painkiller and cough suppressant. This new medication—under the trade name Heroin—was available in American pharmacies without a prescription until 1914.† The 1899 edition of

---

* Some doctors prescribed straight alcohol. In the 1890s, Adolphus Bridger, an influential London physician and the author of such popular medical books as *The Demon of Dyspepsia* and *Man and His Maladies,* told patients suffering from tension and melancholy to drink port and brandy. He wrote that "a suitable form of alcohol"—especially "full-bodied Burgundy, high class claret, port, the better white French, German, and Italian wines, stout or good brandy"—would "do more to restore nervous health" than any other medicine.

† Two years later, Bayer brought out another analgesic, acetylsalicylic acid, under the brand name Aspirin. In time, as Heroin and Aspirin became ubiquitous, both went from being brand names to generic terms. Turn-of-the-century physicians in America and England had a somewhat backward understanding of these medications, often giving Heroin to their patients for physical pain (which, in fairness, made a certain sense) and administering Aspirin for "nervousness" (which did not).

*The Merck Manual,* then as now a respected compendium of the most up-to-date medical information, recommended opium as a standard treatment for anxiety.

The serene confidence with which *The Merck Manual*—as well as the physicians and apothecaries of the time—glibly dispensed recommendations for drugs we now know to be addictive, unhealthy, or useless raises the question of whether we should place much trust in the similarly serene confidence of the physicians and drug manuals of today. Yes, today's researchers and clinicians are armed with data from controlled studies and findings from neuroimaging and blood assays, and they are buttressed—or held back, depending on your perspective—by a more cautious FDA that demands years' worth of animal testing and clinical trials before a drug can be approved for sale. But a hundred years from now, medical historians may once again be marveling at the addictive, toxic, or useless substances we consume in such great quantities today.

For the first half of the twentieth century, barbiturates were the most popular remedy for strained nerves. Originally synthesized in 1864 by a German chemist who combined condensed urea (found in animal waste) with diethyl malonate (which derives from the acid in apples), barbituric acid seemed, at first, to have no productive use. But in 1903, when researchers at Bayer gave barbituric acid to dogs, the dogs fell asleep. Within months, Bayer was marketing barbital, the first commercially available barbiturate, to consumers. (Bayer named the drug Veronal because one of its scientists believed Verona, Italy, to be the most peaceful city on earth.) In 1911, the company released a longer-acting barbiturate, phenobarbital, under the trade name Luminal, which would go on to become the most popular drug in the category. By the 1930s, barbiturates had almost completely displaced their late nineteenth-century predecessors—chloral hydrate and bromides, as well as opium—as the treatment of choice for "nerve troubles."*

---

\* Potassium bromide, a compound introduced at a British medical conference in 1857, was originally used as an antiseizure medication and was, from the late nineteenth century into the early twentieth, popular as a sedative. Eventually, the toxicity and side effects of bromides, ranging from a bitter aftertaste and acne to dizziness, severe nausea, and vomiting, led to their abandonment (today they are used almost exclusively in veterinary medicine for dogs and cats with epilepsy), but their use was widespread enough for long enough that the word "bromide" also came to mean a soporific platitude. Chloral

As early as 1906, so many Americans were taking, and sometimes overdosing on, Veronal that *The New York Times* editorialized against the overprescription of such "quick-cure nostrums," but to little effect: in the 1930s, *The Merck Manual* was still recommending Veronal for the treatment of "extreme nervousness, neurasthenia, hypochondria, melancholia," and other "conditions of anxiety." Veronal and Luminal—advertised as "aspirin for the mind"—dominated what would today be called the anxiety medication market for decades. By 1947, there were thirty different barbiturates being sold under separate trade names in the United States; the three most popular were Amytal (amobarbital), Nembutal (pentobarbital), and Seconal (secobarbital). Since "anxiety" and "depression" didn't officially exist yet, the barbiturates tended to be prescribed for "nerves" (or "nerve troubles"), "tension," and insomnia.

But the barbiturates had two big drawbacks: they were highly addictive, and accidental overdoses were common and often lethal. In 1950, at least a thousand Americans fatally overdosed on barbiturates. (My great-grandmother and Marilyn Monroe, among many others, would go on to do so in the 1960s.) In 1951, *The New York Times* called barbiturates "more of a menace to society than heroin or morphine" and declared that "the matron who regards a pink pill as much of a bedtime necessity as brushing her teeth, the tense business man who gulps a white capsule to ease his nerves before an important conference, the college student who swallows a yellow 'goof ball' to breeze through an examination, and the actor who takes a 'blue angel' to bolster his self-confidence are aware that excessive use of barbiturates is 'not good for the system,' but are ignorant of the extent of the hazard."

You would think that such heavy consumption of barbiturates would have made drug companies keen to develop new and better nostrums. But when Frank Berger, a research scientist at the Wallace Laboratories subsidiary of Carter Products, tried to interest company executives in a new antianxiety medication he had synthesized in the late 1940s, they

---

hydrate, a sleep-inducing agent first synthesized in 1832, was added to doctors' psychotropic toolkit in 1869 after Otto Liebrich, a professor of pharmacology in Berlin, gave the substance to melancholic patients and observed that it alleviated their insomnia. A hundred years later, my great-grandfather would be prescribed chloral hydrate for his tension and insomnia. (Chloral hydrate was also one of the active ingredients, along with alcohol, in the Mickey Finn, a doctored drink that often featured in Depression-era potboilers.)

showed no interest. For one thing, they argued, therapy for anxiety was supposed to focus on psychological issues or unresolved personal problems, not on biology or chemistry—a distinction that from the vantage point of modern biological psychiatry seems quaint. Besides, psychoactive drugs lay outside Carter's usual commercial domain, which consisted of such things as laxatives (Carter's Little Liver Pills), deodorant (Arrid), and depilatory cream (Nair).

Berger had stumbled on the antianxiety properties of this new substance entirely by accident. Born in what is now the Czech Republic in 1913, Berger had, after earning his medical degree at the University of Prague, conducted immunology research that established him as a promising scientist. But when Hitler annexed Austria and seemed poised to claim Czechoslovakia, Berger, who was Jewish, escaped to London.

Unable to find work there, Berger and his wife became homeless, sleeping on park benches and eating at soup kitchens. Eventually, Berger got a job as a doctor in a refugee camp, where he learned English, and then moved on to a job as an antibiotics researcher at the Public Health Laboratory near Leeds.

By 1941, penicillin had been demonstrated to be an effective treatment for bacterial infections. But manufacturing and preserving penicillin in quantities large enough to be useful in fighting infections among Allied soldiers proved vexing. "The mold is as temperamental as an opera singer," lamented one pharmaceutical executive. So Berger, along with hundreds of other scientists, went to work trying to find better extraction and purification techniques for the revolutionary antibiotic. He was particularly successful in developing a method for preserving the mold long enough to distribute it more widely. After his research was published in prestigious scientific journals, a British drug company offered the once-homeless chemist a high-ranking position.

One of the penicillin preservatives Berger tested was a compound called mephenesin, which he had synthesized by modifying a commercially available disinfectant. When he injected mice with mephenesin to test its toxicity, Berger observed something he'd never seen before: "The compound had a quieting effect on the demeanor of the animals."

Berger had, quite by accident, discovered the first of a revolutionary new class of drugs. When mephenesin was found to have a similar sedating effect on humans, the Squibb Corporation, recognizing a commercial opportunity, began distributing mephenesin as a drug to induce relaxation before surgery. Sold under the trade name Tolserol, mephenesin had by 1949 become one of Squibb's most prescribed drugs.

But mephenesin wasn't very potent in pill form, and its effects were short-lived. Berger resolved to develop a more powerful version. In the summer of 1949, he took a job as the president and medical director of Carter's Wallace Labs subsidiary in New Brunswick, New Jersey. There, Berger and his team set to work synthesizing and testing compounds that might prove more potent than mephenesin. Eventually, they identified a dozen (out of the roughly five hundred they synthesized) that seemed promising; after more experiments on animals, they narrowed the list down to four and then to one, called meprobamate, which they patented in July 1950. Berger's team found that meprobamate relaxed mice. The effect on monkeys was even more vivid. "We had about twenty Rhesus and Java monkeys," Berger would later tell the medical historian Andrea Tone. "They're vicious, and you've got to wear thick gloves and a face guard when you handle them." But after they were injected with meprobamate, they became "very nice monkeys—friendly and alert." Further testing revealed meprobamate to be longer lasting than mephenesin and less toxic than barbiturates.

Meanwhile, two new papers in top medical journals were providing the first reports of the therapeutic effects of mephenesin—which, remember, was less potent than meprobamate. One of the studies, conducted by doctors at the University of Oregon, found that when mephenesin was given to 124 patients who had sought treatment from their physicians for "anxiety tension states," more than half experienced a significant reduction in anxiety—to the point where they resembled, in the words of the researchers, "individuals who are pleasantly and comfortably at ease." Other reports from mental hospitals showed similar results. Soon the first small-scale studies of meprobamate were finding the same thing: the drug significantly reduced what doctors of the time tended to call "tension."

These studies were among the first to measure in any kind of systematic way the effects of a drug on the mental states of human beings. Today, when reports on randomized controlled trials of the efficacy of various psychotropic drugs are published by the score every month in newspapers and medical journals, this kind of study seems routine. But at midcentury the notion that psychiatric drugs could be widely and safely prescribed—let alone scientifically measured—was novel.

So novel, in fact, that Carter executives didn't believe there was a market for such a drug. They retained a polling company to ask two hundred primary care physicians whether they would be willing to prescribe a pill that would help patients with the stresses of day-to-day life—and a large majority of them said they would not. Frustrated, Berger persisted on his own, sending meprobamate pills to two psychiatrists he knew, one in New Jersey and one in Florida, for testing. The New Jersey psychiatrist reported back that meprobamate had helped 78 percent of his patients suffering from what we would today call anxiety disorders—they became more sociable, slept better, and in some cases returned to work after being housebound. The psychiatrist in Florida gave the drug to 187 patients and found that 95 percent of those with "tension" improved or recovered on meprobamate.

"When I first came in here, I couldn't even listen to the radio. I thought I was going crazy," one of the Florida psychiatrist's patients reported after a few months on meprobamate. "I now go to football games, shows, and even watch TV. My husband can't get over how relaxed I am."

Berger showed these results—which *The Journal of the American Medical Association* would publish in April 1955—to Henry Hoyt, the president of Carter Products, who finally allowed meprobamate to be submitted for FDA approval. The custom at Carter had been to name compounds after local towns, and so meprobamate had been internally dubbed Milltown, after a small hamlet about three miles from Berger's lab that a guidebook called "tranquil little Milltown." Since place-names cannot be trademarked, Hoyt dropped an *l*, and when the pill came to market in May 1955, meprobamate was called Miltown.

In 1955, barbiturates were still the most popular antianxiety medication; they were marketed as sedatives and had dominated the pharmacy shelves for several decades. Because they had a proven sales record, Berger wanted to market Miltown as a sedative, too. But one night over dinner in Manhattan, his friend Nathan Kline, the research director of Rockland State Hospital, advised against that. "You are out of your mind," Kline said. "The world doesn't need new sedatives. What the world really needs is a tranquilizer. The world needs tranquility. Why don't you call this a tranquilizer? You will sell ten times more." Out of such contingencies—an unexpected side effect of a penicillin preservative, a stray remark at dinner—is the history of psychopharmacology made.

Miltown was brought quietly to market on May 9, 1955. Carter Products sold only $7,500 worth of the drug in each of the first two months it was available. But sales of the compound—which was advertised as being effective for "anxiety, tension, and mental stress"—soon accelerated. In December, Americans bought $500,000 worth of Miltown—and before long they were spending tens of millions of dollars a year on Miltown prescriptions.

In 1956, the drug became a cultural phenomenon. Movie stars and other celebrities sang the praises of the new tranquilizer. "If there's anything this movie business needs, it's a little tranquility," a Los Angeles newspaper columnist declared. "Once you're big enough to be 'somebody' in filmtown you've just got to be knee-deep in tension and mental and emotional stress. The anxiety of trying to make it to the top is replaced by the anxiety of wondering if you're going to stay there. So, big names and little alike have been loading their trusty pillboxes with this little wonder tablet." Lucille Ball's assistant kept a supply of Miltown on the set of *I Love Lucy* to help the actress calm down after spats with her husband, Desi Arnaz. Tennessee Williams told a magazine that he needed "Miltowns, liquor, [and] swimming" to get him through the stress of writing and producing *The Night of the Iguana*. The actress Tallulah Bankhead joked that she ought to have been paying taxes in New Jersey, home of Wallace Labs, because she was consuming so much Miltown. Jimmy Durante and Jerry Lewis publicly praised the drug on televised awards shows. The comedian Milton Berle took to beginning the monologues on his Tuesday night television show with "Hi, I'm Miltown Berle."

With so many prominent champions, Miltown's popularity spread nationally. Magazines wrote about "happy pills" and "peace of mind drugs" and "happiness by prescription." Gala Dalí, the wife of the surrealist painter Salvador Dalí, was such a devotee of Miltown that she convinced Carter Products to commission a $100,000 Miltown art installation from her husband.* Aldous Huxley—whom, based on the drug-addled dystopia he painted in *Brave New World,* you might have expected to be a stern Cassandra about such things—proselytized that the synthesis of meprobamate was "more important, more genuinely revolutionary, than the recent discoveries in the field of nuclear physics."

Within eighteen months of its introduction, Miltown had become the most prescribed and—with the possible exception of aspirin—the most consumed drug in the history of the world. At least 5 percent of Americans were taking it. "For the first time in history," the neurologist Richard Restak would later observe, "the mass treatment of anxiety in the general community seemed possible."

Miltown contributed to a wholesale transformation of the way we think about anxiety. Before 1955, there was no such thing as a tranquilizer—no medication that was designed to treat anxiety per se. (The first use of the word "tranquilizer" in English was by Benjamin Rush, a physician and signatory of the Declaration of Independence, who used the term to describe a chair he had invented to restrain psychotic patients.) But within a few years, American pharmacies were full of dozens of different tranquilizers, and companies were spending hundreds of millions of dollars to develop more.

The confidence of psychiatrists in the new drugs could be overweening. Testifying before Congress in 1957, Frank Berger's friend Nathan Kline enthused that the advent of psychiatric drugs may "be of markedly greater import in the history of mankind than the atom bomb since if these drugs provide the long-awaited key which will unlock the mysteries of the relationship of man's chemical constitution to his psychological behavior and provide effective means of correcting pathological needs there may no longer be any necessity for turning thermonuclear energy to destructive purposes." Kline told a journalist from *BusinessWeek* that meprobamate was good for both economic productivity (because it restored "full efficiency to business executives") and artistic creativity (because it helped writers and artists break free

---

* *Crisalida,* an undulating two-and-a-half-ton tunnel meant to symbolize the Miltown-aided passage to what the painter called "the nirvana of the human soul," stood in the exhibition hall at the annual meeting of the American Medical Association in 1958, surely one of the more avant-garde exhibits ever to grace a medical convention.

of their neuroses and overcome "mental blocks"). This utopian vision of better living through chemistry may have been overblown, but it was broadly shared. By 1960, some 75 percent of all doctors in America were prescribing Miltown. The treatment of anxiety had begun to migrate from the psychoanalyst's couch to the family doctor's office. Soon attempts to resolve conflicts between the id and the superego were being displaced by efforts to better calibrate the neurochemistry of the brain.

*The deficiencies in our description [of the mind] would probably vanish if we were already in a position to replace the psychological terms by physiological or chemical ones.*
—SIGMUND FREUD, *Beyond the Pleasure Principle* (1920)

*The insulin of the nervous.*
—FRENCH PSYCHIATRIST JEAN SIGWALD'S CHARACTERIZATION OF THE NEWLY DISCOVERED DRUG CHLORPROMAZINE (THORAZINE), 1953

Meanwhile, a series of unexpected pharmacological discoveries in France were to have medical and cultural consequences that were perhaps even further reaching than Miltown's.

In 1952, Henri Laborit, a surgeon in Paris, decided to experiment on some of his patients with a compound called chlorpromazine. Chlorpromazine, like so many drugs that would find their way into the modern psychotropic arsenal, had its origins in the rapid growth of the German textile industry in the late nineteenth century—specifically in the industrial dyes developed by chemical companies starting in the 1880s.* Chlorpromazine came into being in 1950, when French researchers synthesized the new compound from phenothiazine, intending to create a more powerful antihistamine. But chlorpromazine failed to

---

* First synthesized as a blue dye in the 1880s, phenothiazine, chlorpromazine's parent compound, was over the decades that followed discovered to have an unlikely array of medicinal properties: it worked as an antiseptic (reducing the risk of infection), an anthelmintic (expelling parasitic worms from the body), an antimalarial (combating malaria), and an antihistamine (preventing allergic reactions). Capitalizing on its bug-killing powers, DuPont started selling phenothiazine to farmers as an insecticide in 1935.

improve on existing antihistamines, so they quickly put it aside. When Laborit asked the chemical company Rhône-Poulenc for some chlorpromazine, he was hoping he would find that its purported qualities as an antihistamine would help mitigate surgical shock by reducing inflammation and suppressing the body's autoimmune response to the trauma of surgery. It did—but to Laborit's surprise, the drug also sedated his patients, relaxing some of them to the point where they were, as he put it, "indifferent" toward the major surgical procedures they were about to undergo.

"Come look at this," Laborit reportedly said to one of the army psychiatrists on the staff of the Val-de-Grâce military hospital, pointing out that the "tense, anxious, Mediterranean-type patients" had become completely calm, even in the face of major threats to their health.

Word got around the hospital, and one of Laborit's surgical colleagues would soon tell his brother-in-law, the psychiatrist Pierre Deniker, about the effects of this new compound. Intrigued, Deniker administered the drug to some of his most psychotic patients on the back wards of a Parisian mental hospital. The results were astounding: violently agitated patients calmed down; the crazy became sane. When one of Deniker's colleagues gave it to a patient who had been nonresponsive for years, the man emerged from his stupor and wanted to leave the hospital and return to his work as a barber. The doctor asked him for a shave, which the patient carefully gave him, and so the doctor discharged him. Not every case was as dramatic, but the calming effects of the drug were powerful. Neighbors reported that the noise emanating from the asylum had dropped significantly. Other small-scale experiments with the drug showed similarly potent results. In 1953, Jean Sigwald, a psychiatrist in Paris, gave chlorpromazine to eight patients suffering from "melancholia with anxiety," and five of them got better. Chlorpromazine was, Sigwald declared, "the insulin of the nervous."

Chlorpromazine came to North America when, one Sunday evening in the spring of 1953, Heinz Edgar Lehmann, a psychiatrist at McGill University in Montreal, read an article while luxuriating in his bath. The article, which had been left in his office by a drug company sales representative, reported on chlorpromazine's effect on French psychotics. ("This stuff is so good that the literature alone will convince him," the salesman had told Lehmann's secretary.) When Lehmann got out of the bath, he ordered a shipment of the compound, and he used it to launch the first North American trial of chlorpromazine, administering it to seventy mentally ill patients at nearby Verdun Protestant Hospital, where he served as clinical director. The results amazed him: within weeks, patients who had been suffering from schizophrenia, major depression, and what we would today call bipolar disorder, among other psychiatric ailments, seemed effectively cured. Many found themselves completely symptom-free; some of those who doctors had thought would be confined to asylums for life left the hospital. It was, Lehmann would later say, "the most dramatic breakthrough in pharmacology since the advent of anesthesia more than a century before."

Smith, Kline & French Laboratories, an American drug company, licensed chlorpromazine and in 1954 brought it to market with the trade name Thorazine. Its arrival transformed mental health care. In 1955, for the first time in a generation, the number of hospitalized mentally ill in the United States declined.*

Together, Thorazine and Miltown reinforced a culturally ascendant new idea—that mental illness was caused not by bad parenting or unresolved Oedipus complexes but by biological imbalances, organic disturbances in the brain that could be corrected with chemical interventions.

*For me, the watches of that long night passed in ghastly wakefulness; strained by dread: such dread as children only can feel.*
—CHARLOTTE BRONTË, *Jane Eyre* (1847)

As it happens, my own decades-long experience with chemical interventions would begin, some twenty-five years later, with Thorazine.

As I approached the end of elementary school, my proliferating array of tics and phobias drove my parents to take me to the psychiatric hospital for the evaluation where it was determined I needed intensive psychotherapy. In seventh grade, I started at a new school. One Mon-

---

* This revolutionized psychiatry. Before 1955, both the acutely psychotic and the moderately neurotic were treated mainly by psychoanalysis or something like it; the working out of psychological issues or childhood traumas in talk therapy was the accepted route to mental health. "No one in their right mind in psychiatry was working on drugs," Heinz Lehmann would later say of the field before the 1950s. "You used shock, or various psychotherapies."

day morning in October, I refused to go. The prospect of separation from my parents, and of exposure to germs, felt too terrifying to endure. But my parents, after calling Dr. L. (the psychiatrist who had conducted the Rorschach test during my evaluation at McLean Hospital and whom I was now seeing for weekly psychotherapy sessions) and Mrs. P. (the social worker who was supposed to be counseling my mother and father about how to be less anxiety-inducing parents), refused to let me refuse. Which led to a melodramatic standoff that would replay itself most mornings for the rest of that school year.

I would wake up crying and clutching my covers, saying I was too scared to go to school. After failing to reason me out of bed, my parents would tear the covers off, and the wrestling match would begin: my father would hold me down while my mother forced me into my clothes as I struggled to escape. Then they'd frog-march me out to the car while I tried to wriggle free. During the seven-minute drive to school, I would sob and beg my parents not to make me go.

As we'd pull into the school parking lot, my moment of reckoning would arrive: Would my parents have to physically remove me from the car, humiliating me in front of merciless schoolmates? School was terrifying—but so was the threat of humiliation. Wiping my tears, I'd get out of the car and begin the gangplank walk to my homeroom. My anxiety was not rational; I had nothing, really, to fear. Yet anyone who has suffered the torments of acute pathological anxiety knows that I am not exaggerating when I say I do not think I would have felt much worse had I been walking to my own beheading.

Stunned by despair, blinking back tears, struggling to control my roiling bowels, I'd sit mutely at my desk, trying not to embarrass myself by bursting into sobs.*

By January, my phobias and separation anxieties had become so consuming that I had begun to drop my friends, and they to drop me; I scarcely socialized with my peers anymore. Engaging in the give-and-

---

* My first glimpse of clinical depression came as I was sitting in class one Friday afternoon that year. I was experiencing my characteristic relief at the prospect of being sprung for the weekend when I had the thought *But on Sunday night this starts all over again,* and I was chilled by the infiniteness of my plight, by the notion that Sunday nights—and Monday mornings—eternally return, and that only death would put a stop to them, and that therefore there was nothing, ultimately, to look forward to that might help me transcend my dread about bad things to come.

take of schoolboy banter had become too stressful, so at lunchtime I preferred to sit quietly beside a teacher. This put me in a position, on the first day back after holiday break that year, to overhear the Spanish teacher tell the French teacher a graphic tale of spending the holidays with friends in Manhattan, where she and her companions had been stricken by a stomach virus that had included prolific amounts of vomiting.*

This was more than I could bear on the first day back after vacation; I left school, went home, and pretty much lost my mind.

Here are the snapshots I can remember from that evening: me throwing things around the house, smashing everything I can get my hands on, while my father tries to grapple me into submission; me lying on the floor, pounding it with my fist, screaming so hard that drool froths from my mouth, yelling that I am so scared and can't take it anymore and want to die; my father, on the phone with Dr. L., talking about whether I should be committed (there is mention of straitjackets and ambulances); my father going to Corbett's, the local drugstore, and coming back with emergency doses of Valium (a minor tranquilizer of the benzodiazepine class, about which more shortly) and liquid Thorazine (which was then known as a major tranquilizer and is now classified as an antipsychotic).

The Thorazine tasted awful. But I was desperate for relief, so I drank it in some orange juice. For the next eighteen months, I was on Thorazine around the clock. And starting later that week, I began also taking imipramine, the tricyclic medication that was the antidepressant of choice prior to the arrival of Prozac in the late 1980s.†

Every day for the next two years, my mother would place one large orange Thorazine pill and an assortment of smaller green and blue imipramine pills on the edge of my plate at breakfast and at dinner. The medication reduced my anxiety enough to keep me out of the hospital. But at a cost: on Thorazine, I became foggy and dehydrated, shuffling along with a dry mouth and hollowed-out emotions and twitching fingers, the result of a common Thorazine side effect known as tardive

---

* Yes, it is a mark of the intensity of my phobic preoccupations that I can today, some thirty years later, still remember the conversation almost verbatim.

† Imipramine did more to determine the modern conception of panic anxiety than any other drug. (More about that in the next chapter.)

dyskinesia. A year earlier, prior to going on Thorazine and imipramine, I had been selected for an elite soccer team. When I showed up the following autumn in a Thorazine stupor, the coaches were baffled. What had happened to the short kid who had embarrassed older players by dribbling circles around them? They now had a kid, still short, who moved slowly, tired easily, and became rapidly dehydrated, a gluey white mucus encrusted around his lips.

Even after I was heavily medicated, my anxiety persisted. I'd make it to school but then get overwhelmed by fear, leave class, and end up in the infirmary with the school nurse, begging her to let me go home. When the confines of the infirmary came to feel too claustrophobic to contain my antic pacing, she would kindly walk around school with me while I tried to calm down.*

Seeing me wandering the campus with the nurse when I should have been in class, my peers naturally wondered what was wrong with me. The mother of an erstwhile friend ran into my mother and asked if I was ill. My mother, prevaricating, said I was fine.

But I was not fine; I was miserable. In photographs from that time, I look hunched and hangdog and sickly, like I am shrinking into myself. I was on antipsychotics and antidepressants and tranquilizers, and I was taking daily walks with the school nurse instead of attending class.

Without Thorazine and imipramine and Valium, I don't know that I would have survived seventh grade. But I did, and by the end of eighth grade my anxious misery had relented somewhat. Dr. L. weaned me off the Thorazine. But since that winter some thirty years ago, I have been on one psychiatric medication or another—and often two,

---

* Compounding matters, my phobia of vomiting metastasized around this time into a fear of choking; I started having trouble swallowing. (Difficulty in swallowing has been a well-recognized symptom of anxiety since at least the late nineteenth century and is known clinically as dysphagia.) I became afraid to eat. My skinny adolescent frame, worn ever thinner by nervous fidgeting, became emaciated. I stopped eating lunch at school. The more trouble I had swallowing, the more I'd obsess about my trouble swallowing, and the worse the trouble would get. Soon I was having trouble swallowing even my saliva. I'd sit there in history class, my mouth full of spit, terrified that if I were called upon to speak, I would choke on my mouthful of saliva or spew it all over my desk—or both. I took to carrying wads of Kleenex around with me everywhere I went, discreetly drooling into them so that I wouldn't have to swallow. By lunchtime each day, my pockets would be full of drenched tissues, which would leach into my pants and make them smell like saliva. Over the course of the day, the tissues would disintegrate, so by evening bits of slobbery Kleenex would be spilling out of my pockets.

Are you surprised to learn that I had but one date in all of middle school and high school?

three, or more at a time—more or less continuously, making me a liv-ing repository of the pharmacological trends in anxiety treatment of the last half century.

*Drug discoveries were of sensational importance for understand-ing psychiatric illness and the basic nature of the human condition: Our personalities, our intellects, our very culture could presumably be boiled down to a sack of enzymes.*
—EDWARD SHORTER, *Before Prozac* (2009)

For a brief period in the 1980s, I took phenelzine, a monoamine oxi-dase inhibitor, or MAOI, whose trade name is Nardil. My experience on MAOIs was not notably successful. I didn't feel any less anxious—but I did do a lot of worrying about whether I would die from complicat-ing side effects of the drug. This is because MAOIs can have danger-ous, even lethal, side effects, especially when combined with the wrong elements. When patients taking MAOIs ingest things—such as wine and other fermented alcohol, aged cheeses, pickled foods, some kinds of beans, and many over-the-counter medications—that contain high levels of an amino acid derivative called tyramine, the health effects can be serious: painful headaches, jaundice, a spike in blood pressure, and in some cases severe internal hemorrhaging. Which means MAOIs may not be ideal for people like me who are, even in the best of circum-stances, prone to hypochondria and health anxiety.

For this reason, among others, while there are still depressed and anxious patients for whom MAOIs remain the most, or the only, effec-tive pharmacological treatment, MAOIs have not been considered a first-line treatment for mood disorders for many years now.* Though MAOIs played only a cameo role in my own psychiatric history, they are important in the scientific and cultural history of anxiety because they were among the first drugs to be specifically tied to a just-emerging neurochemical theory of mental illness. At midcentury the advent of

---

* After trying many alternative remedies, including electroshock therapy, the novelist David Foster Wallace found Nardil to be the most effective treatment for his anxiety and depression. Going off Nar-dil, after experiencing what seems to have been a tyramine-induced side effect, may have precipitated Wallace's downward spiral to suicide in 2008.

MAOIs, in conjunction with the arrival of imipramine and the other tricyclics (about which more shortly), helped create the modern scientific understanding of depression and anxiety.

MAOIs have their origins in the later years of the Second World War, when the German Luftwaffe, bombarding English cities with V-2 rockets, ran low on conventional fuel and had to resort to propelling the rockets with a fuel called hydrazine. Hydrazine is poisonous and explosive, but scientists had found that they could modify it in ways that might be medically useful. When the war ended, drug companies bought the leftover hydrazine supplies at a steep discount. The investment paid off. In 1951, scientists working at Hoffmann–La Roche in Nutley, New Jersey, discovered that two modified hydrazine compounds, isoniazid and iproniazid, inhibited the growth of tuberculosis. Clinical trials ensued. By 1952, both isoniazid and iproniazid were on the market for treatment of tuberculosis.

But these antibiotics had an unexpected side effect. After being treated with them, some patients would become, as newspapers recounted, "mildly euphoric," dancing through the hallways of the tuberculosis wards. Reading these reports, psychiatrists wondered if this mood-elevating effect meant that isoniazid and iproniazid might be used as psychiatric medications. In a 1956 study at Rockland State Hospital in New York, patients with various psychiatric disorders were given iproniazid for five weeks; toward the end of that period the depressed patients had improved markedly. Nathan Kline, the hospital's research director, observed what he called a "psychic energizing" effect, and he began prescribing iproniazid to the melancholic patients in his private practice. Some of these patients, he subsequently reported, experienced "a complete remission of all symptoms." Kline would later declare that iproniazid "was the first cure in all of psychiatric history to act in such a manner." In April 1957, Hoffmann–La Roche began marketing iproniazid with the trade name Marsilid, and it was featured on the front page of *The New York Times*. Marsilid was the first of the MAOIs and one of the first drugs to become known as an antidepressant.

At midcentury the history of neuroscience, such as it was, was brief. Knowledge of how the brain worked was primitive. Debate churned between the "sparks" and the "soups"—between those scientists who believed that transmission of impulses between neurons was electrical and those who believed it was chemical. "When I was an undergraduate student at Cambridge," Leslie Iversen, a professor of pharmacology at Oxford recalled of his time there in the 1950s, "we were taught . . . there was no chemical transmission in the brain—that it was just an electrical machine."

English physiologists had done primitive research on brain chemistry in the late nineteenth century. But not until the 1920s did Otto Loewi, a professor of pharmacology at the University of Graz in Austria, isolate the first neurotransmitter, arguing in a 1926 paper that a chemical called acetylcholine was what mediated the transmission of impulses between one nerve ending and the next.*

Even as sales of Thorazine and Miltown were taking off, the concept of a neurotransmitter—of a chemical that transmitted impulses between brain cells—had not been definitively established.[†] (The psychiatrists who prescribed these drugs, and even the biochemists who developed them, generally had no idea why the drugs had the effects they did.) But discoveries by two researchers in Scotland swung the pendulum forcefully toward the "soups." In 1954, Marthe Vogt, a German neuroscientist at the University of Edinburgh, discovered the first convincing evidence of a neurotransmitter—norepinephrine. Later that year, John Henry Gaddum, a colleague of Vogt's, discovered through a series of unorthodox experiments that serotonin, which until that point was thought to be a gut-based compound involved in digestion, was also a neurotransmitter.[‡] Gaddum took LSD—which he reported made him feel crazy for forty-eight hours and which also, according to labo-

---

* Loewi famously claimed he conceived the experiment, which involved artificially raising and lowering the heart rate of frogs, in a dream he had on Easter Sunday 1923. Thrilled, he scribbled the experiment on a piece of paper by his bed—only to awake the next morning to find that he could neither remember his dream nor decipher his own handwriting. Fortunately, he dreamed the same experiment the following night. This time he remembered it, performed it, and demonstrated for the first time the chemical basis of nerve transmission—work for which he would later be awarded a Nobel Prize.

† Otto Loewi and others had found suggestive evidence of neurotransmitters such as norepinephrine in the bloodstream—but no one had yet isolated any in the brain.

‡ A brief history of early serotonin research: In 1933, the Italian researcher Vittorio Erspamer isolated a chemical compound in the stomach that he named enteramine because it seemed to promote the gut contraction involved in digestion. In 1947, two American physiologists studying hypertension at the Cleveland Clinic found enteramine in the platelets of the blood. Noticing that enteramine caused blood vessels to contract, they renamed the compound serotonin (*sero* for "blood," from the Latin word *serum*, and *tonin* for muscle tone, from the Greek word *tonikos*, tonic). In 1953, when researchers for the first time found traces of serotonin in the brain, they still assumed it was merely the residue of what

ratory measurements, decreased the level of serotonin metabolites in his cerebrospinal fluid. His broad conclusion: Serotonin helps keep you mentally healthy—and therefore a deficiency of serotonin can make you mentally ill. Thus was born the neurotransmitter-based theory of mental health. This would transform the scientific and cultural view of anxiety and depression.

> *Canst thou not . . .*
> *Raze out the written troubles of the brain*
> *And with some sweet oblivious antidote*
> *Cleanse the stuff'd bosom of that perilous stuff*
> *Which weighs upon the heart?*
> —WILLIAM SHAKESPEARE, *Macbeth* (CIRCA 1606)

Bernard "Steve" Brodie had built his reputation as a biochemist making antimalarial drugs during World War II. When Thorazine and Miltown came on the market in the 1950s, he was running a lab at the National Heart Institute of the National Institutes of Health in Bethesda, Maryland. Over the next decade, that lab would revolutionize psychiatry.

The seminal experiments were on reserpine. An extract from the plant *Rauwolfia serpentina* (its root looks like a snake), reserpine had been used for more than a thousand years in India, where it was prescribed for everything from high blood pressure and insomnia to snakebite poisonings and infant colic. But it had also been used, evidently with some success, according to Hindu writings, for treating "insanity." Reserpine had never gotten much attention in the West. But when Thorazine produced such striking results, executives at Squibb wondered if reserpine could compete with it. They provided funding to Nathan Kline, who tested the compound on a group of his patients at Rockland State Hospital: several of them improved dramatically, and a few whose case reports had described them as "crippled" by anxiety became relaxed enough to leave the hospital and resume their lives.

---

had been carried through the bloodstream from the stomach. Only in the ensuing years did serotonin's role as a neurotransmitter become evident.

This led to a much larger study. In 1955, Paul Hoch, the commissioner of mental hygiene for New York, arranged with Governor W. Averell Harriman for $1.5 billion in funding to give reserpine to *every single one* of the ninety-four thousand patients in all of the state's psychiatric hospitals. (FDA regulations would never allow a study like this to be conducted today.) The results: Reserpine worked for some patients but not quite as well as Thorazine—and it had serious, sometimes lethal, side effects. Clinicians largely set it aside as a psychiatric drug.

But not before Steve Brodie and his NIH colleagues had used reserpine to establish a clear link between biochemistry and behavior. Inspired by what John Gaddum had learned about the relationship between LSD and serotonin, Brodie gave reserpine to rabbits to see what it did to their serotonin levels. Brodie found two interesting things: administering reserpine to rabbits decreased the amount of serotonin in their brains, and this decrease in serotonin seemed to produce rabbits who were "lethargic" and "apathetic," mimicking the behavior of people we would today call depressed. Moreover, Brodie and his colleagues found they could induce and diminish "depressed" behavior in the rabbits by manipulating their serotonin levels. Brodie's 1955 paper in *Science* reporting these findings was the first to tie levels of a specific neurotransmitter to behavioral changes in animals. Brodie had, as one medical historian later put it, built a bridge from neurochemistry to behavior.

Brodie's reserpine research intersected in intriguing ways with what psychiatrists were then discovering about MAOIs. To oversimplify a little, brain researchers in the 1950s were just figuring out that neurotransmitters are discharged by "upstream" neurons into the synapses—the tiny spaces between nerve cells—in order to make "downstream" neurons fire. Each neurotransmitter travels quickly from one neuron to the next, where it attaches to a receptor—its molecular mirror image—embedded in the neuron's membrane. Each time one of these neurotransmitters latches onto its receptor on the postsynaptic neuron (serotonin attaching to serotonin receptors, norepinephrine to norepinephrine receptors), the receiving neuron changes shape: its membrane becomes porous, allowing atoms from the outside of the neuron to rush toward the interior, causing a sudden change in the neuron's electric voltage. This change causes the receiving neuron to fire, releasing its own supply of neurotransmitters into the surrounding synapses. These neurotransmitters then land on receptors on still other neurons. This cascade of activity—neurons firing, releasing neurotransmitters, causing other neurons to fire—throughout the one hundred billion neurons and the trillions of synapses in our brain is what gives rise to our emotions, perceptions, and thoughts. Neurons and neurotransmitters are, in ways scientists are still struggling to understand, the physical stuff of emotion and thought.

Early research on iproniazid had revealed that the antibiotic inactivated an enzyme called monoamine oxidase (MAO), whose function is to break down and clear away the serotonin and norepinephrine that build up in the synapses. After a neurotransmitter is squirted into the synapse, it ordinarily gets quickly cleared out by MAO, allowing for the next transmission to happen. But the "inhibition" of the monoamine oxidase enzyme by iproniazid allowed the neurotransmitters to remain in the nerve terminals longer. The extra buildup of these neurotransmitters in the synapses, Brodie's researchers theorized, accounted for iproniazid's antidepressant effects. Sure enough, when rabbits were given iproniazid before reserpine was administered, these rabbits did not become lethargic the way the other reserpine rabbits did. The iproniazid, Brodie and his colleagues concluded, kept the rabbits from getting "depressed" by boosting the levels of norepinephrine and serotonin in their synapses.

This was the moment the pharmaceutical industry awoke to the idea that it could sell psychiatric drugs by marketing them as correcting "chemical imbalances," or deficiencies of certain neurotransmitters. In one of its first advertisements for iproniazid, in 1957, Hoffmann–La Roche promoted the drug as "an amine oxidase inhibitor which affects the metabolism of serotonin, epinephrine, norepinephrine and other amines."

Research on another new drug lent further support to this idea. In 1954, Geigy, a Swiss pharmaceutical company, had tweaked Thorazine's chemical structure to create the compound G22355, which it called imipramine, the first tricyclic. (Drugs in this category have a three-ring chemical structure.) Roland Kuhn, a Swiss psychiatrist who was trying to develop a better sleeping pill, had tried giving imipramine to some of his patients. Because Thorazine and imipramine were chemically similar (only two atoms were different), Kuhn assumed that imipramine, like Thorazine, would have a sedating effect. It didn't: rather than putting patients to sleep, imipramine energized them and elevated their moods. In 1957, after treating more than five hundred patients with imipramine, Kuhn delivered a paper to the International Congress of Psychiatry in Zurich, reporting that even deeply depressed patients had improved dramatically after several weeks on the drug. Their moods lifted, their energy surged, their "hypochondriacal delusions" disappeared, and their "general inhibition" dissipated. "Not infrequently the cure is complete, sufferers and their relatives confirming the fact that they had not been so well for a long time," he declared. Geigy took imipramine out of mothballs and brought it to the European market in 1958 under the trade name Tofranil.*

On the day imipramine was released in the United States, September 6, 1959, *The New York Times* published an article headlined "Drugs and Depression" about both Marsilid (iproniazid, the first MAOI) and Tofranil (imipramine, the first tricyclic). The *Times* called these drugs "anti-depressants"—seemingly the first use of the term in the press or in popular culture.

While some estimates put the number of Americans taking antidepressant medications today at over forty million, there was no such thing as an antidepressant when Roland Kuhn addressed the International Congress of Psychiatry in 1957. The concept simply didn't exist. The MAOIs and the tricyclics had created a new drug category.

---

* Imipramine might never have made it to pharmacies—and the history of biological psychiatry might have been quite different—if not for another accident of history. Kuhn's presentation to the International Congress of Psychiatry was met, as he put it, "with a great deal of skepticism" because "of the almost completely negative view of drug treatment of depression up to that time." In fact, such was the lack of psychiatric interest in drugs that only twelve people attended Kuhn's talk in Zurich. (His talk has since been referred to as the Gettysburg Address of pharmacology—little noted at the time but destined to become a classic.) Geigy, too, was unimpressed. The company shared psychiatry's skepticism about a medicine that could treat an emotional disorder. It had no plans to market imipramine. But one day Kuhn happened to run into Robert Bohringer, a powerful Geigy shareholder, at a conference in Rome. When Bohringer mentioned that he had a deeply melancholic relative in Geneva, Kuhn handed him a bottle of imipramine. Within a few days of starting on it, Bohringer's relative had recovered. "Kuhn is right," Bohringer declared to Geigy executives. "Imipramine *is* an antidepressive." Geigy executives relented and brought the drug to market.

In the early 1960s, Julius Axelrod, an NIH biochemist and a veteran of Steve Brodie's lab, began to identify the effects of imipramine on various chemicals in the brain. Axelrod discovered that imipramine blocked the reuptake of norepinephrine in the synapses. (A few years later, he would find that it also blocked the reuptake of serotonin.) Axelrod theorized that antidepressants' effect on the reuptake of norepinephrine was what accounted for the elevation of mood and the relief of depression. This was a transformative idea: if imipramine blocked the reuptake of norepinephrine, and if it made patients less anxious and depressed, that meant there must be a correlation between norepinephrine and mental health. Marsilid or Tofranil—or cocaine, for that matter, which has a similar effect—seemed to cure anxiety and depression by boosting the levels of norepinephrine in the synapses, delaying its reuptake into the neurons.

Around this time, Joseph Schildkraut was a psychiatrist at the Massachusetts Mental Health Center who believed that anxiety and psychoneurosis were caused by childhood trauma or unresolved psychic conflicts and were therefore best treated by Freudian psychotherapy. Then he gave imipramine to a few of his patients. "These drugs seemed like magic to me," he would say later. "I became aware that there was a new world out there, a world of psychiatry informed by pharmacology." In 1965, he published an article in *The American Journal of Psychiatry*, "The Catecholamine Hypothesis of Affective Disorders: A Review of the Supporting Evidence"; building on the work of Steve Brodie and Julius Axelrod, he argued that depression was caused by elevated brain levels of catecholamines, the fight-or-flight hormones (such as norepinephrine) that are released by the adrenal glands in times of stress. Schildkraut's paper became one of the most cited journal articles in the history of psychiatry, enshrining the chemical imbalance theory of anxiety and depression at the center of the field.

The first pillar of biological psychiatry had been constructed. The Freudian model of psychiatry had sought to treat anxiety and depression by resolving unconscious psychic conflicts. With the advent of the antidepressants, mental illness and emotional disorders were increasingly attributed to malfunctions of specific neurotransmitter systems: schizophrenia and drug addiction were believed to be caused by problems in the dopamine system; depression was a consequence of stress hormones released by the adrenal glands; anxiety resulted from defects in the serotonin system.

But pharmacology's most transformative effect on the history of anxiety was still to come, beginning with studies on imipramine that would reshape the psychiatric establishment's understanding of anxiety.

# CHAPTER 6

# A Brief History of Panic; or, How Drugs Created a New Disorder

*An anxiety attack may consist of a feeling of anxiety alone, without any associated ideas, or accompanied by the interpretation that is nearest to hand, such as the ideas of the extinction of life, or a stroke, or the threat of madness, or the feeling of anxiety may have linked to it a disturbance of one or more of the bodily functions—such as respiration, heart action, vasomotor innervation or glandular activity. From this combination the patient picks out in particular now one, now another, factor. He complains of "spasms of the heart," "difficulty in breathing," "outbreaks of sweating," . . . and such like.*

—SIGMUND FREUD, "ON THE GROUNDS FOR DETACHING
A PARTICULAR SYNDROME FROM NEURASTHENIA UNDER
THE DESCRIPTION OF ANXIETY NEUROSIS" (1895)

*The bases of mental illness are chemical changes in the brain. . . . There's no longer any justification for the distinction . . . between mind and body or mental and physical illness. Mental illnesses are physical illnesses.*

—DAVID SATCHER, U.S. SURGEON GENERAL (1999)

One day I am sitting in my office reading e-mail when vaguely, at the edges of my awareness, I notice I am feeling slightly warm.

*Is it getting hot in here?* Suddenly awareness of the workings of my body moves to the center of my consciousness.

*Do I have a fever? Am I getting sick? Will I pass out? Will I vomit? Will I, in one way or another, be incapacitated before I can escape or get help?*

I am writing a book about anxiety. I am steeped in knowledge of the phenomenon of panic. I know as much as any layperson about the neuromechanics of an attack. I have had thousands of them. You would think that this knowledge and experience would help. And, to be sure, occasionally it does. By recognizing the symptoms of a panic attack early on, I can sometimes head it off, or at least restrict it to what's known as a limited-symptom panic attack. But too often my internal dialogue goes something like this:

*You're just having a panic attack. You're fine. Relax.*

*But what if it's not a panic attack? What if I'm really sick this time? What if I'm having a heart attack or a stroke?*

*It's always a panic attack. Do your breathing exercises. Stay calm. You're fine.*

*But what if I'm not fine?*

*You're fine. Every one of the last 782 times when you were having a panic attack and you thought it might not be a panic attack, it was a panic attack.*

*Okay. I'm relaxing. Breathing in and out. Thinking the calming thoughts the meditation tapes have taught me. But just because the last 782 instances were panic attacks, that doesn't mean the 783rd one is too, right? My stomach hurts.*

*You're right. Let's get outta here.*

Sitting in my office while something like this sequence of thoughts flows through my head, I go from feeling moderately warm to feeling hot. I begin to perspire. The left side of my face starts to tingle, then goes numb. (*See,* I say to myself, *maybe I* am *having a stroke!*) My chest tightens. I am suddenly aware that the fluorescent lights in my office have a strobelike quality and are flickering dizzyingly. I feel a terrible vertiginous teetering, like the furniture in my office is moving around, like I am about to topple forward onto the ground. I grip the sides of my chair for stability. As my dizziness increases and my office swirls around me, my physical surroundings no longer feel quite real; it's as though a scrim has come between me and the world.

My thoughts race, but the three most prominent are: *I'm going to vomit. I'm about to die. I've got to get out of here.*

I bolt unsteadily from my chair, perspiring heavily now. All my focus is on escape: I need to get out—out of my office, out of the building, out of this situation. If I'm going to have a stroke or vomit or die, I want to be out of the building. I'm going to make a break for it.

Desperately hoping that I'm not accosted on my way to the stairs, I open the door and sprint-walk to the elevator vestibule. I push through the fire door to the stairwell and, with a small feeling of relief at having made it this far, begin to climb seven flights down. By the time I reach the third floor, my legs are quaking. If I were thinking rationally—if I could calm my amygdala and make better use of my neocortex—I would conclude, correctly, that this quaking is the natural result of an autonomic fight-or-flight response (which causes trembling in the skeletal muscles) combined with the effects of physical exertion. But too far gone into the catastrophizing logic of panic to access my rational brain, I conclude instead that my quaking legs are a symptom of complete physical breakdown and that I am indeed about to die. As I descend the final two flights, I am wondering whether I will be able to reach my wife from my cell phone to tell her I love her and to ask her to send help before I lose consciousness and possibly expire.

The door from the stairwell to the outside is kept locked. Motion detectors are supposed to sense you coming from the inside and automatically unlock it. For some reason, perhaps because I am going too fast, they fail to activate. I slam into the door at high speed and bounce off, falling backward onto my rear.

I have hit the door with sufficient force to dislodge the plastic frame around the exit sign glowing red above it. The frame falls onto my head with a thud and then clatters to the floor.

The lobby security guard, hearing the racket, pokes his head into the stairwell to find me sitting on the floor in a daze, the exit sign frame by my side. "What's going on in here?" he says.

"I'm sick," I say, and who would say that I am not?


The ancient Greeks believed that Pan, the god of nature, ruled over shepherds and their grazing flocks. Pan was not a noble god: he was short and ugly, ran on stubby goatlike legs, and liked to take naps in caves or bushes by the side of the road. When awakened by passersby, he would issue a bloodcurdling scream that made the hair of anyone who heard it stand on end. Pan's scream, it was said, caused travelers to drop dead from fright. Pan induced terror even in his fellow gods. When the Titans assaulted Mount Olympus (as myth would have it), Pan assured their defeat by sowing fear and confusion in their ranks. The Greeks also credited Pan with their victory at the Battle of Marathon in 490 B.C., where he was said to have put anxiety in the hearts of the enemy Persians. The experience of sudden terror—especially in crowded places—became known as panic (from the Greek *panikos*, literally "of Pan").

Anyone who has suffered the torments of a panic attack knows the turmoil it can unleash—physiological as well as emotional. The palpitations. The sweating. The shaking. The shortness of breath. The feeling of choking and tightness in the chest. The nausea and general gastric distress. The dizziness and blurring of vision. The tingling sensations in the extremities ("paresthesias" is the medical term). The chills and hot flashes. The feelings of doom and gaping existential awfulness.*

David Sheehan, a psychiatrist who has studied and treated anxiety for forty years, tells a story that captures how awful the experience of panic can feel. In the 1980s, a World War II veteran, one of the first infantrymen to land at Normandy on D-day, came to see Sheehan, seeking therapy for panic attacks. Wasn't the experience of storming the beach at Normandy, Sheehan asked him, bullets and blood and bodies flying and falling all around him—with the prospect of his own injury or death quite real, even likely—more frightening and miserable than enduring a panic attack at the dinner table, however ravaged he might feel by the neurotic circuitry of his own mind? Not at all, the man said. "The anxiety he felt landing on the beaches was mild compared to the sheer terror of one of his bad panic attacks," Sheehan reports. "Given the choice between the two, he would gladly again volunteer to land in Normandy."

Today, panic attacks are a fixture of psychiatric medicine and of popular culture. As many as eleven million Americans today will, like me, at

---

* I've just listed ten of the thirteen *DSM* criteria for a panic attack; the other three symptoms are feelings of depersonalization or unreality, fear of losing control or going crazy, and fear of dying. At least four of these thirteen symptoms must be present for a panic attack to have occurred, according to the *DSM*.

some point be formally diagnosed with panic disorder. Yet as recently as 1979, neither panic attacks nor panic disorder officially existed. Where did these concepts come from?

Imipramine.

In 1958, Donald Klein was a young psychiatrist at Hillside Hospital in New York. When imipramine became available, he and a colleague began administering it willy-nilly to most of the two hundred psychiatric patients in their care at Hillside. "We assumed it would be some sort of supercocaine, blasting the patients out of their rut," Klein recalled. "Remarkably, these anhedonic, anorexic, insomniac patients began to sleep better, eat better, after several weeks . . . saying 'the veil has lifted.'"

What most interested Klein was that fourteen of these patients—who had previously been suffering from intermittent acute episodes of anxiety characterized by "rapid breathing, palpitations, weakness, and a feeling of impending death" (symptoms of what was then called, in the Freudian tradition, anxiety neurosis)—experienced significant or complete remission of their anxiety. One patient in particular drew Klein's attention. He would rush in a panic to the nurses' station, saying he was afraid he was about to die. A nurse would hold his hand and talk to him soothingly, and within a few minutes the attack would pass. This recurred every few hours. Thorazine hadn't worked for him. But after the patient had been on imipramine for a few weeks, the nurses noticed that his regular panicky visits to their station stopped. He still reported a generally high level of *chronic* anxiety, but the *acute* paroxysms of it had stopped completely.

This got Klein thinking. That imipramine could block paroxysmal anxiety without stopping general anxiety or chronic worrying suggested there was something wrong with the prevailing theory of anxiety.

When Freud had hung out his shingle as a "nerve doctor" in the late 1880s, the most common diagnosis among the patients he and his peers saw was neurasthenia, a term popularized by the American physician George Miller Beard to refer to the mixture of dread, worry, and fatigue that Beard believed the stresses of the Industrial Revolution had produced. The root cause of neurasthenia was thought to be nerves that had been overstrained by the pressures of modern life; the prescribed remedies for these "tired nerves" were "nerve revitalizers"—nostrums such as mild electrical stimulators or elixirs tinged with opium, cocaine, or alcohol. But Freud became convinced that the feelings of dread and worry that he was seeing in the neurasthenic patients he consulted were based not in tired nerves but in problems of the psyche, which could be resolved through psychoanalysis.

In 1895, Freud wrote a paper about anxiety neurosis, a condition he sought to differentiate from neurasthenia and whose symptoms, as he described them, conform quite closely to the *DSM-V* checklist for panic disorder: rapid or irregular heartbeat, hyperventilation and breathing disturbances, perspiration and night sweats, tremor and shivering, vertigo, gastrointestinal disturbances, and a feeling of impending doom that he called "anxious expectations."

Nothing in all this necessarily contradicted anything that Donald Klein would later glean from his imipramine experiments. But that's because in 1895 Freud still considered anxiety neurosis to be the product not of a "repressed idea" (which is what he believed underlay most psychopathology) but of a biological force. Anxiety neurosis, Freud theorized in these early writings, was the result of either genetic predisposition (a theory that modern molecular genetics supports) or some kind of pent-up physiological pressure—most notably, in Freud's imagining, the pressure caused by thwarted sexual desire.

But in many of his subsequent writings (starting with *Studies on Hysteria* from around this same time), Freud asserted instead that attacks of anxiety—even ones that manifested themselves in acute physical symptoms—emanated from unresolved, and often unconscious, inner psychic conflicts. For nearly thirty years, Freud effectively abandoned the argument that anxiety attacks were a biological problem. He and his followers replaced anxiety neurosis with plain neurosis—a problem that had its basis in psychic discord, not in genes or biology. By the mid-twentieth century, the overwhelming psychiatric consensus was that anxiety was the result of a conflict between the desires of the id and the repressions of the superego—and that, furthermore, anxiety was the foundation of almost all mental illness, from schizophrenia to psychoneurotic depression. One of the main purposes of psychoanalysis—and of most forms of talk therapy—was to help the patient become aware of and contend with the underlying anxiety against which all of his various maladaptive "ego defenses" had been mustered. "The predominant American psychiatric theory was that all psychopathology was secondary to anxiety," Klein later recalled, "which in turn was caused by intrapsychic conflict."

But this didn't square with what Klein was finding in his imipramine studies. If anxiety was the animating force behind all psychopathology, then why didn't imipramine—which seemed to eliminate the panic suffered by patients with anxiety neurosis—help schizophrenics with their psychosis? Maybe, Klein ventured, not all mental illnesses lay on the spectrum of anxiety the way the Freudians thought they did.

The spectrum theory of anxiety held that what determined a mental illness's severity was the intensity of the underlying anxiety: mild anxiety led to psychoneurosis and various neurotic behaviors; severe anxiety led to schizophrenia or manic depression. For many traditional Freudians, the settings—like bridges or elevators or airplanes—that tended to produce acute anxiety attacks had symbolic, and often sexual, significance that accounted for the anxiety they caused.

Balderdash, Klein said. Childhood trauma or sexual repression didn't cause panic; a biological malfunction did.

Klein concluded that these attacks of paroxysmal anxiety—which he would come to call panic attacks—originated in a biological glitch that produced a suffocation alarm response, his term for the cascade of physiological activity that leads to, among other things, what feels like a spontaneous attack of overwhelming terror. Anytime someone starts to asphyxiate, internal physiological monitors detect the problem and send messages to the brain, causing intense arousal, gasping for breath, and an urge to flee—an adaptive survival mechanism. But some people, according to Klein's false suffocation alarm theory, have defective monitors that occasionally fire even when the individual is getting enough oxygen. This causes the person to experience the physical symptoms that make up an anxiety attack. The source of panic is not psychic conflict but crossed physiological wires—wires that imipramine somehow untangled. Klein's data suggested that imipramine eliminated spontaneous anxiety attacks in most patients who suffered them.

When Klein published an initial report on imipramine in *The American Journal of Psychiatry* in 1962, it was received, as he recalled, "like the proverbial lead balloon." Subsequent articles over the next several years, in which he argued that panic anxiety was an illness distinct from chronic anxiety, were received with similar *froideur*. He was attacked from all sides, accused of being an apostate. But because imipramine seemed to cure panic anxiety without affecting feelings of general apprehension and neurosis, Klein remained convinced that panic anxiety had symptoms and physiological causes that were different in kind and not just in degree from other forms of anxiety.

Though he hadn't set out to, Klein had achieved what's known as the first pharmacological dissection: working backward from the effects of drug treatment, he had defined a new illness category, carving out panic anxiety from the more general anxiety that was supposed to underlie the Freudian neuroses.

Klein's pharmacological dissection of anxiety met with enormous hostility from his colleagues. At a conference in 1980, just as the publication of the *DSM-III* was bringing panic disorder into existence, Klein's presentation on how the suffocation alarm response caused panic anxiety was followed immediately by a lecture from John Nemiah, the longtime editor of the prestigious *American Journal of Psychiatry*. Rebutting Klein, Nemiah said that panic anxiety had nothing to do with a suffocation alarm response or problems of biological hardwiring but rather was "the reaction of the individual's ego . . . to the threatened emergence into conscious awareness of unpleasant, forbidden, unwanted, frightening impulses, feelings, and thoughts."

Though Klein's theory has been to some degree officially adopted by American psychiatry since 1980, it remains controversial today. My own current therapist, Dr. W., a PhD psychologist who did his training in the 1960s, laments that Klein's work led to a fundamental shift in how we think about mental illness, moving us from the dimensional model that prevailed through the age of the *DSM-II* to the categorical model that began with the publication of the *DSM-III* in 1980. According to the dimensional model, depression, neurosis, psychoneurosis, panic anxiety, general anxiety, social anxiety, obsessive-compulsive disorder, and so forth all exist along a spectrum emanating from the same roots in what Freud called intrapsychic conflicts (or Dr. W.'s "self-wounds"). According to the categorical model, as laid out in the *DSM* since its third edition, depression, panic anxiety, general anxiety, social anxiety, obsessive-compulsive disorder, and so forth are carved up into discrete categories based on distinctive symptom clusters that are believed to have different underlying biophysiological mechanisms.

Between 1962, when Klein published his first imipramine study, and 1980, when the *DSM-III* was published, the way psychiatry (and the culture generally) thought about anxiety underwent an enormous transformation. "It is hard to recall that fifteen or twenty years ago there was no such concept [as panic anxiety]," marveled Peter Kramer, a psychiatrist at Brown University, in his 1993 book, *Listening to Prozac.* "Neither in medical school nor psychiatry residency, both in the 1970s, did I ever meet a patient with 'panic anxiety.'" Yet today panic disorder is a frequently diagnosed disease (some 18 percent of Americans are estimated to suffer from it), and "panic attack" has transcended the psychiatric clinic to become part of our lingua franca.

Panic disorder was the first psychiatric disease for which the determining factor in its creation was a drug reaction: imipramine cures panic; ipso facto panic disorder must exist. But this phenomenon—in which a drug effectively defined the syndrome for which it was prescribed—would soon recur.

*DSM assigns each slice of craziness with a name and a number. Panic disorder, for example, is disease number 300.21, a diagnostic code. . . . But just because it has a name, is it actually a disease?*
—DANIEL CARLAT, *Unhinged: The Trouble with Psychiatry— a Doctor's Revelations About a Profession in Crisis* (2010)

An advertisement for an October 1956 public talk by Frank Berger, the inventor of Miltown, stated that tranquilizers were effective in treating high blood pressure, worry, jitters, "executive stomach," "boss nerves," and "housewife nerves." None of these ailments were then, or are now, listed as illnesses in the American Psychiatric Association's *Diagnostic and Statistical Manual*—which raises the question of whether Miltown prescriptions were aimed less at treating actual psychiatric disorders than at treating the age itself—at mitigating the effects of what Berger in this talk called "today's pressure living."

Every time new drug therapies come along, they raise the question of where the line between anxiety as psychiatric disorder and anxiety as a normal problem of living should get drawn. We see this again and again throughout the history of pharmacology: the rise of tranquilizers is followed by an increase in anxiety disorders diagnoses; the rise of antidepressants is followed by an increase in the rate of depression.

When the APA published the first edition of the *DSM* in the aftermath of World War II, the governing infrastructure of the profession was still Freudian: the first edition placed all disorders along a spectrum of anxiety. "The chief characteristic of [neurotic] disorders is 'anxiety,'" the manual declared, "which may be directly felt and expressed or which may be unconsciously and automatically controlled by the utilization of various defense mechanisms." The second edition, published in 1968, was even more explicitly psychoanalytic. When the APA decided in the 1970s that it was time for a third edition, the Freudians (who had dominated the task forces that wrote the first two editions) and the biological psychiatrists (who had gotten a boost from the recent findings of pharmacology research) prepared for a pitched battle.

The stakes were high. Doctors and therapists of different schools would see their professional fortunes rise or fall depending on whether the definitions of the diseases they specialized in were narrowed or expanded. Drug company profits would spike or plummet depending on whether the categories that were created could be targeted by—and could help secure FDA approval for—the medications they manufactured.

The publication of the *DSM-III* in 1980 represented at least a partial repudiation of Freudian concepts and a victory for biological psychiatry. (One medical historian called the *DSM-III* a "death thrust" for psychoanalysis.) Out went the neuroses, and in their place came the anxiety disorders: social anxiety disorder, generalized anxiety disorder, post-traumatic stress disorder, obsessive-compulsive disorder, and both panic disorder with agoraphobia and panic disorder without agoraphobia. Donald Klein's pharmacological dissection of panic had prevailed.*

---

* Another way of characterizing this was as a victory of the neo-Kraepelinians over the Freudians. Many scholars consider Emil Kraepelin, not Sigmund Freud, to be the crucial figure in the history of psychiatry. Psychoanalysis, these scholars say, was just a blip; Kraepelin's system of disease classification both predated Freudianism and outlasted it.

But in moving mental illness away from Freudianism and into the realm of medical diagnosis, the new *DSM* pathologized as "disordered" or "ill" many people who once would have been considered merely "neurotic." This was a boon for the drug companies, which now had many more "sick" people for whom to develop and market medication. But did it benefit patients?

That's a complicated question. On the one hand, the medicalization of depression and anxiety helped destigmatize conditions once regarded as shameful character weaknesses, and it allowed people to find relief (often pharmacological) from their misery. The number of

---

In 1890, when Freud was setting up his practice in Vienna, Kraepelin, then a thirty-four-year-old physician, took a professorship in psychiatry at Heidelberg University. While there, Kraepelin became interested in the symptoms of various mental illnesses. He and his residents would draw up a note card for each patient who entered his clinic at Heidelberg and would record on it symptoms and a preliminary diagnosis. Each card would then be placed in the "diagnosis box." Every time a new symptom appeared, and every time a diagnosis was revised, the patient's card would be taken from the box and updated. When the patient was released from the hospital, his or her disposition and final diagnosis would be recorded. Over the years, Kraepelin accumulated many hundreds of such cards, which he would take on vacation to study. "In this manner we were able to get an overview and see which diagnoses had been incorrect and the reasons that had led us to this false conception," he wrote.

This systematic recording of patient symptoms and diagnoses may not seem novel today, but no one had attempted to apply such thorough observation and classification to mental illness before Kraepelin. (Actually, one exception here was astrologers. Through the Enlightenment, astrologers kept meticulous medical records so they could chart symptoms against astrological alignments, looking for correlations that would be useful to them in future diagnoses and treatments. This record keeping may in fact have made astrologers better able to prognosticate the course of diseases than doctors, who acted on intuition rather than systematic observation. Astrologers, in other words, may have been more likely to provide evidence-based medicine than doctors were.) Diagnoses were haphazard and random. Kraepelin's goal in gathering all this data was to try to cleave nature at the joints—to identify the cluster of symptoms that characterized each mental disease and to project their development over the life course. Unlike Freud (who was ambiguous about whether mental illness was a medical disease or a psychosocial problem of "adjustment"), Kraepelin came to believe strongly that psychiatry was a subfield of medicine. Emotional disorders were biological entities that could be identified and differentiated the way measles and tuberculosis were.

Kraepelin used the symptom data he accumulated on his cards as the basis of the psychiatry textbook he published in 1883. Revised multiple times over the years, his *Compendium der Psychiatrie* came to be the most influential psychiatric textbook ever published. By the time of the sixth edition in 1899, it had become the urtext of psychiatric classification.

Even through the middle years of the twentieth century, when psychoanalysis pushed Kraepelin's biological psychiatry to the margins, the Kraepelinian and Freudian systems of disease classification existed side by side. When the first edition of the *Diagnostic and Statistical Manual* was published in 1952, it divided diseases into different illness categories based on symptom clusters, very much the way Kraepelin's nineteenth-century textbooks had. But the terminology that described most of those illnesses was psychoanalytic, so almost everything in the first two editions of the *DSM* blended together into a soup of medical and psychoanalytic nomenclature.

people seeing depression or anxiety disorders as a health problem—as opposed to evidence of personal weakness—grew dramatically between 1980 and 2000, as Prozac and other SSRIs provided additional evidence for the idea of depression as a problem of chemical imbalance.* On the other hand, the expansion of medical categories of mental illness had the effect of drawing countless mentally healthy people into the nets of the pharmaceutical companies. Before the arrival of MAOIs and tricyclics in the late 1950s, depression (and its predecessors) was a rare diagnosis, given to only about *1* percent of the U.S. population. Today, by some official estimates, it's a diagnosis given to up to *15* percent of us. Are we truly that much more depressed in 2011 than we were in 1960? Or have we defined depression and anxiety disorders too broadly, allowing the drug companies to bamboozle us (and our insurance companies) into paying for pills that treat diseases we didn't know we had, diseases that didn't exist before 1980?

The publication of each successive edition of the *DSM* has intended to convey the impression of science advancing. And, to be sure, the *DSM-III, DSM-IV* (which came out in 1994), and *DSM-V* (which came out in 2013) were more empirically grounded than the first two editions. They placed much less influence on etiology—that is, on the presumed causes of different illnesses—and much more on simple symptom description.† But they were still political documents as much as scientific ones, representing the claims of one psychiatric school over another—and the professional interests of psychiatrists above everything else. "It is the task of the APA"—and therefore of the *DSM*—"to protect the earning power of psychiatrists," Paul Fink, the vice president of the American Psychiatric Association, declared in 1986. Stuart Kirk and Herb Kutchins, social workers who have together written two books about the history of the *DSM,* say that the APA's so-called bible is "a book of tentatively assembled agreements" that has led to the "pathologizing of everyday behaviors."

When you probe more deeply into the process that produced

---

* I will say more about this in chapter 7.

† The distinction between, say, generalized anxiety disorder and panic disorder lies not in how the disease is acquired—whether by genes or childhood trauma or unreleased libido—but on whether a person experiences a certain minimum number of symptoms from a checklist.

the *DSM-III*, its pretensions to scientific rigor begin to seem rather strained. For starters, some of its new category distinctions appear awfully arbitrary. (Why does panic disorder require the presence of four symptoms, rather than three or five, from the list of thirteen? Why do symptoms have to persist for six months, and not five or seven, for an official diagnosis of social anxiety disorder?) The head of the *DSM-III* task force, Robert Spitzer, would concede years later that many of its decisions were made haphazardly. If a constituency lobbied hard enough for a disease, it tended to get incorporated—which helps explain why between its second and third editions the *DSM* grew from 100 to 494 pages and from 182 to 265 diagnoses.

David Sheehan worked on the *DSM-III* task force. One night in the mid-1970s, Sheehan recalls, a subset of the task force got together for dinner in Manhattan. "As the wine flowed," Sheehan says, the committee members talked about how Donald Klein's research showed that imipramine blocked anxiety attacks. This did seem to be pharmacological evidence of a panic disorder that was distinct from other kinds. As Sheehan puts it:

> Panic disorder was born. And then the wine flowed some more, and the psychiatrists around the dinner table started talking about one of their colleagues who didn't suffer from panic attacks but who worried all the time. How would we classify him? He's just sort of *generally* anxious. Hey, how about 'generalized anxiety disorder'? And then they toasted the christening of the disease with the next bottle of wine. And then for the next thirty years the world collected data on it.

Sheehan, a tall Irishman who today runs a psychiatric center in Florida, is regarded as something of an apostate by the profession. He cheerfully admits he is out to "sabotage the notion" that panic disorder is truly distinct from generalized anxiety disorder. So his jaundiced version of how generalized anxiety disorder was born should perhaps be viewed with some skepticism. But Sheehan, who has been studying and treating anxiety for decades, makes an important point: Once you create a new disease, it starts to take on a life of its own. Research studies accrete around it, and patients get diagnosed with it, and the concept saturates the psychiatric and popular culture. Generalized anxiety disorder, a disease conceived over a boozy dinner and written into the *DSM* with a fairly arbitrary set of criteria, has now had thousands of studies applied to it, and the FDA has approved multiple drugs for treating it. But what if, as Sheehan contends, there is *no such thing* as generalized anxiety disorder—at least not as a disease distinct from panic disorder or major depression?* If Sheehan is right, a large edifice of diagnosis, prescription, and academic study has been built upon something—generalized anxiety disorder—that is presumed to exist in nature but that in fact does not.

> [*At current rates of Valium use*], *the arrival of the millennium would coincide with the total tranquilization of America.*
> —"BENZODIAZEPINES: USE, OVERUSE, MISUSE, ABUSE,"
> EDITORIAL IN *THE LANCET* (MAY 19, 1973)

Even as Thorazine emptied the asylums and antidepressant prescriptions grew exponentially through the late 1950s, nothing approached the runaway commercial success of Miltown. Hence the instructions given to Leo Sternbach, a chemist at Hoffmann–La Roche in New Jersey: "Invent a new tranquilizer," his bosses told him. So Sternbach thought back to research he had done on heptoxdiazine-based dyes while a postdoctoral student in Poland in the 1930s. What would happen if he chemically modified them a little? He tested more than forty different variations on animals—but none seemed to have a tranquilizing effect. Hoffmann–La Roche abandoned the project. Sternbach was reassigned to work on antibiotics.

But one day in April 1957, a research assistant who was cleaning Sternbach's lab came across a powder (official name: Ro-5-090) that had been synthesized a year earlier but was never tested. Without hope, as Sternbach said later, he sent it over to the animal testers on May 7,

---

* Recall from chapter 2 that some genetic research suggests there is in fact no meaningful difference between depression and generalized anxiety disorder.

his forty-ninth birthday. "We thought that the expected negative result would complete our work with this series of compounds and yield at least some publishable material. Little did we know that this was the start of a program which would keep us busy for many years."

Happy birthday. Sternbach had, mostly by accident and nearly without realizing it, invented the first benzodiazepine: chlordiazepoxide, which would be given the trade name Librium (derived from "equilibrium") and was the forerunner of Valium, Ativan, Klonopin, and Xanax, the dominant antianxiety medications of our age. Because of an error in his chemical process, Ro-5-090 had a molecular structure different from the other forty compounds Sternbach had synthesized. (It had a benzene ring of six carbon atoms connected to a diazepine ring of five carbon atoms and two nitrogen atoms—thus "benzodiazepine.") The director of pharmacological research at Hoffmann–La Roche tested the new substance on cats and mice and discovered, to his surprise, that although it was ten times more potent than Miltown, it did not notably impair the animals' motor function. *Time* reported that keepers at the San Diego Zoo had tamed a wild lynx with Librium. A newspaper headline blared: "The Drug That Tames Tigers—What Will It Do for Nervous Women?"

To gauge chlordiazepoxide's toxicity to humans, Sternbach performed the first test on himself. He reported feeling "slightly soft in the knees" and a little bit drowsy for a few hours, but otherwise he experienced no ill effects. By the time the FDA approved the drug, on February 24, 1960, Librium had already been administered to some twenty thousand people. The early reports in the medical journals raved about its effectiveness. Patients who had previously found that only electroshock therapy could control their anxiety declared that Librium was equally or more effective. A study published in *The Journal of the American Medical Association* in January 1960 reported that when 212 outpatients in New Jersey with a range of psychiatric ailments were given Librium, 88 percent of those with "free-floating anxiety" received some degree of relief. The researchers also found that the drug was effective in treating "phobic reactions," "compulsions" (what we would today label obsessive-compulsive disorder), and "tension." The lead researcher of a separate study proclaimed the development of Librium to be "the most significant advance to date in the psychopharmaceutical treatment of anxiety states."

The drug was shipped to American pharmacies in March 1960. The first Hoffmann–La Roche advertisement for Librium said it was for "the treatment of common anxieties and tension." Within three months, sales of Librium were outpacing sales of Miltown; by the end of the decade, more prescriptions had been written for Librium than for any other medication on earth. Physicians prescribed it for everything from hangovers, upset stomachs, and muscle spasms to all varieties of "tension," "nerves," "neurosis," and "anxiety." (One doctor noted that Librium had the same range of indications as gin.)

Librium remained the most prescribed drug in America until 1969—when it was displaced by another compound synthesized by Leo Sternbach, this one with the mellifluous chemical name 7-chloro-1, 3-dihydro-1-methyl-5-phenyl-2H-1, 4-benzodiazepin-2-one. This new drug lacked Librium's bitter aftertaste, and studies found it to be two and a half times as potent. The marketing department at Hoffman–La Roche dubbed it Valium (from the Latin *valere*, "to fare well" or "to be healthy"), and Valium, in turn, remained America's most popular drug until 1982.* In 1973, Valium became the first drug in the United States to exceed $230 million in sales (more than $1 billion in today's dollars)—even as its predecessor, Librium, continued to remain among the five most prescribed drugs in the country. In 1975, it was estimated that one in every five women and one in every thirteen men in America had taken Librium, Valium, or some other benzodiazepine. One study found that 18 percent of all American *physicians* were regularly taking tranquilizers in the 1970s. Advertisements for the drugs became ubiquitous in the medical journals. "It is ten years since Librium became available," went the text of a typical Librium advertisement from the 1970s. "Ten anxious years of aggravation and demonstration, Cuba and Vietnam, assassination and a devaluation, Biafra and Czechoslovakia. Ten turbulent years in which the world-wide climate of anxiety and aggression has given Librium—with its specific calming action and its

---

* Sternbach would also develop flurazepam (marketed as Dalmane) and clonazepam (marketed as Klonopin). Klonopin, like Valium, is still frequently prescribed today as a long-acting benzodiazepine.

remarkable safety margin—a unique and still growing role in helping mankind to meet the challenge of a changing world."

By the end of the decade, Librium and Valium had made Hoffman–La Roche—"the house that Leo built"—the biggest pharmaceutical company in the world. The benzodiazepines had become the greatest commercial success in the history of prescription drugs.

But as benzodiazepine sales grew through the 1960s and 1970s, so did the backlash against them. Some doctors warned that the drugs were being overprescribed. In 1973, Leo Hollister, a psychiatrist at Stanford, mused, "Whether the increase [in the use of antianxiety agents] is the result of the generally turbulent times which have prevailed in the past decade, or the introduction of new drugs and their widespread promotion, or of sloppy prescribing practices of physicians is uncertain." (If 18 percent of doctors were themselves taking Valium, that might account for some of the sloppiness.)

By the middle of the 1970s, the FDA had collected numerous reports of benzodiazepine dependence. Many patients who had been on high dosages of Valium or Librium for long periods of time would experience excruciating physical and psychological symptoms when they stopped taking the medication: anxiety, insomnia, headaches, tremors, blurred vision, ringing in the ears, the feeling that insects were crawling all over them, and extreme depression—and, in some cases, seizures, convulsions, hallucinations, and paranoid delusions. By the time Ted Kennedy led the 1979 Senate hearings on the hazards of benzodiazepines, critics had a rich literature of horror stories to draw on. Judy Garland's death, among others, was attributed to a toxic combination of benzodiazepines and alcohol. Fears about benzodiazepines were given a broad airing by Barbara Gordon, a star television writer at CBS who had been nearly destroyed by addiction to Valium. Gordon's experience with benzodiazepine dependence, as recounted in her memoir, *I'm Dancing as Fast as I Can,* resonated widely. The book became a *New York Times* best seller in 1979 and a feature film starring Jill Clayburgh in 1982. That was the year Public Citizen, the organization led by the consumer advocate Ralph Nader, published *Stopping Valium,* which alleged rampant benzodiazepine addiction.

Social critics worried that the rampant prescription of Valium was papering over the rough edges of society, medicating away radicalism, dissent, and creativity. "One must consider the broader implications of a culture in which tens of millions of adult citizens have come to use psychoactive drugs to alter virtually every facet of their waking (and sleeping) behavior," warned one doctor at a 1971 academic conference on drug use. "What does that say about the impact of modern technology on our style of life? What changes may be evolving in our value system?"* Marxist intellectuals like Herbert Marcuse attributed widespread pill popping to capitalist alienation. Conspiracy theorists invoked Aldous Huxley's dystopian *Brave New World*, alleging that the government was exerting social control by tranquilizing the masses (which was ironic because Huxley himself was an enthusiastic promoter of tranquilizers). An editorial published in the prestigious British medical journal *The Lancet* in 1973 fretted that at current rates of Valium use, which up to that point had been growing at a clip of seven million prescriptions a year, "the arrival of the millennium would coincide with the total tranquilization of America."†

The looming expiration of Valium's patent in 1985 helped spur the rise of a new benzodiazepine, alprazolam, which the Upjohn Company released with the trade name Xanax in 1981. Entering the market just after the *DSM-III* had introduced anxiety disorders as a clinical category, Xanax got a huge commercial boost from being the first drug specifically approved by the FDA for the treatment of the newly created panic disorder.‡

Many patients—and before long I was one of them—found that

---

* Feminists had related concerns. A series of ads run by Roche in the early 1970s presumed to offer a treatment for spinsterhood: "35, single and psychoneurotic," began a typical full-page advertisement, this one telling the sad story of Jan. "You probably see many . . . Jans in your practice," the ad went on. "The unmarrieds with low self-esteem. Jan never found a man to measure up to her father. Now she realizes she's in a losing pattern—and that she may *never* marry." The cure? Valium. ("You wake up in the morning, and you feel as if there's no point in going on another day like this," Betty Friedan had written in 1963 in *The Feminine Mystique*. "So you take a tranquilizer because it makes you not care so much that it's pointless.")

† As it turned out, Valium use peaked in 1973.

‡ This approval was not without controversy. The first favorable studies of Xanax's effect on panic were published in the *Archives of General Psychiatry*, whose editor at the time, Daniel Freedman, turned out to be on Upjohn's payroll as a member of its Division of Medical Affairs. Critics said this had unduly biased him and that the studies should not have been published because they were poorly constructed and therefore did not actually demonstrate that the drug was effective.

Xanax cut down on panic attacks and reduced physical symptoms like dizziness, palpitations, and gastrointestinal distress, as well as psychological ones like excessive timidity and feelings of dread. (The poet Marie Howe once told a friend of mine who was afraid to fly after 9/11: "You know that little door in your brain marked *Fear?* Xanax closes it.") By 1986, Xanax had overtaken Miltown, Librium, and Valium to become the best-selling drug in history. It has dominated the tranquilizer market ever since.*

*Anxiety and tension seem to abound in our modern culture and the current trend is to escape the unpleasantness of its impact. But when has life ever been exempt from stress? In the long run, is it desirable that a population be ever free from tension? Should there be a pill for every mood and occasion?*

—FROM A DECEMBER 1956 REPORT BY THE NEW YORK
ACADEMY OF MEDICINE

Benzodiazepines have been a leading pharmaceutical treatment for anxiety for more than half a century. But not until the late 1970s did the Italian neuroscientist Erminio Costa—yet another veteran of Steve Brodie's lab at the National Institutes of Health—finally home in on their salient chemical mechanism: their effect on a neurotransmitter called gamma-aminobutyric acid, or GABA, which inhibits the rate at which neurons fire.

Some brief and oversimplified neuroscience: A neurotransmitter called glutamate excites neurons, causing them to fire more rapidly; GABA, on the other hand, inhibits neurons, slowing their firing and calming brain activity. (If glutamate is the main accelerator of the brain circuitry, GABA is the main brake.) Costa discovered that benzodiazepines bind to GABA receptors found on every neuron, amplifying GABA's inhibitory effects and suppressing activity of the central nervous system. In binding to the GABA receptors, benzodiazepines

---

* In 2010, Xanax was the twelfth most commonly prescribed drug in America and the most frequently prescribed psychotropic medication—more widely prescribed than Prozac or any other single antidepressant.

change the receptors' molecular structure in a way that causes the GABA signal to last longer, which in turn causes the neuron to continue firing at a lower rate, calming brain activity.

Knowing even this superficial bit of neuroscience has given me a serviceable metaphor for understanding how my brain produces anxiety and how Xanax reduces it. When my anxiety mounts, my autonomic nervous system gets kicked into fight-or-flight mode, my thoughts start racing, and I start imagining all kinds of catastrophic things; my body feels like it's going haywire. I imagine the firing of my synapses getting faster and faster, like an overheating engine. I take a Xanax, and about thirty minutes later, if I'm lucky, I can almost feel the GABA system putting on the brakes as the benzodiazepines bind to their receptors and inhibit neuronal firing. Everything . . . slows . . . down.

Of course, this is a rather reductionist metaphor. Can my anxiety really be boiled down to how effectively gated my chloride ion channels are or to the speed of neuronal firing in my amygdala? Well, yes, at some level it can. Rates of neuronal firing in the amygdala correlate quite directly with the felt experience of anxiety. But to say that my anxiety is reducible to the ions in my amygdala is as limiting as saying that my personality or my soul is reducible to the molecules that make up my brain cells or to the genes that underwrote them.

In any case, I have a more practical concern: What is this long-term reliance on benzodiazepines doing to my brain? By this point, I have taken benzodiazepines (Valium, Klonopin, Ativan, Xanax) at varying doses and frequencies for more than thirty years. For several years during that time, I have been on tranquilizers around the clock for months at a time.

"Valium, Librium, and other drugs of that class cause damage to the brain. I have seen damage to the cerebral cortex that I believe is due to the use of these drugs, and I am beginning to wonder if the damage is permanent," David Knott, a physician at the University of Tennessee, warned back in 1976. In the three decades since then, scores of articles in scientific journals have reported on the cognitive impairment observed in long-term benzodiazepine users. A 1984 study by Malcolm Lader found that the brains of people who took tranquilizers for a long time physically shrank. (Subsequent studies have shown that different benzodiazepines seem to concentrate the shrinkage in different parts of the brain.) Does this explain why at the age of forty-four, after several decades of intermittently continuous tranquilizer consumption, I feel stupider than I used to?

# CHAPTER 7

# Medication and the Meaning of Anxiety

*When Valium came along, both patients and their doctors were will-*
*ing to define their problems in terms of anxiety. . . . When Prozac, a*
*drug for depression, arrived on the scene, the accent fell on depression*
*as the hallmark of distress.*
—EDWARD SHORTER, *A History of Psychiatry* (1997)

In the spring of 1997, after a difficult year—my parents' divorce, an unhappy job situation, a bad romance—and some months off psychiatric medications, I began, at my therapist's urging, to take Paxil, an SSRI whose generic name is paroxetine.

After a week or so on Paxil, I experienced an infusion of energy that bordered on manic: I slept fewer and fewer hours, but without feeling tired during the day; I could, for the first time in my life, regularly awake in the morning feeling energetic. The mild mania passed, but what followed was a slow brightening of my mood. I ended— finally, after several unsuccessful attempts—my codependent and dysfunctional relationship with my girlfriend of nearly two years. I got a promotion at the small magazine where I was working. I started dating.

At some point that fall, I realized I had not experienced a full-blown panic attack since I'd started on Paxil in April—by far my longest such stretch since middle school. I was experiencing less anxiety, feeling productive and engaged in my work, and enjoying an active social life. My stomach settled. Paxil was magic.

Or was it? Because what was cause and what was effect? That promotion I got at work came along after someone left and I was elevated to fill the position; that would likely have happened even if I hadn't gone on Paxil. Maybe that small boost in my professional status, along with the more interesting and empowering day-to-day responsibilities of the job, bolstered my self-esteem, which in turn gave me the confidence to start sending out freelance work, which in turn made me feel professionally engaged. And while I felt like the Paxil had somehow given me the strength to finally break the stubborn cord of neurotic codependence that had tied me to my girlfriend, maybe I would have done that anyway—and there is no question that, Paxil or no Paxil, being out of that relationship was liberating. (For her, too, I'm sure; we haven't spoken since.) So maybe it was the particular constellation of events that came together that spring—the promotion, the breaking off of a dysfunctional relationship, the end of a dark Boston winter and the arrival of spring—that lifted my anxiety and depression. Maybe Paxil had nothing to do with it.

But I think it did. Beginning with that brief manic boost, my lived experience felt like it was Paxil inflected—and I now know that my clinical trajectory (mild mania, lifting of mood, effecting of positive life changes) is a fairly common one. Of course, another possibility is that what I enjoyed that spring and summer was the placebo effect—the Paxil worked because I *believed* it would work. (With the placebo effect, the power of belief itself, rather than the chemical content of any medication, is the salient mechanism.)

But the Paxil was not magic—or if it was, its magic ran out. Because after trundling merrily along in medicated contentment for ten months, my short-lived feeling of invulnerability was punctured within a period of ten minutes.

In those first months on Paxil, I had—for the first time in twenty years—been able to fly with only moderate anxiety. So one February morning, I drove heedlessly through a fierce New England rainstorm to the airport (how nice not to be in a nervous swivet for days before every plane ride!), boarded my flight, and settled in with my newspaper for the hour-long trip to Washington, D.C. I can't say that I was ever, even in those glorious early days on Paxil, free of flying anxiety. But it was a gentler experience, manifesting itself as butterflies in my stomach, sweat on my palms, and a mild feeling of apprehension—what I imagine many people feel upon takeoff. So there I sat, twenty-eight years old, feeling relatively competent and grown-up (*Here I am*, I thought, *the executive editor of a magazine, flying to Washington on business, reading my* New York Times), confidently insulated from terror by my morning dose of twenty milligrams of Paxil, that little pink pill that had kept me panic-free for a blissful few months, as we taxied and took off.

And then, passing through the dark clouds that were producing the rainstorm below, we ran into turbulence.

It lasted all of ten minutes. Fifteen at most. But the whole time I was convinced we were going to crash—or, worse, that I would get airsick and throw up. Hands shaking, I gulped two Dramamine. Beverage service had been suspended—the flight attendants had been asked to stay seated, which terrified me. But as I looked around the cabin, none of my fellow passengers seemed unduly perturbed. To my left, a man tried to read his newspaper, despite the thrashing and dipping of the plane; to my right, across the aisle, a woman appeared to doze. I, meanwhile, wanted to scream. I desperately wanted the turbulence to end (*Please, God, please make it end now and I'll believe in you and be good and pious forever*) and the Dramamine to take effect, and I craved, above all, unconsciousness, an end to the misery.

Of course, my fears of crashing must not have been completely consuming, because I had, even in that moment, an additional worry: Was my panic so obvious that the other passengers would see it? Logically, one anxiety should have canceled out the other: if we were all going to die, I shouldn't have been worried about an ephemeral moment of earthly embarrassment before plunging into eternal oblivion, right? On the other hand, if I was going to end up embarrassed after the flight, that would mean we *weren't* going to die, right? And at that moment, to be safely on the ground and to not be dead—no matter how embarrassed—was a condition greatly to be desired. But in my amygdala-controlled brain, with my sympathetic nervous system on full alert, there was no room for such clarity of logic. All I could think was, *I'm going to throw up and I'm going to be humiliated and I'm going to die and I'm terrified and all I want is to be out of this situation and never to get on a plane again.*

Then we passed above the clouds, and there was clear sky and sun outside the window, and the ride was completely smooth. The seat belt sign was turned off. Beverage service resumed. My parasympathetic nervous system kicked in, arresting the firing rate of the hyperactive neurons in my turbocharged amygdala, and I sank into a relieved, Dramamine-enhanced exhaustion. Half an hour or so later, we landed uneventfully in Washington.

But the Paxil had stopped working.

Not completely, at least not right away. But the illusion of being surrounded by an invincible anxiety-repelling Paxil force field had been dispelled. This, I now know, is not an infrequent occurrence. Certain SSRI medications can reduce anxiety and cut down on panic attacks— but according to the stress-diathesis model of panic, strong stimuli (like a turbulent flight) are potent enough to break through even medication-adjusted brain chemistry to produce intense anxiety. And this can be, because of the effect the breakthrough has on the thinking (or the "cognitions") of the individual, like a magical spell being broken. (Other times, certain drugs just stop working without such stressful provocation; this phenomenon has been called "the Prozac poop-out.")

After that day, my general anxiety level slowly rose again. My panic attacks began to recur—mild and infrequent at first, then more severe and more often. My flying phobia resurged—I needed to take a large dose of Xanax or Klonopin or Ativan before getting on any flight, and sometimes even that wasn't enough. On my first airplane trip with Susanna, who was later to become my wife, my anxiety got so bad soon after takeoff that I began shaking and gasping frantically, and then, as Susanna looked on in bewilderment, my stomach cramped and I lost control of my bowels. I had planned the trip—three days in London— as a romantic vacation, an attempt to woo and impress her. This was not a good start. Nor was the rest of the trip much better: those parts of the vacation that I did not spend sedated into near catatonia by massive quantities of Xanax I spent quaking in mortal dread of the return flight.

I kept taking Paxil for several years, even after it had lost its panic-repelling magic, out of a combination of inertia and the fear of what might happen if I stopped. But by the spring of 2003, I had been on Paxil for six years, and my anxiety was once again in full bloom. It was time to try something new.

This is what prompted me to see Dr. Harvard, the psychopharma-cologist. During my first visit, he was taking my case history when, as if to demonstrate my disorder, I had a florid panic attack that rendered me breathless and tearful, unable to continue. "Take your time," Dr. Harvard said. "Continue when you're ready." Whether it was the facts of my case history or the vividness of the panic attack I unwillingly dis-played for him, Dr. Harvard seemed surprised to learn that I had gone completely unmedicated for stretches of my life. He seemed amazed. To him, I was a hard case, not equipped for normal human functioning without pharmaceutical assistance.

We discussed the pharmacological options, eventually settling on Effexor, the trade name for venlaxafine, a serotonin-norepinephrine reuptake inhibitor (SNRI), which impedes the absorption—and there-fore boosts the intrasynaptic levels of—both serotonin and norepi-nephrine in the brain. We talked about how to taper slowly off the Paxil, which I did, carefully following his instructions, decreasing the dosage bit by tiny bit over a period of several weeks.

Over the years, I had from time to time considered trying to wean myself off psychiatric medication completely. *After all*, I reasoned, *I'm pretty anxious on medication—how much worse can I be off of it?* So once I finally did manage to taper most of the way off the Paxil, I thought, *Why not, let's try flying solo for a while—no more drugs.* I stopped taking the Paxil and didn't start the Effexor.

Here is what you don't see in those TV and magazine advertise-ments for psychotropic drugs or even, with any real specificity or sym-pathetic understanding, in the clinical literature: the hell of going off them. I've never taken heroin, so I can't say whether this is true (I sus-pect it isn't), but many people claim that withdrawal from Paxil is as bad as withdrawal from heroin. The headaches. The exhaustion. The nausea and stomach cramps. The knee-buckling vertigo. The electric zapping sensation in your brain—a weird but common symptom. And, of course, the surge of anxiety: waking up at dawn every morning to a pounding heart and terrible dread; multiple panic attacks daily.

Despite my desire to try to "be myself" and function without phar-macological assistance for the first time in six years, I couldn't hack it, and so one morning after barely a week off the Paxil, I took my first dose of Effexor. Within minutes, literally, I felt much better: the physical symptoms receded; my state of mind improved.

This cannot actually have been due to the Effexor's therapeutic action—SSRIs and SNRIs generally need several weeks to build up in the synapses enough to start working. More likely, something in the Effexor somehow alleviated the effects of chemical withdrawal from Paxil. But what is cause and what is effect? Were the emotional anxiety and physical misery I felt after going off the Paxil really the effect of chemical withdrawal? Or was this simply what it feels like to be me undrugged? After all, I had been on psychiatric medication for long enough that maybe I had forgotten what it feels like to live in my naked brain.

Or was my misery that spring less the result of ill-fated drug-switching experiments than of the stress in my life? Two dates loomed at the end of that summer. The first was the deadline for the delivery of the manuscript of my first book, which by then had been in gestation for six years (roughly the length of time I'd been on Paxil) and had endured a harrowing journey—from editor to editor and publishing house to publishing house, through the descent into Alzheimer's of my biography's subject and the increasingly intrusive involvement of my subject's powerful family—to get to this point. The other was my wife's due date for the delivery of our first child.* Of the difficulties I endured that summer, it's hard to know exactly which were a response to external stressors and which were drug related. And of those drug-related difficulties, it's hard to know which were withdrawal effects from drugs I was weaning *off* and which were side effects from drugs I was going *on*.

The contrast between what the pharmaceutical industry's promotional materials and the clinical research papers (many of them subsidized by grants from the pharmaceutical industry) say and what the roiling online communities of actual patients say is large. I believe both sides are generally honest and accurate as far as they go (the drugs can have measurable therapeutic benefits; the side effects and withdrawal

---

* The birth of a child ranks high on the famous Holmes and Rahe Stress Scale, which attempts to quantify the effects of various kinds of life stresses on mental and physical health.

symptoms can be awful), but neither one is wholly trustworthy. The drug companies, and the doctors subsidized by them, have a profit-motivated interest in pushing pills; the drug takers are pretty much by definition an unhappy and unstable bunch prone, like me, to being easily thrown by physical symptoms. Studies have shown that people who score high on scales of anxiety sensitivity tend to suffer drug side effects more severely. (A bunch of nonanxious people who took an SSRI would likely be much less bothered by any side effects and would therefore be less likely to complain about them in online forums.) So the antidrug rants of the pill-popping community cannot be taken at face value any more than can the assessment of side effects and withdrawal symptoms in the sometimes boosterish clinical literature.

Though the Effexor eased what seemed to be the physical symptoms of my withdrawal from Paxil, my anxiety and panic persisted—and then increased. When I told Dr. Harvard about this, his response, as the response of psychiatrists and psychopharmacologists so often tends to be, was, "We need to elevate your dosage." The quantity of Effexor I was taking was not sufficient, he said, to correct the "chemical imbalance" in my serotonergic and noradrenergic systems. So I went from taking thirty-seven and a half milligrams to seventy-five milligrams of Effexor three times a day.

At which point my anxiety levels shot through the roof. At night, I would awaken in the grip of a raging panic attack. During the day, I was having multiple panic attacks—and even when I wasn't having one, I felt as though I were about to. Never had I felt such chronic, persistent agitation; I couldn't stop moving and twitching, couldn't bear the feeling of being in my own skin. (The clinical term for this is "akathisia.") Glimmerings of suicide began twinkling at the edge of my consciousness.

I called Dr. Harvard. "I can't take it," I told him. "I think maybe I need to get off the Effexor. I feel like I'm going crazy." "You need to give it more time," he said. And he gave me a prescription for Xanax, which he said would take the edge off my anxiety while giving the Effexor time to work.

Prescribing a benzodiazepine (like Xanax) to overcome the anxiety produced when a patient starts taking an antidepressant SSRI or SNRI (like Effexor) has been standard practice since the late 1990s.

And in my case this worked—a little, for a short time. My anxiety receded somewhat, and the panic subsided, but only if I faithfully took my Xanax around the clock.

To work on my book, I had rented a decrepit office on the third floor of a crummy building in Boston's North End, and to hasten my progress, I had hired a research assistant, Kathy, who shared the space with me. Kathy was an excellent researcher and, when I wasn't feeling panicky, delightful company. But I was embarrassed about my anxiety and felt I had to hide it, which meant leaving when I felt panic coming on. So I was forever contriving errands to get me out of the office.*

Yet again I called Dr. Harvard. And yet again he said, "You're not at a therapeutic level of the Effexor yet. Let's increase the dosage." So I started taking more Effexor, and a few days later my vision blurred and I couldn't urinate. I called Dr. Harvard, and for once he sounded alarmed. "Maybe we'd better get you off the Effexor," he said. But I'd been traumatized by the withdrawal symptoms I'd suffered when I'd stopped taking Paxil, and I told him so. (Discontinuation syndrome is now a clinically acknowledged Paxil phenomenon.) "I'm giving you a prescription for Celexa," he said, using the brand name for citalopram, another SSRI. "Start taking it right away, and continue taking the Xanax."

I did, and within a day my vision cleared and my urine again

---

* Often, escaping the office wasn't enough to stem the tide of panic, so I took to walking several blocks to Old North Church, where Paul Revere's famous one-if-by-land-and-two-if-by-sea lanterns had supposedly been hung in 1775. I'd sit in an austere wooden pew in the back and gaze at the oil painting of Jesus that hangs behind the altar. In that painting, Christ's face looks kindly, his eyes sympathetic. I am not a hard-core atheist, but nor am I a believer—I'm a who-knows-what-explains-all-this agnostic, a skeptic who out of my usual abundance of caution refuses to brazenly deny that God exists for fear of losing Pascal's wager and discovering too late that he does. Yet in those desperate weeks in the summer of 2003, I would sit in Old North Church and pray forthrightly to that painting of Jesus. I'd ask it to please give me peace of mind, or a sign that God existed, something I could grab hold of to steady myself against the assault of my nerves. In my quest for succor, I started reading my way through the Bible and a history of early Christianity, trying to see if I could somehow reason my way to faith and the psychic and existential serenity I thought it might provide.

I couldn't. And while I did find something about the unadorned Puritan simplicity of the church to be calming, my visits there didn't really help, either, especially during the nadir of my Effexor experience. I'd try to calm my breathing—but then I'd get overwhelmed by claustrophobia and panic and have to rush out of the church. I'd often end up shaking on a park bench, probably looking to passing tourists like a homeless person suffering delirium tremens.

flowed, which would seem to suggest those problems had been side effects of the drug. But they might not have been: the tendency of anxiety sufferers to "somaticize"—to convert their neuroses into physical symptoms—means it's possible my blurred vision and recalcitrant bladder were simply physical representations of my anxiety.

The transition from Effexor to Celexa was smoother than the transition from Paxil to Effexor had been, perhaps because I didn't wean off one before going on the other. But since then, despite chronic and intermittently severe anxiety, I've not gone a day without taking an SSRI antidepressant, and I've not adjusted my dosage much, for fear of repeating the Paxil-to-Effexor experience. At times I think wistfully about my early days on Paxil, when I found a modicum of relief, and wonder if I shouldn't switch back and try to achieve again that panic-free nirvana. But the clinical research is full of people who return to drugs they had taken earlier only to find them no longer effective.

And in any case, the experience of weaning off Paxil is not one I want to repeat.

*Medication, medication, medication! What do I got to show for it?*
—*THE SOPRANOS'* TONY SOPRANO TO DR. MELFI AFTER A YEAR ON
PROZAC FOR HIS PANIC ATTACKS

Exploding into the national consciousness with the March 26, 1990, edition of *Newsweek,* whose cover featured a green-and-white capsule alongside the words "A Breakthrough Drug for Depression," fluoxetine, under its trade name Prozac, would become the iconic antidepressant of the late twentieth century—a blockbuster for its manufacturer, Eli Lilly. The first selective serotonin reuptake inhibitor (SSRI) to be released in the United States, Prozac would before long surpass Xanax as the best-selling psychotropic drug in history—even as competing SSRIs (among them Zoloft, Paxil, Celexa, and Lexapro) would soon be on their way to outpacing Prozac.

With the possible exception of antibiotics, SSRIs are the most commercially successful class of prescription drugs in history. By 2002, according to one estimate, some twenty-five million Americans—more than 5 percent of all men and 11 percent of all women—were taking an SSRI antidepressant. The numbers have only grown since then—a 2007 estimate put the number of Americans on SSRIs at thirty-three million. These drugs dominate not only hospital psychiatry and our medicine cabinets but also our culture and natural environment. Books like *Prozac Nation, Prozac Diary,* and *Listening to Prozac* (and, of course, *Talking Back to Prozac*) populated the best-seller lists throughout the 1990s, and Prozac and Lexapro jokes remain a fixture of movies and *New Yorker* cartoons. Trace elements of Prozac, Paxil, Zoloft, and Celexa have been found in the ecosystems of American frogs (causing them developmental delays and anomalies), in the brains and livers of fish in North Texas, and in Lake Mead, America's largest reservoir, which supplies drinking water to Las Vegas, Los Angeles, San Diego, and Phoenix.

Given how completely SSRIs have saturated our culture and our environment, you might be surprised to learn that Eli Lilly, which held the U.S. patent for fluoxetine, killed the drug in development *seven times* because of unconvincing test results. After examining tepid fluoxetine trial outcomes, as well as complaints about the drug's side effects, German regulators in 1984 concluded, "Considering the benefit and the risk, we think this preparation totally unsuitable for the treatment of depression." Early clinical trials of another SSRI, Paxil, were also failures.*

How did SSRIs go from being considered ineffective to being one of the best-selling drug classes in history? In the answer to that question lies a story about how dramatically our understanding of anxiety and depression has changed in a short period of time.

Once again the story begins at Steve Brodie's laboratory at the National Institutes of Health. After leaving Brodie's lab for the University of Gothenburg in Sweden in 1959, Arvid Carlsson gave tricyclic antidepressants to mice with artificially depleted serotonin levels.

---

* A series of studies in the 1980s found imipramine, the tricyclic antidepressant, to be more effective than Prozac for treating patients with depression or panic disorder. Imipramine also trounced Paxil in two studies in the early 1980s of patients with depression. In 1989, Paxil failed to beat a placebo in more than half its trials. Yet four years later, Paxil was approved by the FDA—and by 2000 it was the best-selling antidepressant on the market, outselling Prozac and Zoloft.

Would the antidepressants boost serotonin levels? Yes; imipramine had serotonin-reuptake-inhibiting effects. In the 1960s, Carlsson tried similar experiments with antihistamines. Would they also inhibit the reuptake of serotonin? Again, yes. Carlsson found that an antihistamine called chlorpheniramine had a more powerful and precise effect on the brain's serotonin receptors than did either imipramine or amitriptyline, the two most commonly prescribed tricyclics. Carlsson invoked this finding as evidence to support what he called the serotonin hypothesis of depression. He then set about applying this discovery in pursuit of a more potent antidepressant. "This," the medical historian Edward Shorter has written, "was the birthing hour of the SSRIs."*

Carlsson next experimented with a different antihistamine, brompheniramine (the active ingredient in the cough medication Dimetapp). It, too, blocked the reuptake of serotonin and norepinephrine more robustly than imipramine did. He modified the antihistamine to create compound H102-09, which blocked only the reuptake of serotonin. Working with a team of researchers at Astra, a Swedish pharmaceutical company, Carlsson applied for a patent for H102-09—which had by then been renamed zimelidine—on April 28, 1971. Early clinical trials suggested zimelidine had some effectiveness in reducing depres-

---

* Carlsson wanted to pursue chlorpheniramine clinical trials for patients with anxiety and depression, but he never did. His own lab research, as well as subsequent naturalistic observations, showed that chlorpheniramine may, without any modifications, be as effective as any existing SSRI—which is intriguing because chlorpheniramine has been on the market, under the trade name Chlor-Trimeton, as an over-the-counter medicine for pollen allergies since 1950. In 2006, Einar Hellbom, a Swedish researcher, published a study suggesting that patients diagnosed with panic disorder who took chlorpheniramine for their hay fever experienced a remission of their panic symptoms while on the drug; when the patients went off Chlor-Trimeton, even if they switched to another antihistamine, many of them found their panic attacks returning. Hellbom suggested that perhaps this means an effective nonprescription SSRI antidepressant is sitting on the allergy remedy shelf of your local pharmacy today—even though scarcely any doctors, and certainly no consumers, are aware of its potential in this regard. "If chlorpheniramine had been tested on depression in the nineteen seventies," Hellbom writes, "it is probable that a safe, inexpensive SSRI drug could have been used some 15 years earlier than [Prozac]. . . . Chlorpheniramine might have been the first safe, non-cardiotoxic and well-tolerated antidepressant. Billions of dollars in the development and marketing costs would have been saved, and the suffering of millions of patients alleviated."

This is striking to me because I took Chlor-Trimeton regularly each spring throughout my childhood. I had always attributed the lifting of my depression and anxiety in April and May to the lengthening of the daylight and the approaching end of the school year. But Hellbom's paper leads me to wonder if my brightening mood and decreasing tension each spring were a result of my exposure to Chlor-Trimeton, the accidental SSRI.

sion, and in 1982 Astra started selling it in Europe as the antidepressant Zelmid. Astra licensed Zelmid's North American rights to Merck, which began preparing to release the drug in the United States. Then tragedy struck: some patients taking Zelmid became paralyzed; a few died. Zelmid was pulled from pharmacy shelves in Europe and was never distributed in America.

Executives at Eli Lilly watched these developments with interest. Some ten years earlier, biochemists at the company's labs in Indiana had fiddled with chemical derivatives of a different antihistamine, diphenhydramine (the active ingredient in the allergy medication Benadryl), to create a compound called LY-82816, which had a potent effect on serotonin but only a weak effect on norepinephrine levels. This made LY-82816 the most "clean," or "selective," of the several compounds the researchers tested.* David Wong, an Eli Lilly biochemist, reformulated LY-82816 into compound LY-110140 and wrote up his findings in the journal *Life Sciences* in 1974. "At this point," Wong would later recall, "work on [LY-110140] was an academic exercise." Nobody knew whether there would be a market for even one serotonin-boosting psychiatric medication—and since Zelmid already had a head start of several years in getting through clinical trials and onto the market, Eli Lilly put LY-110140, now called fluoxetine, aside.

But when Zelmid started paralyzing people, Eli Lilly executives realized fluoxetine now had a chance to be the first SSRI on the market in America, so they restarted the research machinery. Though many of the early clinical trials were not notably successful, the drug was approved and released in Belgium in 1986. In January 1988, fluoxetine was released in the United States, marketed as "the first highly specific, highly potent blocker of serotonin uptake." Eli Lilly gave it the trade name Prozac, which a branding firm had thought had "zap" to it.

Two years later, the pill graced the cover of *Newsweek*. Three years after that, Peter Kramer, the Brown psychiatrist, published *Listening to Prozac*.

---

* The tricyclics and MAOIs, in contrast, were "dirty," or "nonselective," in that they affected not just serotonin but also norepinephrine, dopamine, and other neurotransmitters, a fact that was thought to account for their wide range of unpleasant side effects.

When *Listening to Prozac* came out in the summer of 1993, I was twenty-three and on my third tricyclic antidepressant—this time desipramine, whose trade name is Norpramin. I read the book with fascination, marveling at the transformative effects Prozac had had on Kramer's patients. Many of his patients became, as he put it, "better than well": "Prozac seemed to give social confidence to the habitually timid, to make the sensitive brash, to lend the introvert the social skills of a salesman." *Hmm,* I thought. *This sounds pretty good.* My longtime psychiatrist, Dr. L., had been suggesting Prozac to me for months. But reading Kramer, I worried about what Faustian exchange was being made here—what got lost, in selfhood or the more idiosyncratic parts of personality, when Prozac medicated away the nervousness or the melancholy. In his book, Kramer concluded forcefully that for most severely anxious or depressed patients, the bargain was worthwhile. But he worried, too, about what he called "cosmetic psychopharmacology"—the use of psychiatric drugs by "normal" or "healthy" people to become happier, more social, more professionally effective.

Before long, I joined the millions of other Americans taking SSRIs—and I've been on one or another pretty much continuously for going on twenty years. Nevertheless, I can't say with complete conviction that these drugs have worked—or that they've been worth the costs in terms of money, side effects, drug-switching traumas, and who knows what long-term effects on my brain.

After the initial flush of enthusiasm for SSRIs, some of the fears that had surrounded tranquilizers in the 1970s began clustering around antidepressants. "It is now clear," David Healy, the historian of psychopharmacology, has written, "that the rates at which withdrawal problems have been reported on [Paxil] exceed the rates at which withdrawal problems have been reported on any other psychotropic drug ever."*

---

* Ironically, the early commercial success of SSRIs owed a lot to the public furor over Valium addiction in the early 1970s, which had driven benzodiazepines out of favor. When the FDA approved SSRIs for the treatment of depression, that caused the number of depression diagnoses to skyrocket, even as rates of anxiety diagnosis fell. But when the FDA subsequently approved SSRIs for the treatment of anxiety, the number of anxiety diagnoses rose again.

"Paxil is truly addictive," Frank Berger, the inventor of Miltown, said not long before his death in 2008. "If you have somebody on Paxil, it's not so easy to get him off. . . . This is not the case with Librium, Valium and Miltown." A few years ago, my primary care physician told me she had stopped prescribing Paxil because so many of her patients had reported such severe withdrawal effects.

Even leaving aside withdrawal effects, there is now a large pile of evidence suggesting—in line with those early studies of the ineffectiveness of Prozac and Paxil—that SSRIs may not work terribly well. In January 2010, almost exactly twenty years after introducing Americans to SSRIs, *Newsweek* published a cover story reporting on studies that suggested these drugs are barely as effective as sugar pills for the treatment of anxiety and depression. Two massive studies from 2006 showed most patients do not get better taking antidepressants; only about a third of the patients in these studies improved dramatically after a first trial. After reviewing dozens of studies on SSRI effectiveness, the *British Medical Journal* concluded that Prozac, Zoloft, Paxil, and the other drugs in the SSRI class "do not have a clinically meaningful advantage over placebo."*

How can this be? Tens of millions of Americans—including me and many people I know—collectively consume billions of dollars' worth of SSRIs each year. Doesn't this suggest that these drugs are effective?

Not necessarily. At the very least, these massive rates of SSRI consumption have not caused rates of self-reported anxiety and depression to go down—and in fact all this pill popping seems to correlate with substantially higher rates of anxiety and depression.

"If you're born around World War I, in your lifetime the prevalence of depression is about 1 percent," says Martin Seligman, a psychologist at the University of Pennsylvania. "If you're born around World War II the lifetime prevalence of depressions seemed to be about 5 percent. If you were born starting in the 1960s, the lifetime prevalence seemed to be between 10 percent and 15 percent, and this is with lives incomplete"—meaning that in the end the actual rates will be higher.

---

* These findings are controversial and continue to be debated fiercely on psychiatry and psychology blogs.

That's at least a tenfold increase in the diagnosis of depression across just two generations.

The same trend is evident in other countries. In Iceland, the incidence of depression nearly doubled between 1976 (before the arrival of SSRIs) and 2000. In 1984, four years before the introduction of Prozac, Britain reported 38 million "days of incapacity" (sick days) resulting from depression and anxiety disorders; in 1999, after a decade of widespread SSRI use, Britain attributed 117 million days of incapacity to the same disorders—an increase of 300 percent. Health surveys in the United States show that the percentage of working-age Americans who reported being disabled by depression tripled in the 1990s. Here's the most striking statistic I've come across: Before antidepressants existed, some fifty to one hundred people per million were thought to suffer from depression; today, between *one hundred thousand and two hundred thousand* people per million are estimated to have depression. In a time when we have more biochemically sophisticated treatments than ever for combating depression, that's a *1,000 percent increase* in the incidence of depression.

In his 2010 book, *Anatomy of an Epidemic*, the journalist Robert Whitaker marshaled evidence suggesting that SSRIs actually *cause* depression and anxiety—that SSRI consumption over the last twenty years has created organic changes in the brains of tens of millions of drug takers, making them more likely to feel nervous and unhappy. (Statistics from the World Health Organization showing that the worldwide suicide rate has increased by *60 percent* over the last forty-five years would seem to give weight to the idea that the quotient of unhappiness in the world has risen in tandem with SSRI consumption.) Whitaker's argument about drugs causing mental illness is controversial—most experts would dispute it, and it's certainly not proven. What's clear, though, is that the explosion of SSRI prescriptions has caused a drastic expansion in the *definitions* of depression and anxiety disorder (as well as more widespread acceptance of using depression and anxiety as excuses for skipping work), which has in turn caused the number of people given these diagnoses to increase.

*We may look back 150 years from now and see antidepressants as a dangerous and sinister experiment.*
—JOSEPH GLENMULLEN, *Prozac Backlash* (2001)

In America, the question of when and whether to prescribe medications for routine neurotic suffering is bound up with two competing intellectual traditions: our historical roots in the self-denial and asceticism of our Puritan forebears versus the post-baby-boom belief that everyone is entitled to the "pursuit of happiness" enshrined in our founding document. In modern psychiatry, the tension between these two traditions plays out in the battle between Peter Kramer's cosmetic psychopharmacology and what's known as pharmacological Calvinism.

Critics of cosmetic psychopharmacology (including, to some extent, Kramer himself) worry about what happens when millions of mildly neurotic patients seek medication to make themselves "better than well" and when competition to get and stay ahead in the workplace creates a pharmaceutical arms race. The term "pharmacological Calvinism" was coined in 1971 by Gerald Klerman, a self-described "angry psychiatrist" who was out to combat the emerging consensus that if a drug makes you feel good, it must be bad. Life is hard and suffering is real, Klerman and his allies argued, so why should ill-founded Puritanism be allowed to interfere with nervous or unhappy Americans' quest for peace of mind?

The pharmacological Calvinists believe that to escape psychic pain without quest or struggle is to diminish the self or the soul; it's getting something for nothing, a Faustian bargain at odds with the Protestant work ethic. "Psychotherapeutically," Klerman wrote sardonically, "the world is divided into the first-class citizens, the saints who can achieve their cure or salvation by willpower, insight, psychoanalysis or by behavior modification, and the rest of the people, who are weak in their moral fiber and need a crutch." Klerman angrily dismissed such concerns, wondering why we would, out of some sense of misguided moral propriety, deny anxious, depressed Americans relief from their suffering and the opportunity to pursue higher, more meaningful goals.

Why remain mired in the debilitating self-absorption of your neuroses if a pill can free your mind?

Americans are ambivalent about all this. We pop tranquilizers and antidepressants by the billions—yet at the same time we have historically judged reliance on psychiatric medication to be a sign of weakness or moral failure.* A study conducted by researchers at the National Institute of Mental Health in the early 1970s concluded that "Americans believe tranquilizers are effective but have serious doubts about the morality of using them."

Which sounds like a somewhat illogical and self-contradictory position—but it happens to be the one I hold myself. I reluctantly take both tranquilizers and antidepressants, and I believe that they work—at least a little, at least some of the time. And I acknowledge that, as many psychiatrists and psychopharmacologists have told me, I may have a "medical condition" that causes my symptoms and somehow "justifies" the use of these medications. Yet at the same time, I also believe (and I believe that society believes) that my nervous problems are in some way a character issue or a moral failing. I believe my weak nerves make me a coward and a wimp, with all the negative judgment those words imply, which is why I have tried to hide evidence of them—and which is why I worry that resorting to drugs to mitigate these problems both proves and intensifies my moral weakness.

"Stop judging yourself!" Dr. W. says. "You're making your anxiety worse!"

He's right. And yet I can't help concurring with the 40 percent of respondents to that NIMH survey who agreed with the statement "Moral weakness causes mental illness and taking tranquilizers to correct or ameliorate the condition is further evidence of that weakness."

Of course, as we learn more about how genes encode certain temperamental traits and dispositions into our personalities, it becomes harder to sustain the moral weakness argument in quite the same way. If my genes have encoded in me an anxious physiology, how responsible can I be held for the way that I quiver in the face of frightening situations or tend to crumble under stress? With the evidence for a

* Much more so than in, say, France, where tranquilizer consumption rates are higher, but perhaps even less so than in Japan, where SSRI consumption rates are much lower.

strong genetic basis to psychiatric disorders accumulating, more recent surveys about American attitudes toward reliance on psychiatric medication reveal a dramatic shift of opinion. In 1996, only 38 percent of Americans saw depression as a health problem—versus 62 percent who saw depression as evidence of personal weakness. A decade later, those numbers had more than reversed: 72 percent saw depression as a health problem, and only 28 percent saw it as evidence of personal weakness.

*The serotonin theory of depression is comparable to the masturbatory theory of insanity.*
—DAVID HEALY, IN A 2002 SPEECH AT THE INSTITUTE OF
PSYCHIATRY IN LONDON

The deeper one digs into the entwined histories of anxiety and psychopharmacology, the clearer it becomes that anxiety has a direct and relatively straightforward biological basis. Anxiety, like all mental states, lives in the interstices of our neurons, in the soup of neurotransmitters that bathes our synapses. Relief from anxiety comes from resetting our nervous thermostats by adjusting the composition of that soup. Perhaps, as Peter Kramer mused in *Listening to Prozac*, what ailed Camus's stranger—his anhedonia, his anomie—was merely a disorder of serotonin.

And then one digs a little deeper still and none of that is very clear at all.

Even as advances in neuroscience and molecular genetics have allowed us to get more and more precise in drawing connections between this protein and that brain receptor, or between this neurotransmitter and that emotion, some of the original underpinnings of biological psychiatry have been unraveling.

The exaltation of Prozac a quarter century ago created a cult of serotonin as the "happiness neurotransmitter." But from the start, some studies were failing to find a statistically significant difference between the serotonin levels of depressed and nondepressed people. One early study of a group of depressed patients, reported in *Science* in 1976, found that only half had atypical levels of serotonin—and only half of those had serotonin levels that were lower than average, meaning that only a quarter of the depressed patients could be considered serotonin deficient. In fact, an equally large number had serotonin levels that were *higher* than average. Many subsequent studies have produced results that complicate the notion of a consistent relationship between serotonin deficiency and mental illness.

Evidently, the correlation between serotonin and anxiety or depression is less straightforward than once thought. None other than the father of the serotonin hypothesis of depression, Arvid Carlsson, has announced that psychiatry must relinquish it. In 2002, at a conference in Montreal, he declared that we must "abandon the simplistic hypothesis" that a disordered emotion is the result of "either an abnormally high or abnormally low function of a given neurotransmitter." Not long ago, George Ashcroft, who as a research psychiatrist in Scotland in the 1960s was one of the scientists responsible for promulgating the chemical imbalance theory of mental illness, renounced the theory when further research failed to support it. In 1998, Elliot Valenstein, a neuroscientist at the University of Michigan, devoted a whole book, *Blaming the Brain*, to arguing that "the evidence does not support any of the biochemical theories of mental illness."

"We have hunted for big simple neurochemical explanations for psychological disorders," Kenneth Kendler, the editor in chief of *Psychological Medicine* and a professor of psychiatry at Virginia Commonwealth University, conceded in 2005, "and we have not found them."

What if the reason we haven't been able to pinpoint how Prozac and Celexa work is that, in fact, they don't work? "Psychiatric drugs do more harm than good," says Peter Breggin, the Harvard-trained psychiatrist who is a frequent witness in lawsuits against the drug companies. He's backed up by those studies showing that only about a third of patients get better on antidepressants.

But studies have generally not found the response rates to other forms of treatment to be all that much better. And the psychiatrists and psychopharmacologists on the front lines who consistently say that they have seen these drugs work time after time cannot all have been fatally duped by the drug industry's marketing campaigns. Sometimes the statistical reality of the randomized double-blind controlled studies says one thing while the clinical reality (what psychiatrists and primary care physicians observe in and hear from their patients) says another. What to make of all this?

I am willing to believe that, for the most part anyway, both sides in these debates are arguing in good faith. The promedication advocates—the Gerald Klermans and Frank Bergers and Peter Kramers and Dr. Harvards of the world—have a compassionate Hippocratic desire to reduce their patients' anxious suffering with drugs, and they are sincere in their desire to destigmatize anxiety disorders and clinical depression by classifying them as medical problems. The antimedication crusaders—the Peter Breggins and Dr. Stanfords of the world—are sincere in their desire to protect patients and would-be consumers against what they believe to be the profit-minded rapaciousness of the drug companies and to help patients recover from their anxiety on the strength of their own inner resources, rather than on potentially dependency-inducing medications.

I have sympathy for the more reasonable drug industry critics. I can say based not only on the thousands of studies I've pored over but on my own lived experience that in some ways the critics are clearly right—right about the debilitating side effects, right about dependency and withdrawal problems, right to express skepticism about whether these drugs work as well as they're advertised to, right to worry about what the long-term effects of such a heavily medicated society will be. But in some ways, too, I believe, they are wrong. The drugs, many other studies suggest, *can* work—yes, only some of the time, in some people, with sometimes rotten side effects and bad withdrawal symptoms and dependency problems. And, yes, we don't know what long-term damage they're wreaking on our brains. And, yes, the diagnostic categories have been artificially inflated or distorted by the drug companies and the insurance industry. But I can tell you with hard-won personal authority that there is legitimate underlying emotional distress here, which can be quite debilitating, and which these drugs can mitigate, sometimes only a little, sometimes profoundly.

When I talk to Dr. W. about this, he reports that his own clinical experience comports with what I have been finding in my research: there is enormous variability in how different patients respond to different drugs. He once treated a patient whose parents were Holocaust survivors. This woman was deeply depressed; it was clear to Dr. W. that she had internalized their survivors' guilt, a common phenomenon. He worked with her for months to get her to recognize this in an effort to dispel her unhappiness. Nothing helped; her devastating depression persisted week after week. Then she tried Prozac. After a few weeks on the drug, she came for her appointment one day and said, "I feel great." A few weeks later, she deemed herself cured and terminated treatment. Score one for the SSRIs.

But around that same time, Dr. W. had another patient, a man suffering from obsessive-compulsive disorder and low-grade depression. That patient, too, started on Prozac—and within forty-eight hours was in the hospital with acute suicidal ideation. Score one against the SSRIs.*

Dr. W. has a psychopharmacologist colleague with whom he has collaborated for years. Together they have successfully treated many patients with anxiety disorders. Whenever one of their patients gets better, Dr. W. will say to the psychopharmacologist, "It was clearly your drugs that did it." And he will respond to Dr. W., "No, it was clearly your psychotherapy that did it." And then they laugh and congratulate each other on another successful case. But the truth is, as Dr. W. acknowledges, they don't really know what made a given patient recover.

*It is much cheaper to tranquilize distraught housewives living in isolation in tower-blocks with nowhere for their children to play than to demolish these blocks and to rebuild on a human scale, or even to provide play-groups. The drug industry, the government,*

---

* Another colleague of Dr. W.'s—let's call him Dr. G.—was an eminent psychoanalytically trained psychiatrist who, late in his career, fell into a severe clinical depression. Dr. G. checked himself into Chestnut Lodge, a psychoanalytically oriented psychiatric hospital in Rockville, Maryland. For years, Dr. G. had been a professional opponent of biological psychiatry, arguing that Freudian talk therapy was the best way to treat anxiety and depression. But daily sessions of analytic psychotherapy provided Dr. G. no relief from his suffering. Only when he consented to go on antidepressants did his condition improve. Dr. G.'s depression lifted—but he now found himself confronted with a professional crisis: Was psychoanalytic psychotherapy, the foundation on which he'd built his career, a chimera? He died not long thereafter.

*the pharmacist, the tax-payer, and the doctor all have vested inter-*
*ests in "medicalizing" socially determined stress responses.*
—MALCOLM LADER, "BENZODIAZEPINES:
OPIUM OF THE MASSES" (1978)

*Just because I can explain your depression using terms such as "sero-*
*tonin reuptake inhibition" doesn't mean you don't have a problem*
*with your mother.*
—CARL ELLIOTT, *The Last Physician: Walker Percy and*
*the Moral Life of Medicine* (1999)

Before Donald Klein's imipramine experiments, interpreting the
content of one's anxiety mattered a lot: What does your phobia of
heights or rats or trains *mean*? What is it trying to communicate to
you? Imipramine drained anxiety of much of its philosophical meaning.
Developments in pharmacology were showing anxiety to be merely a
biological symptom, a physiological phenomenon, a mechanical process whose content didn't matter.

Yet for philosophers like Kierkegaard and Sartre, anxiety resolutely
*does* have meaning. For them, as well as for psychotherapists who resist
reducing brain states to biology, anxiety is not something to be avoided
or medicated but rather the truest route to self-discovery, the road to
(in the sixties-inflected version of this idea) self-actualization. Dr. W.
believes this.

"Go into the heart of danger," he likes to say, quoting a Chinese
proverb, "for there you will find safety."

For evolutionary biologists, anxiety is a mental and physiological
state that evolved to keep us safe and alive. Anxiety enhances our vigilance, prepares us to fight or flee. Being anxious can helpfully attune us
to physical threats from the world. Freud believed anxiety attunes us
not just to threats from the world but to threats from within ourselves.
Anxiety, in this view, is a sign that our psyche is trying to tell us something. Medicating away that anxiety instead of listening to what it's
trying to tell us—listening to Prozac, as it were, instead of listening to
our anxiety—might not be what's called for if we want to become our
best selves. Anxiety can be a signal that something needs to change—

that we need to change our lives. Medication risks blocking that signal.*

In *Listening to Prozac*, Peter Kramer engages the work of the novelist Walker Percy, whose writing grapples with how to cope with emotional pain and spiritual longing in the age of biological psychiatry. What gets lost, Percy's stories and essays ask, when anxiety and anomie are medicated away?

Percy was well situated to tackle these issues. The "hereditary taint" (as Freud called it) of melancholy ran thick through the bloodlines of his Southern family. His grandfather, his father, and possibly his mother (who drove herself off a bridge) committed suicide; two of his uncles had nervous breakdowns. Percy's father, LeRoy, a lawyer, medicated his depression with alcohol and sought treatment from specialists, traveling to Baltimore to meet with the leading psychiatrists at Johns Hopkins in 1925. But modern psychopharmacology was not yet available, and in 1929 LeRoy succeeded in his second attempt at killing himself, shooting himself in the head with a 20-gauge shotgun.

Walker's response was to study science. Believing that science would eventually explain everything in the cosmos, including the nature of the melancholy that killed so many members of his family, he decided to become a doctor. His medical training hardened his scientific materialism. "If man can be reduced to the sum of his chemical and biological properties," as one of his biographers characterized Percy's reasoning as a young man, "why worry about ideals, or lack thereof?"

But in 1942, Percy contracted tuberculosis and had to drop out of medical school, repairing to a sanatorium in Saranac Lake, New York, to recover. Streptomycin and—note this—isoniazid and iproniazid were still a few years away from being available as tuberculosis remedies, so the prescribed treatment was rest. While at the sanatorium, he fell into a depression and read intensively—lots of Dostoyevsky and Thomas Mann, as well as Kierkegaard and Thomas Aquinas. Feeling physically and emotionally unwell, he underwent a spiritual crisis in

* Edward Drummond, a psychiatrist in New England, used to regularly prescribe benzodiazepine tranquilizers to his patients in order to reduce their anxiety. Today, he strongly believes tranquilizers are a significant *cause* of chronic anxiety. Taking Xanax or Ativan can temporarily alleviate acute anxiety, Drummond says, but at the cost of allowing us to avoid dealing with whatever issues are causing that anxiety.

which he determined that science could not, after all, solve the problem of human unhappiness. Eventually, influenced especially by the writings of Kierkegaard, he decided to make a leap of faith and become a Catholic.* How differently might Percy's life and philosophy have turned out if he had been treated with iproniazid instead of with a curriculum of European novels and existential philosophy? Iproniazid, we now know, would shortly become the MAOI antidepressant Marsilid—a drug that might quickly have both cured his tuberculosis and dispelled his melancholy. He might well have returned to his medical training and never become a novelist. His opinion of biological psychiatry might have become considerably warmer.†

Percy never lost his respect for the scientific method. But he came to distrust the reductionist worldview that claimed science as the philosophical basis of ethics and of all human knowledge. In fact, he came to believe that the high rates of depression and suicide in modern society were owed in part to the cultural triumph of the scientific worldview, which reduced man to a collection of cells and enzymes, without supplying an alternative repository of meaning.

In 1957, Percy wrote a two-part article for *America*, the weekly Jesuit magazine. By focusing on the biological, he said, psychiatry becomes "unable to account for the predicament of modern man." Guilt, self-consciousness, sadness, shame, anxiety—these were important signals from the world and from our souls. Medicating these signals away as symptoms of organic disease risks alienating us further from ourselves. "Anxiety is," Percy wrote, "under one frame of reference a symptom to be gotten rid of; under the other, it may be a summons to an authentic existence, to be heeded at any cost."‡

* Percy's conversion prompted his best friend, the novelist and Civil War historian Shelby Foote, to tell him, "Yours is a mind in full intellectual retreat."
† Peter Kramer makes observations along these lines in *Listening to Prozac*.
‡ Themes of anxiety, nervous disorders, and existential dread run through much of Percy's writing. In *The Second Coming*, Will Barrett, a retired lawyer, must cope with a strange affliction that descends on him after the death of his wife, a feeling of depression accompanied by a disturbance of his internal gyroscope, a hitch in his golf swing, and what his doctors believe may be petit mal seizures. Will suspects his neurotic ailment is caused by the world's being "farcical." But one doctor suspects "a small hemorrhage or arterial spasm near the brain's limbic system." Is Will's unhappiness a problem of meaning? Or a quirk of biology?

As the novel progresses, Will's malaise deepens; his fainting spells become more frequent, and he becomes filled with religious yearning. Eventually, his family commits him to the hospital, where

Many times in his writing, Percy alludes to Kierkegaard's idea that worse than despair is to be in despair and not realize it—to have anxiety but to have built your life around not experiencing it. "We all know perfectly well that the man who lives out his life as a consumer," he writes in "The Coming Crisis in Psychiatry," "a sexual partner, an

---

a doctor diagnoses him with Hausmann's syndrome, a disease (invented by Percy) whose symptoms include, in addition to seizures, "depression, fugues, certain delusions, sexual dysfunction alternating between impotence and satyriasis, hypertension, and what [Dr. Hausmann] called *wahnsinnige Sehnsucht*"—"inappropriate longing." The disease is caused, Will's doctors explain, by a simple pH imbalance and is treated by the simplest of drugs—a hydrogen ion, a single nucleus of one proton. Will is consigned to a nursing home, where his pH levels can be checked every few hours. "Remarkable, don't you think," says his doctor, "that a few protons, plus or minus, can cause such complicated moods? Lithium, the simplest metal, controls depression. Hydrogen, the simplest atom, controls *wahnsinnige Sehnsucht*." Will, ostensibly cured and living his circumscribed nursing-home existence, marvels: "How odd to be rescued, salvaged, converted by the hydrogen ion! A proton as simple as a billiard ball! Did it all come down to chemistry after all? Had he . . . pounded the sand with his fist in a rage of longing . . . because his pH was 7.6?"

Percy, writing here in the late 1970s, when the "catecholamine hypothesis of affective disorders" and "norepinephrine theory of depression" were taking hold, is mocking the pretensions of biological reductionism. By reducing Will's humanity—not only his depression but his ideas and his longings—to his hydrogen molecules, Percy is essaying a critique of modern psychopharmacology, which in his view pathologizes alienation.

Seven years later, on the eve of Prozac's American launch, Percy published an even blunter critique of biological materialism. *The Thanatos Syndrome* featured a character named Thomas More, a psychiatrist who had appeared in an earlier novel, *Love in the Ruins*. In *The Thanatos Syndrome*, Dr. More, who has recently been released from jail, where he had been serving time for illegally selling the benzodiazepine Dalmane at truck stops, returns to his hometown of Feliciana, Louisiana, to find everyone acting strangely. The women of his town have developed a propensity for presenting themselves rearward for sex. His own wife, in addition to exhibiting this predilection, has developed a computerlike aptitude for playing bridge that has propelled her to success in national tournaments. He notes that anxious women have suddenly lost weight and self-consciousness while gaining boldness, sexual voracity, and emotional insensitivity. They shed "old terrors, worries, rages . . . like last year's snakeskin, and in its place is a mild fond vacancy, a species of unfocused animal good spirits." It turns out that some supercilious civic leaders—including the director of the Quality of Life Division, a federal agency that oversees euthanasia programs—have taken it upon themselves to introduce a chemical called heavy sodium into the water supply, like fluoride, in an effort to "improve" the social welfare. Heavy sodium makes people more placid, less self-conscious, and more content. This is not necessarily a good thing: in losing their anxiety and self-consciousness, the citizens of Feliciana are becoming less human. Dosed with heavy sodium, Feliciana's women are no longer "hurting, they are not worrying the same old bone, but there is something missing, not merely the old terrors, but a sense in each of her—her what? her self?" Dr. More is skeptical, but the heavy sodium advocates try to argue him around to their way of thinking. "Tom, we can see it!" one zealous champion tells him. "In a PETscanner! We can see the glucose metabolism of the limbic system raising all kinds of hell and getting turned off like a switch by the cortex. We can see the locus ceruleus and the hypothalamus kicking in, libido increasing—healthy heterosexual libido—and depression decreasing—we can see it!" Mocking the arrogance of biological psychiatry, Percy means to warn that to medicate away guilt, anxiety, self-consciousness, and melancholy is to medicate away the soul.

'other-directed' executive; who avoids boredom and anxiety by consuming tons of newsprint, miles of film, years of TV time; that such a man has somehow betrayed his destiny as a human being."

If anxiolytic medication mutes our anxiety, deafens us to it—allows us to be in despair without knowing it—does that somehow deaden our souls? Percy would seem to believe that it does.

I believe all of this, as far as it goes. I endorse the philosophical stances of Walker Percy and Søren Kierkegaard. And yet how much credibility do I have? After all, here I am, in my thirtieth year of taking psychiatric medications, with citalopram and alprazolam and possibly still some of last night's clonazepam flowing through my bloodstream as I write this—my serotonergic and GABAnergic systems boosted, my glutamate inhibited—agreeing with Peter Breggin that drugs are toxic and with Walker Percy that they diminish the soul. Am I not a terribly compromised vessel for delivering this argument?

And yet so, one might say, was Percy, who took sleeping medications for his chronic insomnia. (And with good reason: his father's brutal insomnia played a large role in driving him to suicide.) Psychiatric medications—for some people, in some situations, some of the time—work. To deny the schizophrenic chemical remission from his psychotic delusions, or the bipolar patient pharmacological relief from his self-endangering manias and crushing depressions—or, yes, the panic-ravaged and housebound individual some medical defense against anxiety—would be cruel. One can be, I believe, skeptical about the claims of the pharmaceutical industry, concerned about the sociological implications of a population that is so heavily medicated, and attuned to the existential trade-offs involved in taking psychiatric medications without being ideologically in opposition to the judicious use of these drugs.

On the other hand, I know I would do well to heed Percy, as well as modern Big Pharma critics like Edward Drummond and Peter Breggin, because the irony of what I have had to ingest in order to write this section on drugs is obvious. I elevated my Celexa dosage, became dependent on Xanax and Klonopin, and consumed heroic quantities of alcohol to keep my anxiety at bay. After forty years of never smoking a single cigarette (because after getting my grandmother to quit smoking in her sixties, I'd promised to never take up the habit myself), I smoked my first one at forty-one. After having been so afraid of recreational narcotics (perhaps an instance of the evolutionary adaptiveness of my innate caution) that I'd never for forty years taken so much as a puff of marijuana nor indulged in any other nonprescribed drug, I resorted in desperation (after reading Freud's enthusiastic papers about it) to trying cocaine and also amphetamines. Many nights I would begin the evening fueled by caffeine and nicotine, which I needed to propel me out of torpor and hopelessness—only to overshoot into quaking, quivering anxiety. Thoughts racing, hands shaking, I would end the evening taking a Klonopin and then perhaps a Xanax and drinking a scotch (and then another and another) to settle down. This is not healthy.

More constructively, I have tried to draw on Kierkegaard and Percy for backbone and solace, and I have also tried yoga and acupuncture and meditation. I would very much like to unlock my "inner pharmacy"— that repository of healthy, natural hormones and neurotransmitters that can be activated, the antidrug New Age healers say, with meditation and biofeedback and better "inner balance"—but despite my best efforts, I'm fumbling with the keys.

# PART IV

# Nurture Versus Nature

# CHAPTER 8

# Separation Anxiety

‖‖‖‖‖‖‖‖‖‖‖‖‖‖‖‖‖‖‖‖‖‖‖‖‖‖‖‖‖‖‖‖‖‖‖‖‖‖‖‖‖‖‖‖‖‖‖‖‖‖‖‖‖‖‖‖‖‖‖‖‖‖‖‖‖‖‖‖‖‖‖‖‖‖‖‖

*The great source of terror in infancy is solitude.*
    —WILLIAM JAMES, *The Principles of Psychology* (1890)

When did my anxiety begin?

Was it when I, as a toddler, would throw epic tantrums, screaming relentlessly and banging my head on the floor?

The questions that confronted my parents were these: Was my behavior merely a slightly extreme but nonetheless typical manifestation of the terrible twos—or did it lie outside the band of the normal? What is the difference between childhood separation anxiety as a normal developmental stage and separation anxiety as a clinical, or preclinical, condition? Where is the line between temperamental inhibition as a normal personality trait and inhibition as a symptom of pathology—a sign of, say, incipient social anxiety disorder?

On the matter of my tantrums, my mother's Dr. Benjamin Spock manual was not dispositive, so she took me to the pediatrician and described my behavior. "Normal," was his conclusion, and his advice, in keeping with the laissez-faire approach to child rearing of the early 1970s, was to let me "cry it out." So my parents would watch in distress as I lay on the floor, screaming and writhing and smashing my head on the ground, sometimes for hours at a time.

Then what to make of my extreme shyness at age three? When my mother took me to my first day of nursery school, she couldn't (or wouldn't—separation anxiety cuts both ways with children and parents) leave because I clung to her leg and whimpered. Still, separation anxiety in a three-year-old is well within the spectrum of normal developmental behavior, and eventually I was able to stay at school for three mornings a week by myself. And while I clearly exhibited signs of an "inhibited temperament"—shy, introverted, withdrawing from unfamiliar situations (and in a lab I probably would have displayed a hair-trigger startle reflex and high levels of cortisol in my blood)—none of this was necessarily evidence of emerging psychopathology.

Today, it's not hard to see that my early behavioral inhibition was a harbinger of my adult neurosis—but that's only in retrospect, seeing my anxiety as an unfolding narrative.

At age six, when I was in first grade, two new problems set in. The first was an intensified resurgence of my separation anxiety (about which more in a moment). The second was the onset of emetophobia, or the fear of vomiting, my original, most acute, and most persistent specific phobia.

The first presenting symptom for some 85 percent of adults with anxiety disorders, according to data collected by Harvard Medical School researchers, is a specific phobia developed as a child. The same data, based on interviews with a quarter of a million people around the world, has also revealed that early experiences with anxiety tend to compound and metastasize. A child who develops a specific phobia— say, a fear of dogs—at age six is nearly five times more likely than a child without a fear of dogs to develop social phobia in her teenage years; that same child is then 2.2 times more likely than a child without an early dog phobia to develop major depression as an adult.

"Fear disorders," says Ron Kessler, the head of the Harvard study, "have a very strong pattern of comorbidity over time, with the onset of the first disorder strongly predicting the onset of a second, which strongly predicts the onset of a third, and so on." ("Comorbidity" is the medical term for the simultaneous presence of two chronic diseases or conditions in a patient; anxiety and depression are often comorbid, with the presence of one predicting the presence of the other.) "Fear of dogs at age five or ten is important not because fear of dogs impairs the quality of your life," Kessler says. "Fear of dogs is important because it makes you *four times more likely* to end up a 25-year-old, depressed, high-school dropout single mother who is drug dependent."*

---

* The strong predictive association between a childhood fear of dogs and adult dysfunction might mean that a dog phobia somehow *causes* later social phobia, depression, or drug addiction. Or it might

While the nature of the link between childhood phobia and adult psychopathology is not clear, the fact of it is—which is why Kessler insists that early diagnosis and treatment is so important. "If it turns out that dog phobia does somehow cause adult psychopathology, then the successful early treatment of phobic children could reduce later incidence of depression by 30 to 50 percent. Even if it's only by 15 percent, that's significant."

The numbers from Kessler's study would seem to lend a statistical fatedness to the progression of my anxiety: from specific phobia at age six to social phobia starting around age eleven to panic disorder in my late teens to agoraphobia and depression in young adulthood. I have been, in my pathogenesis—the development of my pathology—a textbook case.

*Missing someone who is loved and longed for is the key to an under-standing of anxiety.*
—SIGMUND FREUD, *Inhibitions, Symptoms, and Anxiety* (1926)

When I was six years old, my mother started attending law school at night. My father says this was at his instigation, because he'd seen how my mother's mother had become depressed and alcoholic as a stay-at-home suburban housewife without professional aspirations. My mother, for her part, says that it was over my father's objections that she started studying law. She adds, furthermore, that her mother was neither depressed nor an alcoholic. (My mother is presumably the better

---

mean that a childhood fear of dogs and adult depression tend to be produced by the same kinds of environmental circumstances—an impoverished inner-city childhood, say, where dangerous pit bulls are a real threat and where early trauma or deprivation can lay the neural groundwork for later depression. Or it might mean that a fear of dogs and adult depression or drug addiction are different behavioral markers of a shared genetic underpinning—the same genetic coding that predisposes you to fear dogs might also predispose you to depression. Or, finally, maybe a childhood fear of dogs is actually *the very same thing as* adult panic disorder or depression. That is, it might be that childhood phobia and adult depression are the same disease, unfolding over the life cycle through different developmental stages, each stage expressing different symptoms. As I've noted, specific phobias tend to appear early in life—half of all people who will ever have a phobia in their lives first develop it between the ages of six and sixteen—so perhaps a dog phobia is simply the first symptom of a broader disorder, the way a sore throat can augur the onset of a cold.

authority here, but for what it's worth, my grandmother, whom I loved dearly, often did smell appealingly of gin.)

The powerful recrudescence of my separation anxiety coincided with the beginning of my mother's first year in law school. Each day during first grade, I would be driven home from school in a car pool to be greeted by one of a series of neighborhood babysitters. The babysitters were all very nice. Nevertheless, nearly every evening ended the same way: with me pacing around my bedroom waiting desperately for my father to come home from work. Because nearly every night for about four years—and then intermittently for about ten more years after that—I was convinced that my parents were not coming home, that they had died or abandoned me, and that I had been orphaned, a prospect that was unbearably terrifying to me.

Even though every night provided yet another piece of evidence that my parents always did come home, that never provided reassurance. *This time*, I was always convinced, *they're really not coming back.* So I would pace around my room, and sit on the radiator peering hopefully out the window, and listen desperately for the rumble of my father's Volkswagen. He was supposed to be home by no later than 6:30, so as the clock clicked past 6:10 and 6:15, I would begin suffering my nightly paroxysms of anxiety and despair.

Sitting on the radiator, nose pressed up against the window, I'd try to will him home, mentally picturing his return—the Volkswagen turning off Common Street and onto Clark Street, heading up the hill and left onto Clover, then right onto our street, Blake—and then I'd look down the street and listen for the rumble of the car. And . . . nothing. I'd stare at my bedroom clock, my agitation increasing as the seconds ticked by. Imagine you have just been told that a loved one has died in a car crash. Every night produced the same fifteen to thirty minutes of effectively believing I had been told just that—a half hour of exquisite agony during which I was absolutely, resolutely convinced that my parents had died or that they had abandoned me—even as the babysitter blandly played board games with my sister downstairs. And then finally, usually by six-thirty and almost always by seven, the Volkswagen would come motoring down the street and turn into the driveway, and a burst of relief-borne euphoria would cascade through me: *He's home, he's alive, I haven't been abandoned!*

And then the next night I would go through this all over again.

Weekends when my parents went out together were even worse. My fears of abandonment were not rational. Most of the time I was convinced my parents had died in a car crash. Other times I was sure they had simply decided to leave—either because they didn't love me anymore or because they weren't really my parents after all. (Sometimes I thought they were aliens; sometimes I thought they were robots; at times I was convinced that my sister was an adult midget who had been trained to play the part of a five-year-old girl while her colleagues, my parents, performed whatever experiments they were carrying out before abandoning me.)

My mother, more attuned to my anxiety than my father was, clued into how I would start my worrying well in advance of when they had promised to be home. So when they were leaving and I would ask, ritually, "What's the latest you'll be back?" my mother would announce a time fifteen or twenty minutes later than when she actually estimated they would return. But I cottoned on to this gambit soon enough, so I would factor in that extra time and begin my worried pacing forty-five minutes or an hour before the stated latest time. And my mother, picking up on *this*, moved her stated return time still later, but I would pick up on *that*—and we were off and running on a kind of arms race of stated and assumed return times that eventually rendered anything she said meaningless to me, so my anxiety would rise from the moment they left.

This weekend worrying went on, I hate to say, for a long time. As a young teenager, I sometimes called (or forced my sister to call) parties my parents were at to make sure they were still alive. On several occasions I woke neighbors (and once the minister of the Episcopal church around the block) by banging on their doors late in the evening to tell them that my parents weren't home and that I thought they might be dead and to please call the police. When I was six, this was embarrassing to my parents; when I was thirteen, it was mortifying.

By the time I was twelve, even being alone in my room at night—down the hall from my parents, less than fifteen feet away—had become an ordeal. "Do you *promise* everything will be okay?" I would ask my mother when she tucked me in at night. As my emetophobia got worse, I worried I would wake up vomiting. This made me anxious and queasy at bedtime. Feeling that way one night, I told my mother, "I'm not feeling well. Can you please be especially on the alert tonight?" She said she would be. But then a few nights later, I must have been feeling even more nervous than usual, because I said, "Can you please be especially, especially, *especially* on the alert tonight?" I remember the exact wording because I began asking that question every night. Eventually, this escalated into a ritual, one with a precise and weird sequence to it, that persisted until I went to college.

"Do you *promise* everything will be okay?"

"I promise."

"And will you be especially, especially, especially, especially, *especially* three hundred fifty-seven and a quarter times on the alert?"

"Yes."

Like a psalm, with the stress always on the fifth "especially," every night for years.

My separation anxiety affected nearly every aspect of my life. I was a reasonably coordinated athlete as a preadolescent, but here's how my first baseball practice ended: with me, age six, crying in the dugout, alongside a kindly but puzzled coach. (I never went back.)

Here's how my first beginners' swimming lesson ended: with me, age seven, fearfully, tearfully refusing to get in the pool with the other children.

Here's how my first soccer practice ended: with me, age eight, crying on the sideline with the babysitter who'd brought me, resisting entreaties to join the other boys doing drills.

Here's how I spent my first morning at day camp, when I was five: sobbing by my cubby, crying that I missed my mommy and wanted to go home.

Here's how I spent the first two hours at my first (and only) overnight at camp, when I was seven: sobbing in the corner with a passel of befuddled counselors trying, serially and without success, to console me.

Here's how I spent the drive to college with my parents: sobbing in the backseat, consumed by anxiety and anticipatory homesickness, worried that my parents would not love me after I went away to college—"away," in this case, being a mere three miles from my parents' house.

Why could I never feel assured of my parents' love or protection?

Why were ordinary childhood activities so difficult? What existential reassurance was I seeking in my nightly call-and-response with my mother?

> *The first anxiety is the loss of the object in the form of maternal care;*
> *after infancy and throughout the rest of life loss of love . . . becomes a*
> *new and far more abiding danger and occasion for anxiety.*
> —SIGMUND FREUD, *The Problem of Anxiety* (1926)

In 1905, Sigmund Freud wrote, "Anxiety in children is nothing other than an expression of the fact that they are feeling the loss of the person they love," and so-called separation anxiety has remained a focus of researchers and clinicians ever since. Decades of studies by psychologists, primatologists, anthropologists, endocrinologists, ethologists, and others have revealed again and again, in myriad ways, the paramount significance of the early mother-child bond in determining the lifelong well-being of the child. The nature of that mother-child relationship starts getting established at the moment the infant enters the world—with "the trauma of birth," as the early Freudian psychoanalyst Otto Rank put it—if not earlier than that. Experiences in the womb and during infancy can have profound effects on a child's sense of well-being that last for decades—and that can even, according to recent research, persist into subsequent generations of offspring.

Yet for all his astuteness about the role of early childhood experiences in predicting lifelong emotional health, Freud was for most of his career strangely blind to the ways early parent-child relationships affect the human psyche. This seems to have been especially true in the case of his own psyche.

For many years, Freud endured a debilitating phobia of train travel. The train phobia first presented itself, according to Freud's own account, in 1859, when he was three years old. His father's wool business had collapsed, prompting the Freuds to relocate from Freiberg, a small Austro-Hungarian town (now Příbor, in the Czech Republic), to Vienna. When the family arrived at the train station in Freiberg, young Sigmund was filled with dread: the gas-jet lights that illuminated the station made him think of "souls burning in hell"; he was terrified that the train would depart without him, taking his parents and leaving him behind. For years thereafter, train travel caused him anxiety attacks.

His life was circumscribed by his travel phobia. For a long time, he professed a desire to visit Rome—but was deterred from going by what he came to call his "Rome neurosis." When compelled to travel anywhere by train with his family, he would book himself into a separate compartment from his wife and children because he was ashamed to have them witness his fits of anxiety. He compulsively insisted on getting to railway stations hours in advance of departure because he forever retained the intense fear of being left behind that he first experienced as a three-year-old.

A modern therapist might naturally attribute Freud's travel phobia to his childhood fears of abandonment. Freud himself did not. Rather, as he wrote to his friend Wilhelm Fliess in 1897, he believed that what prompted his anxiety was seeing his mother naked in their train compartment while en route from Freiberg to Vienna. Witnessing this at a time when his "libido toward matrem had awakened" must have aroused him sexually, Freud surmised, and even as a three-year-old he would have known the taboo nature of such incestuous desire and would therefore have repressed it. This act of repression, he theorized, generated anxiety that he neurotically transmuted into a phobia of trains. "You yourself have seen my travel anxiety at its height," he reminds Fliess.

Tellingly, Freud couldn't actually recall seeing his mother nude on the train; he just supposed that he must have and that he'd then pushed the image down into his unconscious. From this (strained) supposition he generalized that all train phobia derives from repressed sexual desire and that those who are "subject to attacks of anxiety on the journey" are actually protecting themselves "against a repetition of the painful experience by a dread of railway-travel."

On the basis of this (quite likely imagined) experience, Freud over the years elaborated his Oedipus complex and concluded that this was "a universal event in early childhood." He would eventually make the Oedipus complex the centerpiece of his psychoanalytic theory of neurosis.*

---

* According to Freud's theory of the Oedipus complex, a boy's greatest anxiety is that his father will castrate him as punishment for sexually desiring his mother, and a girl's greatest anxiety is generated by her envy of the penis she lacks. This was largely derived from Freud's own recollection of, as he wrote Fliess, "being in love with my mother and jealous of my father."

Was my own separation anxiety as a young boy—and are my abiding anxiety and dependency issues as an adult—attributable to my repressed sexual feelings for my mother? It certainly never felt that way to me. Of course, Freud would say that it *wouldn't* have felt that way: his whole point was that such feelings are repressed into the unconscious and transmuted into anxiety about other things—trains or heights or snakes or whatever. And in support of Freud, I confess there is this: The name of my first crush, in fifth grade, was Anne; the name of my first postcollege girlfriend, whom I dated for three years, was Ann; the girl I dated immediately after Ann, for nearly two years, was named Anna; the girl I left Anna for was named Anne; and my wife's name is Sus*ann*a. My mother's name? Anne, of course. I used to joke that dating all those Anns, Annes, and Annas reduced the likelihood I would call any of them by the wrong name—because even the wrong name would sound like the right one. But Freud would say that what I was really in danger of calling them—that what I was seeking with all those Anns, Annes, and Annas—was Mom. Lending still further Oedipal determinism to my romantic relations is the fact that my paternal grandmother was also named Anne—meaning that my father also married a woman with the same name as his mother.

But there is, of course, a less sexual explanation for how Freud's early childhood experiences might have produced his lifelong anxiety and train phobia.

The first years of Freud's life were colored by loss, and by the wavering attention of his mother, Amalia. Shortly after he was born, in 1856, his mother got pregnant again, giving birth to another son, Julius. Less than a year later, Julius died, felled by an intestinal infection. At the time, the Freud family lived in a one-room apartment, so it's likely that Sigmund, as a toddler, witnessed at close hand his brother's death and his parents' reaction to it. Some of Freud's biographers have suggested that Julius's death sent Amalia into a depression that would have made her remote and unavailable to Sigmund. (Depression in mothers of children this age can be highly predictive of anxiety and depression in those children later in life.) With his mother emotionally unavailable, Freud naturally turned to an alternative maternal figure—the nursemaid, a Czech Catholic woman, who cared for him in the early years of his life. But while Sigmund was still a small child, the nursemaid was caught stealing and sent tó jail; he never saw her again.

The logical conclusion here would seem to be that Freud's train phobia was a response to the fear of abandonment produced by this string of childhood losses—the death of his brother, the emotional unavailability of his mother, and the sudden disappearance of his primary caretaker. But Freud remained fixated on proving the rightness of his sexual explanations of anxiety and his Oedipus complex. He would exile from the fold anyone (including Alfred Adler, Carl Jung, and Otto Rank) who dared question their centrality.

> *All anxiety goes back to the anxiety at birth.*
> —OTTO RANK, *The Trauma of Birth* (1924)

Later in his career, as Freud moved from his repressed libido theory of anxiety to his intrapsychic conflict theory, he began to take more account of the way in which parent-child relations—"object relations," in the psychoanalytic argot—related to anxiety.

The final shifts in Freud's theory of anxiety were motivated by his disavowal of a book written by one of his most devoted acolytes. Otto Rank, the secretary of Freud's Vienna Psychoanalytical Society, had intended *The Trauma of Birth*, published in 1924, as a tribute to his mentor. (The book is dedicated to Freud, "the explorer of the unconscious, creator of psychoanalysis.") Rank's basic argument, elaborated at great length, was that birth—both the physical act of passing through the uterine canal and the psychological fact of separation from the mother—is so traumatic that the experience becomes the template for all future experiences of anxiety. In making this claim, Rank was building on what Freud himself had already argued. "The act of birth is the first experience of anxiety, and thus the source and prototype of the affect of anxiety," Freud had written in a footnote to the second edition of *The Interpretation of Dreams* in 1908, and he repeated this notion in a speech he gave to the Vienna Psychoanalytical Society the following year.*

---

* James Strachey, a British psychoanalyst and translator of Freud's works, speculated that Freud's linking of childbirth and anxiety dated to the early 1880s, when, while working as a physician, he heard

But *The Trauma of Birth* was a work of such extravagant interpretive brio that Freud, though no stranger to extravagant interpretive leaps himself, found it alienating and bewildering, and he devoted a full chapter of *The Problem of Anxiety* to renouncing it.* Rank's arguments forced Freud to wrestle once more with the ways in which early life experiences are relevant to anxiety. This led him to revise his own theory of it.

In the final chapter of *The Problem of Anxiety*, Freud gives brief attention to what he called the "biological factor," by which he meant "the protracted helplessness and dependence of the young of the human species."

Freud writes that "the human infant is sent into the world more unfinished than the young [of other species]"—meaning that humans emerge much more highly dependent on their mothers for their survival than do other animals.† The infant seems to be born with an instinctive sense that the mother can provide sustenance and succor, and learns very quickly that whereas the mother's presence equals safety and comfort, her absence equals danger and discomfort. Observing this, Freud concluded that the earliest human anxiety, and thus to some degree the source of all subsequent ones, is a reaction to "the loss of the object"— the "object" being the mother. "This biological factor of helplessness thus brings into being the need to be loved which the human being is destined never to renounce," Freud writes. The first anxiety is about the loss of a mother's care; throughout the balance of life, "loss of love . . . becomes a new and far more abiding danger and occasion for anxiety."

In the final pages of *The Problem of Anxiety*, Freud briefly develops the idea that phobic anxiety in adults is the residue of human evolu-

---

secondhand about a midwife who had declared that there is a lifelong connection between birth and being frightened.

* Rank believed the birth trauma explained everything—from territorial conquests like Alexander the Great's (motivated by an "attempt to gain sole possession of the mother" from the father) to revolutions like the French (an attempt to overthrow "masculine dominance" and return to the mother) to phobia of animals ("a rationalization . . . of the wish—through the desire to be eaten—to get back again into the mother's womb") to the apostles' dedication to Jesus Christ ("they could see in him one who had overcome the birth trauma"). Some of Freud's later disciples would denounce Rank, not without reason, as insane.

† Most animals emerge from the uterus or the egg dependent to some extent on parental care for their survival, but the majority of them are relatively less dependent than humans are at birth.

tionary adaptations: phobias of such things as thunderstorms, animals, strangers, being alone, and being in the dark represent "the atrophied remnants of innate preparedness" against real dangers that existed in the state of nature. For early man and woman, being alone, or in the dark, or bitten by a snake or a lion—and, of course, the separation of an infant from his mother—were legitimate mortal threats. In all of this, Freud was anticipating the work of the biologists and neuroscientists who would study phobias in the decades ahead.*

In other words, Freud was, in his seventies, in an addendum to one of his final works, finally moving closer to what would become the modern scientific understanding of anxiety. But by then it was too late. Freud's followers were off to the races with "Oedipus conflicts" and "penis envy" and "castration anxiety"—and "inferiority complexes" (Adler) and the "collective unconscious" (Jung) and "death instincts" (Melanie Klein) and "oral and anal fixations" (Karl Abraham) and so-called "phantasies" about "the good breast and the bad breast" (Klein again). For a generation, as the field grew in the years leading up to and following the Second World War, the prevailing psychoanalytic view was that anxiety was caused by dammed-up sexual drives.

> *While parents are held to play a major role in causing a child to develop a heightened susceptibility to fear, their behaviour is seen not in terms of moral condemnation but as having been determined by the experiences they themselves had as children.*
> —JOHN BOWLBY, *Separation: Anxiety and Anger* (1973)

The person most responsible for unlocking the mysteries of separation anxiety, and for installing the concept near the center of mod-

---

* Freud did retain for psychoanalysis some interpretative élan by positing that childhood phobias become overly severe or persist into adulthood only when they become the outer fears (of rats or heights or darkness or thunder or open spaces—or mayonnaise, a noted phobia in the literature) onto which inner psychic conflicts get projected. Phobias, in this view, are the outward symbolic representations of the threats that the id (with its wanton impulses that must be repressed) and the superego (with its strict demands of conscience and morality) place on the ego.

ern psychiatry, was the British psychoanalyst John Bowlby, who did as much as anyone to rescue psychoanalysis from its more torturous theoretical overreaching. Trained in the 1930s by Freud's protégé Melanie Klein, Bowlby would go on to develop what has become known as attachment theory—the idea that an individual's anxiety level derives largely from the nature of the relationship with early attachment figures, most commonly the mother.

Bowlby was born in 1907 to an aristocratic surgeon who ministered to the king of England, and he would later claim that his "was a very stable background." But it's not hard to see that Bowlby's clinical and research interests, like Freud's, were informed by his own childhood experiences. Bowlby's mother, according to the psychologist Robert Karen, was "a sharp, hard, self-centered woman who never praised the children and seemed oblivious to their emotional lives"; Bowlby's father, generally absent, was "something of an inflated bully." The Bowlby children ate completely apart from their parents until they were twelve years old—at which age they would be permitted to join their parents only for dessert. By the time Bowlby turned twelve, he'd already been away from home, at boarding school, for four years. Publicly, he would always say his parents had sent him away because they wanted to protect him from the bombs they feared German zeppelins would drop on London during the First World War; in private, however, he confessed that he'd hated boarding school and that he wouldn't send a dog away so young.*

Psychoanalysts before Bowlby were generally uninterested in the day-to-day relationship between parents and children. What interest they did have was focused on breast-feeding, toilet training, and (especially) instances in which a child witnessed his parents having sexual intercourse. Anyone who placed undue emphasis on a child's real experience—as opposed to on his internal fantasies—"was regarded as pitifully naive," Bowlby would later recall. Once, while still a medical student, he watched with dismay as a series of case studies presented at

---

* Robert Karen observes that almost everything Bowlby wrote about the needs of young children throughout his long career "could be seen as an indictment of the type of upbringing to which he'd been subjected."

the British Psychoanalytic Society traced patients' emotional disorders to childhood fantasies. Unable to bear it any longer, he blurted: "But there *is* such a thing as a *bad* mother!" This sort of thing did not endear him to the psychoanalytic establishment.

In 1938, while still in good standing with the mandarins of psychoanalysis, he was assigned as a supervisor a doyenne of the Freudian establishment, Melanie Klein.*

Bowlby would soon come to find himself at odds with many of Klein's views—such as that babies were seething miasmas of hatred, libido, envy, sadism, death instincts, and rage against the restraining superego and that neuroses arose because of conflicts between the "good breast" and the "evil breast." Klein herself was by most accounts an unpleasant person; Bowlby would later describe her as "a frightfully vain old woman who manipulated people." But what most appalled him was Klein's disregard for the actual relationship between mother and child. The first case he treated under Klein's supervision was an anxious, hyperactive young boy. Bowlby noticed right away that the boy's mother was "an extremely anxious, distressed woman, who was wringing her hands, in a very tense, unhappy state." To him it seemed obvious that the mother's emotional problems were contributing to the boy's and that a sensible course of treatment would include counseling for the mother. But Klein forbade Bowlby to talk to the woman. When the mother was eventually admitted to a mental hospital after a nervous breakdown, Klein's response was exasperation at having to find a new patient, since there was no longer anyone who could bring the boy to his appointments. "The fact that this poor woman had had a breakdown was of no clinical interest to [Klein] whatever," Bowlby would say later. "This horrified me, to be quite frank. And from that point onwards my mission in life was to

---

* Born in Vienna and trained as a nursery school teacher, Klein would go on, after the end of an unhappy marriage, to be psychoanalyzed by two of Freud's closest disciples, Sándor Ferenczi and Karl Abraham, and then herself to become one of Freud's most important followers and interpreters. In 1926, Klein, forty-four years old, moved to London, where she was exalted by Ernest Jones, the head of the British Psychoanalytic Society and the most ardent protector of Freud's legacy. Klein's arrival in London—and in particular her disagreements with Freud's daughter Anna Freud over the analysis and treatment of children—precipitated a rift in the society between the Kleinians and the (Anna) Freudians that would last through World War II.

demonstrate that real-life experiences have a very important effect on development."

In 1950, the chief of the mental health section of the World Health Organization, Ronald Hargreaves, commissioned from Bowlby a report on the psychological problems of the thousands of European children rendered homeless by the disruptions of World War II. Bowlby's report, *Maternal Care and Mental Health,* urged governments to recognize that a mother's affection was as important for mental health "as are vitamins and proteins for physical health." Strange as it may seem now, in 1950 there wasn't much recognition of the effects of parenting on psychological development—especially within psychiatry, where treatment still often focused on the processing of inner fantasies.*

Bowlby's early research focused on what happened when children, through the intrusions of war or illness, were separated from their mothers. Psychoanalytic and behaviorist theory held that separations from the mother didn't really matter as long as the child's basic needs (food, shelter) were taken care of. Bowlby found that not to be true at all: when young children were separated from their mothers for any substantial period of time, they tended to display acute distress. Bowlby wondered if the effects of prolonged separation in young childhood could lead to mental illness later on. The children who became clingy upon postseparation reunions, Bowlby suspected, were those who would grow up to be needy, neurotic adults; those who became hostile were those who would eschew intimacy and have difficulty forming deep relationships.

Throughout the 1940s and 1950s, while serving as head of the children's department at a health clinic in London, he began to explore how the early day-to-day relationship between mother and child— what he would come to call the attachment style—affected the child's psychological well-being. He found the same patterns again and again.

---

* In his initial work on hysteria, in the early 1890s, Freud had argued that adult neuroses were the product of *actual* early childhood traumas, mostly of a sexual nature—but by 1897 he had revised his view to support his emerging notion of the Oedipus complex, arguing now that adult neuroses were the result of repressed childhood *fantasies* about having sex with the opposite-sex parent and murdering the same-sex parent. Adults without neuroses were those who had successfully worked through their Oedipus complexes; adults with neuroses were those who hadn't.

When mothers had "secure attachment" relationships with their infants or toddlers—the mothers calm and available but not smothering or overprotective—the children were calmer, more adventurous, happier; they struck a healthy balance between maintaining proximity to their mothers and exploring their environment.

Securely attached children were able to create what Bowlby called "an internal working model" of their mothers' love that they could carry out into the world with them throughout their lives—an internalized feeling of psychological security, a sense of being loved and of being safe in the world. But when the mothers had "insecure" or "ambivalent" attachment relationships with their toddlers—if the mothers were anxious and overprotective or emotionally cold and withdrawn—the children were more anxious and less adventurous; they would cling to their mothers and become very agitated in response to any separation.

Over the next four decades, Bowlby and his colleagues would develop a typology of attachment styles. Secure attachment in childhood predicted low anxiety levels and a healthy degree of intimacy in adult relationships. Ambivalent attachment—which described those children who clung most anxiously, who displayed high levels of physiological arousal in novel situations, and who were much more concerned with monitoring their mothers' whereabouts than in exploring the world—predicted high levels of anxiety in adulthood.* Avoidant attachment in a child—which described those kids who tended to withdraw from their mothers after separations—predicted a dislike of intimacy in adulthood.†

The person most responsible for helping Bowlby develop this tax-

---

* Adult romantic relationships among those with ambivalent attachment styles tend to be characterized by clinginess and fear of abandonment.

† Adult avoidants tend to shun close relationships and are often workaholics; just as they preferred their toys to their mothers as children, they prefer work to family as adults. (Though those with avoidant attachment styles appear to be less anxious than those with ambivalent attachment styles, Bowlby came to believe that was not the case; a series of studies beginning in the 1970s have demonstrated that during separations the avoidant children exhibited increased levels of physiological arousal—elevated heart rates, increased excretion of stress hormones in the bloodstream, and so forth—of the sort associated with anxiety. The child seems to be feeling a physically manifested distress, but he is able—adaptively, or not—to suppress visible expression of the emotion.)

onomy of attachment styles was the psychologist Mary Ainsworth. In 1929, Ainsworth was a freshman at the University of Toronto plagued by feelings of inadequacy. That year she took a course in abnormal psychology from William Blatz, a psychologist whose security theory held that a young child's sense of well-being derives from proximity to his parents and that the child's ability to grow and develop depends on the constancy of his parents' availability. Drawn to Blatz by her own abiding sense of insecurity, Ainsworth went on to do graduate work in psychology, eventually becoming, in 1939, a lecturer in the University of Toronto's psychology department. But when her husband decided to attend graduate school in England, she had to find work in London. A friend directed her to an advertisement in *The Times,* placed by a psychoanalyst seeking research help on a project about the developmental effects of early childhood separation from the mother. Keen to understand her relationship with her own mother, who had been self-absorbed and distant, Ainsworth applied. John Bowlby hired her—and with that began the central partnership in the development of attachment theory.

Ainsworth made two signature contributions to the field. The first was in the mid-1950s, when she accompanied her husband to Kampala, Uganda. In Kampala, Ainsworth identified twenty-eight unweaned babies from local villages and began observing them in their homes, studying attachment behavior in a natural environment. She kept meticulous records, tracking breast-feeding, toilet training, bathing, thumb sucking, sleeping arrangements, expressions of anger and anxiety, and displays of happiness and sadness, and she watched how the mothers interacted with the children. It was the most extensive naturalistic observation of this sort yet conducted.

When Ainsworth first arrived in Uganda, she agreed with both the Freudians and the behaviorists that the emotional attachment babies invested in their mothers was a secondary association with feeding: mothers provided breast milk, which provided comfort, so babies came to associate that feeling of comfort with the mother; there was nothing inherent in the maternal relationship itself, distinct from the provision of food, that was psychologically significant. But as Ainsworth totted up her meticulous observations, she changed her mind. The Freudians and behaviorists were wrong, she concluded, and Bowlby was right. When the babies began to crawl on their own and to explore the world around them, they would repeatedly return to their mothers—either physically or by exchanging a reassuring glance and a smile—and appeared always to remain conscious of exactly where their mothers were. Describing what she observed when the babies first began to crawl, Ainsworth wrote that the mothers seemed to provide the "secure base" from which these excursions can be made without anxiety. The secure base would go on to become a crucial element of Bowlby's attachment theory.

Ainsworth noticed that whereas some babies clung fiercely to their mothers at almost all times and cried inconsolably when separated from them, others seemed indifferent, tolerating separations without evident distress. Did this mean that the uninterested babies loved their mothers less than the clinging babies and were somehow less attached to them? Or, as Ainsworth came to suspect, did this mean that the clinging babies were in fact the *less* securely attached ones?

Ainsworth ultimately deemed seven of the twenty-eight Ugandan babies "insecurely attached." She studied them carefully. What made them so anxious and clingy? For the most part, these insecure babies seemed to receive the same quantity of maternal care as the other ones; the insecure babies had not suffered inordinate or traumatic separations that would explain their anxiety. But as she looked more closely, Ainsworth began to notice things about the mothers of these insecure babies: some of them were "highly anxious," distracted by their own preoccupations—often they had been deserted by their husbands or had disordered family lives. Still, she wasn't able to point conclusively to specific maternal behaviors that generated separation anxiety or insecure attachment.

In 1956, Ainsworth moved to the United States and began teaching at Johns Hopkins. Determined to find out whether attachment behaviors were culturally universal, she decided to contrive an experiment that could test this.

Thus was born what Ainsworth called the strange situation experiment, which has been a staple of child development research ever since. The procedure was simple. A mother and child would be placed in an unfamiliar setting—a room with a lot of toys in it—and the baby would be free to explore. Then, with the mother still present, a stranger would enter the room. How would the baby react? Then the mother would exit the room, leaving the baby with the stranger. How would the baby react to that? Then the mother would come back. How would the baby respond to the reunion? This could be repeated without the stranger—the mother would leave the child alone in the room and then return a while later. All of this would be observed by researchers sitting behind a two-way mirror. Over the ensuing decades, thousands of repetitions of this experiment produced mountains of data.

The experiments yielded some interesting insights. In the first phase of the experiment, the babies would explore the room and look at the toys while checking in frequently with the mothers—suggesting that babies' psychological need to operate from a "secure base" is indeed universal across cultures. But babies varied a lot in how distressed they would become when separated from their mothers: about half of them cried after their mothers left the room, and some babies became severely distressed and had a hard time recovering. When their mothers returned, the distressed babies would both cling to and hit them, displaying both anger and anxiety. Ainsworth labeled these insecure babies "ambivalent" in their attachment. Even more fascinating to Ainsworth than the ambivalent babies were those she would come to label "avoidant" in their attachment style: these babies seemed completely indifferent to their mothers' departures and rarely got perturbed. Superficially, they seemed quite healthy and well adjusted. But Ainsworth would come to believe—and a lot of research would eventually be produced to support the idea—that the independence and equanimity these avoidant babies displayed were in fact the product of a defense mechanism, an emotional numbing designed to cope with maternal rejection.

As Ainsworth collected her data, the most telling fact to emerge was the powerful correlation between a mother's parenting style and her child's general level of anxiety. Mothers of the children identified by researchers as securely attached were quicker to respond to their children's signals of distress, tended to hold and caress their children for longer, and derived more apparent pleasure from doing so than did the mothers of the ambivalent and avoidant children. (The mothers of securely attached children didn't necessarily interact *more* with them, but they interacted *better*, being more affectionate and responsive.) The mothers of the avoidant children displayed the most rejecting behavior; the mothers of the ambivalent children displayed the most anxiety and also by far the most unpredictability in their responses to their children—sometimes they were loving, sometimes rejecting, sometimes distracted. Ainsworth would later write that the predictability of maternal response helped dictate a child's confidence and self-esteem later in life; those mothers who predictably responded to distress signals quickly and warmly had calmer, happier babies who became more confident, independent children.

Over the next few decades, the connection between attachment style and psychological health was repeatedly confirmed by a host of different measures.* A series of influential longitudinal studies begun by researchers at the University of Minnesota in the 1970s have found that securely attached children are happier, more enthusiastic, and more persistent and focused when working on experimental tasks than anxiously attached children are and that they have better impulse control. On almost every test the researchers devised, the securely attached children did better than the ambivalently attached ones: they had higher self-esteem, stronger "ego resiliency," and less anxiety and were more independent; they were even better liked by their teachers. They also displayed greater empathy for others—probably because the insecurely attached children were too self-preoccupied to be much attuned to anyone else. The securely attached children just seemed to enjoy life more: none of the ambivalently attached children smiled, laughed, or expressed delight at the same level as the securely attached children. Many of the ambivalently attached children tended to fall apart when subjected to even minor stress.

These effects persisted for years, even decades. Teenagers who had been securely attached as toddlers had an easy time making friends—but those who had been ambivalently attached were overwhelmed by the anxiety of navigating social groups and often ended up friendless and alienated. Studies found that adults with mothers who had ambivalent attachment styles tended to procrastinate more, to have more difficulty concentrating, to be more easily distracted by concerns about their interpersonal relations, and—perhaps as a result of all this—to have

---

* As a result of Bowlby and Ainsworth's influence, by the 1980s the psychology departments of American universities were thickly populated with attachment scholars.

lower average incomes than those with mothers who had either secure or avoidant attachment styles. Many studies from the last thirty years have suggested that insecure attachment as a baby and young child is highly predictive of emotional difficulty as an adult. A two-year-old girl with an ambivalent attachment to her mother is on average much more likely to become an adult whose romantic relations are plagued by jealousy, doubt, and anxiety; she will always be seeking—likely without success—the secure, stable relationship that she did not have with her mother. The daughter of an anxious and clingy mother will herself likely grow up to be an anxious and clingy mother.

*A mother who, due to adverse experiences during childhood, grows up to be anxiously attached is prone to seek care from her own child and thereby lead the child to become anxious, guilty, and perhaps phobic.*

—JOHN BOWLBY, *A Secure Base* (1988)

During the postwar decades, neurochemical research would demonstrate that when an infant or an adult is stressed, a cascading series of chemical reactions in the brain produces anxiety and emotional distress; returning to a secure base (the mother or a spouse) releases endogenous opiates that make the individual relax and feel safe. Why should this be so?

Back in the 1930s, John Bowlby, already absorbed in his studies of the mother-child bond, discovered the work of the early ethologists. Ethology, the scientific study of animal behavior, suggested that many of the attachment behaviors Bowlby had been observing in humans were universal to all mammals, and it supplied an evolutionary explanation for these behaviors.

The evolutionarily adaptive benefit of early attachment behaviors is not hard to figure: holding offspring near helps a mother to keep them safe until they are fit to fend for themselves. Thus it was possible, Bowlby realized, to explain separation anxiety almost purely in terms of natural selection: there's an adaptive value to psychological mechanisms that encourage mothers and children of whatever species to stick close to one another by producing distress when they are separated; those children most predisposed to cling to their mothers in times of distress may gain a Darwinian advantage over their peers.

In yanking the sources of anxiety out of the realm of fantasy and into the world of ethology, Bowlby alienated his psychoanalytic colleagues.* When Bowlby first presented his emerging research findings in the early 1950s, he was attacked from two sides—by the psychoanalysts and the behaviorists. For the behaviorists, the mother-child bond had no inherent importance; its relevance to separation anxiety derived from the "secondary gains"—the provision of food, the soothing presence of the breast—that the child came to associate with his mother's presence. For the behaviorists, an attachment wouldn't even exist distinct from the specific needs—mainly for food—that the mother met. Bowlby disagreed. Attachment behaviors—and separation anxiety—were biologically hardwired into animals, including humans, independent of the association between food and mothers. In defense of this argument, Bowlby cited Konrad Lorenz's influential 1935 paper "The Companion in the Bird's World," in which Lorenz had revealed that goslings could become attached to geese, and sometimes even to objects, that did *not* feed them.†

Freudians argued that Bowlby's reliance on animal models of behavior gave short shrift to the intrapsychic processes—such as the battle between the id and superego—that set the human mind apart from other animals'. Once, after Bowlby presented an early paper on separation anxiety to the British Psychoanalytic Society, the organization dedicated multiple subsequent sessions to the presentations of all the critics who wanted to "bash" him. There were calls to "excommunicate" him for his apostasy.

---

* Despite what Freud wrote late in his life about the evolutionary roots of phobic anxiety, his conversion to this line of thinking came too late to influence his followers, who were now spreading the gospel of psychoanalysis around the globe. Through at least World War II, psychoanalytic theorists still viewed castration fears, the repressive superego, and the sublimated death instincts as the "cornerstones"—in Bowlby's word—of anxiety. (Bowlby believed that if Freud had had a fuller understanding of Darwin's work, psychoanalysis would have more convincingly incorporated biological principles into its corpus.)

† When Bowlby made a series of presentations, "The Nature of the Child's Tie to His Mother," to his colleagues in the British Psychoanalytic Society in the late 1950s, he tried to place himself and his work squarely within the Freudian tradition. The reactions against him were harsh. "What's the use to psychoanalyze a goose?" the psychoanalyst Hanna Segal would later ask (channeling Ogden Nash), mocking Bowlby's resort to ethology. "An infant can't follow its mother; it isn't a duckling," another analyst said dismissively.

As psychoanalytic criticism of Bowlby swelled, he received a bracing injection of support from the world of animal research when, in 1958, Harry Harlow, the president of the American Psychological Association and a psychologist at the University of Wisconsin, published an article in the *American Psychologist* called "The Nature of Love." In it, Harlow described the series of experiments that are now a fixture of every introductory psychology course.

The experiments came about by happenstance. Many of the rhesus monkeys in Harlow's lab had been contracting fatal diseases, so he took sixty infant monkeys from their mothers a few hours after birth to be raised in a germ-free environment. It worked: the separated monkeys stayed free of disease, and their physical development seemed normal, even though they remained apart from their mothers. But Harlow observed some strange things about their behavior. For one, they clung desperately to the cloth diapers used to line the cage floors. Those monkeys who were placed in mesh cages without diapers seemed to struggle physically to survive; they did better if given a mesh cone covered in terry cloth.

This gave Harlow an idea for how he might test a hypothesis that he, like Bowlby, had always found suspect: the notion, advanced by both the psychoanalysts and the behaviorists, that a baby becomes attached to his mother only because she feeds him. Even granting that the mother's association with food may provide a "secondary-reinforcing agent" (in behaviorist terminology), Harlow didn't think that those early feedings were enough to account for the maternal bond—the love and affection—that persisted for decades afterward. Could his separated rhesus monkeys, Harlow wondered, be used to research the origins of a child's love of his mother? He decided to try.

He separated eight rhesus babies from their mothers and placed each in its own cage, along with two contraptions he called surrogate mothers. One of the two mothers in each cage was made of wire mesh; the other was made of wood but was covered with terry cloth. In four of the cages, a rubber nipple offering milk was affixed to the mesh surrogate; in the other four, the nipple was affixed to the cloth-covered one. If the behaviorist supposition was correct and attachment was merely a by-product of association with feeding, then the infants should always have been drawn to the surrogate possessing the nipple.

That's not what happened. Instead, all eight monkeys bonded with the cloth mother—and spent sixteen to eighteen hours a day clinging to it—*even when the wire mother provided the feeding nipple.* This was a devastating blow to the behaviorist theory of separation anxiety. If the monkeys were more likely to bond with a soft and cuddly object that *didn't* feed them than with a wire one that *did,* hunger relief could not be the operative association in the bonding process, as the behaviorists had assumed.*

By coincidence, Bowlby attended the American Psychological Association meeting in Monterey, California, where Harlow first presented his "Nature of Love" paper. Bowlby immediately recognized the relevance of Harlow's work to his own, and the two men made common cause. In the ensuing years, other studies would replicate Harlow's initial findings. For Bowlby, this was vindication, armor against the assaults of the Freudians and the behaviorists. "Thereafter," Bowlby would later write, "nothing more was heard of the inherent implausibility of our hypotheses; and criticism became more constructive."

The Harlow study would prove even more relevant to Bowlby's ideas about attachment relationships than either man knew at the time. In later years, the monkeys from Harlow's initial study suffered lasting effects from the separation experiment. As intensely as the babies had seemed to bond with the inanimate cloth surrogates, this was clearly no replacement for a real mother-child relationship: for the remainder of their lives, these monkeys had trouble relating to their peers and exhibited abnormal social and sexual behavior. They were abusive, even murderous, parents. When presented with novelty or stress, they became much more anxious, inhibited, and agitated—which is exactly what Bowlby had observed in his studies of humans who had endured separations or difficult relations with their mothers. All of this was haunting confirmation of the long-term effects of early experiences with separation and attachment.†

* There were other parallels between the monkeys' behavior and what Bowlby had observed in human babies. When Harlow introduced a new object into their cages, the monkeys would rush to the cloth mother in agitation and rub up against it until they felt soothed; after they calmed down, they would begin to investigate and play with the object, using the cloth mother as—to invoke the phrase that Bowlby and Ainsworth would soon be using—"a secure base."

† As so often seems to be the case across the history of psychology, Harlow was unable to apply to

In the ensuing decades, hundreds of other animal experiments have supported these findings. Robert Hinde, an ethologist at Cambridge University, showed that when infant monkeys were separated from their mothers for only a few days, they were still more timid than control monkeys when placed in a novel situation five months later. A subsequent paper by Harry Harlow observed that certain key maternal styles—such as "near total acceptance of her infant (the infant can do no wrong)" and close supervision of the infant's "beginning sallies beyond her arm's reach"—were predictive of well-adjusted adult monkeys. Recent studies of rhesus monkeys have found that the "initiation of ventral contact" (or hugging, in plain English) reduces sympathetic nervous system arousal; those monkeys that received fewer hugs from their mothers were less likely to explore the environment—and were more likely to display anxious or depressive behavior as adults. In other words, when monkey mothers coddled and protected their babies, those babies grew up healthy and happy—which is precisely what Mary Ainsworth noted in her meticulous long-term observations of mother-infant interactions among humans.

*Remember when you are tempted to pet your child that mother love is a dangerous instrument.*
—JOHN WATSON, *Psychological Care of Infant and Child* (1928)

The experiments of Harlow, Hinde, and their contemporaries had been fairly crude; the separations they forced were severe, and the situations they set up were not analogous to real life. But in 1984, a group of researchers at Columbia University devised a way of approximating more closely the range of separation and attachment behaviors that occur in the wild.

The idea behind the variable foraging demand (VFD) paradigm, as the researchers called it, was that changing the availability of the mother's food supply could produce changes in the way she interacted with her offspring. (Primatologists already knew this from extensive

---

his own life what he learned from his research on parent-child relationships: he died alcoholic and depressed, estranged from his children.

observations in the wild.) In what have become known as VFD experiments, researchers manipulate how easy or hard it is for monkey mothers to get food: during low-foraging-demand periods, food is left freely exposed in containers strewn around the primates' enclosure; during high-foraging-demand periods, food is more difficult to get, buried in wood chips or hidden under sawdust. In a typical VFD experiment, a two-week period during which food is easy to find is followed by a two-week period when it's hard to find.

Unsurprisingly, the mothers are more stressed, and less available to tend to their offspring, during high-foraging-demand periods than they are during low-foraging-demand periods. Bonnet macaques whose mothers are subjected to extended high-foraging-demand periods have, on average, more social and physical problems growing up. But episodes of *variable* foraging demand turn out to be even more stressful than extended high-foraging-demand periods—that is, the mothers are more stressed when food is unpredictably unavailable than when it is consistently hard to find.

Jeremy Coplan, the director of neuropsychopharmacology at State University of New York Downstate Medical Center, has been conducting VFD experiments for fifteen years. He says that these experiments appear to induce a "functional emotional separation" between mother and infant. The stressed mother becomes "psychologically unavailable" to her infant, in the way that a stressed-out human mother (like Amalia Freud) might become distracted and inattentive to her children.

The shifts in behavior might appear subtle—the stressed mothers still respond to the babies, they just tend to do so more slowly and less effectively than the unstressed mothers—but the effects can be potent. In a series of experiments, Coplan and his colleagues found that the children of the VFD mothers had higher levels of stress hormones in their blood than the children of the non-VFD mothers—an indication that the mother's anxiety was being transmitted to the child. The remarkable thing was the duration of the correlation between the mother's anxiety and the child's stress hormones: when Coplan examined those original VFD children ten years after the first experiment, their levels of stress hormones were still higher than those of a control group. When they were injected with anxiety-provoking chemicals, their responses were hyperreactive compared with other monkeys'.

Evidently, these VFD monkeys had become permanently more anxious: they were less social, more withdrawing, and more likely to display subordinate behavior; they also showed an elevated level of autonomic nervous system activity and a compromised immune response. Here was powerful physiological evidence of what Bowlby had argued half a century earlier: early child-rearing experiences—not just the obviously traumatic ones but subtle ones—have psychological and physical effects on the well-being of the child that persist even into adulthood. Coplan's team concluded that even brief disruptions in the mother-child relationship can alter the development of neural systems "central to the expression of adult anxiety disorders."*

Versions of this experiment repeated many times over the last twenty years have continually found similar results: brief periods of childhood stress, and even mild strains on the mother-child relationship, can have lasting consequences on a primate's neurochemistry.† There's even some evidence that the *grandchildren* of the VFD mothers will have elevated cortisol levels from birth, as the effects of those brief early weeks of mild stress get transmitted from generation to generation.

Researchers have found analogous evidence in the descendants of

---

* Related research on rodents finds the same thing: the amount of licking and grooming that a mother rat lavishes on her pups has a powerful effect on the pups' tolerance for stress throughout their lifetimes—the more licking and grooming a rat receives as a pup, the more resistant to stress it will be as an adult. The rats who receive extra maternal licking display reduced autonomic nervous system activity—a diminished level of activity in the hypothalamic-pituitary-adrenal axis—and a concomitant increased tolerance for stress. These well-licked rats have what researchers call an "augmented 'off' switch" for the stress response; after just four days of extra maternal licking, they show reduced activity in the amygdala. In contrast, those rats that receive low levels of maternal grooming exhibit an exaggerated stress response.

These effects can be adaptive even when they might seem to be negative. Rats who as pups received low levels of grooming and licking are more fearful and quicker to learn to avoid frightening environments—a useful adaptation in a harsh or dangerous environment. In fact, that dangerous environment may, in the state of nature, have been what produced the low levels of licking and grooming in the first place, as the mothers were focused on finding food or avoiding external threats rather than on lavishing affection on their children. Rats who receive high levels of maternal affection are less fearful, more adventurous, and slower to learn to avoid threats—useful adaptations in a stable environment but liabilities in a dangerous one.

† Neuroscience research has begun to find suggestive evidence for the specific mechanisms by which early life stress generates later psychopathology. In essence, elevated levels of stress hormones in childhood correlate with adverse effects on the brain's serotonin and dopamine systems, which are strongly implicated in clinical anxiety and depression. Neuroimaging studies also show that protracted childhood stress tends to have what scientists call neuropathological consequences: for instance, the hippocampus, a part of the brain crucial to creating new memories, shrinks.

trauma victims: the children and even grandchildren of Holocaust survivors exhibit greater psychophysiological evidence of stress and anxious arousal—such as elevated levels of various stress hormones—than do ethnically similar children and grandchildren of cohorts who were not exposed to the Holocaust. When these grandchildren are shown stressful images having nothing directly to do with the Holocaust—for instance, of violence in Somalia—they display more extreme responses, both in behavior and physiology, than do their peers. As John Livingstone, a psychiatrist who specializes in treating trauma victims, told me, "It's as though traumatic experiences get plastered into the tissues of the body and passed along to the next generation."

By now scores of studies support the idea that the quantity and quality of a mother's affection toward her children has a potent effect on the level of anxiety those children will experience later in life. A recent study published in the *Journal of Epidemiology and Community Health* followed 462 babies from their birth in the early 1960s in Providence, Rhode Island, through their midthirties. When the study subjects were infants, researchers observed their interactions with their mothers and rated the mothers' level of affection on a scale ranging from "negative" to "extravagant." (Most mothers—85 percent of them—were rated "warm," or normal.) When psychologists interviewed the study subjects thirty-four years later, those whose mothers had shown affection that was "extravagant" or "caressing" (the second highest level) were less likely to be anxious or to experience psychosomatic symptoms than their peers.

This would seem to suggest that John Bowlby was right—that if you want to raise a well-adjusted, nonanxious child, the best approach is *not* the one prescribed by the ur-behaviorist John Watson, who once averred, "Remember when you are tempted to pet your child that mother love is a dangerous instrument." In his famous 1928 book on child rearing, Watson warned that a mother's affection could have dangerous effects on a child's developing character. "Never hug and kiss them, never let them sit in your lap," he wrote. "If you must, kiss them once on the forehead when they say good night. Shake hands with them in the morning. Give them a pat on the head if they have made an extraordinarily good job of a difficult task." Treat children, in other words, "as though they were young adults." Bowlby, who had himself been treated that way as a boy, believed more or less the opposite: if you want to instill a secure base in the child and a resistance to anxiety and depression, be unstinting in the provision of love and affection.

By 1973, when he published his classic *Separation: Anxiety and Anger,* Bowlby was convinced that almost all forms of clinical anxiety in adults* could be traced to difficult early-childhood experiences with the primary attachment figure—almost always the mother. Recent research continues to add to the substantial pile of evidence supporting this idea. In 2006, new results from the forty-year longitudinal Minnesota Study of Risk and Adaptation from Birth to Adulthood found that infants with insecure attachments were significantly more likely than infants with secure or avoidant attachments to develop anxiety disorders as adolescents. Insecure attachment in infancy leads to fears of abandonment in later childhood and adulthood and gives rise to a coping strategy based on "chronic vigilance"—those babies who anxiously scan the environment to monitor the presence of their erratically available mothers tend to become adults who are forever anxiously scanning the environment for possible threats.

Bowlby's attachment theory has an elegant simplicity and a plausible, easily understood evolutionary basis. If your parents provided a secure base when you were an infant and you were able to internalize it, then you will be more likely to go through life with a sense of safety and psychological security. If your parents failed to provide one, or if they did provide one but it was disrupted by trauma or separation, then you are more likely to endure a life of anxiety and discontent.

> *They fuck you up, your mum and dad.*
> *They may not mean to, but they do.*
> —from PHILIP LARKIN, "THIS BE THE VERSE" (1971)

I recently came across a diary that I kept briefly in the summer of 1981, when I was eleven years old. Some months earlier I had started

---

* The exception was specific animal phobias, which Bowlby, like Freud, believed came from evolutionary adaptations gone awry.

seeing the child psychiatrist who would treat me for twenty-five years, Dr. L., who was trained as a Freudian. At his instigation, I was using the diary to free-associate in pursuit of the root cause of my emotional problems. I must say it was somewhat dispiriting for my early middle-aged self to discover my eleven-year-old self already so anxious and self-absorbed, wondering on the pages of the journal which source bore greater responsibility for my abiding anxiety and discontent: Was it the tyrannical camp counselor who had, when I was six, yelled at me and sent me—alone among the merry campers of the Sachem tribe at the Belmont Day Camp—to the baby pool because I was shaking and crying, afraid to get into the big pool on my own? Or was it the neighbor who had, when I was four, slapped me in the face in front of all my preschool peers when I broke down into hysterical sobs at the birthday party for her son Gilbert because I was scared and wanted my mommy?

Evidently, my narcissism and quest for self-knowledge are endlessly recursive: I dig back into the past at age forty-three, seeking the roots of my anxiety, and discover . . . myself, at age eleven, digging back into the past, seeking the roots of my anxiety.

We had just returned from a family vacation, and much of the diary is an enumeration of the fears and perceived injustices I had endured on the trip.

1. Afraid of motion sickness on plane.
2. 1st night homesickness, can't sleep.
3. Don't like the food.
4. Restaurant: mummy getting mad and not talking to me because I complained about wanting to go home.
5. Afraid of unsanitariness.
6. Afraid thin air in mountains will make me sick.
7. Daddy forcing me to eat. Getting mad when I eat and not letting me eat when I complain . . .
8. Dad not listening to me, and hitting me when I persisted in asking.
9. I was really scared and upset when I saw what may have been throw up on the rug downstairs. I felt awful and scared.

10. On the plane ride back, person throws up. I am terrified. Feel sad, depressed, and scared.

The trip diary ends: "I just feel like hiding my head and being hugged and loved by my mummy and daddy but they are not sympathetic about my fear at all."

Not long ago, I e-mailed my mother a transcription of the diary and then called to ask if she thought that she had expressed more or less affection for my sister and me than her peers had for their children.

"About the same," she said. Then she thought for a moment. "Actually," she said, "I consciously withheld affection."

Stunned, I asked her why.

"I thought it was for your own good," she said, and went on to explain.

Her own mother, my grandmother Elaine Hanford, had expressed ample affection for my mother and her sister and had always been present for them, physically and otherwise. Elaine built her life around catering to her daughters' needs. Every day when my mother came home from elementary school for lunch, Elaine was there to make it for her. My mother felt loved and cared for—and coddled. And so when she started to struggle with panic attacks and agoraphobia and emetophobia and other phobias as a young adult, she wondered if maybe her anxiety was so intense because she had felt *too* loved and safe in her mother's abundant care. So in an effort to spare my sister and me the anxiety she endured, she denied us the outward expressions of unconditional love she had received.

John Watson would have approved.

But while my mother spared us affection, she didn't spare us overprotection. Overprotection and withheld affection can be a pernicious combination. It can lead to feeling not only unloved (because you're not receiving affection) but also incompetent and helpless (because someone's doing everything for you and assuming you can't do it yourself).

My mother physically dressed me until I was nine or ten years old; after that, she picked out my clothes for me every night until I was fifteen. She ran my baths for me until I was in high school. By middle school, many of my friends were taking public transportation to downtown Boston to hang out, staying home alone during school vacations while their parents were at work, and shopping for (and buying and riding) motorbikes. Even if I had been inclined to take the subway to Boston or to ride motorbikes—and, believe me, I wasn't—I wouldn't have been allowed to: I wasn't permitted to walk more than a few streets away from our suburban neighborhood because there were streets my mother deemed too busy to cross and neighborhoods she deemed too dangerous to traverse. (This in a sleepy commuter suburb where a violent crime was a once-in-a-decade affair.) Anytime my sister and I were home while my parents were at work, we had the company of a babysitter. By the time I was a young teenager, this was getting a bit weird—as I realized one day when I discovered, to our mutual discomfort, that the babysitter was my age (thirteen).

My mother did all this out of genuine anxious concern. And I welcomed the excess of solicitude: it kept me swaddled in a comforting dependency. As embarrassing as it was to be told in front of my peers that I couldn't walk downtown with them unless my mother came with us, I didn't want her to relinquish her protective embrace. The dyad between mother and child implicates the behavior of each—I craved overprotection; she offered it. But our relationship deprived me of autonomy or a sense of self-efficacy, and so I was a clingy and dependent elementary school student, and then a clingy and dependent teenager, and I then grew up to be—as my long-suffering wife will tell you—a dependent and anxious adult.

"Adults with agoraphobia are more likely to rate their parents as low on affection and high on overprotection." (That's from a 2008 paper, "Attachment and Psychopathology in Adulthood.") "Adults with agoraphobia report more childhood separation anxiety than a control group." (A 1985 study published in *The American Journal of Psychiatry*.) "[Infants with insecure] attachments [are] significantly more likely than infants with secure attachments to be diagnosed with anxiety disorders." (A 1997 study published in the *Journal of the American Academy of Child and Adolescent Psychiatry*.) "Your parents—anxious, overprotective mother and alcoholic, emotionally absent father—were a classically anxiety-producing combination." (That's from my first psychiatrist, Dr. L., whom I recently tracked down and interviewed, nearly thirty years after my first appointments with him.) And then there's the neurobiological evidence for all this: "Human adults who reported

extremely low-quality relationships with their parents evidenced significantly more release of dopamine in the ventral striatum [a portion
of subcortical material deep in the forebrain] and a higher increase in
salivary cortisol [a stress hormone] during a stressful event than individuals who reported extremely high-quality parental relations. Such
an effect suggests that early human caregiving may similarly affect the
development of systems that underlie stress reactivity." (A 2006 study
published in *Psychological Science*.) As I write this, I have in my office a
stack of articles nearly two feet high reinforcing these and related findings. Which proves that my anxiety is largely a function of my childhood relationship with my mother.

Except, of course, that it doesn't prove anything of the sort.

CHAPTER 9

# Worriers and Warriors:
# The Genetics of Anxiety

*The manner and conditions of mind are transmitted to the children through the seed.*
—HIPPOCRATES (FOURTH CENTURY B.C.)

*Such as the temperature of the father is, such is the son's, and look what disease the father had when he begot him, his son will have after him. I need not therefore make any doubt of melancholy, but that it is an hereditary disease.*
—ROBERT BURTON, *The Anatomy of Melancholy* (1621)

*Daddy, I'm nervous.*
—MY DAUGHTER, AT AGE EIGHT

I could blithely blame my anxiety on the behavior of my parents—my father's drinking, my mother's overprotectiveness and phobias, their unhappy marriage and eventual divorce—were it not for, among other reasons, this inconvenient fact: my children, now nine and six, have recently developed anxiety that, to a distressing degree, parallels my own.

My daughter, Maren, has always had, like me, an inhibited temperament—shy and withdrawing in unfamiliar situations, risk averse in her approach to the world, and highly reactive to stress or any kind of novelty. More strikingly, when she was in first grade she developed an obsessive phobia of vomiting. When a classmate of hers threw up during math, she couldn't get the image out of her head. "I can't stop thinking bad thoughts," she said, and my heart broke.

Have I—despite my decades of therapy, my hard-won personal and scholarly knowledge of anxiety, my wife's and my informed efforts at inoculating our children against it—bequeathed to Maren my disorder, as my mother bequeathed it to me?

Unlike my mother, I never revealed my emetophobia to my daughter before she developed it herself. I have tried not to betray evidence of my anxiety to Maren, knowing that to do so might be to pass it on to her through what psychologists call modeling behavior. My wife is not an anxious person; she has none of the nervously overprotective tendencies that, expressed for so many years by my mother, I had thought reduced my sister and me to such states of neurotic dependency. And we are both, my wife and I, loving and nurturing, and we strive to be emotionally present for our kids in ways that my parents sometimes were not.

Or so we like to think.

And yet here is my daughter exhibiting symptoms very similar to mine and at almost the same age I first developed them. Somehow, despite our best efforts at providing emotional prophylaxis, Maren seems to have inherited my nervous temperament—and, remarkably, *the exact same phobic preoccupation.* Which happens to be, moreover, a preoccupation I share with my mother.

Is it possible, my wife asks, that so idiosyncratic a phobia can be genetically transmitted?

One would think not. And yet we have here the evidence of three generations on my mother's side with the same phobia. And unless Maren has picked up on subtle or unconscious cues (which, I concede, is possible), she cannot have "learned" the phobia from me through some kind of behavioral conditioning, as I thought I might have learned mine from my mother.

While observers since Hippocrates have noted that temperaments are heritable, and while the modern field of behavioral genetics is revealing with increasing precision—down to the individual nucleotide—the relationship between the molecules we inherit and the emotions we're predisposed to, no one has yet identified a gene, or even a set of genes, for emetophobia. Nor, for that matter, has anyone reduced anxiety—or any behavioral trait—to pure genetics. But in recent years, thousands of studies have pointed to various genetic bases for clinical anxiety in its different forms.

Some of the earliest research on the genetics of anxiety studied twins. In the most basic studies, researchers compared rates of anxiety disorder between sets of identical and fraternal twins. If, say, panic disorder were completely genetic, that would mean in a set of identical twins—genetic copies—you would never find just one with the disease. But that's not the case. When one twin has the disorder, the other is much more likely than a randomly selected person from the population to have the disease—but not *guaranteed* to have it. This suggests that while panic disorder—like height or eye color—has a powerful genetic component, the disease is not completely genetic.

In 2001, Kenneth Kendler, a psychiatrist at Virginia Commonwealth University, compared the rates of phobic disorders among twelve hundred sets of fraternal and identical twins, determining that genes account for about 30 percent of the individual differences in vulnerability to anxiety disorders. Subsequent studies have tended to roughly support Kendler's findings. Meta-analyses of genetic studies conclude that if you don't have any close relatives with generalized anxiety disorder, your odds of having it yourself are less than one in twenty-five—but having a single close relative with the disorder boosts your odds of developing it to one in five.

Wait, you might object, this doesn't prove a genetic basis for anxiety. Couldn't the high probability of the same mental illness occurring in members of the same family be a result of their sharing what researchers call a pathogenic environment, one that is predictive of anxiety or depression? If twins share a traumatic upbringing, mightn't that engender in both of them a higher susceptibility to mental illness?

Certainly. While genes may predispose a person to schizophrenia or alcoholism or anxiety, there is almost always some environmental contribution to the disease. Still, the number of studies on the heritability of anxiety is climbing into the tens of thousands, and the overwhelming conclusion of almost all of them is that your susceptibility to anxiety—both as a temperamental tendency and as a clinical disorder—is strongly determined by your genes.

This would not have surprised Hippocrates or Robert Burton or Charles Darwin or any number of observers who long predate the era of molecular genetics. Once a family tree has one or two individuals with anxiety disorder or depression, then you will likely find the rest of the tree stippled with anxiety and depression. Researchers call this phenomenon "familial aggregation due to genetic risk."*

Does "familial aggregation" mean that my daughter, like my mother and me, is biologically predestined to be anxious, perhaps genetically fated to develop nervous illness? On my mother's side of the family alone, there is, in addition to my mother and my daughter and me, my son, Nathaniel, now six, who has separation anxiety that threatens to become as bad as mine ever was; my sister, who has struggled since age twelve with anxiety and has tried as many drug treatments as I have; another blood relative who has similarly wrestled his whole life with anxiety and depression and a nervous stomach and who has been medicated off and on for decades; that relative's older brother, who was diagnosed with clinical depression in the early 1980s, at the tender age of eight, and who vomited from anxiety before school nearly every day for a year; and my mother's father, ninety-two years old, who today takes a variety of antianxiety and antidepressant medications. Looking further back into my ancestry, I have discovered that my mother's father's grandfather was painfully reserved and hated dealing with people, dropping out of Cornell to start a "quiet life" cultivating fruit orchards ("The outdoor life saved him," his daughter-in-law would say later), and that my grandfather's aunt suffered from severe anxiety, depression, and a famously nervous stomach.

And then there is my grandfather's father Chester Hanford, whose anxiety and depression were severe enough that he had to be institutionalized multiple times, leaving him frequently incapacitated during the last thirty years of his life.

---

* In 2011, Giovanni Salum, a Brazilian psychiatrist, released the results of one of the largest-scale studies of the heritability of anxiety disorders ever conducted. Surveying data on ten thousand people, Salum found that a child who has no relatives with an anxiety disorder has only a one-in-ten chance of developing one himself. If that same child has one relative with an anxiety disorder in his family, his odds of developing an anxiety disorder rise to three in ten. And if a large majority of members have an anxiety disorder, the child's odds rise to *eight* in ten.

*I suspect that most, but not all, of the large number of human tem-
peraments are the result of genetic factors that contribute to the pro-
files of molecules and receptor densities that influence brain function.*
    —JEROME KAGAN, *What Is Emotion?* (2007)

*It frequently happens that hysteria in the mother frequently begets
hysteria in the son.*
    —JEAN-MARTIN CHARCOT, *Lectures on Diseases of the
    Nervous System,* VOLUME 3 (1885)

Jerome Kagan, a developmental psychologist at Harvard, has spent
sixty years studying the effect of heredity on human personality. In longitudinal studies extending across decades, he has consistently found
that about 10 to 20 percent of infants are, from the time they are a few
weeks old, demonstrably more timid than other infants. These infants
are fussier, sleep more poorly, and have faster heart rates, more muscle
tension, and higher levels of cortisol in their blood and of norepinephrine in their urine. They exhibit faster startle reflexes (meaning that in
response to a sudden noise they twitch nanoseconds faster and show
greater increases in pupil dilation). In fMRI scans, the fear circuits of
their brains—namely, the amygdala and the anterior cingulate—show
higher-than-normal neuronal activity. These physiological measures
remain consistently higher for these children than for other children
throughout their lifetimes. Whether they are tested at six weeks, seven
years, fourteen years, twenty-one years, or older, they continue to have
higher heart rates, faster startle reflexes, and more stress hormones than
their low-reactive peers.

Kagan has labeled as inhibited the temperament of these children
with high-reactive physiology. "We believe that most of the children
we refer to as 'inhibited' belong to a qualitatively distinct category of
infants who were born with a lower threshold for arousal to unexpected
changes in the environment or novel events," Kagan says. "For these
children, the prepared reaction to novelty that is characteristic of all
children is exaggerated."

A few years ago, Kagan and his colleagues took brain scans of a group of twenty-one-year-olds they had been studying for nineteen years. In 1984, when Kagan had first observed these subjects as two-year-olds, he had described thirteen of them as inhibited and the other nine as uninhibited. Two decades later, when Kagan showed pictures of unfamiliar faces to all twenty-two test subjects, now young adults, the thirteen who had been identified as inhibited displayed significantly more amygdala response than the nine who had been identified as uninhibited. Kagan believes that your genes determine the reactivity of your amygdala—and we know from other research that the reactivity of your amygdala, in turn, helps determine how you will react to stress.

Those infants or toddlers identified as inhibited are more likely to become shy, nervous adolescents—and then shy, nervous adults—than their peers. They are much more likely to develop clinical anxiety or depression as teens or adults than their less physiologically reactive peers. Even those high-reactive babies who don't grow up to get officially diagnosed with anxiety disorders tend to remain more nervous, on average, than their peers.

In believing that temperament is innate and largely fixed from birth, Kagan falls squarely in the intellectual tradition that stretches back to Hippocrates, who in the fourth century B.C. argued that personality and mental health derived from the relative balance of the four humors in the body: blood, phlegm, black bile, and yellow bile. According to Hippocrates, as noted in chapter 1, a person's relative humoral balance accounted for his temperament: whereas someone with relatively more blood might have a lively or "sanguine" temperament and be given to hot-blooded explosions of temper, someone with relatively more black bile might have a melancholic temperament. Hippocrates's theory of humoral balance directly anticipates, metaphorically anyway, the serotonin hypothesis of depression and other modern theories of the relation between chemical imbalances in the brain and mental health. For instance, Hippocrates attributed what we would by the mid-twentieth century be calling neurotic depression—and what we would today call generalized anxiety disorder (*DSM* code 300.02)—to an excess of black bile (*melain chole*). As Hippocrates described it, this condition was characterized by both physical symptoms ("pains at the abdomen, breathlessness . . . frequent burps") and emotional ones ("anxiety, restlessness, dread . . . fear, sadness, fretfulness" often accompanied and usually caused by "meditations and worries exaggerated in fancy").

Hippocrates may have had the wrong explanatory metaphor, but modern science is proving him to have been basically right about temperament's fixity and biological basis. Kagan, now in his eighties, is semiretired, but four major longitudinal studies started by him or by a former protégé, Nathan Fox at the University of Maryland, are still under way. All four are reaching conclusions that support Kagan's long-held theory that the anxious temperament is an innate, genetically determined phenomenon that characterizes a relatively fixed percentage of the population.* His studies have repeatedly found that those 15 to 20 percent of infants who react strongly to strangers or novel situations are much more likely to grow up to develop anxiety disorders than their less physiologically reactive peers. If you are born highly reactive and inhibited, you tend to stay highly reactive and inhibited. In decades of longitudinal studies, only rarely has Kagan seen anyone move from one temperamental category to another.

All of which would seem to complicate, if not undermine, what I said about attachment theory in the previous chapter. Indeed, Kagan believes John Bowlby, Mary Ainsworth, and their colleagues were largely wrong about how anxiety gets transmitted from one generation to the next. In Kagan's view, insecure attachment style per se does not produce an anxious child. Rather—and I'm oversimplifying a little—*genes* produce a mother with an anxious temperament; that temperament, in turn, leads her to demonstrate an attachment style that psychologists observe to be insecure. The mother then transmits this anxiety to her children—not primarily, as Bowlby and Ainsworth would have it, through her nervous parenting style (though, to be sure, that may intensify the transmission), but rather by the passing on of her anxious genes. Which, if true, would make it harder to break the transmission of anxiety from generation to generation through changes

---

* This squares with what studies have found about the relatively fixed percentage of soldiers who are especially prone to break down when exposed to combat stress.

in parenting behavior—and which might explain why, despite our best efforts, my wife and I have been unable to prevent our children from developing signs of incipient anxiety disorders.

John Bowlby cited animal studies to buttress his theory of attachment. But Jerome Kagan can also cite animal studies to rebut Bowlby and support his own theory of temperament. In the 1960s, researchers at the Maudsley Hospital in London bred what became known as the Maudsley strain of reactive rats, which responded to stress with pronounced anxious behavior. These breeding experiments were performed without the benefit of modern genomics. Researchers simply observed rat behavior, noted the "emotionally reactive" ones (mainly by measuring their defecation rates when placed in open spaces), and mated them with one another—and in so doing managed to produce this highly anxious strain. (By the same selective breeding technique, they also produced a strain of nonreactive rats, which responded *less* fearfully than average to open spaces and other stressors.) This seemed to be evidence of a potent hereditary component to anxiety in rat populations.

Modern experimental techniques have advanced beyond selective breeding. Scientists are now able to chemically switch different mouse genes on or off, allowing researchers to observe how the genes affect behavior. By deactivating certain genes, researchers have created mice that, for instance, no longer experience anxiety, and in fact cannot recognize real danger, because their amygdalae have stopped working. Researchers, churning out hundreds of studies of this sort a year, have so far identified at least seventeen genes that seem to affect various parts of the fear neurocircuitry in mice.

For instance, Eric Kandel, a Nobel Prize–winning neuroscientist at Columbia, has discovered one gene (known as *Grp*) that seems to encode a mouse's ability to acquire new phobias through fear conditioning and another gene (known as stathmin) that regulates innate levels of physiological anxiety. Mice whose *Grp* gene has been switched off cannot learn to associate a neutral tone with an electric shock the way normal mice do. Mice whose stathmin gene has been switched off become daredevils: instead of instinctively cowering on the edge of open spaces like normal mice, they venture boldly into exposed areas.

Evolution has conserved many genes, so humans and rodents share many of the same ones. Consider *RGS2,* a gene that in both mice and humans seems to regulate the expression of a protein that modulates serotonin and norepinephrine receptors in the brain. After it was noted that mice without the *RGS2* gene displayed markedly anxious behavior and "elevated sympathetic tone" (meaning their bodies were on constant low-grade fight-or-flight alert), a series of studies on humans by Jordan Smoller and his team at Harvard Medical School found a relation between certain variations of the *RGS2* gene and human shyness. In one study of children from 119 families, the kids who displayed characteristics of a "behaviorally inhibited" temperament tended to have the same variant of the *RGS2* gene. Another study, of 744 college students, found that students with the "shy" variant of the gene were more likely to describe themselves as introverted. A third study revealed how the gene exerts its effect on the brain: when fifty-five young adults were placed in a brain scanner and shown pictures of angry or fearful faces, those with the relevant *RGS2* variation were more likely to show increased "neuronal firing" in the amygdala and the insula, a part of the cortex associated not only with limbic system expressions of fear but also with "interoceptive awareness," that explicit consciousness of inner bodily functions that can give rise to "anxiety sensitivity." A fourth study, of 607 people who lived through the severe Florida hurricane season of 2004, found that those who had the relevant variant of the *RGS2* gene were more likely to have developed an anxiety disorder in the aftermath of the hurricanes.

None of these studies prove that simply having a certain variant of the *RGS2* gene *causes* anxiety disorder. But they do suggest that the *RGS2* gene affects the functioning of fear systems in the insula and the amygdala—and that individuals who have the "shy" variant of the gene are more likely to have hyperactive amygdalae and to experience higher levels of autonomic arousal in social situations and therefore to be shy or introverted. (Shyness and introversion are both predisposing factors in the anxiety disorders.)

Lauren McGrath, a researcher in the Psychiatric and Neurodevelopmental Genetics Unit at Massachusetts General Hospital, studied 134 babies over nearly twenty years. When the babies were four months old, McGrath's team divided them into groups of (using Kagan's terms) "high-reactives" and "low-reactives." At four months, the high-reactives cried and moved more in response to the movement of a mobile than the low-reactives did; at fourteen and twenty-one months, those same high-reactives still tended to demonstrate fearful reactions in response to novel situations. Eighteen years later, McGrath's team tracked down the original study subjects and looked at the structure and reactivity of their amygdalae. Sure enough, the babies identified as high-reactives at four months had larger, more hyperactive amygdalae at age eighteen than the low-reactives did—yet more evidence that the amygdala's response to novelty is a strong predictor of temperamental anxiety level. In a final wrinkle, McGrath's team, using new genetic coding techniques, discovered that high amygdala reactivity at age eighteen was highly correlated with a particular variation on a specific gene known as *RTN4*. McGrath and her colleagues hypothesize that the *RTN4* gene helps determine how hyperreactive your amygdala will be, which in turn helps determine whether your temperament will be high-reactive or low-reactive—which in turn helps determine your vulnerability to clinical anxiety.

This alphabet soup of genetic studies—hundreds if not thousands of which are being conducted at any given time—can seem inanely reductionist. A few years ago, I read a *New York Times* article about studies attributing a correlation between certain variants of two human genes—*AVPR1a* and *SLC6A4*—and a "talent for creative dance performance."* The good news, I suppose, is that if this changes how we think about character and fate, it might also change how we think about courage and cowardice, shame and disease, stigma and mental illness. If extreme anxiety is owed to genetic anomalies, should it be any more shameful than multiple sclerosis or cystic fibrosis or black hair, all diseases or traits encoded by the genes?

Fifty years ago, we could plausibly blame the behavior of our mothers for all manner of neuroses and unhappiness and bad behavior. Today,

---

* To be sure, genetic researchers grant that anxious emotion, or a talent for dancing, must have multiple genetic (and environmental) causes. But the trend toward reducing emotions to their underlying neurochemical correlates, and to the genes that underwrote them, can seem inexorable.

we can perhaps still blame our mothers—but it may be more plausible to blame the *genes* they conferred upon us than the *behaviors* they displayed or the emotional wounds they inflicted.

> *For that which is but a flea-biting to one, causeth insufferable torment to another.*
> —ROBERT BURTON, *The Anatomy of Melancholy* (1621)

A number of private companies will, in exchange for a drop of your saliva and a hefty fee, sequence part of your genome in order to provide information about your relative risk factor for various diseases. A few years ago, I paid a few hundred dollars to a company called 23andMe, and so I now know that my genes have left me with, all things being equal, a modestly higher than average likelihood of getting gallstones, a modestly lower than average likelihood of developing type 2 diabetes or skin cancer, and a roughly average likelihood of suffering a heart attack or developing prostate cancer. I also learned that I am, according to my genotype, a "fast caffeine metabolizer," that I am at "typical" risk for heroin addiction and alcohol abuse, and that I have fast-twitch sprinter's muscles. (I also learned that I have "wet" earwax.)

I was hoping to find out which variants I have of two particular genes, each of which has at different times been dubbed the "Woody Allen gene." The first gene, known as *COMT*, is found on chromosome 22 and encodes the production of an enzyme (catechol-O-methyltransferase) that breaks down dopamine in the prefrontal cortex of the brain. The second gene, *SLC6A4*, also known as the *SERT* gene, is found on chromosome 17 and encodes for how efficiently serotonin gets ferried across the synapses of your neurons.

The *COMT* gene has three variants.* One (known as val/val) encodes for a high level of the enzyme that breaks down dopamine very effectively; the others (val/met and met/met) encode for lower levels that break down less dopamine and leave more of it in the synapses.

---

* Let me stipulate here that I am not a genetic scientist, and that I am oversimplifying a vast and complex body of research. For an easy-to-understand book about psychiatric genetics by an expert, I recommend *The Other Side of Normal: How Biology Is Providing the Clues to Unlock the Secrets of Normal and Abnormal Behavior* by Jordan Smoller.

Recent studies have found that people with the met/met version tend to have a harder time regulating their emotional arousal. The excess levels of dopamine, researchers speculate, are linked to "negative emotionality" and to an "inflexible attentional focus" that leaves people unable to tear themselves away from obsessional preoccupation with frightening stimuli—traits that are, in turn, linked to depression, neuroticism, and, especially, anxiety. People with the met/met variant show an inability to relax after exposure to apparently threatening stimuli, even when those stimuli are revealed to be not dangerous after all. In contrast, the val/val variant was associated with *less* intense experiencing of negative emotions, a *less* reactive startle reflex, and *less* behavioral inhibition.*

David Goldman, the chief of human neurogenetics at the National Institutes of Health, has labeled *COMT* the "worrier-warrior gene." Those who possess the val/val version, according to Goldman, are "warriors": under stressful conditions, this gene variant gives them a beneficial increase in the extracellular brain level of dopamine, which presumably makes them less anxious and less susceptible to pain and allows them to focus better. The extra dopamine also gives them "better working memory" while under stress. I would imagine that, for example, the NFL quarterback Tom Brady—who is legendary for his ability to make quick, smart decisions while under tremendous pressure (throwing the ball accurately to the correct receiver even as thousands of pounds of linebacker are bearing down on him at high speed and millions of people are watching and judging him)—has the warrior variant. But there are situations in which the worrier version, which 25 percent

---

* Many studies have supported the connection between the met/met variant of the *COMT* gene and unusually high levels of anxiety—though, interestingly, mainly in women. One study, conducted by investigators at the National Institute on Alcohol Abuse and Alcoholism, looked at two disparate groups of women—Caucasians from suburban Maryland and Plains Indians from rural Oklahoma—and found that in both populations women with the met/met variant reported much higher levels of anxiety than did women with the other variants. (The met/met variant also correlated with having only a quarter to a third of the typical quantity of the catechol-O-methyltranferase enzyme in the brain.) When women with the met/met variant were placed in an EEG machine, they exhibited a "low-voltage alpha brain-wave pattern," which has been found to be associated with both anxiety disorders and alcoholism. In short, the study revealed a connection not only between the gene and enzyme levels, and between enzyme levels and brain activity, but also between brain activity and subjectively experienced levels of anxiety. Another study, conducted among both German and American populations in 2009, found that people with the met/met version of the gene exhibited higher-than-average physiological startle responses when shown a series of unpleasant pictures and were, according to standard personality tests, higher in general anxiety.

of the world population has, confers evolutionary advantages. Studies have shown that carriers of the met/met version perform better on cognitive tasks requiring memory and attention when *not* under severe stress; this suggests the worriers may be better at evaluating complex environments and therefore at avoiding danger. Each version confers a different adaptive strategy: those with the worrier variant are good at staying out of danger; those with the warrior variant act effectively once they're in danger.*

The *SERT* gene also has three variants: short/short, short/long, and long/long (these get abbreviated to s/s, s/l, and l/l). Starting in the mid-1990s, many studies have found that people with one or more short *SERT* allele (that is, those with the s/s or s/l variant of the gene) tend to process serotonin less efficiently than those with only long alleles— and that when carriers of short-allele polymorphisms are shown fear-producing images, they display more amygdala activity than carriers of the l/l pairing. This correlation between a specific gene and activity in the amygdala, researchers hypothesize, helps account for the higher rates of anxiety disorder and depression that other studies were finding in people with the s/s version.

In the absence of life stress, people with the s/s and s/l genotypes weren't any likelier to become depressed than people with the l/l genotypes. When stressful situations arose, however—whether in the form of financial, employment, health, or relationship problems—those individuals with short versions were more likely to become depressed or suicidal. Put the other way around, those people with the l/l vari-

---

* These different evolutionary strategies seem to apply even in fish. Lee Dugatkin is a professor of biology at the University of Louisville who studies guppy behavior. Some guppies are bold; some are timid. Bold male guppies, Dugatkin observes, are more likely than timid male guppies to attract females to mate with. But the bold guppies, in their brazenness, are also more likely to swim near predators and get eaten. The timid guppies thus tend to live longer—and therefore to prolong the time during which they have opportunities to mate. Both types of guppies, the bold and the timid, represent a viable evolutionary strategy: Be bold and mate more but be more likely to die young—or be timid, mate less, and be more likely to live longer. There's an adaptive value to being a bold guppy—but there's also an adaptive value to being a timid one. It's not hard to see the same evolutionary strategies at work among human populations. Some people live boldly, mate promiscuously, take risks, and tend to die young (think of the bold and tragic Kennedy clan); others live timidly, mate less, are risk averse, and tend to be less likely to die prematurely in accidents.

ant seemed partly insulated against depression and anxiety even when under stress.*

Kerry Ressler, a psychiatrist at Emory University, has produced similar findings about other genes. Ressler has discovered that whereas some genotypes seem to confer increased vulnerability to certain forms of anxiety disorder, other genotypes seem to confer *almost complete resistance to them.* For instance, a gene called *CRHR1* encodes the structure of brain receptors for corticotropin-releasing hormone (CRH), which is released during activation of the fight-or-flight response or during times of prolonged stress. To oversimplify a little, there are three variants of this gene: C/C, C/T, and T/T (the letters refer to the sequence of proteins that encode the amino acids that make up your DNA). Looking at a group of five hundred people from inner-city Atlanta who had suffered high rates of poverty, trauma, and child abuse, Ressler found that the variant of the *CRHR1* gene you inherited strongly predicted the likelihood of your developing depression as an adult if you were abused as a child. One homozygous version of the gene (C/C) was associated with child abuse victims being *very likely* to develop clinical depression in adulthood; the heterozygous version of the gene (C/T) was associated with a *moderate likelihood* of depression in adulthood; and, most fascinatingly, the other homozygous version of the gene (T/T) was *not associated at all* with depression in adulthood—the T/T version of the gene seems to confer on these child abuse victims almost complete immunity to depression. Child abuse seemed to have had *no long-term psychological effect at all* on those with this version of the gene.

Ressler has also discovered similar findings in studies on the gene responsible for coding the feedback sensitivity of glucocorticoid receptors. Variations in this gene, known as *FKBP5,* seem to have a powerful effect on the susceptibility of children to post-traumatic stress disorder.

---

* Not every study has borne out the initial hypothesis that having a short version of the *SERT* allele makes you more susceptible to anxiety or depression. For instance, while epidemiological studies consistently find that rates of clinical anxiety and depression are *lower* in Asia than in Europe and North America, genetic testing has found that the prevalence of the s/s *SERT* allele is markedly *higher* among East Asian populations than among Western ones—which raises intriguing questions about how culture and social structure interact with genetics to affect the rates and intensity of anxiety among individuals in different societies.

Whereas one variant of the *FKBP5* gene seems to be associated with high rates of PTSD, another variant seems to confer strong resistance: kids with the G/G variant developed PTSD at only around a third the rate of kids with other variants.

Research like this suggests that your susceptibility to nervous breakdown is strongly determined by your genes. Certain genotypes make you especially vulnerable to psychological breakdown when subjected to stress or trauma; other genotypes make you naturally resilient. No single gene, or even set of genes, programs you to be anxious per se. But certain gene combinations program you to have either a high or a low level of hypothalamic-pituitary-adrenal activity: if you were born with a sensitive autonomic nervous system and then get exposed to stress in early childhood, your HPA system gets sensitized even further, so it's always hyperactive later in life, producing an excessively twitchy amygdala—which in turn primes you to develop depression or anxiety disorders. If, however, you were born with genes encoding low baseline levels of HPA activity, you will tend to have a high level of immunity to the effects of even severe stress.

Here, it seems, is at least a partial explanation for what the Oxford scholar Robert Burton had observed back in 1621 in *The Anatomy of Melancholy:* "For that which is but a flea-biting to one, causeth insufferable torment to another."

Would finding out that I have the warrior version of the *COMT* gene be a relief because it would mean that I am not, after all, genetically doomed to high levels of "neuroticism" and "harm avoidance"? Or would discovering that I have, say, the long/long version of the *SERT* gene make me feel even worse than I already do: to be blessed with the genes for easygoingness and resilience and yet to feel so anxious and neurotic—how pathetic would that be? I'd be learning that I had somehow managed to squander a generous genetic inheritance.

In her 1937 book, *The Neurotic Personality of Our Time,* Karen Horney, a disciple of Freud, writes about how a standard behavioral tic of the neurotic is to reduce himself to nothing—*I am such a loser,* he says to himself, *look at all the obstacles that impede me and the handicaps that confine me; it's a wonder that I can function at all*—in order to relieve the pressure to accomplish anything. The neurotic secretly (sometimes without even knowing it) nurtures a powerful ambition to achieve as a means of compensating for a weak sense of self-worth. But the fear of failing to accomplish, or of having his poor self-worth confirmed by manifest lack of achievement despite a sincere effort to succeed, is too unbearable to abide. So as a psychological self-defense tactic, the neurotic plays up the infirmities that ostensibly make achieving success difficult. Once these handicaps and disadvantages are established, the pressure is off: anything a neurotic accomplishes merits extra credit. And if the neurotic fails? Well, that's what playing up all these deficits has aimed to prepare for: How could you expect anything but failure given the barriers stacked against him? Thus to discover that I have the neurotic version of the *COMT* gene or the anxious-depressive *SERT* gene might at some level prove to be a relief. *See,* I could say, *here's proof that my anxiety is "real." It's right there in my genes. How can anyone expect me—how can I expect myself—to do anything much more than muddle anxiously along? It's a wonder I've been able to accomplish anything given my disordered constellation of genes! Now let me huddle under the covers and watch soothing television shows.*

Late one night, the report on my *COMT* gene arrived.* I am heterozygous (val/met), which means, based on the limited data so far, I am neither warrior nor worrier but something in between. (A 2005 study at San Diego State University did find that people—mainly women—with the val/met variant tended to be more introverted and neurotic.) Some time later, I received the results from the genotyping of my *SERT* gene: I'm short/short—meaning I've got the variant that many studies have found is predictive of anxiety disorders and depression when coupled with life stress. If current genetic research is to be believed, I should—based on my genotype—be anxious and harm avoidant, inordinately susceptible to suffering and pain.

Shouldn't this be liberating? If being anxious is genetically encoded,

---

* I asked my brother-in-law, a medical student and former biochemistry major, to take the raw genomic data that 23andMe provided and plug it into open-source genome databases to figure out what variant I have of the *COMT* gene. And though 23andMe does not currently provide clients with even the raw data on *SERT* variants, I prevailed upon some neuroscientist friends of mine to test me for it, on the condition that I not reveal their names since they receive federal grant funding and are not supposed to perform the test on anyone who is not officially part of a study.

a medical disease, and not a failure of character or will, how can I be blamed or shamed or stigmatized for it?

But ceding responsibility for your temperament and personality and baseline level of anxiety to hereditary bad luck—however well based in genetic science this may be—quickly bleeds into vexing philosophical territory. The same building blocks of nucleotides, genes, neurons, and neurotransmitters that make up my anxiety also make up the rest of my personality. To the extent that genes encode my anxiety, they also encode my self. Do I really want to attribute the "me-ness" of me to genetic factors completely beyond my control?

> *The enigmatic phobias of early childhood deserve mention once again. . . . Certain of them—the fear of being alone, of the dark, of strangers—we can understand as reactions to the danger of object loss; with regard to others—fear of small animals, thunderstorms, etc.—there is the possibility that they represent the atrophied remnants of an innate preparedness against reality dangers as is so well developed in other animals.*
>
> —SIGMUND FREUD, *The Problem of Anxiety* (1926)

How could something as idiosyncratic as a specific phobia have gotten passed from my mother to me to my daughter? Can a simple phobia be genetic?

Recall that Freud, late in his career, observed that certain common phobias—fear of the dark, fear of being alone, fear of small animals, fear of thunderstorms—seem to have evolutionarily adaptive roots, representing "the atrophied remnants of an innate preparedness against reality dangers such as is so well developed in other animals." By this logic, certain phobias are so common because they arise from instinctive fears that have been evolutionarily selected for.

In the 1970s, Martin Seligman, a psychologist at the University of Pennsylvania, elaborated this notion into what he called preparedness theory: certain phobias are common because evolution has selected for brains primed to have exaggerated fear responses to dangerous things. Cro-Magnons who innately feared—and who therefore avoided—

falling off cliffs or getting bitten by poisonous snakes or bugs or being exposed to predators in open fields were more likely to survive.

If the human brain is predisposed to develop fears of certain things, that casts one of the most famous experiments in the history of psychology in a new light. What if John Watson misinterpreted the Little Albert experiment that I discussed in chapter 2? What if the real reason Albert developed such a profound phobia of rats, and so readily generalized it to other furry creatures, was not that behavioral conditioning is so powerful but that the human brain has a natural predisposition to fear small furry things? Rodents, after all, can carry lethal diseases. Early humans who acquired a prudent fear of rats would have had an evolutionary advantage that made them more likely to survive. So it may be that neither the outward projections of inner psychic conflict (as the early Freud would have it) nor the power of behavioral conditioning (as Watson had it) is the primary reason so many people today develop rodent phobias; rather, it may be the connection of such fears to an atavistic response that is readily triggered.

For a long time, primatologists believed monkeys emerged from the womb with an innate fear of snakes. When researchers would observe a monkey encounter a snake (or even a snakelike object), the monkey would react fearfully—seemingly a clear instance of purely innate preparedness, of an inborn fear somehow handed down through the genes. But Susan Mineka, a psychologist at Northwestern University, discovered that monkeys who have been separated from their mothers and raised in captivity display no fear when they first encounter a snake. Only after infant monkeys have observed their mothers reacting fearfully to a snake—or after they have watched a video of another monkey reacting fearfully to a snake—do they later exhibit fearful behavior when exposed to a snake themselves. This suggests young monkeys *learn* to be afraid of snakes from watching their mothers—which in turn would seem to be strong evidence that the phobia is acquired by environmental learning rather than through the genes. But Mineka discovered another wrinkle: she found that monkeys could *not* easily acquire fears of things that were not intrinsically dangerous. Young monkeys who were shown videos of other monkeys reacting fearfully to a snake subsequently developed the fear of snakes—but monkeys shown (artfully spliced) videos of other monkeys reacting fearfully to flowers or rabbits did *not* develop fears of flowers or rabbits. Evidently, a combination of social observation and intrinsic danger is necessary to produce phobic-like behavior in monkeys.

Arne Öhman, the Swedish psychologist whose work on social anxiety I mentioned in chapter 4, points out that while all humans are evolutionarily primed to acquire certain adaptive fears, most people do not develop phobias. This is evidence, Öhman argues, that there is genetic variation in how sensitive our brains are to even those stimuli we are evolutionarily primed to fear. Some people—like my mother, my daughter, my son, and me—have a genetically encoded propensity to acquire fears and to have them be more intense than average.*

In support of Seligman's preparedness theory, Öhman found that those phobias—including acrophobia (fear of heights), claustrophobia (enclosed spaces), arachnophobia (spiders), murophobia (rodents), and ophidiophobia (snakes)—that would have had clear adaptive relevance in our early evolutionary history were much harder to extinguish with exposure therapy than phobias of objects like horses or trains that were not historically "fear relevant." Furthermore, Öhman found that even phobias of guns and knives—which are clearly "fear relevant" today but would not have been for Neanderthals and other evolutionary forebears—were much easier to extinguish than fears of snakes and rats, suggesting that the fears we are most readily primed for, and least easily rid of, were inscribed in our genes relatively early in primate evolution.

But what, if anything, is evolutionarily useful about emetophobia? Vomiting is adaptive; it can rid us of toxins that could kill us. What would account for a genotype for such a phobia?

One speculative possibility is that emetophobia is genetically

---

* Interestingly, different phobias seem to trigger different parts of our neurocircuitry and to have different genetic roots. This is true to my own experience. As phobic as I am of flying and of heights and of vomiting and of cheese, I have no inordinate fear of snakes or rats or other animals; in fact, the animal kingdom may be one of the few areas where I'm actually less fearful than I ought to be. I have been badly bitten by a dog (which resulted in a trip to the emergency room when I was eight), by a snake (I once had a pet bull snake named Kim), and was once viciously attacked by, of all things, a kangaroo, which I'd mistakenly thought wanted a hug. (Long story.) I'd be much happier covered in a pile of (nonpoisonous) snakes and rats than flying through even the mildest turbulence.

derived from an impulse that *is* evolutionarily adaptive: avoiding *other people* who are vomiting. Instinctively running away from regurgitating peers might have saved those early hominids from being exposed to ambient toxins that could have poisoned them. Another possibility is that an array of genetically conferred temperamental traits and behavioral and cognitive predispositions, plus a high innate level of physiological reactivity, combined to enhance a vulnerability to phobic anxiety—and maybe especially, somehow, to this particular phobic anxiety. My mother, my daughter, and I all have high-reactive physiologies, with jittery amygdalae and bodies always on DEFCON 4 alert, which make us constantly hypervigilant about danger. My mother—like my daughter and like me—is a high-octane worrier; at times, she emits a nervous thrum that is practically audible. Our physiological reactivity and inhibited temperaments make all three of us more generally nervous, and more likely to experience intense negative emotion when exposed to a frightening stimulus, than someone with a low-reactive, uninhibited temperament.

Here's a conversation I had with my daughter the night before a trip to Florida not long after she turned six.

"I'm afraid of the plane ride tomorrow."

"There's nothing to be afraid of," I say, trying to project calm. "What is it about the plane that makes you scared?"

"The safety instructions."

"The *safety instructions*? What about the safety instructions?"

"The part where they talk about crashing."

"Oh, planes are very safe. The plane's not going to crash."

"Then why do they have the instructions telling you what to do if it *does* crash?"

"That's just because there's special rules that say flight attendants have to give us the instructions in order to keep us extra safe. But flying is much safer than driving in a car."

"Then how come we don't have to listen to safety instructions when we get in the car?"

"Susanna," I yell down the stairs, "can you come talk to Maren about something?"

Maren seems to have come by her fear of flying without any overt instruction from me. She was already temperamentally equipped to worry about things, to scan the environment for potential threats; the natural cast of her mind—like mine, like my mother's, like those of typical patients with generalized anxiety disorder—is such that she seeks out and worries (in the original sense of "playing with it," turning it over in her mind to consider it from every angle) every worst-case scenario. Her dawning awareness of the safety instructions, with their references to water landings and crash positions, stimulated her anxiety.

Both my children share my gift for catastrophizing—for always imagining, and worrying about, the worst-case scenario, even if that scenario is not statistically likely. If I detect a small bump on my face while shaving, I immediately worry that it is not (as is most likely) a burgeoning pimple but rather a malignant and possibly fatal tumor. If I feel a twinge in my side, I instantly worry that it is not a strained muscle or a digestive blip but rather the onset of acute appendicitis or liver cancer. If, while driving into the sunlight, I feel a bit of dizziness, I am convinced that it is not a trick of the flickering light but rather an early sign of a stroke or a brain tumor.

Some time later, we were once again preparing to fly off for a family vacation. Maren clutched the armrests on the plane before takeoff, keenly attentive to every clank and whir from the aircraft's innards, asking after each one if the noise meant that the plane was broken.

"No, it doesn't," my wife said.

"But how do you *know*?"

"Maren, would we ever put you somewhere that was dangerous?"

Another noise from the engine: *Clank!* "But what about *that* noise," Maren says, tears in her eyes. "Does *that* noise mean the plane is broken?"

Sigh. The apple has fallen all too close to the tree.*

---

* I should say here that perhaps because both my children have received early psychotherapy for their anxiety—to help them take control of what we call their "worry brains"—they both seem to be less anxious than they were a few years ago. Maren is still emetophobic, but she's developed techniques for managing her fear, and she's less anxious—and in fact quite self-confident—in most areas of her life. Nathaniel remains an imaginative catastrophizer, but his separation anxiety has become a little less severe. Temperamentally, they will probably remain prone to anxiety for their entire lives—but my hope is that they will be able to manage their fear, and even harness it in productive ways, in such a fashion that they will be able to thrive despite it.

*And that which is more to be wondered at, [melancholy] skips in
some families the father, and goes to the son, "or takes every other,
and sometimes every third in a lineal descent, and doth not always
produce the same, but some like, and a symbolizing disease."*
—ROBERT BURTON, *The Anatomy of Melancholy* (1621)

*The patient has been shown to be a perfectionist, ambitious to suc-
ceed though not in an egocentric way, and sensitive to small degrees
of failure. Whether such psychodynamic explanations give the cause
of the depression is not known. Anxiety seems the larger feature.*
—FROM CHESTER HANFORD'S 1948 MCLEAN HOSPITAL REPORT

As unnerving as it has been to watch my children's anxiety develop
along lines similar to mine, it's been equally so to discover the similarities between my great-grandfather's neuroses and my own. If there is
such behavioral similarity between my mother and me, and between
me and my kids, then mightn't the anxious genotype run all the way
from my great-grandfather through my children—five generations (at
least) of the hereditary taint?

Chester Hanford died the summer I turned six. I mainly recall him
as a gentle, kindly presence, simultaneously distinguished and decrepit,
sitting in his wheelchair in my grandparents' living room in suburban
New Jersey, or in his room at the nursing home nearby, wearing a burgundy blazer, a dark tie, and gray flannel slacks. After his death in 1975,
he remained a presence in our house, gazing out with wise, sad eyes
from various photos and living on in a letter to him from President
Kennedy that hung on the living room wall alongside a picture of the
two of them campaigning together with Jacqueline Kennedy.

When I was growing up, I knew only about Chester's accomplishments: his long and successful deanship at Harvard; his respected academic publications on municipal government; his association with JFK
over the course of several decades, from Kennedy's undergraduate years
to his time in the White House. Only when I got older did I begin to
glean the dark bits: that he had suffered from anxiety and depression;
that he had undergone multiple courses of electroshock therapy; that

he had been institutionalized for extended periods many times between the late 1940s and the mid-1960s and had been forced into premature semiretirement (giving up his deanship) and then full retirement (leaving Harvard) as a result; and that he had spent some portion of his final decades moaning in a fetal ball in the bedroom of his home in western Massachusetts.

What was the cause of Chester's afflictions? Was the problem primarily what we would today call an anxiety disorder or clinical depression? How closely did his anxieties resemble mine?

According to his psychiatric records from several hospitals, Chester's general existential fears and anxieties were akin to my own. Does this mean I share—whether owing to the transmission of specific genes or to a neurotic family culture established by our ancestors—a specific psychiatric disease in common with my great-grandfather? Or merely that, in an inversion of Tolstoy, all psychoneurotics are unhappy in the same way?

Reading about my great-grandfather—especially after having learned a little bit about behavioral genetics—has kindled a sense of deep uneasiness, because so much about him reminds me of myself. His nervousness. His fears of public speaking. His tendency to procrastinate.* His obsessive hand washing.† His fixation on his bowels.‡ His relentless self-criticism. His lack of self-esteem despite his respectable job. His ability to project a demeanor of seeming imperturbability and good cheer while roiling with internal torment.§ His emotional and practical dependence on his more outgoing, more together wife.¶

His first institutionalization, at age fifty-six, seems to have been

---

* From a 1948 "diagnostic impressions" report: "He was overconscientious and overly self-critical, a person of high energy and work output, but a procrastinator."

† From a report by his principal psychiatrist during his sojourn at McLean in May 1953: "It has been noted that he is developing an increasing hand-washing ritual. This has not been taken up in psychotherapy sessions since I feel it is important not to give him the impression that we are unduly critical of his personal activities."

‡ From a handwritten physician's note from the spring of 1948: "The patient has had an irritable large bowel . . . for years." From another note some years later: "Patient chronically worried about his bowels."

§ "Patient is very pleasant," a nurse noted, observing Chester as he ambled around the ward during his second stint at McLean. "Gives the impression that nothing could upset him."

¶ "He has also been quite a burden on his wife." That's from a psychiatrist's notes during Chester's third stay at McLean.

precipitated by the anxiety he felt about a series of lectures he was to give to graduate students. "He had read a good deal this past fall," his principal psychiatrist wrote after Chester was admitted to McLean Hospital in 1948, "but began to fear that he could not organize the material into lectures." He felt that other professors were better than he was and that he was not enough of a scholar to produce satisfactory lectures. In the late spring of 1947, Chester "became very upset over his inability to organize his work and be creative. Anxiety overwhelmed him. He became quite depressed and wept at times."

Chester's psychotherapists tried to get him to quiet his superego. "The patient's sense of self-criticism has been attacked as a factor in his depression, and shows itself to be more rigid and excessive than his talents and virtues warrant." (Over the years, my own therapists have tried to do the same thing—only they generally don't call it a superego anymore; they call it an "inner critic" or a "critical self.") In my great-grandfather's case, this didn't work. Despite abundant evidence of his effectiveness as a scholar and an administrator, he couldn't subdue his feelings of ineffectuality and inferiority. ("He is not glad to think back over his great usefulness to the college as in any way ameliorating his present plight of uselessness," his psychiatrist wrote.) The objective evidence suggests that he was a figure who commanded considerable respect among both students and academic peers. Yet by the fall of 1947, he had come to believe himself a fraud, unequal to the task of composing lectures of sufficient interest and cogency for his students.

How did this happen? This was a man who had manifestly thrived in his professional and family life. He had had tenure at Harvard for decades, had written a well-used political science textbook, and had been the academic dean of the college for many years. He had been married for thirty-two years. He enjoyed an active social life as a modest grandee of the Cambridge scene and often presided over morning chapel services for undergraduates. A father, a grandfather, a Harvard professor and dean, a member in good standing of the community—he had all the outward trappings of success, stability, and happiness. Yet inwardly he was crumbling.

Today, my grandfather says that until his father broke down completely for the first time in the late 1940s, he had never seen any evidence that his father was anxious or depressed. Yet, according to his medical records, Chester had always been "a rather nervous person," with a habit of—as his wife, Ruth, had first noticed when they were courting—constantly blinking his eyes. (Modern researchers sometimes use a measurement they call eyeblink frequency as a gauge of physiological anxiety.) Ruth also recalled the anxiety he had suffered over a series of lectures he had to give as a young assistant professor, reporting to his doctors that he had become "quite apprehensive and sleepless" for days in advance. Combing through old correspondence, I came across a letter Chester had written to Ruth while he was a junior professor at Harvard during the First World War, in which he declared that he almost hoped to be drafted for combat—because dodging bullets on the battlefield would be less nerve-racking than having to give lectures to undergraduates.

All of this suggests that Chester had a nervous disposition—what Jerome Kagan would call a behaviorally inhibited temperament—that was almost certainly, to some degree, hereditary. Both his father and a maternal aunt were prone to various forms of anxiety and depression. But this nervous disposition, this behavioral inhibition, was not, for the first fifty years of his life, unduly debilitating: as apprehensive and susceptible to worry and insomnia as he could sometimes be, he progressed steadily along a dignified professional path, gaining esteem and respect as he went.

So why, after more than five decades of managing his worry and melancholy, did he finally crack in the winter of 1947, surprising even himself?* According to the stress-diathesis model of mental illness, clinical disorders like anxiety and depression often erupt when a genetic susceptibility to psychiatric disease combines with life stressors that overwhelm the individual's ability to cope. Certain people are blessed with genotypes programmed to withstand even severe trauma; other people, like my great-grandfather (and, presumably, me), are less naturally resilient and lose the ability to cope when the stress of life becomes too heavy.

---

* "Mr. Hanford remarked that he had once visited one of his students in the [neuropsychiatric] ward at the Mass General and was quite impressed with the way the doors, etc., were kept locked," his psychiatrist noted. "He said, 'I never expected that I would find myself under the same circumstances; I always felt that I could take care of myself.'"

My great-grandfather was able to carry on his work until the Second World War. But as various colleagues were deployed to the war effort, his teaching load increased. "This put added strain on him," his principal psychiatrist later reported, "and he became quite nervous and anxious about his ability to continue." He became chronically tired. After years of hosting a salon at his home in Cambridge, he found himself too fatigued to entertain or even to socialize at all; dealing with people was too much of a strain. He suggested to James Conant, the president of Harvard, that he might resign. (For the moment, Conant requested that he stay on as dean.)

In the spring of 1945, a close friend died. Already feeling worried and on edge, he became after this (according to his wife) perpetually "jittery"—a condition that was compounded as he surveyed the casualty lists from the war and saw the names of many of his former students. After years of teaching undergraduates, Chester suddenly could no longer organize his lectures. On several occasions, his wife had to write the lectures for the freshman seminar he taught.

At the urging of his family physician, Roger Lee, he took a month off in the summer of 1946. "He felt better after this," his records report, "and was able to continue fairly well through the next school year." But the following spring, he again became upset over his inability to organize his work; he worried his lectures were inferior. He also worried obsessively about a trivial financial matter. Depression descended. He was able to carry out his teaching and administrative duties during the day, but at night he was driven to weeping by tension and sadness. Dr. Lee advised him to cut back on his workload, and so, in the fall of 1947, he retired as dean and returned to his full-time position in the government department, teaching courses in political science.

At which point he deteriorated rapidly. By mid-October, he had become "overtired, nervous, and upset about his lectures and felt that he could not carry on." He would stay up until two in the morning revising his lectures and yet still could not sleep because he was dissatisfied with his drafts, and so he would rise early the next day to begin work again. "He began to think he was not any good any more as a lecturer," his McLean Hospital records say. "He began to think that other professors were better and that he was not up to his own standard." The week before he was finally admitted to the hospital for the first time, he had become "even more apprehensive" about his lectures. At times he "wept bitterly," and he had begun talking of suicide.

In the "diagnostic impressions" section of Chester's intake file, the hospital's psychiatric director reports: "The patient gives the impression of having been an extremely valuable person in his professional life, as well as very kindly and helpful in his personal relations. He was overconscientious and overly self-critical, a person of high energy and work output, but a procrastinator. He was a worrier, and has a history of previous depression. Thus he has anxious and obsessional character traits. The change back from administrative to scholastic duties cut down the amount of satisfactory activity and of personal contacts, and increased the amount of contemplative, self-conscious and self-critical thinking. Dependent and despairing attitudes increased. He might be diagnosed as *psychoneurosis, reactive depression.* The prognosis seems fairly good for an easing of the present symptoms but the future of his adjustment is doubtful."

If Chester Hanford's psychoneurotic ailments and his genotype— and, to a lesser degree, his life circumstances—are similar to my own, does that mean a fate like his awaits me? ("The future of his adjustment is doubtful.") Does my heredity doom me to a similar downward spiral if I am subjected to too much stress? What might already have become of me if I had not had recourse to, at various times, the readily available antipsychotics, tricyclic and SSRI antidepressants, and benzodiazepines that were unavailable to my great-grandfather, who developed his affliction before the flowering of modern psychopharmacology? If my great-grandfather had had access to, say, Xanax or Celexa, would he have been spared the multiple rounds of electroshock and insulin coma therapy, not to mention the months spent moaning in his bed in a fetal ball?

Impossible to say, of course. Whatever quotient of anxious and depressive genes we may share, Chester Hanford and I are different people, living in different times under different cultural conditions, with different experiences and different stresses. Maybe Celexa wouldn't have worked on Chester Hanford. (As we have seen, the clinical evidence on SSRIs is mixed.) And, who knows? Maybe I could have muddled through without Thorazine and imipramine and Valium and desipramine and Prozac and Zoloft and Paxil and Xanax and Celexa and Inderal and Klonopin.

But somehow I don't think so. Which is what makes the similarities between us so disconcerting—and what makes me wonder if the difference between Holding It Together (as I'm doing now and as Chester Hanford anxiously did for so many years before finally breaking down) and Failing to Do So is some ingested chemical compounds that in whatever mysterious and imperfect way interact with my genotype to keep me suspended, tenuously, over the abyss.

My great-grandfather's first stay at McLean Hospital was relatively Edenic compared with his subsequent ones. Over the course of seven weeks, he had daily psychotherapy sessions, swam, played badminton and cards, read books, and listened to the radio. He also took various medications, which provide a representative snapshot of the pharmaco-therapy of the time.*

In Chester's daily psychotherapy sessions, his psychiatrist tried to boost his self-esteem and to reduce his anxiety by getting him to be less rigid in his thinking. Gradually, whether it was the talk therapy, the badminton, the drugs, the respite from work, or the passage of time, his anxiety lifted. (For what it's worth, his principal psychiatrist gave greatest credit to the testosterone injections and the regular physical exercise.) He was released from the hospital on April 12, less depressed and no longer actively suicidal. But in his discharge records, his psychiatrist stated ominously that while the symptoms of anxiety had momentarily abated, his worry-prone temperament would likely trouble him again.

A year later, he was back, readmitted on March 28, 1949, feeling, as the hospital director noted, "tense, anxious, depressed, and self-deprecatory" and suffering from "insomnia and an inability to concen-

---

* He took methyltestosterone, an anabolic steroid given to him by injection, which at midcentury was considered a standard treatment for depression in men; Oreton, a synthetic testosterone that today seems to be prescribed only to boys suffering delayed puberty; chloral hydrate, the old-fashioned nineteenth-century ethanol-chlorine derivative that remained popular as a sedative and sleep aid until the arrival of benzodiazepines; and Donatal, a potent combination of phenobarbital (the barbiturate in Luminal) and hyoscyamine and atropine (which are both plant derivatives from the deadly nightshade family), which was prescribed for his agitated bowels and nerves.

trate on his work." The day before returning to McLean, he had told Roger Lee, his family physician, that he wanted to kill himself but "did not have the guts for suicide." Dr. Lee advised that he admit himself again to the hospital.

Chester acclimated to life in a psychiatric hospital more quickly this time, and within ten days he already seemed to the staff to be more relaxed. But he was still talking about the same issues as on his previous admission—the anxiety, tension, and practical difficulties he was having in composing his lectures and the general inferiority he felt relative to his faculty peers.*

As the doctors successfully "reassured him as to his own considerable value in the college community," he became within a few weeks "a good deal more sociable and relaxed." His psychiatrists believed that the combination of "relief from the responsibilities of work" and the positive boost he got from the injections of testosterone allowed his confidence to build up fairly quickly, and he was able to leave the hospital within a month.†

My great-grandfather was at least somewhat improved for a time. He resumed his full teaching responsibilities at the college and returned to his scholarly work. For several years, it seems, he felt well and worked productively and effectively.

Then he fell to pieces.

At a faculty meeting on January 22, 1953, his colleagues noticed that he seemed "very tense," "depressed," and "disturbed." That spring, his depression became severe and his anxiety rose; he couldn't work. Most alarmingly, as his wife reported, he spent his days walking around the house "shrieking." "Oh! Lord, lift up my soul," he would moan loudly. "Today, this is the end of everything, this is the end of everything. I

---

* As his principal psychiatrist writes, "In talking with him I have laid a good deal of stress on his previous value as an individual in his work for the college. I have led him to take more satisfaction in his executive and teaching accomplishments. Thus it has been possible to somewhat relax his self-critical attitude."

† On April 29, 1949, Chester was returned to the care of his wife and his personal physician, Dr. Lee, his file noting, "There are some evidences of tension and depression still present, but it has been possible for him to be discharged home as improved."

shouldn't have let myself go." Feeling "very strongly that he was losing control of himself," he sought an emergency consultation with Dr. Lee, who recommended that he return to the hospital. On May 5, 1953, he was admitted to McLean for the third time in five years.

During his psychiatric exam upon admission, he was terribly anxious, and his sense of shame about his anxiety and depression was palpable.* By now he had developed symptoms of what would today be called obsessive-compulsive disorder: he washed his hands constantly, and he shaved and changed shirts multiple times a day.

Because testosterone injections seemed to have relieved his depression during his earlier stints at McLean, the doctors started him on a large dose. This time, however, "the sense of well-being engendered by the testosterone" could not overcome his symptoms. His psychiatrists judged that talk therapy and drugs would be insufficient to elevate his mood.

And so, on May 19, with his ready acquiescence, Chester Hanford underwent his first round of electroshock therapy with Kenneth Tillotson.† During each session, Chester would be sedated and strapped tightly to a bed. Orderlies would attach electrodes to various points on his skin and slip in a mouth guard so he wouldn't bite off his own tongue. Then a switch would be flipped, and several hundred volts of current would pass through his body, which would twitch and convulse on the bed.

After each session, he would feel a little confused and have a mild headache—both common symptoms of electroshock. But within a day of his first session, he told his doctors he was feeling considerably better. A few days later, he had his second round of treatment. After that, the nurses on his ward noticed that he seemed "more relaxed, more pleasant, and more outgoing." He stopped ruminating about his problems. He seemed markedly less anxious. A week later, after a third round of electroshock, the transformation was profound: he "looked well," was sleeping and eating, and was "laughing a great deal." The

---

* "His colleagues recently have given him support during his illness these past five years, and actually he is not carrying the workload he should, and he knows it," one psychiatrist noted. "He has also been quite a burden on his wife who has found it necessary to prepare some of his lectures for him."

† During this same period, Dr. Tillotson also administered electroshock treatment to the poet Sylvia Plath, who recorded the experience in her novel, *The Bell Jar*.

nurses reported him to be "much less fearful than when he came in," no longer "running around asking the nurses whether he can do this or that." He began spending a great deal of time in the gym with other patients, playing badminton and bowling—activities that he had earlier implied to his psychiatrist were beneath the dignity of a sixty-two-year-old Harvard professor. The electroshock therapy, it seemed, had restored (or injected) a sense of fun.

After a fourth round of treatment, on June 2, he reported himself "relaxed" and eager to return to work. His wife, who visited him frequently, was amazed: her husband was, she told his psychiatrists, "more the way he was many years ago." Chester himself told the staff that he felt "more like himself." To me this sounds uncannily like what Peter Kramer reported in *Listening to Prozac:* that the patients he put on Prozac in the 1990s had told him the medication made them feel "more like themselves."

We still have remarkably little understanding of how electroshock therapy works. Metaphorically, electroshock seems to function the way hitting Ctrl+Alt+Delete on your computer does; it reboots the system, restoring the settings on the neural operating system. The outcome statistics are compelling. Though the practice went out of vogue in the 1970s and 1980s—in part because Jack Nicholson's portrayal of an electroshock patient in the movie version of Ken Kesey's novel *One Flew over the Cuckoo's Nest* convinced people the technique was barbaric—modern studies show that the recovery rates from severe depression may be higher with electroshock than with any kind of drug or talk therapy. The experience of my great-grandfather, at least in the short term, would seem to bear that out.

Could there be any more compelling evidence that anxiety and depression are irreducibly "embodied" or "enmattered," in the fashion observed since Aristotle? By his third trip to the psychiatric hospital, Chester Hanford's psychiatrists seem largely to have given up on talking or psychoanalyzing him out of his depression and anxiety; his personality and character seemed so fixed as to resist "adjustment." But zapping his brain with a few hundred volts of electricity, on the other hand—rewiring the connections—seemed to do the trick just fine. After four electroshock treatments, the hospital director wrote that Chester "showed tremendous improvement."

On June 9, 1953, about a month after entering the hospital, a cheerful Chester was discharged into the care of his wife. They promptly left for vacation in Maine, where for the first time in years he eagerly anticipated the arrival of the fall semester and a new crop of students to teach.

I wish Chester Hanford's story ended on this hopeful note. But in time his anxiety returned, and he was compelled to retire. Throughout the 1950s and 1960s, he went regularly to McLean—and, later, to the New England Deaconess Hospital in downtown Boston—for more electroshock therapy. At one point, a too-potent drug cocktail nearly killed him. For a period in the late 1950s, his anxieties and compulsions got so bad that his doctors considered performing a prefrontal leucotomy—a partial lobotomy. (Ultimately, he was spared.)

For the balance of his lifetime, he kind of limped along. He would be okay for stretches—and then for stretches he wouldn't be. Even when he wasn't okay, he could pull himself together for appearance's sake. My mother recalls a summer day in the mid-1960s when a party was planned at the Hanford home in western Massachusetts. Family and friends from all over New England were to be gathering that evening. Throughout the day of the party, a haunted moaning emanated from Chester's bedroom; my mother cringed to think what his appearance at the party would be like—if he could manage an appearance at all. Yet as twilight fell and the party began, he emerged downstairs as a gracious, even sociable host. And then the next day he retreated again to his room, to his fetal curl and his moaning.

My parents recall Chester seeming less anxious and agitated during his years in the nursing home—a fact that my father suspects may be explained by the generous doses of Valium administered there. Benzodiazepines may, finally, have successfully tranquilized his anxiety into submission. Or perhaps being liberated from the stresses of work relaxed him.

In immersing myself so deeply in the psychopathologies of my greatgrandfather, and in identifying rather strongly with them, I—as hypochondriacal and prone to worry as I am—have naturally grown concerned that the hereditary taint will soon reduce me, too, to permanent weeping and shaking in my room.

When I tell Dr. W. about this, he says, "As you know, I don't place a lot of stock in genetic determinism."

I cite some of the recent studies suggesting a powerful heritable component to anxiety disorders and depression.

"Okay, but you're three generations removed from your great-grandfather," he says. "You share only a fraction of his genes."

True enough. And in any case, genes and environment interact in complex ways. "[A genetically] inherited reaction to potential danger may be a boon or a bane," says Daniel Weinberger, the lead researcher on one of the first *SERT* gene studies. "It can place us at risk for an anxiety disorder, or in another situation it may provide an adaptive positive attribute such as increased vigilance. We have to remember that anxiety is a complicated multidimensional characteristic of human experience and cannot be predicted by any form of a single gene."

Dr. W. and I talk about the way academic conferences on anxiety have been placing increasing emphasis on how the psychological traits of resilience and acceptance can be crucial bulwarks against both anxiety and depression; much of the cutting-edge research and treatment focuses in particular on the importance of cultivating resilience.

"Yes!" Dr. W. says. "We need to work on making you more resilient."

When I tell him what I've learned about the serotonin transporter gene, and about how people with certain genotypes are far more likely to live anxious, unhappy, and unresilient lives, Dr. W. reminds me how much he dislikes the modern emphasis on the genetics and neurobiology of mental illness because it hardens the notion that the mind is a fixed and immutable structure, when in fact it can change throughout a lifetime.

"I know," I say. I've read about the recent findings on neuroplasticity—about the way the human brain can keep forming new neuronal connections into old age. I tell him that I understand the importance of resilience in combating anxiety. But how, I ask, do I gain that quality?

"You're already more resilient than you know," he said.

# CHAPTER 10

# Ages of Anxiety

*The philosophic study of the several branches of sociology, politics,*
*charities, history, education, shall never be even in the direction of*
*scientific precision or completeness until it shall have absorbed some,*
*at least, of the suggestions of this problem of American nervousness.*
—GEORGE MILLER BEARD, *American Nervousness* (1881)

In April 1869, a young doctor in New York named George Miller
Beard, writing in the *Boston Medical and Surgical Journal*, coined a term
for what he believed to be a new and distinctively American affliction,
one he had seen in thirty of his patients: "neurasthenia" (from *neuro* for
"nerve" and *asthenia* for "weakness"). Referring to it sometimes as "nervous exhaustion," Beard argued that neurasthenia afflicted primarily
ambitious, upwardly mobile members of the urban middle and upper
classes—especially "the brain-workers in almost every household of the
Northern and Eastern States"—whose nervous systems were overtaxed
by a rapidly modernizing American civilization. Beard believed that he
himself had suffered from neurasthenia but had overcome it in his early
twenties.

Born in a small Connecticut village in 1839, Beard was the son of a
Congregational minister and the grandson of a physician. After attending prep school at Phillips Academy in Andover, Massachusetts, he
went on to Yale, where he began to suffer from the array of nervous
symptoms that would afflict him for the next six years and that he
would later observe in his patients: ringing in the ears, pains in the side,
dyspepsia, nervousness, morbid fears, and "lack of vitality." By his own
account, Beard's anxious suffering was prompted largely by his uncertainty about what career to pursue—though there is also evidence that

he anguished over his lack of religious commitment. (Two of Beard's older brothers had followed his father into the ministry; in his diary, he chastises himself for his indifference to spiritual concerns.) Once he decided to become a physician, however, his doubts left him and his anxiety dissipated. He entered medical school at Yale in 1862, determined to help others plagued by the anxious suffering that had once afflicted him.

Influenced by Darwin's recent work on natural selection, Beard came to believe that cultural and technological evolution had outstripped biological evolution, putting enormous stress on the human animal—particularly those in the business and professional classes, who were most driven by status competition and the burgeoning pressures of capitalism. Even as technological development and economic growth were improving material well-being, the pressure of market competition—along with the uncertainty that took hold as the familiar verities fell away under the assault of modernity and industrialization—produced great emotional stress, draining American workers' stock of "nerve force" and leading to acute anxiety and nervous prostration. "In the older countries, men plod along in the footsteps of their fathers, generation after generation, with little possibility and therefore little thought of entering a higher social grade," Beard's colleague A. D. Rockwell wrote in the *New York Medical Journal* in 1893. "Here, on the contrary, no one is content to rest with the possibility ever before him of stepping higher, and the race of life is all haste and unrest. It is thus readily seen that the primary cause of neurasthenia in this country is civilization itself, with all that term implies, with its railway, telegraph, telephone, and periodical press intensifying in ten thousand ways cerebral activity and worry."*

Beard believed that constant change, combined with the relentless striving for achievement, money, and status that characterized American life, produced rampant nervous weakness.† "American nervous-

---

* Anxiety seems to be woven into the American spirit—as Alexis de Tocqueville observed as early as the 1830s. "Life would have no relish for the [people who live in democracies] if they were delivered from the anxieties which harass them, and they show more attachment to their cares than aristocratic nations to their pleasures," he wrote in *Democracy in America*.

† It also produced drug dependence. Just as the postwar affluence of the 1950s would lead to the frantic gobbling of Miltown, Librium, and Valium, the competitive pressures of the late nineteenth century

ness is the product of American civilization," he wrote. The United States had invented nervousness as a cultural condition: "The Greeks were certainly civilized, but they were not nervous, and in the Greek language there is no word for that term."* Ancient cultures could not have experienced nervousness, he argued, because they didn't have steam power, the periodical press, the telegraph, the sciences, and the mental activity of women: "When civilization, plus these five factors, invades any nation, it must carry nervousness and nervous disease along with it." Beard also argued that neurasthenia affected only the more "advanced" races—especially the Anglo-Saxon—and religious persuasions; he observed that "no Catholic country is very nervous." (On its face, this is a dubious proposition, and Beard had no real evidence to buttress it. On the other hand, rates of anxiety in modern Mexico, a primarily Catholic country, are much lower than in the United States. A 2002 World Health Organization study found that Americans are four times more likely to suffer from generalized anxiety disorder than Mexicans—and some research has found that Mexicans recover from anxiety attacks twice as quickly as Americans. Interestingly, when Mexicans immigrate to the United States, their rates of anxiety and depression soar.)

Neurasthenia was a self-flattering diagnosis, since it was thought to affect primarily the most competitive capitalists and those with the most refined sensibilities. It was a disease of the elites; in Beard's estimation, 10 percent of his own patient load was made up of other physicians, and by 1900 "nervousness" had definitively become a mark of distinction—a signifier of both high class and cultural refinement.†

---

produced an alarming rise in the number of "opiate eaters." Writing in *Confessions of an American Opium Eater: From Bondage to Freedom* in 1895, Henry G. Cole argued that "our mechanical inventions, the spread of our commerce . . . our ambition for political honors; and grasping for petty offices for gain; our mad race for speedy wealth, which entails feverish excitements . . . [and] a growth so rapid, and in some ways so abnormal, [have combined to produce] the mental strain [that] has been too much for the physical system to bear; till finally, the overworked body and the overtaxed body must . . . find rest in the repeated use of opium or morphine."

* Elsewhere, Beard wrote that anxiety was "modern, and originally American; and no age, no country, and no form of civilization, not Greece, not Rome, nor Spain, nor the Netherlands, in their days of glory, possessed such maladies."

† Some years earlier, the elites of Georgian Britain—the period extending from the early 1700s until Queen Victoria ascended to the throne in 1837—had adopted a similar "nervous culture," which claimed for itself the same kind of self-flattering class connotations that would be characteristic of

Beard's books contain case studies and elaborate symptomatologies that sound strikingly contemporary to the modern ear. In *A Practical Treatise on Nervous Exhaustion*, published in 1880, he expatiates for hundreds of pages on the symptoms of nervous exhaustion. "I begin with the head and brain," he writes, "and go downwards." The list includes tenderness of the scalp; dilated pupils; headache; "*Muscoe Volitantes*, or floating specks before the eyes"; dizziness; ringing in the ears; softness of voice (a voice "wanting in clearness and courage of tone"); irritability; numbness and pain in the back of the head; indigestion;

---

American neurasthenia: the idea that the nervous systems of those of better breeding and more creative sensibilities were unusually susceptible to hypochondriasis and nervous collapse. This culture, like that of the Renaissance, tended to glamorize individuals with sensitive nervous systems while providing both medical and psychological explanations for their delicate constitutions. As anatomists continued to unlock the secrets of the human nervous system, scientists of this era variously described the nerve network as a system of fibers, strings, pipes, and cords, venturing explanations that attributed the system's functioning to hydraulics, electricity, mechanics, and so forth. The crucial concept in all these explanations was the nervous breakdown—the idea being that when the nervous system was overstrained, it would break down, producing both mental and physical symptoms and often general prostration. Beginning in the 1730s, the malfunctions of the nervous system that led to breakdown were often called "nervous distempers," which encompassed everything from hysteria and hypochondria to "the vapors"—mental and physical complaints that in more recent times would be labeled psychoneurotic or psychosomatic.

In striking contrast to the stiff-upper-lip ideals of the Victorian era that would follow, the British elites of the eighteenth century wallowed in, and even cultivated, their nervous disabilities. "Nervous self-fashioning"—painting oneself as the victim of one's nerves—was common. From 1777 to 1783, James Boswell, Samuel Johnson's biographer, wrote a monthly essay for *The London Magazine* under the pen name the Hypochondriack, and in his own diary he minutely tracked every subtle shift in his endless litany of emotional and physical symptoms. Boswell was obsessed with his digestive system. "From this day follow Mr. [John] Locke's prescription of going to stool every day regularly after breakfast," he wrote in his journal early in October 1764. "It will do your health good, and it is highly necessary to take care of your health." (Yes, that John Locke—the one who wrote *Two Treatises of Government* and is the father of constitutional liberalism. Most people turn to Locke for his thoughts on political philosophy; Boswell did so for his advice on digestive hygiene. If you're curious what Locke's prescription was, well, so was I—so I tracked it down, and here's what I found in section 24 of *Some Thoughts Concerning Education:* "If a man, after his first eating in the morning, would presently solicit nature, and try whether he could strain himself so as to obtain a stool, he might in time, by constant application, bring it to be habitual.")

Nervous disorders of various kinds were believed to be so widespread during this time that, despite the various physiological explanations given for them, they were viewed as a cultural condition as much as a medical one. One prominent British physician claimed that a third of the population was "destroyed or made miserable by the Diseases." (The popularity of nervous illness during this time was not confined to England. In 1758, Joseph Raulin, the personal physician to Louis XV of France, wrote that "the vapors" had become "a veritable social plague, an endemic disease in the cities [of the Continent].")

nausea; vomiting; diarrhea; flatulence ("with annoying rumbling in the bowels these patients complain of very frequently"); frequent blushing ("I have seen very strong, vigorous men, who have large muscular power and great capacity for physical labor, who, while in a neurasthenic state, would blush like young girls"); insomnia; tenderness of the teeth and gums; alcoholism and drug addiction; abnormal dryness of the skin; sweating of the hands and feet ("A young man under my care is so distressed [by his sweating] that he threatens suicide unless he is permanently cured"); excess salivation (or, alternatively, dry mouth); back pain; "heaviness of the loins and limbs"; heart palpitations; muscle spasms; dysphagia (difficulty swallowing); cramps; tendency to get hay fever; sensitivity to changes in the weather; "profound exhaustion"; ticklishness; itching; hot flashes; cold chills; cold hands and feet; temporary paralysis; and gaping and yawning. On the one hand, this panoply of symptoms is so broad as to be meaningless; these are the symptoms, more or less, of being alive. On the other hand, this litany resonates with the twenty-first-century neurotic's—it sounds, in fact, not unlike my weekly catalog of hypochondriacal complaint.

Neurasthenia also encompassed what we would today call phobia. Beard's case studies range from the lightning phobic ("One of my patients tells me she is always watching the clouds in summer, fearing that a storm may come. She knows this is absurd and ridiculous, but she declares she cannot help it. In this case the symptom was inherited from her grandmother; and even in her cradle, as she is informed by her mother, she suffered in the same way") to the agoraphobic ("One of my cases, a gentleman of middle life, could walk up Broadway without difficulty, because shops and stores, he said, offered him an opportunity of retreat, in case of peril. He could not, however, walk up Fifth Avenue, where there are no stores, nor in side streets, unless they were very short. He could not pay a visit to the country in any direction, but was hopelessly shut up in the city during the hot weather. One time, in riding in the stage up Broadway, on turning onto Madison Square, he shrieked with terror, to the astonishment of the passengers. The man who possessed this interesting symptom was tall, vigorous, full-faced, and mentally capable of endurance"); from the claustrophobic (who fear enclosed spaces) to the monophobic (who fear being alone; "One man was so afraid to leave the house alone he paid a man $20,000 to be his constant companion"); from the mysophobic (who fears contamination and must wash her hands two hundred times a day) to the panophobic (who fears everything). One of Beard's patients had a morbid fear of drunken men.

By the turn of the century, the language and imagery of neurasthenia had permeated deep into American culture. If you yourself didn't suffer from it, you surely knew people who did. Political rhetoric and religious sermons addressed it; consumer advertisements offered remedies for it. Magazines and newspapers published articles about it. Theodore Dreiser and Henry James populated their novels with neurasthenic characters. The language of neurasthenic distress ("depression," "panic") crept into economic discourse. Nervousness, it seemed, had become the default psychological state and cultural condition of modern times. Disrupted by the transformations of the Industrial Revolution and riven by Gilded Age wealth inequality, the United States was rife with levels of anxiety unmatched in human history.

Or so Beard claimed. But was it really?

According to the latest figures from the National Institute of Mental Health, some forty million Americans, or about 18 percent of the population, currently suffer from a clinical anxiety disorder. Recent editions of *Stress in America*, a report produced each year by the American Psychological Association, have found a badly "overstressed nation" in which a majority of Americans describe themselves as "moderately" or "highly" stressed, with significant percentages of them reporting stress-related physical symptoms such as fatigue, headache, stomach troubles, muscle tension, and teeth grinding. Between 2002 and 2006, the number of Americans seeking medical treatment for anxiety increased from 13.4 million to 16.2 million. More Americans seek medical treatment for anxiety than for back pain or migraine headaches.

Surveys by the Anxiety and Depression Association of America find that nearly half of all Americans report "persistent or excessive anxiety" in their daily work lives. (Other surveys find that three out of four Americans believe there is more workplace stress today than in the past.) A study published in the *American Psychologist* found that 40 percent more people said they'd felt an impending nervous breakdown in 1996 than had said so in 1957. Twice as many people reported experiencing symptoms of panic attacks in 1995 as in 1980.* According to a national survey of incoming freshmen, the anxiety levels of college students are higher today than at any time in the twenty-five-year history of the survey. When Jean Twenge, a professor of psychology at San Diego State University, looked at survey data from fifty thousand children and college students between the 1950s and the 1990s, she found that the average college student in the 1990s was more anxious than 85 percent of students in the 1950s and that "'normal' schoolchildren in the 1980s reported higher levels of anxiety than child psychiatric patients in the 1950s." (Robert Leahy, a psychologist at Weill Cornell Medical College, characterized this finding colorfully in *Psychology Today:* "The average high school kid today has the same level of anxiety as the average psychiatric patient in the 1950s.") The baby boomers were more anxious than their parents; Generation X was more anxious than the boomers; the millennials are turning out to be more anxious than Generation X.

Rates of anxiety seem to be increasing all around the world. A World Health Organization survey of eighteen countries concluded that anxiety disorders are now the most common mental illness on earth, once again overtaking depression. Statistics from the National Health Service reveal that British hospitals treated four times as many people for anxiety disorders in 2011 as they did in 2007 while issuing record numbers of tranquilizer prescriptions. A report published by Britain's Mental Health Foundation in 2009 concluded that a "culture of fear"—marked by a shaky economy and hyperbolic threat-mongering by politicians and the media—had produced "record levels of anxiety" in Great Britain.

Given the "record levels of anxiety" we seem to be seeing around the world, surely we must today be living in the most anxious age ever—more anxious even than George Beard's era of neurasthenia.

How can this be? Economic disruption and recent global recession notwithstanding, we live in an age of unprecedented material affluence.

---

* This is not surprising, considering that panic attacks did not officially exist until the publication of the *DSM-III* in 1980.

Standards of living in the industrialized West are, on average, higher than ever; life expectancies in the developed world are, for the most part, long and growing. We are much less likely to die an early death than our ancestors were, much less likely to be subjected to the horrors of smallpox, scurvy, pellagra, polio, tuberculosis, rickets, and packs of roving wolves, not to mention the challenges of life without antibiotics, electricity, or indoor plumbing. Life is, in many ways, easier than it used to be. Therefore shouldn't we be *less* anxious than we once were?

Perhaps in some sense the price—and surely, in part, the source— of progress and improvements in material prosperity has been an increase in the average allotment of anxiety. Urbanization, industrialization, the growth of the market economy, increases in geographic and class mobility, the expansion of democratic values and freedoms—all of these trends, on their own and in concert, have contributed to vastly improved material quality of life for millions of people over the last several hundred years. But each of these may also have contributed to rising anxiety.

Until the Renaissance, there was scarcely any concept of social, political, technological, or any other kind of progress. This lent a kind of resignation to medieval emotional life that may have been adaptive: the sense that things would always be as they were was depressing but also comforting—there was no having to adapt to technological or social change; there were no hopes for a better life in danger of being dashed. While life was dominated by the fear—and expectation—of eternal damnation (one Franciscan preacher in Germany put the odds in favor of damnation for any given soul at a hundred thousand to one), medieval minds were not consumed, as ours are, with the hope of advancement and the fear of decline.

Today, especially in Western capitalist democracies, we also probably have more choice than ever in history: we are free to choose where to live, whom to court or marry, what line of work to pursue, what personal style to adapt. "The major problem for Americans is that of choice," the late sociologist Philip Slater wrote in 1970. "Americans are forced into making more choices per day, with fewer 'givens,' more ambiguous criteria, less environmental stability, and less social structural support, than any people in history." Freedom of choice generates great anxiety. Barry Schwartz, a psychologist at Swarthmore College, calls this "the paradox of choice"—the idea that as the freedom to choose increases, so does anxiety.

Maybe anxiety is, in some sense, a luxury—an emotion we can afford to indulge only when we're not preoccupied by "real" fear. (Recall that William James made a version of this argument in the 1880s.) Perhaps precisely because medieval Europeans had so many genuine threats to be *afraid* of (the Black Death, Muslim invaders, famine, dynastic turmoil, constant military conflict, and death, always death, imminently present—the average life expectancy during the Middle Ages was thirty-five years, and one out of every three babies died before reaching the age of five), they were left with little space to be *anxious,* at least in the sense that Freud, for example, meant neurotic anxiety— anxiety generated from within ourselves about things we don't really have rational cause to be afraid of. Perhaps the Middle Ages were relatively free of neurotic anxiety because such anxiety was a luxury no one could afford in their brief, difficult lives. In support of this proposition are the surveys showing that people in developing nations have lower rates of clinical anxiety than Americans despite life circumstances that are materially more difficult.

Moreover, political and cultural life in the Middle Ages was largely organized to minimize, even eliminate, the sorts of social uncertainties we contend with today. "From the moment of birth," the psychoanalyst and political philosopher Erich Fromm observed, "[the medieval person] was rooted in a structuralized whole, and thus life had a meaning which left no place, and no need, for doubt. A person was identical with his role in society; he was a peasant, an artisan, a knight, and not *an individual* who *happened* to have this or that occupation." One argument for why twenty-first-century life produces so much anxiety is that social and political roles are no longer understood to have been ordained by God or by nature—we have to *choose* our roles. Such choices, research shows, are stressful. As sodden with fear and darkness and death as the Middle Ages were, Fromm and others argue, they were likely freer of anxiety than our own time is.

The "dizziness of freedom," as Kierkegaard described it, produced by the ability to make choices, can have political implications: it can generate anxiety so intense that it creates a yearning to return to the comforting certainties of the primary ties—a yearning for what Fromm called "the escape from freedom." Fromm argued that this anxiety led many working-class Germans to willingly submit to Hitler in the 1930s. Paul Tillich, a theologian who grew up in Weimar Germany, similarly explained the rise of Nazism as a response to anxiety. "First of all a feeling of *fear* or, more exactly, of indefinite anxiety was prevailing," he writes of 1930s Germany. "Not only the economic and political, but also the cultural and religious, security seemed to be lost. There was nothing on which one could build; everything was without foundation. A catastrophic breakdown was expected every moment. Consequently, a longing for security was growing in everybody. A freedom that leads to fear and anxiety has lost its value; better authority with security than freedom with fear." Herbert L. Matthews, a *New York Times* correspondent who covered Europe between the wars, also observed that Nazism provided relief from anxiety: "Fascism was like a jail where the individual had a certain amount of security, shelter, and daily food." Arthur Schlesinger, Jr., writing a few years after the end of the Second World War, observed the same thing about Soviet Communism: "It has filled the 'vacuum of faith' caused by the waning of established religion; it provides the sense of purpose which heals internal agonies of anxiety and doubt." In periods of social disruption, when old verities no longer obtain, there's a danger that, as Rollo May put it, "people grasp at political authoritarianism in their desperate need for relief from anxiety."

One implication of the neurobiologist Robert Sapolsky's work is that human social and political systems that are highly fluid and dynamic generate more anxiety than systems that are static. Sapolsky points out that "for 99 percent of human history" society was "most probably strikingly unhierarchical" and therefore probably less psychologically stressful than in the modern era. For hundreds of thousands of years, the standard form of human social organization was the hunter-gatherer tribe—and such tribes were, judging from what we know of the bands of hunter-gatherers that still exist today, "remarkably egalitarian." Sapolsky goes so far as to say that the invention of agriculture, a relatively recent development in the scope of human history, "was one of the great stupid moves of all times" because it allowed for the stockpiling of food and, for the first time in history, "the stratification of society and the invention of classes." Stratification created relative poverty, making possible the invidious comparison and producing the occasion for status anxiety.

Jerome Kagan, among others, has argued that historical changes in the nature of human society have led to mismatches between our evolutionary hardwiring and what modern culture values. Qualities such as excessive timidity, caution, and concern with the opinions of others that would have been socially adaptive in early human communities are much "less adaptive in an increasingly competitive, mobile, industrialized, urban society than these traits had been several centuries earlier in a rural, agricultural economy of villages and towns," Kagan writes. In preliterate cultures, all members of a community generally shared the same values and sources of meaning. But starting sometime around the fifth century B.C., humans have increasingly lived in communities of strangers with diverse values—a trend that hyperaccelerated during the Renaissance and again during the Industrial Revolution. As a result, and especially since the Middle Ages, "a different kind of uncomfortable feeling was evoked by reflection on the adequacy of self's skills or status and the validity of one's moral premises," Kagan argues. "These feelings, which were labeled anxiety, ascended to the position of the alpha emotion in the hierarchy of human affects." Perhaps the human organism is not equipped to live life as society has lately designed it—a harsh zero-sum competition where the only gains to be had are at the expense of someone else, where "neurotic competition" has displaced solidarity and cooperation. "Competitive individualism militates against the experience of community, and the lack of community is a centrally important factor in contemporaneous anxiety," Rollo May argued in 1950.

By 1948, when W. H. Auden won the Pulitzer Prize for *The Age of Anxiety*, his six-part poem depicting man adrift ("as unattached as tumbleweeds") in an uncertain industrial world, anxiety seemed to have leached out of the realm of psychiatry to become a general cultural condition. During the 1950s, with America newly ascendant after the Second World War, the best-seller list was already stippled with books about how to achieve nervous relief. On the heels of Dale Carnegie's best-selling 1948 *How to Stop Worrying and Start Living* came a passel of books bearing titles like *Relax and Live* and *How to Con-*

*trol Worry and Cure Your Nerves Yourself* and *The Conquest of Fatigue and Fear,* suggesting that America was in the grip of what one social historian called "a national nervous breakdown." On March 31, 1961, a *Time* magazine cover story (featuring an image of Edvard Munch's *The Scream*) declared that the present era "is almost universally regarded as the Age of Anxiety." The British and American best-seller lists of the 1930s, a much more unstable time, were similarly populated with self-help books about "tension" and "nerves." *Conquest of Nerves: The Inspiring Record of a Personal Triumph over Neurasthenia* went through multiple printings in 1933 and 1934. *You Must Relax: A Practical Method of Reducing the Strains of Modern Living,* a book by an American physician named Edmund Jacobson, reached the top of the *New York Times* best-seller list in 1934.

In linking anxiety to uncertainty, Auden was both falling into a long historical tradition and anticipating modern neuroscience. One of the earliest uses of the word "anxiety" in English associated it with chronic uncertainty: the seventeenth-century British physician and poet Richard Flecknoe wrote that the anxious person "troubles herself with every thing" or is "an irresolute person" who "hovers in his every choice like an empty Ballance with no weight of Judgment to incline him to either scale. . . . When he begins to deliberate he never makes an end." (The first among the *Oxford English Dictionary*'s definitions of "anxiety" is "uneasiness about some *uncertain* event" [emphasis added].) Recent neurobiological investigations have revealed that uncertainty activates the anxiety circuits of the brain; the amygdalae of clinically anxious people are unusually sensitive to uncertainty. "Intolerance of uncertainty appears to be the central process involved in high levels of worry," Michel J. Dugas, a psychologist at Penn State, has written. Patients with generalized anxiety disorder "are highly intolerant of uncertainty," he says. "I use the metaphor of 'allergy' to uncertainty . . . to help them conceptualize their relationship with uncertainty." Between 2007 and 2010, there was a 31 percent increase in the number of news articles employing the word "uncertainty." No wonder we're so anxious.

Except maybe we're relatively less anxious than we think. Because if you read far enough back into the cultural history of nervousness and melancholy, each successive generation's claim to be the most anxious starts to sound much like the claims of the generations that preceded and followed it. When the British physician Edwin Lee, writing in *A Treatise on Some Nervous Disorders* in 1838, argued that "nervous complaints prevail at the present day to an extent unknown at any former period, or in any other nation," he sounds not only like George Miller Beard after him but also like the British naval surgeon Thomas Trotter before him. "At the beginning of the nineteenth century, we do not hesitate to affirm that nervous disorders . . . may now be justly reckoned two thirds of the whole with which civilized society is afflicted," Trotter wrote in *A View of the Nervous Temperament*, published in 1807.* Eighty years before Trotter, George Cheyne, the most prominent "nerve doctor" of his day, argued that the "atrocious and frightful symptoms" of the nervous affliction he had dubbed "the English Malady" were "scarce known to our ancestors, and never r[ose] to such fatal heights nor afflict[ed] such numbers and any other known nation."†

Some intellectual historians have traced the birth of modern anxiety to the work of the seventeenth-century Oxford scholar Robert Burton.‡ Burton was not a doctor, and he scarcely left his study, so busy was he for dozens of years reading astonishingly widely and scribbling away at his mammoth tome, *The Anatomy of Melancholy*, but his influence on Western literature and psychology has been lasting. Sir William Osler, the inventor of the medical residency system and one of the most influential doctors of the late nineteenth century, called *The Anatomy of Melancholy* "the greatest medical treatise ever written by a layman." John Keats, Charles Lamb, and Samuel Taylor Coleridge all treasured it and drew on it for their own work. Samuel Johnson, for his

---

* Trotter warned that an "epidemic" of nervousness threatened not only the "national character" of Britain but also its national security, since in their weakened states, British citizens were ripe for being invaded and conquered. (Trotter's fears about the country's epidemic of nervous weakness were intensified by Napoleon, who was marauding around the Continent.)

† Cheyne claimed that a third of the British population was afflicted with the nervous condition known variously as "spleen," "the vapours," or "hypochondria"—what would today be clustered in the *DSM* under the umbrellas of the anxiety or depressive disorders. (Note that Cheyne is claiming a level of anxious affliction for the England of the 1730s that is comparable to what the National Institute of Mental Health claims for America today.)

‡ Citing the reports of other writers, Burton claimed that the frequency of melancholia—which subsumed the modern diagnoses of both anxiety and depression—was "so common in this crazed age of ours" that "scarce one in a thousand is free from it."

part, told James Boswell that it was "the only book that ever took him out of bed two hours sooner than he wished to rise." Completed in 1621, when Burton was forty-four and then revised and expanded multiple times over the following seventeen years, *The Anatomy of Melancholy* is an epic work of synthesis that ranges across all of history, literature, philosophy, science, and theology up to that time. Originally published in three volumes, the work swelled as Burton tinkered and added (and added some more) in the years before his death in 1640; my own copy, a paperback facsimile of the sixth edition, is 1,382 pages of very small type.

Much of what Burton writes is absurd, nonsensical, self-contradictory, boring, in Latin, or all of the above. But it is also full of good humor and dark pessimism and consoling wisdom about the human condition (it's easy to see why Samuel Johnson was so taken with it), and in his exuberant travels through what seems like everything ever written, he managed to gather all of the extant human knowledge about melancholy in a single work and to establish for later writers and thinkers the terrain on which they would operate. The work is also clearly informed by his own depression and, like Augustine's *Confessions* and Freud's *Interpretation of Dreams*, draws insight not only from the expert testimony of others but from his own deep introspection. "Other men get their knowledge from books," he writes. "I get mine from melancholizing." Of course, a lot of Burton's knowledge does come from books—he cites thousands of them—and part of what makes the book so interesting is Burton's ability to objectify his subjective experience.*

Though parts of Burton's book were already outdated and ridiculous when he published it, some of his insights and observations are quite modern. His clinically precise description of a panic attack would pass muster with the *DSM-V*: "Many lamentable effects this fear causeth in men, as to be red, pale, tremble, sweat; it makes sudden cold and heat to come over all the body, palpitation of the heart, syncope, etc."

---

* I feel a kinship with Burton because he freely conceded that he wrote about melancholy to combat his own: "I write of melancholy, by being busy to avoid melancholy." (I write of anxiety to avoid being anxious.)

And here's a passable description of what would today be diagnosed as generalized anxiety disorder: "Many men are so amazed and astonished with fear, they know not where they are, what they say, what they do, and that which is worst, it tortures them many days before with continual affrights and suspicion. It hinders most honourable attempts, and makes their hearts ache, sad and heavy. They that live in fear are never free, resolute, secure, never merry, but in continual pain: that, as Vives truly said, *Nulla est miseria major quam metus,* no greater misery, no rack, nor torture like unto it; ever suspicious, anxious, solicitous, they are childishly drooping without reason, without judgment, 'especially if some terrible object be offered,' as Plutarch hath it."*

Burton piles up hundreds upon hundreds of theories about anxiety and depression, many of which contradict each other, but in the end the treatments he emphasizes might be boiled down to getting regular exercise, playing chess, taking baths, reading books, listening to music, using laxatives, eating right, practicing sexual moderation, and, above all, keeping busy. "There is no greater cause of melancholy than idleness, 'no better cure than business,'" he wrote, citing the Arabian physician Rhasis. Channeling the wisdom of the Epicureans and the Stoics (and, from the East, the Buddhists), he advises modesty of ambition and an acceptance of what one has as a path to happiness: "If men would attempt no more than what they can bear, they should lead contented lives and, learning to know themselves, would limit their ambition; they would perceive then that nature hath enough without seeking such superfluities and unprofitable things, which bring nothing

---

* Plutarch, the biographer and historian, described vividly and accurately how what we would today call clinical depression can bring with it an escalation of anxiety. Anyone who has suffered the torturous insomnia of agitated depression—where anxiety begets sleeplessness and sleeplessness begets more anxiety—will recognize the clinical aptness of Plutarch's description. To the depressed person, he writes, "every little evil is magnified by the scaring spectres of his anxiety. . . . Asleep or awake he is haunted alike by the spectres of his anxiety. Awake, he makes no use of his reason; and asleep, he enjoys no respite from his alarms. His reason always slumbers; his fears are always awake. Nowhere can he find an escape from his imaginary terrors."

Plutarch was not a physician—but Galen, born not long after Plutarch died, was. Describing an epidemic of anxiety that sounds remarkably modern, Galen wrote of having seen "tremors in the hearts of healthy young people and adolescents weak and thin from anxiety and depression" and patients with "scarce, turbulent, and interrupted sleep, palpitations, vertigo" and "sadness, anxiety, diffidence, and the belief of being persecuted."

with them but grief and molestation. As a fat body is more subject to diseases, so are rich men to absurdities and fooleries, to many casualties and cross inconveniences."

Trying to directly compare levels of anxiety between eras is a fool's errand. Modern poll data and statistics about rising and falling levels of tranquilizer consumption aside, there is no magical anxiety meter that can transcend the cultural particularities of place and time to objectively measure levels of anxiety—which, like any emotion, is in some sense an inherently subjective and culturally bound thing. But if anxiety is a descendant of fear, and if fear is an evolutionary impulse designed to help prolong the survival of the species, then anxiety is surely as old as the human race. Humans have always and ever been anxious (even if that anxiety gets refracted in different ways in different cultures); some relatively fixed proportion of us have always been more anxious than others. As soon as the human brain became capable of apprehending the future, it became capable of being apprehensive about the future. The ability to plan, the ability to imagine the future—with these come the ability to worry, to dread the future. Did Cro-Magnons suffer nervous stomachs when predators lurked outside the cave? Did early hominids find their palms getting sweaty and their mouths dry when interacting with higher-status members of the tribe? Were there agoraphobic cavemen or Neanderthals who endured performance anxiety or fear of heights? I imagine there were, since these proto–*Homo sapiens* were the products of the same evolution that has generated our own capacity for anxiety, and they possessed the same, or very similar, physiological equipment for fear.

Which suggests that anxiety is an abiding part of the human condition. "In our day we still see our major threats as coming from the tooth and claw of physical enemies when they are actually largely psychological and in the broadest sense spiritual—that is they deal with meaninglessness," Rollo May wrote in 1977 in the foreword to his revised edition of *The Meaning of Anxiety*. "We are no longer prey to tigers and mastodons but to damage to our self-esteem, ostracism by our group, or the threat of losing out in the competitive struggle. The form of anxiety has changed, but the experience remains relatively the same."

PART V

# Redemption and Resilience

# CHAPTER II

# Redemption

*The capacity to bear anxiety is important for the individual's self-realization and for his conquest of his environment. . . . Self-actualization occurs only at the price of moving ahead despite such shocks. This indicates the constructive use of anxiety.*
—KURT GOLDSTEIN, *Human Nature in the Light of Psychopathology* (1940)

Starting when I was ten years old, I saw the same psychiatrist once or twice a week for twenty-five years. Dr. L. was the psychiatrist who, when I was taken to McLean Hospital as a comprehensively phobic ten-year-old, administered my Rorschach test. When I started therapy with him in the early 1980s, he was approaching fifty, tall and lanky, balding a little, with a beard in the classic Freudian style. Over the years, the beard came and went a few times, and he lost more of his hair, which turned, over time, from brown to salt-and-pepper to white. He moved his office from one place (where he lived with his first wife) to another (where he lived with his second wife) to a third (where he leased space from an eye doctor) to a fourth (where, in keeping with his migration in a New Age direction, he shared a waiting room with a massage therapist and an electrologist) to, finally, the last time I visited him, a building by the ocean on Cape Cod (where he'd moved his practice and where his office is once again connected to his house).

Trained at Harvard in the 1950s and early 1960s, Dr. L. came of professional age in the late stages of the psychoanalytic heyday, when Freudianism still dominated. When I first encountered Dr. L., he was a believer both in medication and in such Freudian concepts as neurosis and repression, Oedipus complexes and transference. Our first sessions, in the early 1980s, were filled with Rorschach tests and free-associating and discussions of early memories from my youngest years. Our last sessions, in the mid-2000s, were focused on role-playing and "energy work"; he also spent a lot of time during those latter years trying to get me to sign up for a special kind of yoga program that is today defending itself in federal court against multiple allegations that it is a brainwashing cult.

Here's some of what we did in our sessions together over a quarter century: looked at picture books (1981); played backgammon (1982–85); played darts (1985–88); experimented sporadically with various cutting-edge psychotherapeutic methods of a progressively more New Age complexion, such as hypnotism, facilitated communication, eye movement desensitization and reprocessing, inner-child therapy, energy systems therapy, and internal family systems therapy (1988–2004). I was the beneficiary, or possibly the victim, of seemingly every passing trend in psychotherapy and psychopharmacology.

A few years ago, when embarking on the research for this book, I decided to track down Dr. L. for an interview. His inability to cure me notwithstanding, who better to help me figure out my anxiety than the man who had worked for decades to treat me? So I wrote to him to tell him what I was working on and to ask if I might interview him about my many years of therapy with him and look at any old case files of mine he still had. He said he didn't have my files anymore but that he would be happy to talk. So on a cold afternoon in late November, I drove from Boston out the length of Cape Cod to Provincetown, brisk and barren in the off-season. It had been more than five years since I'd last seen or spoken to him, and I was anxious (of course) about how the meeting would go. Wanting to maintain a journalistic composure—and to avoid falling into old dependent habits of relating to him (he'd been a father figure for twenty-five years)—I popped a Xanax beforehand and briefly considered stopping at a liquor store for a sedating nip of vodka.* I pulled into his driveway in the midafternoon.

Waiting on his back deck, he waved and gestured me up the steps and into his office, where he greeted me warmly, if a little warily, won-

---

* That I even contemplated this, of course, suggests that those decades of therapy with Dr. L. were not terribly effective; my dependencies are now chemical.

dering, I suspect, if I had come to gather evidence for a malpractice suit. (His e-mail correspondence leading up to this meeting, about my case files and so forth, had all seemed carefully worded, as though vetted by a lawyer.) By then in his late seventies, he still looked lithe and fit and appeared younger than his years. We sat down and I caught him up on what I'd been doing the past few years, and then we began talking about my anxiety.

What, I asked, did he remember about my case from when I originally showed up at the psychiatric hospital more than two decades earlier?

"I remember it pretty clearly," he said. "You were a very distressed child."

I asked him about my emetophobia, which had already presented itself forcefully by the time I was ten. "It was a dramatic fantasy that vomiting would make your body come apart," he said. "Your parents didn't help you to reality-test, and you merged with that phobia."

Did he remember how he and the team at the mental hospital interpreted my Rorschach test? I had recently approached the records department at McLean Hospital to ask whether archivists could find my original evaluation file, but it had been moved off-site some years ago, and no one had been able to track it down. The only image I could recall was one that I remembered looking like a wounded bat, its wings torn, unable to escape from its cave. "That likely had something to do with your feelings of being abandoned or being enveloped," Dr. L. said. "A sense of lack of safety and of enormous vulnerability."

I asked him what he thought had produced that vulnerability.

"There was a whole host of causal factors. We knew there were deficits in the parents."

He spoke first about my father, whom he knew very well, having counseled him when my mother left him for the managing partner of her law firm.* "When you were growing up, your father had a very

---

* This, by the way, led to a rather complex web of conflicts of interest. On the Sunday in the autumn of 1995 that my mother announced to him she might want a divorce, my father, desperate to save the marriage, stopped drinking completely for the first time in years and, in a gesture that was completely out of character, acquiesced to emergency couples' counseling. For years before that, my father, despite footing the bill for my sister's and my shrinks, disdained psychotherapy. "How was your wacko lesson?" he'd ask jeeringly after I'd had an appointment. He did this so often that the term became a part of the

strong 'knower,' which meant that parts of himself stood strongly in judgment. He didn't have a lot of tolerance for anxious behavior. Your

---

family's lingua franca, and eventually my sister and I were referring without irony to our wacko lessons. ("Mom, can you give me a ride to my wacko lesson on Wednesday?") In 1995, Dr. L. had recently hung out a shingle—with his new wife, Nurse G.—as a relationship counselor. So my parents began seeing Dr. L. and Nurse G. (who was also a licensed clinical social worker) in intensive couples' therapy. Which would have been fine except that I—by then in my midtwenties—was still seeing Dr. L. as my principal psychotherapist. So my appointments with Dr. L. started to run something like this:

> DR. L.: How are you?
> ME: Well, I had kind of a rough week. I had a panic attack when—
> DR. L.: How are your parents doing?
> ME: What?
> DR. L.: Have you talked to your mother or father in the last couple of days? Has your mother said anything about whether she's still seeing Michael P.?

As it happened, my mother *was* still seeing Michael P. and in fact would soon be setting up house with him.

Unmoored by my mother's departure, my father started seeing Dr. L. for psychotherapy on an individual basis. By this point, we might as well have had Dr. L. on family retainer. He had just provided six months of marriage counseling to my parents, was seeing my father at least once a week, and was still seeing me. To make this web of psychopathology even more incestuous, my mother had started seeing Nurse G. on an individual basis.

My own therapy sessions with Dr. L. came to be dominated by his questions about his new star patient, my father. I couldn't blame Dr. L. for finding my father the more interesting patient. After all, while he'd been seeing me for more than fifteen years, he'd only been seeing my dad for a few months. Being able to talk to my father about his relationship with me, and then to talk to me about my relationship with my father, surely provided an intriguing *Rashomon*-like fascination for Dr. L. He was seeing my father, his wife was seeing my mother, he and his wife were seeing my mother and father together, and he was seeing me—a kaleidoscopic game of family telephone, with Dr. L. and Nurse G. as the switchboard operators.

My dad entered therapy emotionally wrecked by his separation, profoundly shaken, and drinking heavily. He completed therapy less than two years later, happy, productive, remarried, and deemed (by himself and by Dr. L.) to be much more "self-actualized" and "authentic" than he had been. He was in and out of therapy with Dr. L. in eighteen months. Whereas I was entering my nineteenth year of therapy with Dr. L. and was still as anxious as ever.

A few years ago, my wife asked my father what had happened when he graduated from therapy with Dr. L. Had Dr. L. said anything about me when he did? He had. Dr. L., my father recalled, had told him that I wasn't anywhere near ready to graduate and that I had "serious issues" I still needed help with.

Which, I suppose, was manifestly the case. But wasn't one of those issues the fact that my own father—whose stern critical assessments of my life and work over the years had likely contributed to the leakiness of my self-esteem—had, in borrowing my therapist and advancing from temporary basket case to cured in no time at all as I languished in purgatorial neurotic stasis, confirmed yet again my general inferiority and incompetence? When my father graduated, I felt like a schoolchild whose younger sibling has just sped past him in the accelerated class: my father, starting therapy years (decades!) after me, shot through quickly to graduation with honors, while I, trapped in remedial classes, repeated third grade for the nineteenth time.

anxiety would make him blow up with anger. He had no empathy. When you got anxious, he would judge it and want to fix it. He couldn't just help you sit with it. He couldn't soothe you."

Dr. L. paused for a moment. "He couldn't soothe himself, either. He would judge his anxiety. In his mind, anxiety is weakness. It makes him angry."*

What about my mother?

"She was too anxious herself to be very effective at helping you cope with your own anxiety," Dr. L. said. "She organized her life around trying not to be anxious. So when *you* got anxious, *she* would get anxious. A parent-child unit like that, the child takes on the anxiety of the parent but doesn't know where it came from. Her anxiety became yours, and you couldn't handle it, and she couldn't help you.

"You had problems with 'object constancy,'" he continued. "You couldn't carry an internal image of your parents. Whenever you were away from them, you were in fundamental doubt about whether you were being abandoned. Your parents could never settle down enough to give you the assurance they were on the planet."†

Dr. L. said he believed this separation anxiety was compounded by my mother's overprotectiveness. "The message you got from your mother was, *You can't take it—don't take risks because the anxiety will be too overwhelming.*"

I tell him it sounds like he's mainly attributing my anxiety to psycho-

---

* *My father's anger.* Among the darker moments of my childhood was this: One night when I was fourteen, I woke up at three in the morning with one of my bouts of screaming panic. Hearing me cry, my father lost control. He stormed into my room, trailed by my mother, and started hitting me repeatedly, telling me to shut up. This made me cry harder. "You twerp, you pathetic little twerp!" he shouted as he picked me up and threw me. I hit the wall and slid to the floor. As I lay there, racked by sobbing while my father looked down at me, I could see my mother standing impassively in the doorway. I have a predisposition toward feeling lonely even when surrounded by friends and family; in that moment, I felt more lonely than ever before or since. (Here, for confirmation-of-memory purposes, is an entry from my dad's diary, which he began keeping after my mother left him and which he kindly shared with me a few years ago: "At about age 11, however, Scott began to become very anxious and was particularly phobic about vomiting. He began to manifest some behavioral oddities that Anne detected and which I denied. Anne was right, and, acerbically reviling my psychological blindness, Dr. Sherry [a pediatric psychiatrist] recommended an evaluation at McLean. This process led into Scott's now extended psychotherapy with Dr. [L.]. The initial rigmarole was terrible, however. Scott got much worse and in particular couldn't sleep at night. He had to take Thorazine and imipramine. In frustration I often got verbally and even physically abusive.")

† This comports with the Bowlby-Ainsworth attachment theory concept of the secure base.

dynamic issues—to the relationship I had with my parents. But doesn't modern research suggest that vulnerability to anxiety is largely genetic? Doesn't, for instance, Jerome Kagan's work on the links between genes and temperament, and between temperament and anxiety, suggest that anxious character is hardwired into the genome?

"Look, maybe having an 'inhibited temperament' made things worse for you," he said. "But my own view is that even if you hadn't had that kind of genetically produced temperament, your mother's personality might still have given you issues. Neither she nor your father could offer what you needed. You couldn't soothe yourself.

"Yes," he continued, "there's evidence that you've got neurochemical problems produced by your genes. And your mother's personality was a bad match for your genetic temperament. But a gene predisposing you to an illness doesn't necessarily give you that illness. Geneticists say, 'We'll map the genes and find out the trouble.' *No! Not true!* Even with breast cancer, sometimes only an environmental factor—like nutrition—will catalyze a genetic predisposition to cancer into actual cancer."

I observe that medication—Xanax, Klonopin, Celexa, alcohol—is more effective at soothing me than my parents ever were, or than Dr. L. was, or than my own self-will (whatever that may consist of) is. Doesn't that suggest that my anxiety is a medical problem more than a psychological one, regardless of what my parents' shortcomings may have been? That anxiety is a problem embedded in the body, in the physical brain rather than some disembodied mind or psyche—a problem that leaches up from body to brain to mind rather than seeping down from mind to brain to body?

"False dichotomy!" he says emphatically, standing up to pull a book off his shelf: *Descartes' Error.* In it, the neurologist Antonio Damasio explains that Descartes was wrong to argue that the mind and body are distinct. The mind-body duality is not in fact a duality, Dr. L. says, paraphrasing Damasio. The body gives rise to the mind; the mind imbues the body. The two cannot be differentiated. "Neocortical function"—that is, the mind—"makes us who we are," Dr. L. says. "But the limbic system"—which is autonomous and unconscious—"may be just as relevant, if not more, in determining who we are. The neocortex can't make a decision without the emotional system playing in."

To illustrate the inseparability of body and mind, Dr. L. talked about the effects of trauma. (He had recently been to Sri Lanka, where he coached psychotherapists on how to work with survivors of the 2004 tsunami.) The experience of trauma or abuse, he explained, gets stored in the body, "woven into the bodily tissue."

"Consider Holocaust survivors," he said. "Even grandkids of Holocaust survivors carry extra anxiety that is measurable at a physiological level. They tend to have more anxious triggers. If they see a movie with victims of violence in Somalia, they respond to it much more strongly." This is true, he said, not just of the children of Holocaust survivors but of their grandchildren and even great-grandchildren. "They've got something plastered into their bodies via the experience of their parents or grandparents. The trauma doesn't even belong to them, but it affects them." (I think here of my father's Holocaust fixation, the books about Nazis piled always on his bedside table, the World War II documentaries always running on the TV. His mother and father had escaped Germany before the Holocaust; so did much of the rest of the family, but not before his uncles and grandfather were beaten up on Kristallnacht.)

I asked Dr. L. how much he thought the psychiatric field had changed since he entered it nearly fifty years ago, especially regarding its thinking about the causes and treatment of anxiety.

"Freudians were about 'insight' *über alles*," he said. "If you had insight about your neurosis, the expectation was that you could control it. *Wrong!*"

Dr. L.'s treatments of choice these days are, depending on your point of view, either high-tech and cutting-edge or New Age and weird: for instance, eye movement desensitization and reprocessing, which involves moving your eyes back and forth while reliving a trauma, and internal family systems therapy, based on the work of the psychiatrist Richard Schwartz, which involves training a patient to gain control of his multiple selves through the "conducting self" and helping him to develop a better, more strengthening relationship with his vulnerable inner child. In my latter years of therapy with Dr. L., I spent a lot of time moving from chair to chair in his office, inhabiting different "selves" and "energies," and talking to my inner child.

"We used to have a monolithic view of mood and personality disorders," Dr. L. continued. "But now we realize we have little packets of personality; they have their own sets of beliefs and values." The key to treatment, he says, is to make the patient conscious of these multiple selves and to help him manage the selves that carry trauma or anxiety.

"Today," he said, "we now know much more about the neurocircuitry of anxiety. Sometimes you need to medicate. But newer, better psychiatry alters the brain chemistry—alters it in the same way drugs do."

"Am I doomed by my neurocircuitry?" I asked. "I went to therapy with you for twenty-five years, and have seen multiple other therapists, and have tried multiple methods of treatment. And yet here I am, advancing into middle age, and still suffering from chronic and often debilitating anxiety."

"No, you're not doomed," Dr. L. said. "We now know enough about neuroplasticity to understand that the circuitry is always growing. You can always modify the software."


Even if I can't fully recover from my anxiety, I've come to believe there may be some redeeming value in it.

Historical evidence suggests that anxiety can be allied to artistic and creative genius. The literary gifts of Emily Dickinson, for example, were inextricably bound up with her anxiety. (She was completely housebound, and in fact rarely left her bedroom, after age forty.) Franz Kafka yoked his neurotic sensibility to his artistic sensibility; so, of course, did Woody Allen. Jerome Kagan, the Harvard psychologist, argues that T. S. Eliot's anxiety and high-reactive physiology helped make him a great poet. Eliot was, Kagan observes, a "shy, cautious, sensitive child"—but because he also had a supportive family, good schooling, and "unusual verbal abilities," Eliot was able to "exploit his temperament" to become an outstanding poet.

Perhaps most famously, Marcel Proust transmuted his neurotic sensibility into art. Marcel's father, Adrien, was a physician specializing in nervous health and the author of an influential book called *The Hygiene of the Neurasthenic*. Marcel read his father's work, as well as books by many of the other leading nerve doctors of his day, and incorporated their work into his; his fiction and nonfiction are "saturated with the vocabulary of nervous dysfunction," as one critic has put it. At various points throughout *Remembrance of Things Past*, characters either comment on or embody the idea that, as Aristotle first observed, nervous suffering can give rise to great art. For Proust, refinement of artistic sensibility was directly tied to a nervous disposition. From the high-strung comes high art.*

From the high-strung can also come, at least some of the time, great science. Dean Simonton, a psychologist at the University of California, Davis, who has spent decades studying the psychology of genius, estimates that a third of all eminent scientists suffer from anxi-

---

* Consider also such nervous invalid intellectuals as David Hume, James Boswell, John Stuart Mill, George Miller Beard, William James, Alice James, Gustave Flaubert, John Ruskin, Herbert Spencer, Edmund Gosse, Michael Faraday, Arnold Toynbee, Charlotte Perkins Gilman, and Virginia Woolf, every single one of whom suffered debilitating nervous prostration early (and sometimes late) in their careers. During young adulthood, David Hume, who would become one of the bright stars of the Scottish Enlightenment, abandoned his studies in the law and entered upon a far more precarious career in philosophy. In the spring of 1729, following a period of intense intellectual exertion, Hume broke down. He felt, as he later wrote in a letter to a doctor documenting his ills, physically exhausted and emotionally distraught; he couldn't concentrate on the book he was trying to write (which would eventually become the famous *Treatise of Human Nature*), and he suffered terrible stomach pains, rashes, and heart palpitations that incapacitated him for the better part of five years. Much in the way Darwin later would, Hume sampled the full range of remedies on offer in the hope of finding a cure for what he called his nervous "distemper": he took water treatments at spas and went for walks and rides in the country; he took the "Course of Bitters and Anti-hysteric Pills" and "an English Pint of Claret Wine every Day" prescribed by his family's physician. Writing to another doctor in search of succor, Hume asked "whether among all those Scholars you have been acquainted with you have ever known any affected in this manner? Whether I can ever hope for a Recovery? Whether I must long wait for it? Whether my Recovery will ever be perfect, and my Spirits regain their former Spring and Vigor, so as to endure the Fatigue of deep and abstruse thinking?" In the event, Hume did recover: after he published *A Treatise of Human Nature* in 1739, he seems not to have suffered further, and he went on to become perhaps the most important philosopher ever to write in English.

The political philosopher John Stuart Mill endured a similar nervous breakdown. In the fall of 1826, when he was twenty years old, Mill experienced a complete emotional collapse, which he would years later recount in the famous fifth chapter, "A Crisis in My Mental History," of his autobiography. Through the "melancholy winter" of that year, he was, he writes, in an unrelenting state of "depression," "dejection," and "dulled nerves." He found himself so paralyzed by his "irrepressible self-consciousness" that he could scarcely function. (This puts one in mind of the novelist David Foster Wallace, another genius done in by his acute anxiety.) After eighteen months of this unremitting misery, Mill wrote, "a small ray of light broke in upon my gloom" while he was reading the memoirs of a French historian: he needed, he decided, to become less repressed and analytic and to develop his emotional and aesthetic faculties. The arduous education imposed on him by his "grim and exacting" father had, he realized, robbed him of a normal childhood and of an inner emotional life. "The cultivation of the feelings became one of the cardinal points in my ethical and philosophical creed," he wrote. By becoming more attuned to his emotions (which he cultivated by, for instance, reading the poetry of Wordsworth), he was evidently able to leave anxiety and depression behind.

ety or depression or both. He surmises that the same cognitive or neurobiological mechanisms that predispose certain people to developing
anxiety disorders also enhance the sort of creative thinking that produces conceptual breakthroughs in science. When Sir Isaac Newton
invented calculus, no one knew about it for ten years—because he was
too anxious and depressed to tell anyone. (For several years, he was too
agoraphobic to leave his house.) Perhaps if Darwin had not been forc-
ibly housebound by his anxiety for decades on end, he would never have
been able to finish his work on evolution. Sigmund Freud's career was
nearly derailed early on by his terrible anxiety and self-doubt; he overcame it to become a cult figure and a major intellectual influence on
generations of psychotherapists. Once his reputation as a great man of
science had been established, Freud and his acolytes sought to engrave
in stone the image of him as the eternally self-assured wise man. But
his early letters reveal otherwise.*

---

* Ernest Jones, the original guardian of Freud's legacy, once claimed that only "uninteresting details"
had been excised from the collection of Freud's letters he published. But among those strategically
omitted letters were some 130 to his friend Wilhelm Fliess, many of them consisting of a litany of
neurotic, hypochondriacal complaint.

"I have not been free of symptoms for as much as half a day, and my mood and ability to work
are really at a low ebb," Freud wrote Fliess in early May 1894. The omitted letters are full of symptom
reports, repeated over and over again. By his own account, Freud suffered migraine headaches, pains
all over his body, all kinds of stomach distress, and endless heart palpitations that led him to predict
in one letter that he would die in his early fifties of a "ruptured heart." His (failed) attempts to wean
himself from cigar smoking would cause a resurgence of physical symptoms: "I feel aged, sluggish, not
healthy." When his father died in 1896, he reported a seemingly phobic preoccupation with death, what
he called his "death delirium."

This is hardly the image of the stoical, self-assured master of the mind that he sought to project.
"It is too distressing for a medical man who spends every hour of the day struggling to gain an understanding of the neuroses not to know whether he is suffering from a justifiable or a hypochondriacal
mild depression," Freud told Fleiss. His letters are replete with melancholic, self-lacerating thoughts:
he believes that he will die in obscurity, that his work is "rubbish," that all his labors will amount to
nothing. At times, it seems he cannot possibly survive, let alone thrive, in the field he has chosen. "I
have been through some kind of neurotic experience," he wrote on June 22, 1897, plagued by "twilight
thoughts, veiled doubts, with barely a ray of light here or there."

"I still do not know what has been happening to me," he noted a couple of weeks later. "Something from the deepest depths of my own neurosis set itself against any advance in the understanding
of the neuroses."

In August 1897, Freud wrote to Fliess from Bad Aussee, Austria, where he was vacationing with
his family. Freud was not happy: he was "in a period of bad humor" and "tormented by grave doubts
about my theory of the neuroses." His vacation was doing nothing toward "diminishing the agitation
in my head and feelings." Despite his growing practice, Freud wrote, "the chief patient I am preoc-

No, anxiety is not, by itself, going to make you a Nobel Prize–winning poet or a groundbreaking scientist. But if you harness your anxious temperament correctly, it might make you a better worker. Jerome Kagan, who has spent more than sixty years studying people with anxious temperaments, believes that anxious employees are better employees. In fact, he says, he learned to hire only people with high-reactive temperaments as research assistants. "They're compulsive, they don't make errors, they're careful when they're coding data," he told *The New York Times*. They "are generally conscientious and almost obsessively well-prepared." Assuming they can avoid succumbing to full-blown anxiety disorders, "worriers are likely to be the most thorough workers and the most attentive friends," as *The Times* put it. Other research supports Kagan's observation. A 2012 study by psychiatrists at the University of Rochester Medical Center found that conscientious people who were highly neurotic tended to be more reflective, more goal oriented, more organized, and better at planning than average; they tended to be effective, "high-functioning" workers—and to be better at taking care of their physical health than other workers. ("These people are likely to weigh the consequences of their actions," Nicholas Turiano, the lead researcher, said. "Their level of neuroticism coupled with conscientiousness probably stops them from engaging in risky behaviors.") A 2013 study in the *Academy of Management Journal* found that neurotics contribute more than managers predicted to group projects, while extroverts contribute less, with the contributions of the neurotics becoming even more valuable over time. The director of the study, Corinne Bendersky, an associate professor at UCLA's Anderson School of Management, says that if she were staffing a team for a group project, "I would staff it with more neurotics and fewer extroverts than my initial instinct would lead me to do." In 2005 researchers at the University of Wales published a paper, "Can Worriers Be Winners?," reporting that financial managers high in anxiety tended to be the best, most effective money managers, as long as their worrying was accom-

---

cupied with is myself." The following summer, on another vacation, he reported unhappily that his work was progressing poorly and that he was bereft of motivation. "The secret of this restlessness is hysteria," he concluded remarkably, assigning to himself the affliction that he had staked his career on curing.

panied by high IQs. Smart people who worry a lot, the researchers concluded, tend to produce the best results.*

Unfortunately, the positive correlation between worrying and job performance disappeared when the worriers had low IQs. But some evidence suggests that excessive worrying is itself allied to high IQ. Dr. W. says that his anxious patients tend to be his smartest patients. (In his experience, anxious lawyers have tended to be particularly smart—skilled not only at foreseeing complex legal eventualities but also at imagining worst-case scenarios for themselves.) Dr. W.'s anecdotal observations are supported by recent scientific data. Some studies have found the correlation to be quite direct: the higher your IQ, the more likely you are to worry; the lower your IQ, the less likely you are to worry. A study published in 2012 in *Frontiers in Evolutionary Neuroscience* found that high IQ scores correlated with high levels of worry in people diagnosed with generalized anxiety disorder. (Anxious people are very smart at plotting out possible bad outcomes.) Jeremy Coplan, the lead author of that study, says that anxiety is evolutionarily adaptive because "every so often there's a wild-card danger." When such a danger arises, anxious people are more likely to be prepared to survive. Some people, Coplan says, are effectively stupid enough that they are "incapable of seeing any danger, even when danger is imminent"; moreover, "if these folks are in positions as leaders, they are going to indicate to the general populace that there's no need to worry." Coplan, a professor of psychiatry at the State University of New York Downstate Medical Center, says that anxiety can be a good trait in political leaders—and that lack of anxiety can be dangerous. (Some commentators have suggested, based on findings like Coplan's, that the main cause of the economic crash of 2008 was politicians and financiers who were either stupid or insufficiently anxious or both.)

The correlations aren't universal, of course: there are plenty of brilliant daredevils and stupid worriers. And, as always, this comes with the proviso that anxiety is productive mainly when it is not so excessive

---

* "Anxiety is an important component of motivated cognition, essential for efficient functioning in situations that require caution, self-discipline and the general anticipation of threat," the researchers wrote.

as to be debilitating. But if you are anxious, perhaps you can take heart from the growing collection of evidence suggesting that anxiety and intelligence are linked.

Anxiety may also be tied both to ethical behavior and to effective leadership. My wife once mused aloud about what I might lose if I were to be fully cured of my anxiety—and about what *she* might lose if I were to lose my anxious temperament.

"I hate your anxiety," she said, "and I hate that it makes you unhappy. But what if there are things that I love about you that are connected to your anxiety? What if," she asked, getting to the heart of the matter, "you're cured of your anxiety and you become a total jerk?"

I suspect I might—because it may be that my anxiety lends me an inhibition and a social sensitivity that make me more attuned to other people and a more tolerable spouse than I otherwise would be. Evidently, fighter pilots have unusually high divorce rates—a fact that may be tied to their having low levels of anxiety and a corresponding low baseline autonomic arousal, which together are tied not only to a need for adventure (indulged by flying a fighter plane or having extramarital affairs) but also to a certain interpersonal obtuseness, a lack of sensitivity to their partners' subtle social cues.* Anxious people, because they are vigilantly scanning the environment for threats, tend to be more attuned than adrenaline junkies to other people's emotions and social signals.

The notion of a connection between anxiety and morality long predates the findings of modern science or my wife's intuition. Saint Augustine believed fear was adaptive because it helps people behave morally. (That's also what both Thomas Burgess and Charles Darwin believed about anxiety and blushing: fear of misbehavior helps primates and humans behave "rightly," preserving social comity.) The pragmatist philosophers Charles Sanders Peirce and John Dewey believed that the human aversion to experiencing negative emotions like anxiety, shame, and guilt provides a kind of internal psychological incentive to behave ethically. Furthermore, psychological studies of criminals have found

---

* The Air Force reportedly has the highest divorce rate in the U.S. armed services, and nine out of ten fighter-pilot divorces are initiated by wives.

them to be low in anxiety, on average, and to have low-reactive amyg-dalae. (Criminals also tend to have lower-than-average IQs.)

In earlier chapters, I discussed how hundreds of studies on primates conducted over the last half century have found in various ways that the combination of certain genes and small amounts of early life stress can lead to lifelong anxious and depressive behavior in humans and other animals. But recent studies on rhesus monkeys by Stephen Suomi, the chief of the Laboratory of Comparative Ethology at the NIH, have found that when anxious monkeys were taken in early life from their anxious mothers and given to nonanxious mothers to be raised, a fas-cinating thing happened: these monkeys grew up to display *less* anxiety than their genetic siblings—and they also, intriguingly, *tended to become the alpha males of the troop.* This suggests that some quotient of anxiety not only enhances your odds of living longer but also, under the right circumstances, can equip you to be a leader.

My anxiety can be intolerable. It often makes me miserable. But it is also, maybe, a gift—or at least the other side of a coin I ought to think twice about before trading in. Perhaps my anxiety is linked to what-ever limited moral sense I can claim. What's more, the same anxious imagination that sometimes drives me mad with worry also enables me to plan effectively for unforeseen circumstances or unintended conse-quences that other, less vigilant temperaments might not. The quick social judging that is allied to my performance anxiety is also useful in helping me to size up situations quickly and to manage people and defuse conflict.

Finally, at some brute evolutionary level, my anxiety might actually help keep me alive. I am less likely than you bold and heedless people (you fighter pilots and con artists, with your low baseline autonomic arousal) to die in an extreme sporting accident or to provoke a fight that leads to my getting shot.*

In his 1941 essay "The Wound and the Bow," the literary critic Edmund Wilson writes of the Sophoclean hero Philoctetes, the son of a king, whose suppurating, never-healing snakebite wound on his

---

* On the other hand, I'm more likely to die prematurely from some stress-related disease.

foot is linked to a gift for unerring accuracy with his bow and arrow—his "malodorous disease" is inseparable from his "superhuman art" for marksmanship.* I have always been drawn to this parable: in it lies, as the novelist Jeanette Winterson put it, "the proximity of wound to gift," the insight that in weakness and shamefulness is also the potential for transcendence, heroism, or redemption. My anxiety remains an unhealed wound that, at times, holds me back and fills me with shame—but it may also be, at the same time, a source of strength and a bestower of certain blessings.

---

* Wilson's essay is about how art and psychological suffering are linked in writers like Sophocles, Charles Dickens, Ernest Hemingway, James Joyce, and Edith Wharton.

# CHAPTER 12

# Resilience

*Anxiety cannot be avoided, but it can be reduced. The problem of the management of anxiety is that of reducing anxiety to normal levels, and then to use this normal anxiety as stimulation to increase one's awareness, vigilance, zest for living.*
— ROLLO MAY, *The Meaning of Anxiety* (1950)

The essayist, poet, and lexicographer Samuel Johnson was, famously, a melancholic intellectual in the classic mode, suffering badly from what Robert Burton called the "Disease of the learned." In 1729, when he was twenty years old, Johnson found himself "overwhelmed with an horrible hypochondria, with perpetual irritation, fretfulness, and impatience; and with a dejection, gloom, and despair, which made existence misery," as James Boswell reported in his *Life of Samuel Johnson*. "From this dismal malady he never afterwards was perfectly relieved." ("That it was, in some degree, occasioned by a defect in his nervous system appears highly probable," Boswell surmised.) It was, as another biographer records, "an appalling state of mind, in which feelings of intense anxiety alternated with feelings of utter hopelessness." Many contemporaries noted Johnson's strange tics and twitches, which suggests he may have had OCD. He also seemed to have what would today be called agoraphobia. (He once wrote to the local magistrate asking to be excused from jury duty because "he came very near fainting . . . in all public places.") Johnson himself refers to his "morbid melancholy" and was ever worried that his dejection would tip over into full-blown madness. In addition to dipping regularly into Burton's *Anatomy of Melancholy*, Johnson read widely in both classic and contemporary medical texts.

Desperate to hold on to his sanity, Johnson—like Burton before him—seized on the idea that idleness and slothful habits were breeding grounds for anxiety and madness and that the best way to combat them was with steady occupation and regular habits, such as rising at the same time early each morning. "Imagination," he would say, "never takes such firm possession of the mind, as when it is found empty and unoccupied." So he was always at pains to occupy himself and to try to impose a regimen on his daily habits. What most endears Johnson to me is his lifelong, and plainly futile, attempts to start getting up earlier in the morning. A representative sampling from his journals:

> September 7, 1738: "O Lord, enable me . . . in redeeming the time which *I have spent in Sloth.*"
>
> January 1, 1753: "To rise early To lose no time."
>
> July 13, 1755: "I will once more form *a scheme of life* . . . (1) to rise early."
>
> Easter Eve 1757: "Almighty God . . . *Enable me to shake off sloth.*"
>
> Easter Day 1759: "Give me thy Grace to break the chain of evil custom. Enable me to shake off idleness and Sloth."
>
> September 18, 1760: "Resolved . . . To rise early . . . To oppose laziness."
>
> April 21, 1764: "My purpose is from this time (1) To reject . . . idle thoughts. To provide some useful amusement for leisure time. (2) To avoid Idleness. To rise early."
>
> The next day (3:00 a.m.): "Deliver me from the distresses of vain terrour . . . Against loose thoughts and idleness."
>
> September 18, 1764: "I resolve to rise early, *Not later than six if I can.*"
>
> Easter Sunday 1765: "I resolve *to rise at eight* . . . I purpose to rise at eight because though I shall not yet rise early it will be much earlier than I now rise, for I often lye till two."
>
> January 1, 1769: "I am not yet in a state to form many resolutions; I purpose and hope to *rise* . . . *at eight, and by degrees at six.*"
>
> January 1, 1774 (2:00 a.m.): "To rise at *eight* . . . The chief cause of my deficiency has been a life *immethodical and unset-*

*tled*, which breaks all purposes . . . and perhaps leaves too much leisure to imagination."

Good Friday 1775: "When I look back upon resoluti[ons] of improvement and amendments, which have year after year been broken . . . why do I yet try to resolve again? I try because Reformation is necessary and despair is criminal . . . My purpose is from Easter day to rise early, not later than eight."

January 2, 1781: "*I will not despair.* . . . My hope is (1) to rise at eight, or sooner. . . . (5) to avoid idleness."

Johnson never was able to sustain his early rising, and he spent many nights working until nearly dawn or roaming the streets of London tormented by his fears and phobias.*

Johnson's journal entries, you will have noted, span more than forty years—from his twenties until his early seventies—and it is hard to know which is more affecting: the futility of his efforts to shake off sloth and to rise early or his earnest commitment to continuing to try despite his knowledge of that futility. (As he wrote in his journal on June 1, 1770, "Every Man naturally persuades himself that he can keep his resolutions, nor is he convinced of his imbecility but by length of time and frequency of experiment.") Walter Jackson Bate, Johnson's greatest modern biographer, first compiled many of these entries in the 1970s, when psychobiography in the Freudian mode was in vogue. Bate suggested that these entries—and Johnson's continuing exhortations to improve himself generally—were evidence of a superego that was too perfectionistic in its demands, and he argued that the constant berating by Johnson's superego, along with the low self-esteem that naturally accompanied it, accounted for Johnson's "depressive anxiety" and his many psychosomatic symptoms. For Johnson, the "danger" of indolence was that, as his friend Arthur Murphy noted, "his spirits, not employed abroad, turned inward with hostility against himself. His reflections on his own life and conduct were always severe; and, wishing

---

* Recent research on sleep cycles suggests that difficulty in rising early is not (entirely) a character failing but rather a biologically hardwired trait: some people's circadian rhythms make them what researchers call "morning doves," leaping easily out of bed in the morning and fading at night, whereas other people are "night owls," productively burning the midnight oil and unable to get out of bed in the morning.

to be immaculate, he destroyed his own peace by unnecessary scruples." When Johnson surveyed his life, Murphy wrote, "he discovered nothing but a barren waste of time, with some disorders of body, and disturbances of mind, very near to madness. His life, he says, from his earliest youth, was wasted in a morning bed; and his reigning sin was a general sluggishness, to which he was always inclined, and, in part of his life, almost compelled, by morbid melancholy and weariness of mind." In this striving for perfection in order that he might think well of himself, Johnson exhibits the classic traits of what Karen Horney, the influential Freudian psychoanalyst, called the neurotic personality. According to Bate, Johnson's writing, "which often anticipates . . . modern psychiatry," was concerned with "how much of the misery of mankind comes from the inability of individuals to think well of themselves, and how much envy and other evils spring from this." As Johnson himself put it, his strong interest in biography as a literary form—his work includes *The Lives of the Poets* and other biographical sketches—was motivated by an interest not so much in understanding how a man "was made happy" or how "he lost the favour of his prince" but in understanding "how he became discontented with himself."

But here's an instructive fact: As unhappy with himself as he was, and as frequently as he berated himself for his lassitude and for lying in bed until two, Johnson was enormously productive. Johnson, despite churning out essays for money ("no man but a blockhead" would ever do otherwise, as he famously said), was no mere hack. Some of his writings—his protonovel *Rasselas,* his poem *The Vanity of Human Wishes,* the best of his essays—are fixtures of the Western canon. *The Works of Samuel Johnson* occupies sixteen thick volumes on my shelf—and that's not even including the work for which he is most famous, the massive dictionary he compiled. Clearly, Johnson's self-assessments of skillfulness and accomplishment were at odds with the reality—which, modern clinical research has shown, is often the case in people of melancholy disposition.*

In his persistent efforts toward self-improvement, and in keeping

---

* Actually, an intriguing body of research has found that clinically depressed people tend to be *more* accurate in their self-assessments than healthy people, suggesting that an ample quotient of self-delusion—of thinking you're better or more competent than you in fact are—is useful for good mental health and professional success.

up his great writerly productivity in the face of emotional torment, Johnson exhibited a form of resilience—a trait that modern psychology is increasingly finding to be a powerful bulwark against anxiety and depression. Anxiety research, which has traditionally focused on what's wrong with pathologically anxious people, is focusing more and more on what makes healthy people resistant to developing anxiety disorders and other clinical conditions. Dennis Charney, a professor of psychiatry and neuroscience at the Ichan School of Medicine at Mount Sinai, has studied American prisoners of war in Vietnam who did *not*, despite the traumas they endured, become depressed or develop PTSD. A number of studies by Charney and others have found that the qualities of resilience and acceptance were what allowed these POWs to ward off the clinical anxiety and psychological breakdown that afflicted many others. The ten critical psychological elements and characteristics of resilience that Charney has identified are optimism, altruism, having a moral compass or set of beliefs that cannot be shattered, faith and spirituality, humor, having a role model, social supports, facing fear (or leaving one's comfort zone), having a mission or meaning in life, and practice in meeting and overcoming challenges. Separate research has suggested that resilience is associated with an abundance of the brain chemical neuropeptide Y—and while it's unclear which way the causation goes (does a resilient temperament produce NPY in the brain, or does NPY in the brain produce a resilient temperament, or is it, most likely, a combination of both?), some evidence suggests NPY levels have a strong genetic component.*

I lament to Dr. W. that, based on thirty years of futile effort so far, my prospects for achieving a recovery from anxiety sufficiently transcendent to provide an uplifting ending to this book seem dismal. I talk to him about the emerging research on resilience, which is fascinating and hopeful—but then I note, as I've done before, that I don't feel very resilient. In fact, I say, I've now got tangible proof that I'm genetically

---

* As we saw in chapter 9, the research of Jerome Kagan, Kerry Ressler, and others suggests that genes play a large role in determining one's innate levels of nervousness and resilience.

predisposed to be *not* resilient: I'm biologically hardwired, at a cellular level, to be anxious and pessimistic and *non*resilient.

"This is why I keep telling you I hate all the modern emphasis on the genetics and neurobiology of mental illness," he says. "It hardens the notion that the mind is a fixed and immutable structure, when in fact it can change throughout the life course."

I tell him that I know all that. And I know, furthermore, that gene expression is affected by environmental factors and that, in any event, reducing a human being to either genes or environment is absurdly reductionist.

And yet I still don't feel much capacity for resilience.

"You're more resilient than you know," he says. "You're always saying 'I can't handle this' or 'I can't handle that.' Yet you handle a lot for someone with anxiety—you handle a lot, period. Just think about what you've had to deal with while trying to complete your book."

As my deadline for delivering this book crept paralyzingly closer, I took a part-time leave from my day job as a magazine editor so I could focus on writing. This decision was not without risk: advertising my dispensability at a company that had been downsizing, in an industry (print journalism) that was radically contracting and possibly dying, and in an economy that was the worst since the Great Depression was hardly the best way to maximize my job security. But increasingly panicked that I was going to miss my deadline and have to plunge my family into bankruptcy, I calculated that the leave was a necessary gamble. My hope was that the time freed up by going on temporary leave, combined with the pressure of the looming deadline, would create the conditions necessary for a spasm of productivity.

That didn't happen. This did:

The very day that my leave was to begin, my heretofore healthy wife fell ill with a mysterious and protracted ailment that led to multiple doctor's appointments (internists, allergists, immunologists, endocrinologists) and a series of inconclusive diagnoses (lupus, rheumatoid arthritis, Hashimoto's thyroiditis, Graves' disease, and others). A few days after that, my completely law-abiding wife was charged (wrongly and absurdly; it's a long story) with a felony that required thousands of dollars in legal expenses and several trips to court to combat. Around this same time, my mother's second husband left her for another woman, and they (my mother and my soon-to-be ex-stepfather) began divorce proceedings that I feared would leave her impoverished. My father's start-up company, which I had hoped would help fund my kids' college education, lost its funding and folded. And so as I sat at my computer day after day on my ostensible book leave, I spent less time writing than I did worrying about my wife's health and compulsively checking our dwindling bank balances as money flowed out much faster than it was flowing in.

And then one early morning in August—the final month of my leave—I awoke to crashing thunder and a driving rain. Suddenly branches and stones started pummeling my bedroom window. As I leapt from bed and ran from the room, the window exploded inward. (My wife and kids were out of town.) I made for the basement, passing the kitchen just as the ceiling caved in—a tree had fallen on the roof. Cabinets were ripped from the walls and pitched to the floor. Light fixtures dropped from above and dangled in the air, suspended by sizzling wires. A swath of insulation unfurled from what remained of the ceiling, hanging there like a panting tongue. Shingles rained from above, splattering onto the linoleum. Rain poured through the gaping hole in the roof.

I ran through the living room just as another tree toppled onto the house. All four windows in the room shattered at once, glass flying everywhere. Dozens of trees were falling, some of them pulled up by their roots, others split in two about eighty feet up from the ground.

I scrambled down the stairs, intending to take refuge underground. But when I got to the basement, three inches of water already covered the ground, and the level was rising fast. I stood on the bottom step, thoughts racing, wondering what was going on (hurricane? nuclear attack? earthquake? tornado? alien invasion?)* and trying to figure out what to do.

Standing there in my boxer shorts, I became conscious of the thunderous pounding of my heart. My mouth was dry, my breathing was quick, my muscles were tense, my heart was racing, adrenaline was coursing through my bloodstream—my fight-or-flight response was

* It was, my insurance company would later conclude, "a tornadic event."

fully activated. As I felt my heart thudding, it occurred to me that my physical sensations were like those of a panic attack or an episode of phobic terror. But even though the danger now was so much more real than during a panic attack, even though I was aware that I might get hurt or even (who knows?) die as the roof caved in and giant trees tumbled, I was less unhappy than I would be during a panic attack. I was scared, yes, but I was marveling at Nature's force, her ability to tear down my seemingly solid house around me and to knock down scores of big trees. It was actually sort of . . . exciting. A panic attack is worse.*

The next several weeks were spent dealing with insurance claims and disaster recovery technicians and real estate agents and movers—and not at all working on my book. As the precious days of my dwindling leave ticked away, I again found myself in an excruciating bind. If I didn't go back to work, I feared, I would lose my job; if I did go back to work, I'd probably miss my book deadline (and maybe lose my job anyway). Worse still would be to finally receive the external confirmation of my inner conviction all these years: that I am a failure—weak, dependent, anxious, shameful.

"Scott!" Dr. W. said when I was going on in this fashion. "Are you listening to yourself? You've already written one book. You're supporting a family. You *have* a job."

Later that day he e-mailed me:

> *As I was writing my notes today after we met, it occurred to me that you need to better internalize positive feedback. . . . Your capabilities are far from the picture of inadequacy that you carry around in your head. Please try and absorb.*

I wrote back:

> *I'll try to absorb these comments—but I immediately discount or back away or rationalize them.*

---

* As if to confirm that, two nights later I woke up with a stomachache, which instantly triggered miserable body-quaking panic that had me desperately gulping vodka and Xanax and Dramamine in headlong pursuit of unconsciousness—probably putting myself at more risk of death than the house-destroying storm did.

He responded:

*Scott, the automatic response is to discount positive feedback. That is why it is so difficult to change. But the beginning of that process is a pushback against the negative juggernaut.*

*Trying is all anyone can ask.*

The irony, of course, is that, as Dr. W. keeps telling me, the route to mental health and freedom from anxiety is to deepen my sense of what he calls, drawing on the work of the cognitive psychologist Albert Bandura, self-efficacy. (Bandura believed that repeatedly proving to oneself one's competence and ability to master situations, and doing so in spite of feelings of anxiety, depression, or vulnerability, builds up self-confidence and psychological strength that can provide a bulwark against anxiety and depression.) Yet writing this book has required me to wallow in my shame, anxiety, and weakness so that I can properly capture and convey them—an experience that has only reinforced how deep and long-standing my anxiety and vulnerability are. Of course, I suppose that even as writing this book has intensified my sense of shame, anxiety, and weakness and has accentuated those feelings of "helpless dependency" that, according to the psychiatrists at McLean Hospital, did in my great-grandfather, it has also helped me appreciate that my efforts to withstand their corrosive effect provide some evidence that I have the resources to overcome them. Maybe by tunneling into my anxiety for this book I can also tunnel out the other side. Not that I can escape my anxiety or be cured of it. But in finishing this book, albeit a book that dwells at great length on my helplessness and inefficacy, maybe I am demonstrating a form of efficacy, perseverance, productivity—and, yes, resilience.

Maybe I am not, for that matter—despite my dependency on medication, despite my flirtations with institutionalization, despite the genotype of pathology handed down to me by my ancestors, despite the vulnerability and what sometimes feels like the unbearable physical and emotional agony of my anxiety—as weak as I think I am. Consider the opening sentence of this book: "I have an unfortunate tendency to falter at crucial moments." That statement feels true to me. ("The neurotic,"

Karen Horney writes in *The Neurotic Personality of Our Time,* "tenaciously insists on being weak.") And yet, as Dr. W. is always pointing out, I *did* survive my wedding and have managed (so far) to remain productive and gainfully employed for more than twenty years despite often debilitating anxiety.

"Scott," he says. "Over the last few years, you've run a magazine and edited many of its cover stories, worked on your book, taken care of your family, and coped with the destruction of your house and with the normal vicissitudes and challenges of life." I point out that I've managed all this only with the help of (sometimes heavy) medication—and that anything I've accomplished has been accompanied by constant worry and frequent panic and has been punctuated by moments of near-complete breakdown that leave me always at risk of being exposed for the anxious weakling that I am.

"You have a handicap—anxiety disorder," he says. "Yet you manage it and, I would say, even thrive despite it. I still think we can cure you of it. But in the meantime, you need to recognize that, given what you're up against, you've accomplished a lot. You need to give yourself more credit."

Maybe finishing this book and publishing it—and, yes, admitting my shame and fear to the world—will be empowering and anxiety reducing.

I suppose I'll find out soon enough.

# Acknowledgments

This book might not exist if Kathryn Lewis had not, unbeknownst to me, shown an e-mail with my inchoate thoughts to Sarah Chalfant of the Wylie Agency—and it would almost certainly not exist if Sarah had not then tracked me down and spurred me, patiently but relentlessly, to produce an actual proposal. Scott Moyers, during his stint at the Wylie Agency, held my hand through some dark times, providing both wisdom and invaluable practical advice. Andrew Wylie is as legend has him: a great and fearsome agent—you want him on your side. No one is a greater champion of writers than Andrew.

Marty Asher, a sympathetic editor, immediately grasped what I was trying to do, and his enthusiasm for the book brought it to Knopf. Marty's warmth and his many kindnesses sustained the book (and me) through some difficult stretches.

I owe Sonny Mehta triply: first for signing off on Marty's original acquisition of the book; second for his patience as the writing dragged on; and third for assigning the manuscript to Dan Frank for editing. Dan's ministrations made this book so much better. I have worked as an editor for twenty years, so I like to think I know good editing when I encounter it: Dan is a brilliant editor and a kind man. Amy Schroeder helped untangle my prose. Jill Verrillo, Gabrielle Brooks, Jonathan Lazzara, and Betsy Sallee, among others, make it a pleasure to be a Knopf author.

I am grateful for fellowships at the Yaddo and MacDowell colonies, which gave me time and space to work.

Lots of people contributed ideas, steered me to useful sources, or provided support in other ways: Anne Connell, Meehan Crist, Kathy Crutcher, Toby Lester, Joy de Menil, Nancy Milford, Cullen Murphy, Justine Rosenthal, Alex Starr, and Graeme Wood. Alane Mason, Jill Kneerim, and Paul Elie all provided helpful early feedback on the book proposal before it was fully formed. Alies Muskin, executive director at the Anxiety and Depression Association of America, was generous with her time and her Rolodex.

My brother-in-law, Jake Pueschel, provided valuable research assistance, tracking down hundreds of scholarly articles for me and, more essentially, helped me to process and interpret my genetic data. Jake's parents, my mother- and father-in-law Barbara and Kris Pueschel, provided both child care and moral support—and tolerated my too-frequent absences from family events while I raced to meet deadlines.

At *The Atlantic*, I am grateful to colleagues (and former colleagues) who endured my periodic absences and filled in for me while I worked on the book, among them Bob Cohn, James Fallows, Geoff Gagnon, James Gibney, Jeffrey Goldberg, Corby Kummer, Chris Orr, Don Peck, Ben Schwarz, Ellie Smith, and Yvonne Rolzhausen. (On the business side, *Atlantic* president Scott Havens, Atlantic Media president Justin Smith, and Atlantic Media chairman and owner David Bradley showed blessed forbearance in allowing me time to work on this book.) More than any other *Atlantic* colleagues, though, I owe Jennifer Barnett, Maria Streshinsky, and James Bennet, who were exceedingly generous in working around the problems my absences caused. I worry I've taken years off James's life.

Despite everything, I am grateful to Dr. L., Dr. M., Dr. Harvard, Dr. Stanford, and various other therapists and social workers and hypnotists and pharmacologists who are not named or got left on the cutting room floor. I am unreservedly and ongoingly grateful to Dr. W.: thank you for helping keep me afloat.

I want to thank my family—especially my dad, my mom, my sister, and my grandfather. I love them all. None of them (with the qualified exception of my father) were happy I was writing this book—and they were all even unhappier to be included in it themselves. (I am especially grateful to my father for sharing his diary with me.) I have tried to be as accurate and objective as my memory and the limited documentary record permit. Some family members would dispute aspects of what I have written here. I worry that some in my family view my revelations about Chester Hanford as a desecration of his memory and a posthumous despoiling of his dignity. For what it's worth, I respect him tremendously, and I hope that in my own anxious struggle I can live up to the standards of grace, decency, kindness, and perseverance he embodied. (I owe special thanks to my grandfather, who—though he made clear he didn't want to know what was in his father's psychiatric records—was willing to let me find out and helped me navigate probate court to secure them.)

As ever, my deepest thanks go to my wife, Susanna. Early on, she logged many hours at the National Institutes of Health Library, tracking down scientific articles and books. She also went far beyond any reasonable expectation of spousal support in helping me fight through legal thickets and bureaucratic impediments to gain access to the mental health records of my great-grandfather. Most important, if you've read this book, you know that holding me together can sometimes be challenging, unrewarding work. That work falls most heavily on Susanna—and for that I owe her more than I can ever repay.

# Notes

CHAPTER 1: THE NATURE OF ANXIETY

8  accounting for 31 percent of the expenditures: Figure on anxiety and mental health care expenditures comes from "The Economic Burdens of Anxiety Disorders in the 1990s," a comprehensive report published in *The Journal of Clinical Psychiatry* 60, no. 7 (July 1999).

8  "lifetime incidence" of anxiety disorder: Ronald Kessler, an epidemiologist at Harvard, has spent decades studying this. See, for instance, his paper "Lifetime Prevalence and Age-of-Onset Distributions of DSM-IV Disorders in the National Comorbidity Survey Replication," *Archives of General Psychiatry* 62, no. 6 (June 2005): 593–602.

8  A study published: R. C. Kessler et al., "Prevalence and Effects of Mood Disorders on Work Performance in a Nationally Representative Sample of U.S. Workers," *The American Journal of Psychiatry* 163 (2006): 1561–68. See also "Economic Burdens."

8  the median number of days: U.S. Bureau of Labor Statistics, "Table R67: Number and Percent Distribution of Nonfatal Occupational Injuries and Illnesses Involving Days Away from Work by Nature of Injury or Illness and Number of Days Away from Work, 2001."

8  Americans filled fifty-three million prescriptions: *Drug Topics,* March 2006.

8  Xanax prescriptions jumped 9 percent nationally: "Taking the Worry Cure," *Newsweek,* February 24, 2003. See also Restak, *Poe's Heart,* 185.

8  the economic crash caused prescriptions: Report from Wolters Kluwer Health, a medical information company, cited in Restak, *Poe's Heart,* 185.

9  A report published in 2009: Mental Health Foundation, *In the Face of Fear,* April 2009, 3–5.

9  A recent paper: "Prevalence, Severity, and Unmet Need for Treatment of Mental Disorders in the World Health Organization World Mental Health Surveys," *The Journal of the American Medical Association* 291 (June 2004): 2581–90.

9  A comprehensive global review: "Prevalence and Incidence Studies of Anxiety Disorders: A Systematic Review of the Literature," *The Canadian Journal of Psychiatry* 51 (2006): 100–13.

9  other studies have reported similar findings: For instance, "Global Prevalence

of Anxiety Disorders: A Systematic Review and Meta-regression," *Psychological Medicine* 10 (July 2012): 1–14.

9   Primary care physicians report: See, for instance, "Content of Family Practice: A Data Bank for Patient Care, Curriculum, and Research in Family Practice— 526,196 Patient Problems," *The Journal of Family Practice* 3 (1976): 25–68.

9   One large-scale study from 1985: "The Hidden Mental Health Network: Treatment of Mental Illness by Non-psychiatric Physicians," *Archives of General Psychiatry* 42 (1985): 89–94.

9   one in three patients complained: "Panic Disorder: Epidemiology and Primary Care," *The Journal of Family Practice* 23 (1986): 233–39.

9   20 percent of primary care patients: "Quality of Care of Psychotropic Drug Use in Internal Medicine Group Practices," *Western Journal of Medicine* 14 (1986): 710–14.

11  "Woody Allen gene": See, for instance, Peter D. Kramer, "Tapping the Mood Gene," *The New York Times*, July 26, 2003. See also Restak, *Poe's Heart*, 204–12.

11  "The real excitement here": Thomas Insel, "Heeding Anxiety's Call" (lecture, May 19, 2005).

13  "as vain as a child's story": Roccatagliata, *History of Ancient Psychiatry*, 38.

14  "if one's body and mind": Maurice Charlton, "Psychiatry and Ancient Medicine," in *Historical Derivations of Modern Psychiatry*, 16.

14  "All that philosophers have written": Charlton, "Psychiatry and Ancient Medicine," 12.

17  One study found that children: See, for instance, Rachel Yehuda et al., "Transgenerational Effects of Posttraumatic Stress Disorder in Babies of Mothers Exposed to the World Trade Center Attacks During Pregnancy," *The Journal of Clinical Endocrinology and Metabolism* 90, no. 7 (July 2005): 4115 Rachel Yehuda et al., "Gene Expression Patterns Associated with Posttraumatic Stress Disorder Following Exposure to the World Trade Center Attacks," *Biological Psychiatry* 66(7)(2009): 708–11.

17  "Myself and fear were born twins": Quoted in Hunt, *Story of Psychology*, 72.

18  There's also evidence that: See, for instance, "The Relationship Between Intelligence and Anxiety: An Association with Subcortical White Matter Metabolism," *Frontiers in Evolutionary Neuroscience* 3, no. 8 (February 2012). (Also on high Jewish IQ: Steven Pinker, who in 2007 gave a lecture called "Jews, Genes, and Intelligence," says "their average IQ has been measured at 108 to 115." Richard Lynn, author of the 2004 article "The Intelligence of American Jews," says Jewish intelligence is half a standard deviation higher than the European average. Henry Harpending, Jason Hardy, and Gregory Cochran, University of Utah authors of the 2005 research report "Natural History of Ashkenazi Intelligence," state that their subjects "score .75 to 1.0 standard deviations above the general European average, corresponding to an IQ of 112–115.")

19  An influential study: "The Relation of Strength of Stimulus to Rapidity of Habit-Formation," *The Journal of Comparative Neurology and Psychology* 18 (1908): 459–82.

19  "We then face the prospect": *Los Angeles Examiner*, November 4, 1957, quoted in Tone, *Age of Anxiety*, 87.

19 "Van Gogh, Isaac Newton": *Los Angeles Examiner,* March 23, 1958, quoted in Tone, *Age of Anxiety,* 87.

19 "Without anxiety, little would be accomplished": Barlow, *Anxiety and Its Disorders,* 9.

22 "I awoke morning after morning": James, *Varieties of Religious Experience,* 134.

28 Petraeus . . . "rarely feels stress at all": Steve Coll, "The General's Dilemma," *The New Yorker,* September 8, 2008.

CHAPTER 2: WHAT DO WE TALK ABOUT WHEN WE TALK ABOUT ANXIETY?

35 "usually linked with a strong": Jaspers, *General Psychopathology,* 113–14.

36 "a sense of foreboding": Lifton, *Protean Self,* 101.

36 "the internal precondition of sin": Niebuhr, *Nature and Destiny,* vol. 1, 182.

36 "the most pervasive psychological phenomenon": Hoch and Zubin, *Anxiety,* v.

36 "The mentalistic and multi-referenced term": Theodore R. Sarbin, "Anxiety: Reification of a Metaphor," *Archives of General Psychiatry* 10 (1964): 630–38.

36 "to feelings": Kagan, *What Is Emotion?,* 41.

37 "as wine to vinegar": See, for instance, "Three Essays on the Theory of Sexuality," in Freud, *Basic Writings.*

37 "with a manual stimulation": Quoted in Roccatagliatia, *History of Ancient Psychiatry,* 204.

37 "It is almost disgraceful": Freud, *Problem of Anxiety,* 60.

38 "When a mother is afraid": Horney, *Neurotic Personality,* 41.

39 Studies of the: *DSM-II:* See, for instance, R. Spitzer and J. Fleiss, "A Re-analysis of the Reliability of Psychiatric Diagnosis," *The British Journal of Psychiatry* 125 (1974): 341–47; Stuart A. Kirk and Herb Kutchins, "The Myth of the Reliability of *DSM," Journal of Mind and Behavior* 15, nos. 1–2 (1994): 71–86.

40 "stress tradition": For more on the stress tradition, see the section "Anxiety and the Stress Tradition" in Horwitz and Wakefield, *All We Have to Fear,* 200–4.

40 "a sister, *fidus Achates*": Burton, *Anatomy,* 261.

40 "are affrighted still": Ibid., 431.

40 "Don't allow the sum total": Breggin, *Medication Madness,* 331.

42 Moreover, the brain of a research subject: Kagan, *What Is Emotion?,* 83.

43 humans whose amygdalae get damaged: See, for instance, "Fear and the Amygdala," *The Journal of Neuroscience* 15, no. 9 (September 1995): 5879–91.

44 "the final and most exciting contest": Cannon, *Bodily Changes,* 74.

45 "The progress from brute to man": James, *Principles of Psychology,* 415.

45 "One day": Quoted in Fisher, *House of Wits,* 81.

47 "Contrary to the view of some humanists": LeDoux, *Emotional Brain,* 107.

47 Even *Aplysia californica:* This comes from the research of Eric Kandel, which is described in Barber, *Comfortably Numb,* 191–96.

47 "It is not obvious": Kagan, *What Is Emotion?,* 17.

47 "entering a seemingly involuntary state": Barlow, *Anxiety and Its Disorders,* 35.

48 "How many hippos worry": Sapolsky, *Zebras,* 182.

48 "A rat can't worry": Quoted in Stephen Hall, "Fear Itself," *The New York Times Magazine,* February 28, 1999.

51  "Theta activity is a rhythmic burst": Gray and McNaughton, *Neuropsychology of Anxiety*, 12.

53  "This remark of Plato": Maurice Charlton, "Psychiatry and Ancient Medicine," in Galdston, *Historic Derivations*, 15.

54  Meditation led to decreased density: G. Desbordes et al., "Effects of Mindful-Attention and Compassion Meditation Training on Amygdala Response to Emotional Stimuli in an Ordinary, Non-meditative State," *Frontiers of Human Neuroscience* 6 (2012): 292.

54  Other studies have found that Buddhist monks: See, for instance, Richard J. Davidson and Antoine Lutz, "Buddha's Brain: Neuroplasticity and Meditation," *IEEE Signal Processing Magazine* 25, no. 1 (January 2008): 174–76.

54  suppress their startle response: See, for instance, R. W. Levenson, P. Ekman, and M. Ricard, "Meditation and the Startle Response: A Case Study," *Emotion* 12, no. 3 (June 2012): 650–58; for additional context, see Tom Bartlett, "The Monk and the Gunshot," *The Chronicle of Higher Education*, August 21, 2012.

54  even old-fashioned talk therapy: Richard A. Friedman, "Like Drugs, Talk Therapy Can Change Brain Chemistry," *The New York Times*, August 27, 2002.

54  "My theory": William James first articulated this in "What Is an Emotion?," an article he published in *Mind*, a philosophy journal, in 1884.

55  When researchers at Columbia: S. Schachter and J. E. Singer, "Cognitive, Social, and Physiological Determinants of Emotional State," *Psychological Review* 69, no. 5 (1962): 379–99. Joseph LeDoux has a good description of this experi-ment, and of the history of the James-Lange theory, in *Emotional Brain*, 46–49.

55  "fear of death, conscience, guilt": Tillich, "Existential Philosophy," *Journal of the History of Ideas* 5, no. 1 (1944): 44–70. (This later appeared in Tillich's 1959 book *Theology of Culture*.)

57  the moment an anxious patient: See, for instance, Gabbard, "A Neurobiologi-cally Informed Perspective on Psychotherapy," *The British Journal of Psychiatry* 177 (2000): 11; A. Öhman and J. J. F. Soares, "Unconscious Anxiety: Phobic Responses to Masked Stimuli," *Journal of Abnormal Psychology* (1994); John T. Cacioppo et al., "The Psychophysiology of Emotion," *Handbook of Emotions* 2 (2000): 173–91.

58  Richard Burton could not bear: Shawn, *Wish*, 10.

59  how to eliminate fear responses in cats: Joseph Wolpe, *Psychotherapy by Reciprocal Inhibition* (Stanford, Calif.: Stanford University Press, 1958), 53–62.

61  "chimney sweeping": Breger, *Dream*, 29.

CHAPTER 3: A RUMBLING IN THE BELLY

69  "scare the hell out of the patient": David Barlow "Providing Best Treatments for Patients with Panic Disorder," Anxiety and Depression Association of American Annual Conference, Miami, March 24, 2006.

69  phobia cure rate of up to 85 percent: Lauren Slater, "The Cruelest Cure," *The New York Times*, November 2, 2003.

69    Barlow himself has a phobia: "A Phobia Fix," *The Boston Globe,* November 26, 2006.

70    "It's from 1979": J. K. Ritow, "Brief Treatment of a Vomiting Phobia," *American Journal of Clinical Hypnosis* 21, no. 4 (1979): 293–96.

75    "a phobia and a beef-steak": Northfield, *Conquest of Nerves,* 37.

75    as many as 12 percent: Harvard Medical School, *Sensitive Gut,* 71.

75    First identified in 1830: Ibid., 72.

75    In one well-known set of experiments: William E. Whitehead et al., "Tolerance for Rectosigmoid Distention in Irritable Bowel Syndrome," *Gastroenterology* 98, no. 5 (1990): 1187; William E. Whitehead, Bernard T. Engel, and Marvin M. Schuster, "Irritable Bowel Syndrome," *Digestive Diseases and Sciences* 25, no. 6 (1980): 404–13.

76    an article in the medical journal *Gut:* Ingvard Wilhelmsen. "Brain-Gut Axis as an Example of the Bio-psycho-social Model," *Gut* 47, supp. 4 (2000): 5–7.

77    "nervous in origin": Walter Cannon, "The Influence of Emotional States on the Functions of the Alimentary Canal," *The American Journal of the Medical Sciences* 137, no. 4 (April 1909): 480–86.

77    between 42 and 61 percent: Andrew Fullwood and Douglas A. Drossman, "The Relationship of Psychiatric Illness with Gastrointestinal Disease," *Annual Review of Medicine* 46, no. 1 (1995): 483–96.

77    40 percent overlap between patients: Robert G. Maunder, "Panic Disorder Associated with Gastrointestinal Disease: Review and Hypotheses," *Journal of Psychosomatic Research* 44, no. 1 (1998): 91.

78    "Fear brings about diarrhea": Quoted in Roccatagliata, *History of Ancient Psychiatry,* 106.

78    "People attacked by fear": Quoted in Sarason and Spielberger, *Stress and Anxiety,* vol. 2, 12.

79    "90 percent redness": Wolf and Wolff, *Human Gastric Function,* 112.

85    One of the more alarming: Richard W. Seim, C. Richard Spates, and Amy E. Naugle, "Treatment of Spasmodic Vomiting and Lower Gastrointestinal Distress Related to Travel Anxiety," *The Cognitive Behaviour Therapist* 4, no. 1 (2011): 30–37.

85    weeping at a sad play: Alvarez, *Nervousness,* 123.

85    The nervousness and hypersensitivity: Ibid., 266.

85    "The stomach specialist has to be": Ibid., 11.

85    "day and night for a week": Ibid., 22.

86    "a tense, high-pressure type of sales manager": Ibid., 17.

86    "the cruelest prank of nature": Ibid.

87    A study published in: Angela L. Davidson, Christopher Boyle, and Fraser Lauchlan, "Scared to Lose Control? General and Health Locus of Control in Females with a Phobia of Vomiting," *Journal of Clinical Psychology* 64, no. 1 (2008): 30–39.

88    As the British physician and philosopher: Tallis, *Kingdom of Infinite Space,* 193.

89    "Age 56–57": Quoted in Desmond and Moore, *Darwin,* 531.

89    "Diary of Health": Cited at length in Colp, *To Be an Invalid,* 43–53.

90    "knocked up": Desmond and Moore, *Darwin,* 530.

90    "We liked Dr. Chapman": Quoted in Colp, *To Be an Invalid,* 84.

91  "What the devil is this": Hooker, *Life and Letters of Joseph Dalton Hooker,* vol. 2, 72.

91  "Darwin's Illness Revealed": Anthony K. Campbell and Stephanie B. Matthews, "Darwin's Illness Revealed," *Postgraduate Medical Journal* 81, no. 954 (2005): 248–51.

91  "bad headache": Bowlby, *Charles Darwin,* 229.

91  "Charles Darwin and Panic Disorder": Thomas J. Barloon and Russell Noyes Jr., "Charles Darwin and Panic Disorder," *The Journal of the American Medical Association* 277, no. 2 (1997): 138–41.

91  "neurotic hands": Edward J. Kempf, "Charles Darwin—the Affective Sources of His Inspiration and Anxiety Neurosis," *The Psychoanalytic Review* 5 (1918): 151–92.

91  one pseudoscholarly paper: Jerry Bergman, "Was Charles Darwin Psychotic? A Study of His Mental Health" (Institute of Creation Research, 2010).

92  "the most miserable which I ever spent": Darwin, *Autobiography,* 28.

92  "I was out of spirits": Ibid., 28.

92  "I dread going anywhere": *Life and Letters of Charles Darwin,* vol. 1, 349.

92  "I have therefore been compelled": Darwin, *Autobiography,* 39.

92  He installed a mirror: Quammen, *Reluctant Mr. Darwin,* 62.

93  In addition to Dr. Chapman's ice treatment: Sources include Bowlby, *Charles Darwin;* Colp, *To Be an Invalid;* Desmond and Moore, *Darwin;* Browne, *The Power of Place;* and Quammen, *The Reluctant Mr. Darwin;* among others.

93  "a very bad form of vomiting": Bowlby, *Charles Darwin,* 300.

93  "I have been bad": Ibid., 335.

93  "I have been very bad": Ibid., 343.

93  "strive to suppress their feelings": Ibid., 11.

94  "I must tell you": Ibid., 375.

94  "Without you, when I feel sick": Desmond and Moore, *Darwin,* 358.

94  "O Mammy I do long": Bowlby, *Charles Darwin,* 282.


CHAPTER 4: PERFORMANCE ANXIETY

98  Starting when he was thirty: Oppenheim, *"Shattered Nerves,"* 114.

98  "To that": Davenport-Hines, *Pursuit of Oblivion,* 56.

98  "mystifying and scandalously sudden retirement": Quoted in Marshall, *Social Phobia,* 140.

99  "They . . . to whom a public examination": "Memoir of William Cowper," *Proceedings of the American Philosophical Society* 97, no. 4 (1953): 359–82.

99  "My head was reeling": Gandhi, *Autobiography.* (I was pointed to this source by chapter 5 of Taylor Clark's *Nerve.*)

99  "Thomas Jefferson, too, had his law career disrupted": All Jefferson material here is drawn from Joshua Kendall's *American Obsessives,* 21.

100  a career-ending panic attack: Mohr, *Gasping for Airtime,* 134.

100  "I had all these panic attacks": "Hugh Grant: Behind That Smile Lurks a Deadly Serious Film Star," *USA Today,* December 17, 2009.

100  Elfriede Jelinek, the Austrian novelist: "A Gloom of Her Own," *The New York Times Magazine,* November 21, 2004.

102 Sigmund Freud took cocaine to medicate: See, for instance, Kramer, *Freud,* 42.

102 The first case study of erythrophobia: Casper, Johann Ludwig, "Biographie d'une idée fixe" (translated into French, 1902), *Archives de Neurologie,* 13, 270-287.

102 "It is not a simple act": Darwin, *Expression,* 284.

103 "the soul might have sovereign power": Burgess, *Physiology or Mechanism of Blushing,* 49.

103 Writing in 1901, Paul Hartenberg: Hartenberg, *Les timides et la timidité* (Félix Alcon, 1901).

103 The term "social phobia" first appeared: Pierre Janet, *Les obsessions et la psychiatrie* (Alcan, 1903).

104 "the socially promoted show of shame": Ken-Ichiro Okano, "Shame and Social Phobia: A Transcultural Viewpoint," *Bulletin of the Menninger Clinic* 58, no. 3 (1994): 323–38.

105 In 1985, Liebowitz published an article: Michael Liebowitz et al., "Social Phobia," *Archives of General Psychiatry* 42, no. 7 (1985): 729–36.

105 As recently as 1994: "Disorders Made to Order," *Mother Jones,* July/August 2002.

107 One study has found: See Manjula et al., "Social Anxiety Disorder (Social Phobia)—a Review," *International Journal of Pharmacology and Toxicology* 2, no. 2 (2012): 55–59.

110 Studies at the University of Wisconsin: See Davidson et al., "While a Phobic Waits: Regional Brain Electrical and Autonomic Activity in Social Phobias During Anticipation of Public Speaking," *Biological Psychiatry* 47 (2000): 85–95.

111 "When I see anyone anxious": "On Anxiety," in Epictetus, *Discourses,* ch. 13.

112 Kathryn Zerbe, a psychiatrist: See, for instance, Kathryn J. Zerbe, "Uncharted Waters: Psychodynamic Considerations in the Diagnosis and Treatment of Social Phobia," *Bulletin of the Menninger Clinic* 58, no. 2 (1994): A3. See also Capps, *Social Phobia,* 120–25.

113 "Highly anxious people read facial expressions": "Anxious Adults Judge Facial Cues Faster, but Less Accurately," *Science News,* July 19, 2006.

113 "this barometer can cause them": "Whaddya Mean by That Look?," *Los Angeles Times,* July 24, 2006.

114 Arne Öhman, a Swedish neuroscientist: See, for instance, Arne Öhman, "Face the Beast and Fear the Face: Animal and Social Fears as Prototypes for Evolutionary Analyses of Emotion," *Psychophysiology* 23, no. 2 (March 1986): 123–45.

114 "doing something foolish": Marshall, *Social Phobia,* 50.

114 A National Institute of Mental Health study: K. Blair et al., *The American Journal of Psychiatry* 165, no. 9 (September 2008): 193–202; K. Blair et al., *Archives of General Psychiatry* 65, no. 10 (October 2008): 1176–84.

115 "Generalized-social-phobia-related dysfunction": K. Blair et al., "Neural Response to Self- and Other Referential Praise and Criticism in Generalized Social Phobia," *Archives of General Psychiatry* 65, no. 10 (October 2008): 1176–84.

115 they are not consciously aware of seeing: For instance, Murray B. Stein et al., "Increased Amygdala Activation to Angry and Contemptuous Faces in Generalized Social Phobia," *Archives of General Psychiatry* 59, no. 11 (2002): 1027.

116 "Unconsciously perceived signals of threat": Zinbarg et al., "Neural and Behavioral Evidence for Affective Priming from Unconsciously Perceived Emotional

Facial Expressions and the Influence of Trait Anxiety," *Journal of Cognitive Neuroscience* 20, no. 1 (January 2008): 95–107.

117 Murray Stein, a psychiatrist: Murray B. Stein, "Neurobiological Perspectives on Social Phobia: From Affiliation to Zoology," *Biological Psychiatry* 44, no. 12 (1998): 1277.

118 the social hierarchies of particular baboon populations: See, for instance, Robert Sapolsky, "Testicular Function, Social Rank and Personality Among Wild Baboons," *Psychoneuroendocrinology* 16, no. 4 (1991): 281–93; Robert Sapolsky, "The Endocrine Stress-Response and Social Status in the Wild Baboon," *Hormones and Behavior* 16, no. 3 (September 1982): 279–92; Robert Sapolsky, "Stress-Induced Elevation of Testosterone Concentrations in High Ranking Baboons: Role of Catecholamines," *Endocrinology* 118 no. 4 (April 1986): 1630.

118 the happiest-seeming and least stressed monkeys: Gesquiere et al., "Life at the Top: Rank and Stress in Wild Male Baboons," *Science* 333, no. 6040 (July 2011): 357–60.

119 monkeys with enhanced serotonergic function: See, for instance, Raleigh et al., "Serotonergic Mechanisms Promote Dominance Acquisition in Adult Male Vervet Monkeys," *Brain Research* 559, no. 2 (1991): 181–90.

119 altered serotonin function in certain brain regions: For instance, Lanzenberger et al., "Reduced Serotonin-1A Receptor Binding in Social Anxiety Disorder," *Biological Psychiatry* 61, no. 9 (May 2007): 1081–89.

119 Prozac and Paxil can be: See, for instance, van der Linden et al., "The Efficacy of the Selective Serotonin Reuptake Inhibitors for Social Anxiety Disorder (Social Phobia): A Meta-analysis of Randomized Controlled Trials," *International Clinical Psychopharmacology* 15, supp. 2 (2000): S15–23; Stein et al., "Serotonin Transporter Gene Promoter Polymorphism Predicts SSRI Response in Generalized Social Anxiety Disorder," *Psychopharmacology* 187, no. 1 (July 2006): 68–72.

119 when nonanxious, nondepressed people take SSRIs: See, for instance, Wai S. Tse and Alyson J. Bond, "Serotonergic Intervention Affects Both Social Dominance and Affiliative Behaviour," *Psychopharmacology,* 161 (2002): 324–330

119 the monkeys that rise the highest: See, for instance, Morgan et al., "Social Dominance in Monkeys: Dopamine D2 Receptors and Cocaine Self-Administration," *Nature Neuroscience* 5 (2002): 169–74; Morgan et al., "Predictors of Social Status in Cynomolgus Monkeys (*Macaca fascicularis*) After Group Formation," *American Journal of Primatology* 52, no. 3 (November 2118): 115–31.

119 people diagnosed with social anxiety disorder: See, for instance, Stein and Stein, "Social Anxiety Disorder," *Lancet* 371 (2008): 1115–25.

119 One 2008 study found that half: Arthur Kummer, Francisco Cardoso, and Antonio L. Teixeira, "Frequency of Social Phobia and Psychometric Properties of the Liebowitz Social Anxiety Scale in Parkinson's Disease," *Movement Disorders* 23, no. 12 (2008): 1739–43.

119 Multiple recent studies have found: See, for instance, Schneier et al., "Low Dopamine D2 Reception Binding Potential in Social Phobia," *The American Journal of Psychiatry* 157 (2000): 457–59.

120 Murray Stein, among others: Stein, Murray B., "Neurobiological Perspectives on Social Phobia: from Affiliation to Zoology," *Biological Psychiatry* 44, no. 12

(1998): 1277–85. See also David H. Skuse and Louise Gallagher, "Dopaminergic-Neuropeptide Interactions in the Social Brain," *Trends in Cognitive Sciences* 13, no. 1 (2009): 27–35.

121 where you fall on the spectrum: See, for instance, Seth J. Gillihan et al., "Association Between Serotonin Transporter Genotype and Extraversion," *Psychiatric Genetics* 17, no. 6 (2007): 351–54.

121 But Robert Sapolsky has found: Sapolsky, "Social Status and Health in Humans and Other Animals," *Annual Review of Anthropology* 33 (2004): 393–418.

121 In the late 1990s, Dirk Hellhammer: Dirk Helmut Hellhammer et al., "Social Hierarchy and Adrenocortical Stress Reactivity in Men," *Psychoneuroendocrinology* 22, no. 8 (1997): 643–50.

125 In 1908, two psychologists: Robert M. Yerkes and John D. Dodson, "The Relation of Strength of Stimulus to Rapidity of Habit-Formation," *The Journal of Comparative Neurology and Psychology* 18, no. 5 (1908): 459–82.

125 Bertoia . . . "couldn't hit and sometimes bobbled fielding plays": Tone, *The Age of Anxiety*, 113–14.

130 "like a song that got in my head": Quoted in Ballard, *Beautiful Game*, 76.

131 "disreturnophobia": "Strikeouts and Psych-Outs," *The New York Times Magazine*, July 7, 1991.

131 The explicit monitoring theory of choking: Sian L. Beilock and Thomas H. Carr, "On the Fragility of Skilled Performance: What Governs Choking Under Pressure?," *Journal of Experimental Psychology: General* 130, no. 4 (2001): 701.

131 Beilock has found that she can: For more on this, see Beilock, *Choke*.

132 a neural "traffic jam" of worry: Quoted in Clark, *Nerve*, 208.

133 "found himself in such disgrace": Herodotus, *Histories*, vol. 4, bk. 7.

133 inure their soldiers to anxiety: Gabriel, *No More Heroes*, 104.

133 and also valerian, a mild tranquilizer: Ibid., 139.

133 Researchers at Johns Hopkins University: "Stress Detector for Soldiers," *BBC World News*, May 29, 2002.

134 The *Anglo-Saxon Chronicle* recounts: Cited in Gabriel, *No More Heroes*, 51.

134 "at best a constitutionally inferior human being": Herman, *Trauma and Recovery*, 21.

134 A 1914 article: "The Psychology of Panic in War," *American Review of Reviews* 50 (October 1914): 629.

134 "hyperconsiderate professional attitude": Quoted in Barber, *Comfortably Numb*, 73.

134 "because only such a measure would prevent": Quoted in Bourke, *Fear*, 219.

134 "It is now time that our country": Ibid.

135 General George Patton of the U.S. Army denied: Shephard, *War of Nerves*, 219.

135 dishonorably discharged for cowardice: Jeffrey Gettleman, "Reduced Charges for Soldier Accused of Cowardice in Iraq," *The New York Times*, November 7, 2003.

135 the first person to be formally diagnosed: Jacob Mendes Da Costa, "On Irritable Heart: A Clinical Study of a Form of Functional Cardiac Disorder and Its Consequences," *The American Journal of the Medical Sciences* 121, no. 1 (1871): 2–52.

135 Studies of "self-soiling rates": Collins, *Violence*, 46.

135 A survey of one U.S. combat division: Paul Fussell, "The Real War, 1939–45," *The Atlantic*, August 1989.

136 Another survey of World War II infantrymen: Kaufman, "'Ill Health' as an Expression of Anxiety in a Combat Unit," *Psychosomatic Medicine* 9 (March 1947): 108.

136 "Hell . . . all that proves": Quoted in Clark, *Nerve*, 234.

136 "I could feel a twitching": Manchester, *Goodbye, Darkness*, 5.

136 "Now, those who fail to register": Christopher Hitchens, "The Blair Hitch Project," *Vanity Fair*, February 2011.

136 needed a man "with iron nerve": Alvarez, *Nervousness*, 18.

137 Comprehensive studies conducted during World War II: See, for instance, Grinker and Spiegel, *Men Under Stress*.

138 "These people will be able to collect": Leach, *Survival Psychology*, 24.

138 "uncontrolled weeping": Ibid., 25.

138 civilians with preexisting neurotic disorders: Janis, *Air War*, 80.

138 "Neurotics turned out to be": Bourke, *Fear*, 231.

138 "looking as worried as they have felt": Felix Brown, "Civilian Psychiatric Air-Raid Casualties," *The Lancet* 237, no. 6144 (May 1941): 689.

138 One fascinating study of stress: V. A. Kral, "Psychiatric Observations Under Severe Chronic Stress," *The American Journal of Psychiatry* 108 (1951): 185–92.

139 "unprecedented in over 30 years": Kathleen E. Bachynski et al., "Mental Health Risk Factors for Suicides in the US Army, 2007–8," *Injury Prevention* 18, no. 6 (2012): 405–12.

139 more than 10 percent of Afghanistan veterans: Hoge et al., "Mental Health Problems, Use of Mental Health Services, and Attrition from Military Service After Returning from Deployment to Iraq or Afghanistan," *JAMA* 259, no. 9 (2006): 1023–32.

140 army veterans diagnosed with post-traumatic stress disorder: Boscarino, Joseph, "Post-traumatic Stress Disorder and Mortality Among U.S. Army Veterans 30 Years After Military Service," *Annals of Epidemiology* 16, no. 4 (2006): 248–56.

140 the suicide rate reached a ten-year high: "Mike Mullen on Military Veteran Suicide," Huffington Post, July 2, 2012.

141 "were some of the greatest": Charles A. Morgan et al., "Relationship Among Plasma Cortisol, Catecholamines, Neuropeptide Y, and Human Performance During Exposure to Uncontrollable Stress," *Psychosomatic Medicine* 63, no. 3 (2001): 412–22.

141 Some individuals with high NPY: "Intranasal Neuropeptide Y May Offer Therapeutic Potential for Post-traumatic Stress Disorder," *Medical Press*, April 23, 2013.

141 Administering NPY via a nasal spray: Charles A. Morgan III et al., "Trauma Exposure Rather Than Posttraumatic Stress Disorder Is Associated with Reduced Baseline Plasma Neuropeptide-Y Levels," *Biological Psychiatry* 54, no. 10 (2003): 1087–91.

142 Researchers at the University of Michigan: Brian J. Mickey et al., "Emotion Processing, Major Depression, and Functional Genetic Variation of Neuropeptide Y," *Archives of General Psychiatry* 68, no. 2 (2011): 158.

142 with more glucocorticoid receptors: Mirjam van Zuiden et al., "Pre-existing High Glucocorticoid Receptor Number Predicting Development of Posttraumatic Stress Symptoms After Military Deployment," *The American Journal of Psychiatry* 168, no. 1 (2011): 89–96.

143 "[Russell] used to throw up all the time": George Plimpton, "Sportsman of the Year Bill Russell," *Sports Illustrated*, December 23, 1968.

144 he ordered that the pregame warm-up: See, for instance, John Taylor, *The Rivalry: Bill Russell, Wilt Chamberlain, and the Golden Age of Basketball* (New York: Random House, 2005).

144 "one of the great mysteries in the history of sport": "Lito Sheppard Says Donovan McNabb Threw Up in the Super Bowl," *CBSPhilly*, July 8, 2013.

145 "You must wonder what makes a man": Gay Talese, "The Loser," *Esquire*, March 1964.

145 Hoping to conquer his anxiety: This section on Pisa in wartime is drawn from Arieti, *Parnas*.

## CHAPTER 5: "A SACK OF ENZYMES"

153 Reportedly, it did: "Restless Gorillas," *Boston Globe*, September 28, 2003; "Restless and Caged, Gorillas Seek Freedom," *Boston Globe*, September 29, 2003.

154 "In my last serious depression": Quoted in, among many other places, Kramer, *Freud*, 33. For more on Freud's use of cocaine, see Markel, *An Anatomy of Addiction*.

155 "I take very small doses": Davenport-Hines, *Pursuit of Oblivion*, 154.

155 It is an irony of medical history: This irony has been noted by Peter Kramer, among others.

156 they were ingesting alcohol: Tone, *Age of Anxiety*, 10.

156 "a suitable form of alcohol": Quoted in Shorter, *Before Prozac*, 15.

156 The 1899 edition of *The Merck Manual:* Tone, *Age of Anxiety*, 10.

158 "quick-cure nostrums": Topics of the Times, *The New York Times*, January 23, 1906.

158 *The Merck Manual* was still recommending: Tone, *Age of Anxiety*, 22.

158 "more of a menace to society": Quoted in Tone, *Age of Anxiety*, 25.

158 But when Frank Berger: Much of the history of Frank Berger and Miltown in these pages draws heavily from Andrea Tone's *Age of Anxiety*, Edward Shorter's *Before Prozac*, and Mickey Smith's *Small Comfort*.

159 "The mold is as temperamental": Quoted in Tone, *Age of Anxiety*, 34.

159 "The compound had a quieting effect": Taylor Manor Hospital, *Discoveries in Biological Psychiatry*, 122.

160 "We had about twenty Rhesus": Quoted in Tone, *Age of Anxiety*, 43.

160 "individuals who are pleasantly": Henry H. Dixon et al., "Clinical Observations on Tolserol in Handling Anxiety Tension States," *The American Journal of the Medical Sciences* 220, no. 1 (1950): 23–29.

161 The New Jersey psychiatrist reported back: Borrus, "Study of Effect of Miltown (2-Methyl-2-n-Propyl-1,3-Propoanediol Dicarbamate) on Psychiatric States," *The Journal of the American Medical Association*, April 30, 1955, 1596–98.

161   The psychiatrist in Florida: Lowell Selling, "Clinical Use of a New Tranquilizing Drug," *The Journal of the American Medical Association*, April 30, 1955, 1594–96.

161   "You are out of your mind": Quoted in Tone, *Age of Anxiety*, 52.

162   Carter Products sold only $7,500: "Onward and Upward with the Arts: Getting There First with Tranquility," *The New Yorker*, May 3, 1958.

162   In December, Americans bought $500,000: Restak, *Poe's Heart*, 187.

162   "If there's anything this movie business needs": Quoted in Tone, *Age of Anxiety*, 57.

162   Lucille Ball's assistant kept a supply: Tone, *Age of Anxiety*, 57.

162   "Miltowns, liquor, [and] swimming": Ibid.

162   The actress Tallulah Bankhead: Ibid., 58.

162   "Hi, I'm Miltown Berle": Restak, *Poe's Heart*, 187.

162   a $100,000 Miltown art installation: Tone, *Age of Anxiety*, 76.

163   "For the first time in history": Restak, *Poe's Heart*, 187.

163   "be of markedly greater import": Testimony of Nathan S. Kline, *False and Misleading Advertisements (Prescription Tranquilizing Drugs): Hearings Before a Subcommittee of the Committee on Government Operations*, 4.

163   Kline told a journalist: "Soothing, but Not for Businessmen," *BusinessWeek*, March 10, 1956.

164   By 1960, some 75 percent: Tone, *Age of Anxiety*, 90.

165   "tense, anxious, Mediterranean-type patients": Shorter, *History of Psychiatry*, 248.

165   "the insulin of the nervous": Shorter, *Before Prozac*, 49.

165   "This stuff is so good": Valenstein, *Blaming the Brain*, 27.

166   "the most dramatic breakthrough": Tone, *Age of Anxiety*, 80.

166   "No one in their right mind": Valenstein, *Blaming the Brain*, 27.

170   may have precipitated Wallace's downward spiral: See, for instance, D. T. Max, "The Unfinished," *The New Yorker*, March 9, 2009.

171   "was the first cure": Kline, *From Sad to Glad*, 122.

171   the "sparks" and the "soups": Valenstein, *Blaming the Brain*, 60–62.

172   "When I was an undergraduate student": Quoted in Abbott, Alison, "Neuroscience: The Molecular Wake-up Call," *Nature* 447, no. 7143 (2007): 368–70.

172   Gaddum took LSD: Shorter, *Before Prozac*, 69.

174   to give reserpine to *every single one:* Valenstein, *Blaming the Brain*, 69–70.

174   administering reserpine to rabbits: Healy, *Creation of Psychopharmacology*, 106, 205–6.

174   Brodie's 1955 paper: Alfred Pletscher, Parkhurst A. Shore, and Bernard B. Brodie, "Serotonin Release as a Possible Mechanism of Reserpine Action," *Science* 122, no. 3165 (1955): 374–75.

174   built a bridge from neurochemistry to behavior: Healy, *Antidepressant Era*, 148.

175   In one of its first advertisements: Shorter, *Before Prozac*, 52.

176   "Not infrequently the cure is complete": Roland Kuhn, "The Treatment of Depressive States with G 22355 (Imipramine Hydrochloride)," *The American Journal of Psychiatry* 115, no. 5 (1958): 459–64.

176   another accident of history: Healy, *Antidepressant Era*, 52, 58; Barondes, *Better Than Prozac*, 31–32; Shorter, *Before Prozac*, 61.

177   "These drugs seemed like magic to me": Shorter, *Before Prozac*, 62.

177   In 1965, he published an article: Joseph J. Schildkraut, "The Catecholamine

Hypothesis of Affective Disorders: A Review of Supporting Evidence," *The American Journal of Psychiatry* 122, no. 5 (1965): 509–22.

### CHAPTER 6: A BRIEF HISTORY OF PANIC

182 "The anxiety he felt landing": Sheehan, *Anxiety Disease,* 37.

183 "We assumed it would be": Donald F. Klein, "Commentary by a Clinical Scientist in Psychopharmacological Research," *Journal of Child and Adolescent Psychopharmacology* 17, no. 3 (2007): 284–87.

183 significant or complete remission of their anxiety: Donald F. Klein, "Anxiety Reconceptualized," *Comprehensive Psychiatry* 21, no. 6 (1980): 411.

184 "The predominant American psychiatric theory": Quoted in Kramer, *Listening to Prozac,* 80.

185 an initial report on imipramine: Donald F. Klein and Max Fink, "Psychiatric Reaction Patterns to Imipramine," *The American Journal of Psychiatry* 119, no. 5 (1962): 432–38.

185 "like the proverbial lead balloon": Quoted in Kramer, *Listening to Prozac,* 84.

185 Subsequent articles over the next several years: Donald F. Klein, "Delineation of Two Drug-Responsive Anxiety Syndromes," *Psychopharmacology* 5, no. 6 (1964): 397–408; Klein and Oaks, "Importance of Psychiatric Diagnosis in Prediction of Clinical Drug Effects," *Archives of General Psychiatry* 16, no. 1 (1967): 118.

186 "the reaction of the individual's ego": Quoted in Kramer, *Listening to Prozac,* 84.

187 "It is hard to recall": Kramer, *Listening to Prozac,* 77.

187 An advertisement for an October 1956 public talk: Tone, *The Age of Anxiety,* 111.

189 "In this manner we were able": Shorter, *History of Psychiatry,* 105.

189 Actually, one exception here was astrologers: MacDonald, *Mystical Bedlam,* 13–35.

190 "It is the task of the APA": Caplan, *They Say You're Crazy,* 234.

190 "a book of tentatively assembled agreements": Kutchins and Kirk, *Making Us Crazy,* 28.

191 "As the wine flowed": David Sheehan, "Rethinking Generalized Anxiety Disorder and Depression" (remarks at a meeting of the Anxiety Disorders of America Association, Savannah, Ga., March 7, 2008).

192 "Invent a new tranquilizer": The account of Sternbach's discoveries is drawn from, among other sources, Baenninger et al., *Good Chemistry,* 65–78; Tone, *Age of Anxiety,* 120–40.

193 "We thought that the expected negative result": Leo Sternbach, "The Discovery of Librium," *Agents and Actions* 2 (1972): 193–96.

193 tamed a wild lynx with Librium: Smith, *Small Comfort,* 74.

193 "The Drug That Tames Tigers": Quoted in Davenport-Hines, *Pursuit of Oblivion,* 327.

193 "slightly soft in the knees": Tone, *Age of Anxiety,* 130.

193 88 percent of those with "free-floating anxiety": Joseph M. Tobin and Nolan D. C. Lewis, "New Psychotherapeutic Agent, Chlordiazepoxide Use in Treatment of Anxiety States and Related Symptoms," *The Journal of the American Medical Association* 174, no. 10 (1960): 1242–49.

194 "the most significant advance to date": Harry H. Farb, "Experience with Librium in Clinical Psychiatry," *Diseases of the Nervous System* 21 (1960): 27.

194 "the treatment of common anxieties": Shorter, *Before Prozac*, 100.

194 Librium had the same range: M. Marinker, "The Doctor's Role in Prescribing," *The Journal of the Royal College of General Practitioners* 23, supp. 2 (1973): 26.

194 Valium became the first drug: Restak, *Poe's Heart*, 191.

194 one in every five women: Valenstein, *Blaming the Brain*, 56.

194 18 percent of all American *physicians*: George E. Vaillant, Jane R. Brighton, and Charles McArthur, "Physicians' Use of Mood-Altering Drugs: A 20-Year Follow-up Report." *The New England Journal of Medicine* (1970).

194 "It is ten years since Librium": Quoted in Smith, *Small Comfort*, 113.

195 "Whether the increase": Hollister, *Clinical Use of Psychotherapeutic Drugs*, 111.

196 "One must consider the broader implications": D. Jacobs, "The Psychoactive Drug Thing: Coping or Cop Out?," *Journal of Drug Issues* 1 (1971): 264–68.

196 "35, single and psychoneurotic": See, for instance, *The American Journal of Psychiatry* 126 (1970): 1696. The advertisement also ran in the *Archives of General Psychiatry*.

196 "the arrival of the millennium": Quoted in Smith, *Small Comfort*, 91.

198 "Valium, Librium, and other drugs": Quoted in Whitaker, *Anatomy of an Epidemic*, 137.

198 the brains of people who took tranquilizers: M. H. Lader, M. Ron, and H. Petursson, "Computed Axial Brain Tomography in Long-Term Benzodiazepine Users," *Psychological Medicine* 14, no. 1 (1984): 203–6. For additional overview, see "Brain Damage from Benzodiazepines," *Psychology Today*, November 18, 2010.

### CHAPTER 7: MEDICATION AND THE MEANING OF ANXIETY

208 By 2002, according to one estimate: M. N. Stagnitti, *Trends in Antidepressant Use by the U.S. Civilian Non-institutionalized Population, 1997 and 2002*, Statistical Brief 76 (Rockville, Md.: Agency for Healthcare Research and Quality, May 2005).

209 a 2007 estimate put the number: United Press International, "Study: Psych Drugs Sales Up," March 28, 2007.

209 Trace elements of Prozac: See, for instance, "In Our Streams: Prozac and Pesticides," *Time*, August 25, 2003; "River Fish Accumulate Human Drugs," *Nature News Service*, September 5, 2003; "Frogs, Fish, and Pharmaceuticals: A Troubling Brew," CNN.com, November 14, 2003; "Prozac in the Water," *Governing* 19, no. 12 (September 2006); "Fish on Prozac Are Violent and Obsessive," Smithsonian .com, November 12, 2012.

209 "Considering the benefit and the risk": Healy, *Let Them Eat Prozac*, 39.

209 A series of studies in the 1980s: Breggin, *Talking Back to Prozac*, 49. See also Healy, *Let Them Eat Prozac*, 37.

210 "This": Shorter, *Before Prozac*, 172.

210 In 2006, Einar Hellbom: Einar Hellbom, "Chlorpheniramine, Selective Serotonin-Reuptake Inhibitors (SSRIs) and Over-the-Counter (OTC) Treatment," *Medical Hypotheses* 66, no. 4 (2006): 689–90. See also Einar Hellbom and

Mats Humble, "Panic Disorder Treated with the Antihistamine Chlorphenira-mine," *Annals of Allergy, Asthma, and Immunology* 90 (2003): 361.

211 David Wong, an Eli Lilly biochemist: Healy, *Let Them Eat Prozac*, 39.

211 a branding firm had thought: "Eternal Sunshine," *The Observer*, May 12, 2007.

212 "It is now clear": Quoted in Barber, *Comfortably Numb*, 55.

213 "Paxil is truly addictive": Quoted in Shorter, *Before Prozac*, 44.

213 "do not have a clinically meaningful": Joanna Moncrieff and Irving Kirsch, "Efficacy of Antidepressants in Adults," *British Medical Journal* 331, no. 7509 (2005): 155.

213 "If you're born around World War I": Quoted in Barber, *Comfortably Numb*, 106.

214 In Iceland, the incidence of depression: Tómas Helgason, Helgi Tómasson, and Tómas Zoega, "Antidepressants and Public Health in Iceland: Time Series Analysis of National Data," *The British Journal of Psychiatry* 184, no. 2 (2004): 157–62.

214 Britain reported 38 million: Joanna Moncrieff and Joceline Pomerleau, "Trends in Sickness Benefits in Great Britain and the Contribution of Mental Disorders," *Journal of Public Health* 22, no. 1 (2000): 59–67.

214 depression tripled in the 1990s: Robert Rosenheck, "The Growth of Psycho-pharmacology in the 1990s: Evidence-Based Practice or Irrational Exuberance," *International Journal of Law and Psychiatry* 28, no. 5 (2005): 467–83.

214 *1,000 percent increase:* See, for instance, Healy, *Let Them Eat Prozac*, 20. See also McHenry, "Ethical Issues in Psychopharmacology," *Journal of Medical Ethics* 32 (2006): 405–10.

214 the worldwide suicide rate has increased: www.who.int.

215 if a drug makes you feel good: Greenberg, *Manufacturing Depression*, 193.

215 "Psychotherapeutically": Gerald L. Klerman, "A Reaffirmation of the Efficacy of Psychoactive Drugs," *Journal of Drug Issues* 1 (1971): 312–19.

216 "Americans believe tranquilizers are effective": Dean I. Manheimer et al., "Popular Attitudes and Beliefs About Tranquilizers," *The American Journal of Psychiatry* 130, no. 11 (1973): 1246–53.

217 only 38 percent of Americans: Mental Health America, Attitudinal Survey 2007.

217 only half had atypical levels of serotonin: Marie Asberg et al., "'Serotonin Depression'—a Biochemical Subgroup Within the Affective Disorders?," *Science* 191, no. 4226 (1976): 478–80.

218 "abandon the simplistic hypothesis": "CINP Meeting with the Nobels, Montreal, Canada, June 25, 2002: Speaker's Notes—Dr. Arvid Carlsson," *Collegium Internationale Neuro-Psychopharmacologicum Newsletter* (March 2003).

218 Not long ago, George Ashcroft: L. McHenry, "Ethical Issues in Psychopharmacology," *Journal of Medical Ethics* 32, no. 7 (2006): 405–10.

218 "the evidence does not support": Valenstein, *Blaming the Brain*, 96.

218 "We have hunted for big simple": Kenneth S. Kendler, "Toward a Philosophical Structure for Psychiatry," *The American Journal of Psychiatry* 162, no. 3 (2005): 433–40. For more on the decaying of the serotonin hypothesis, see Jeffrey R. Lacasse and Jonathan Leo, "Serotonin and Depression: A Disconnect Between the Advertisements and the Scientific Literature," *PLoS Medicine* 2, no. 12 (2005): e392.

222 "If man can be reduced": Tolson, *Pilgrim*, 129.

223 "Yours is a mind": Quoted in Ibid., 191.

223  His opinion of biological psychiatry: Peter Kramer makes observations along these lines in *Listening to Prozac*.

223  "unable to account for the predicament": This essay is reprinted in Percy's collection *Signposts in a Strange Land*.

224  "We all know perfectly well": Quoted and discussed in, among other sources, Elie, *The Life You Save*, 276; Elliott and Chambers, *Prozac as a Way of Life*, 135.

CHAPTER 8: SEPARATION ANXIETY

230  "Fear disorders": Ron Kessler, "Comorbidity of Anxiety Disorders with Other Physical and Mental Disorders in the National Comorbidity Survey Replication" (presentation at ADAA conference, Savannah, Ga., March 7, 2008).

235  "Anxiety in children": Freud, *Three Essays*.

235  "souls burning in hell": Breger, *Dream of Undying Fame*, 9.

236  "libido toward matrem had awakened": Gay, *Freud*, 11.

236  "You yourself have seen": Breger, *Freud*, 18.

236  "subject to attacks of anxiety": Kramer, *Freud*, 20.

236  "a universal event in early childhood": *Complete Letters of Freud to Fliess*, 272.

239  "biological factor": Freud, *Problem of Anxiety*, 99.

239  "the human infant is sent": Ibid.

239  "loss of love": Ibid., 119.

240  "the atrophied remnants of innate preparedness": Ibid., 117.

241  "was a very stable background": Karen, *Becoming Attached*, 30.

241  "a sharp, hard, self-centered woman": Ibid., 31.

241  "could be seen as an indictment": Ibid.

242  "But there *is* such a thing": Bowlby, *Separation*, viii.

242  "a frightfully vain old woman": Karen, *Becoming Attached*, 44.

242  "an extremely anxious, distressed woman": Ibid., 45.

242  "The fact that this poor woman": Ibid.

245  When Ainsworth first arrived in Uganda: This account of Ainsworth's time in Uganda draws heavily on her book *Infancy in Uganda* and on chapter 11 of Robert Karen's *Becoming Attached*.

248  none of the ambivalently attached children: Karen, *Becoming Attached*, 180.

250  Konrad Lorenz's influential 1935 paper: Konrad Z. Lorenz, "The Companion in the Bird's World," *The Auk* 54, no. 3 (1937): 245–73.

250  "What's the use to psychoanalyze a goose?": Quoted in Karen, *Becoming Attached*, 107.

250  calls to "excommunicate" him: Issroff, *Winnicott and Bowlby*, 121.

251  published an article in: Harry Frederick Harlow, "The Nature of Love," *American Psychologist* (1958): 673–85.

252  "Thereafter": Bowlby, *Secure Base*, 26.

253  when infant monkeys were separated: See, for instance, Yvette Spencer-Booth and Robert A. Hinde, "Effects of 6 Days Separation from Mother on 18- to 32-Week-Old Rhesus Monkeys," *Animal Behaviour* 19, no. 1 (1971): 174–91.

253  A subsequent paper by Harry Harlow: Harry F. Harlow and Margaret Harlow, "Learning to Love," *American Scientist* 54, no. 3 (1966): 244–72.

253 "initiation of ventral contact": See, for instance, Stephen J. Suomi, "How Gene-Environment Interactions Can Shape the Development of Socioemotional Regulation in Rhesus Monkeys," *Emotional Regulation and Developmental Health: Infancy and Early Childhood* (2002): 5–26.

253 The idea behind the variable foraging demand: See, for instance, Mathew et al., "Neuroimaging Studies in Nonhuman Primates Reared Under Early Stressful Conditions," *Fear and Anxiety* (2004).

253 he died alcoholic and depressed: See, for instance, Blum, *Love at Goon Park.*

255 the amount of licking and grooming: See, for instance, Christian Caldji et al., "Maternal Care During Infancy Regulates the Development of Neural Systems Mediating the Expression of Fearfulness in the Rat," *Proceedings of the National Academy of Sciences* 95, no. 9 (1998): 5335–40.

255 lasting consequences on a primate's neurochemistry: See, for instance, Jeremy D. Coplan et al., "Variable Foraging Demand Rearing: Sustained Elevations in Cisternal Cerebrospinal Fluid Corticotropin-Releasing Factor Concentrations in Adult Primates," *Biological Psychiatry* 50, no. 3 (2001): 200–4.

255 There's even some evidence: See, for instance, Tamashiro, Kellie L. K., "Metabolic Syndrome: Links to Social Stress and Socioeconomic Status," *Annals of the New York Academy of Science* 1231, no. 1 (2011): 46–55.

256 the children and even grandchildren: See, for instance, Joel J. Silverman et al., "Psychological Distress and Symptoms of Posttraumatic Stress Disorder in Jewish Adolescents Following a Brief Exposure to Concentration Camps," *Journal of Child and Family Studies* 8, no. 1 (1999): 71–89.

256 A recent study published: Maselko et al., "Mother's Affection at 8 Months Predicts Emotional Distress in Adulthood," *Journal of Epidemiology & Community Health* 65, no. 7 (2011): 621–25.

257 a coping strategy based on "chronic vigilance": See, for instance, L. Alan Sroufe, "Attachment and Development: A Prospective, Longitudinal Study from Birth to Adulthood," *Attachment and Human Development* 7, no. 4 (2005): 349–67.

260 "Adults with agoraphobia are more likely": Corine de Ruiter and Marinus H. Van Ijzendoorn, "Agoraphobia and Anxious-Ambivalent Attachment: An Integrative Review," *Journal of Anxiety Disorders* 6, no. 4 (1992): 365–81.

260 "Adults with agoraphobia report": Dozier et al., "Attachment and Psychopathology in Adulthood," in *Handbook of Attachment*, 718–44.

260 "[Infants with insecure] attachments": Warren, et al., "Child and Adolescent Anxiety Disorders and Early Attachment," *Journal of the American Academy of Child & Adolescent Psychiatry* 36, no. 5 (1997): 637–44.

260 "Human adults who reported": Hane, Amie Ashley, and Nathan A. Fox, "Ordinary variations in maternal caregiving influence human infants' stress reactivity," *Psychological Science* 17.6 (2006): 550–556.

CHAPTER 9: WORRIERS AND WARRIORS

264 In 2001, Kenneth Kendler: Kenneth S. Kendler et al., "The Genetic Epidemiology of Irrational Fears and Phobias in Men," *Archives of General Psychiatry* 58, no. 3 (2001): 257. See also Kenneth S. Kendler, John Myers, and Carol A. Prescott,

"The Etiology of Phobias: An Evaluation of the Stress-Diathesis Model," *Archives of General Psychiatry* 59, no. 3 (2002): 242.

264 Meta-analyses of genetic studies: See, for instance, Hettema et al., "A Review and Meta-Analysis of the Genetic Epidemiology of Anxiety Disorders," *The American Journal of Psychiatry* 158, no. 10 (2001) 1568–78.

265 one of the largest-scale studies: Giovanni Salum, "Anxiety 'Density' in Families Predicts Disorders in Children" (presentation at ADAA conference, March 28, 2011).

266 "We believe that most of the children": quoted in Restak, *Poe's Heart,* 64; see also Kagan, *Unstable Ideas,* 161-163.

267 Kagan and his colleagues took brain scans: These studies are described in Robin Marantz Henig, "Understanding the Anxious Mind," *The New York Times Magazine,* September 29, 2009.

269 Mice whose *Grp* gene: See, for instance, Gleb P. Shumyatsky et al., "Identification of a Signaling Network in Lateral Nucleus of Amygdala Important for Inhibiting Memory Specifically Related to Learned Fear," *Cell* 111, no. 6 (2002): 905–18.

269 Mice whose stathmin gene: See, for instance, Gleb P. Shumyatsky et al., "Stathmin, a Gene Enriched in the Amygdala, Controls Both Learned and Innate Fear," *Cell* 123, no. 4 (2005): 697–709.

270 In one study of children: Smoller et al., "Influence of *RGS2* on Anxiety-Related Temperament, Personality, and Brain Function," *Archives of General Psychiatry* 65, no. 3 (2008): 298–308.

270 Another study, of 744 college students: Cited in Smoller et al., "Genetics of Anxiety Disorders: The Complex Road from DSM to DNA," *Depression and Anxiety* 26, no. 11 (2009): 965–75.

270 A third study revealed: Leygraf et al., "*RGS2* Gene Polymorphisms as Modulators of Anxiety in Humans," *Journal of Neural Transmission* 113, no. 12 (2006): 1921–25.

270 A fourth study, of 607 people: Koenen et al., "*RGS2* and Generalized Anxiety Disorder in an Epidemiologic Sample of Hurrican-Exposed Adults," *Depression and Anxiety* 26, no. 4 (2009): 309–15.

270 Lauren McGrath, a researcher: "Unique Study Identifies Gene Associated with Anxious Phenotypes," *Medscape News,* March 29, 2011.

271 "talent for creative dance performance": R. Bachner-Melman et al., "*AVPR1a* and *SLC6A4* Gene Polymorphisms Are Associated with Creative Dance Performance," *PLoS Genetics* 1, no. 3 (2005): e42.

273 tend to have a harder time: See, for instance, "Catechol O-methyltransferase Val158met Genotype and Neural Mechanisms Related to Affective Arousal and Regulation," *Archives of General Psychiatry* 63, no. 12 (2006): 1,396. Also, Montag et al., "COMT Genetic Variation Affects Fear Processing: Psychophysiological Evidence," *Behavioral Neuroscience* 122, no. 4 (1008): 901.

273 One study, conducted by investigators: Enoch et al., "Genetic Origins of Anxiety in Women: A Role for a Functional Catechol-o-methyltransferase Polymorphism," *Psychiatric Genetics* 13, no. 1 (2003): 33–41.

273 Another study, conducted among both: Armbruster et al., "Variation in Genes

Involved in Dopamine Clearance Influence the Startle Response in Older Adults," *Journal of Neural Transmission* 118, no. 9 (2011): 1281–92.

273 David Goldman, the chief of human neurogenetics: See, for instance, Stein et al., "Warriors versus Worriers: The Role of COMT Gene Variants," *CNS Spectrums* 11, no. 10 (2006): 745–48. Also, "Finding the 'Worrier-Warrior' Gene," *Philadelphia Inquirer,* June 2, 2003.

274 These different evolutionary strategies: Cited in Stein and Walker, *Triumph over Shyness,* 21.

274 Starting in the mid-1990s: For instance, Lesch, et al., "Association of Anxiety-Related Traits with a Polymorphism in the Serotonin Transporter Gene Regulatory Region," *Science* 274, no. 5292 (1996): 1527–31. Also, Hariri, Ahmad R., et al., "Serotonin Transporter Genetic Variation and the Response of the Human Amygdala." *Science* 297, no. 5580 (2002): 400–403. (For a good, non-technical overview of this research, see Dobbs, "The Science of Success," *The Atlantic,* December 2009.)

275 Ressler found that the variant: Charles F. Gillespie et al., "Risk and Resilience: Genetic and Environmental Influences on Development of the Stress Response," *Depression and Anxiety* 26, no. 11 (2009): 984–92. See also Rebekah G. Bradley et al., "Influence of Child Abuse on Adult Depression: Moderation by the Corticotropin-Releasing Hormone Receptor Gene," *Archives of General Psychiatry* 65, no. 2 (2008): 190; Kerry J. Ressler et al., "Polymorphisms in CRHR1 and the Serotonin Transporter Loci: Gene× Gene× Environment Interactions on Depressive Symptoms," *American Journal of Medical Genetics, Part B: Neuropsychiatric Genetics* 153, no. 3 (2010): 812–24.

275 Variations in this gene: Ibid. See also Elisabeth B. Binder et al., "Association of FKBP5 Polymorphisms and Childhood Abuse with Risk of Posttraumatic Stress Disorder Symptoms in Adults," *The Journal of the American Medical Association* 299, no. 11 (2008): 1291–305; Divya Mehta et al., "Using Polymorphisms in FKBP5 to Define Biologically Distinct Subtypes of Posttraumatic Stress Disorder: Evidence from Endocrine and Gene Expression Studies," *Archives of General Psychiatry* (2011): archgenpsychiatry-2011.

277 A 2005 study at San Diego State University: Stein, Murray B., Margaret Daniele Fallin, Nicholas J. Schork, and Joel Gelernter. "COMT Polymorphisms and Anxiety-related Personality Traits." *Neuropsychopharmacology* 30, no. 11 (2005): 2092–2102.

278 In the 1970s, Martin Seligman: Martin E. P. Seligman, "Phobias and Preparedness," *Behavior Therapy* 2, no. 3 (1971): 307–20.

279 monkeys could *not* easily acquire fears: Susan Mineka and Arne Öhman, "Born to Fear: Non-associative Vs. Associative Factors in the Etiology of Phobias," *Behaviour Research and Therapy* 40, no. 2 (2002): 173–84.

280 This is evidence, Öhman argues: Öhman and Mineka, "Fears, Phobias, and Preparedness: Toward an Evolved Module of Fear and Fear Learning," *Psychological Review* 108, no. 3 (2001): 483.

CHAPTER 10: AGES OF ANXIETY

295 "the brain-workers in almost every household": Beard, *A Practical Treatise,* 1.

296 "In the older countries": A. D. Rockwell, "Some Causes and Characteristics of Neurasthenia," *New York Medical Journal* 58 (1893): 590.

296 "American nervousness is the product": Beard, *American Nervousness*, 176.

297 "The Greeks were certainly civilized": Ibid., 96.

297 "modern, and originally American": Ibid., vii–viii.

297 "When civilization, plus these five factors": Ibid., 96.

298 The crucial concept in all these explanations: See, for instance, Micale, *Hysterical Men*, 23.

298 "I begin with the head and brain": Beard, *Practical Treatise*, 15.

298 "destroyed or made miserable": Quoted in Micale, *Hysterical Men*, 35.

298 "a veritable social plague": Quoted in Micale, *Hysterical Men*, 35.

299 "One of my patients tells me": Ibid., 53.

299 "One of my cases": Ibid., 54.

299 "One man was so afraid": Ibid., 60.

300 neurasthenia had permeated deep: For a detailed exploration of this, see Lutz, *American Nervousness;* Schuster, *Neurasthenic Nation.*

300 "overstressed nation": American Psychological Association, *Stress in America,* 2010.

300 increased from 13.4 million to 16.2 million: IMS Health Data, National Disease & Therapeutic Index, Diagnosis Visits, 2002–2006.

300 More Americans seek medical treatment: Ibid.

300 A study published in the *American Psychologist:* Swindle et al., "Responses to Nervous Breakdowns in America over a 40-year period," *American Psychologist* 55, no. 7 (2000): 740.

301 Twice as many people reported: Goodwin, Renee D., "The Prevalence of Panic Attacks in the United States: 1980 to 1995," *Journal of Clinical Epidemiology* 55, no. 9 (2003): 914–16.

301 the average college student in the 1990s: Twenge, *Generation Me*, 107.

301 "The average high school kid today": "How Big a Problem is Anxiety?" *Psychology Today*, April 30, 2008.

301 A World Health Organization survey: Kessler et al., "Lifetime Prevalence and Age-of-Onset Distributions of Mental Disorders in the World Health Organization's World Mental Health Survey Initiative," *World Psychiatry* 6, no. 3 (207): 168.

301 Statistics from the National Health Service: "Anxiety Disorders Have Soared Since Credit Crunch," *The Telegraph*, January 1, 2012.

301 "culture of fear": Mental Health Foundation, *Facing the Fear*, April 2009.

302 the odds in favor of damnation: LeGoff, *Medieval Civilization*, 325.

302 "The major problem for Americans": Slater, *Pursuit of Loneliness*, 24.

303 "the paradox of choice": Schwartz, *Paradox of Choice*, 2, 43.

303 "From the moment of birth": Fromm, *Escape from Freedom*, 41.

304 "First of all a feeling": Tillich, *Protestant Era*, 245.

304 "Fascism was like a jail": Quoted in May, *Meaning of Anxiety*, 12.

304 "It has filled the": *The New York Times*, February 1, 1948.

304 "people grasp at political authoritarianism": May, *Meaning of Anxiety*, 12.

304 "for 99 percent of human history": Sapolsky's discussion of this appears in *Zebras*, 378–83.

305 excessive timidity, caution, and concern: Kagan, *What Is Emotion?*, 14.

305  "Competitive individualism militates against": May, *Meaning of Anxiety,* 191.

306  "troubles herself with every thing": Hunter and Macalpine, *Three Hundred Years of Psychiatry,* 116.

306  "Intolerance of uncertainty appears to be": Michel J. Dugas, Mark H. Freeston, and Robert Ladouceur, "Intolerance of Uncertainty and Problem Orientation in Worry," *Cognitive Therapy and Research* 21, no. 6 (1997): 593–606.

306  a 31 percent increase: Scott Baker, Nicholas Bloom, and Steven Davis, "Measuring Economic Policy Uncertainty" (Chicago Booth Research Paper 13-02, 2013).

307  "nervous complaints prevail at the present day": Quoted in Oppenheim, *"Shattered Nerves,"* 14.

307  "At the beginning of the nineteenth century": Quoted in Micale, *Hysterical Men,* 81.

307  "atrocious and frightful symptoms": Cheyne, *The English Malady,* xxx.

308  "Other men get their knowledge": Burton, *Anatomy,* Book I, 34.

308  "I write of melancholy": Ibid., 21.

308  "Many lamentable effects this fear causeth": Ibid., 261.

309  "Many men are so amazed": Ibid.

309  "There is no greater cause": Ibid., 21.

309  "If men would attempt no more": Ibid., 50.

310  "In our day we still see": May, *Meaning of Anxiety,* xiv.

### CHAPTER 11: REDEMPTION

320  Eliot was, Kagan observes: Kagan has made this observation in numerous places.

320  "saturated with the vocabulary": Micale, *Hysterical Men,* 214.

321  "whether among all those Scholars": Quoted in Ibid.

321  Dean Simonton, a psychologist: Simonton, "Are Genius and Madness Related? Comtemporary Answers to an Ancient Question," *Psychiatric Times* 22, no. 7 (2005): 21–23. See also "The Case for Pessimism," *Businessweek,* August 13, 2004.

322  But his early letters reveal otherwise: Letters quoted here are from Masson, *Complete Letters.*

323  "They're compulsive, they don't make errors": Quoted in Robin Marantz Henig, "Understanding the Anxious Mind," *The New York Times Magazine,* September 29, 2009.

323  A 2012 study by psychiatrists: Nicholas A. Turiano et al., "Big 5 Personality Traits and Interleukin-6: Evidence for 'Healthy Neuroticism' in a US Population Sample," *Brain, Behavior, and Immunity* (2012).

323  A 2013 study in the *Academy of Management Journal:* Corrine Bendersky and Neha Parikh Shah, "The Downfall of Extroverts and the Rise of Neurotics: The Dynamic Process of Status Allocation in Task Groups, Academy of Management Journal," AMJ-2011-0316.R3.

323  "I would staff it with more neurotics and fewer extroverts": "Leadership Tip: Hire the Quiet Neurotic, Not the Impressive Extrovert," *Forbes,* April 11, 2013.

323  In 2005, researchers at the University of Wales: Adam M. Perkins and Philip J. Corr, "Can Worriers Be Winners? The Association Between Worrying and Job Performance," *Personality and Individual Differences* 38, no. 1 (2005): 25–31.

324 high IQ scores correlated with high levels: Jeremy D. Coplan et al., "The Relationship Between Intelligence and Anxiety: An Association with Subcortical White Matter Metabolism," *Frontiers in Evolutionary Neuroscience* 3 (2012).

325 a certain interpersonal obtuseness: See Winifred Gallagher, "How We Become What We Are," *The Atlantic,* September 1994.

326 But recent studies on rhesus monkeys: Stephen J. Suomi, "Risk, Resilience, and Gene-Environment Interplay in Primates," *Journal of the Canadian Academy of Child and Adolescent Psychiatry* 20, no. 4 (November 2011): 289–97.

## CHAPTER 12: RESILIENCE

330 the constant berating by Johnson's superego: Bate, *Samuel Johnson,* 117–27.

332 The ten critical psychological elements: Charney, "The Psychobiology of Resilience to Extreme Stress: Implications for the Treatment and Prevention of Anxiety Disorders," keynote address at ADAA conference, March 23, 2006.

336 the work of the cognitive psychologist: See, for instance, Albert Bandura, "Self-Efficacy: Toward a Unifying Theory of Behavioral Change," *Psychological Review* 84, 191–215; Albert Bandura, "The Assessment and Predictive Generality of Self-Percepts of Efficacy," *Journal of Behavior Therapy and Experimental Psychiatry* 13, 195–99.

# Bibliography

Aboujaoude, Elias. *Compulsive Acts: A Psychiatrist's Tales of Ritual and Obsession.* Berkley: University of California Press, 2008.

Ackerman, Diane. *An Alchemy of Mind: The Marvel and Mystery of the Brain.* New York: Scribner, 2004.

Adler, Alfred. *The Neurotic Constitution: Outlines of a Comparative Individualistic Psychology and Psychotherapy.* Translated by Bernard Glueck. New York: Moffat, Yard, 1917.

———. *Problems of Neurosis.* New York: Cosmopolitan Book Corporation, 1930.

———. *Understanding Human Nature.* Greenberg Publishers, 1927.

Aggleton, John, ed. *The Amygdala: A Functional Analysis.* 2nd ed. New York: Oxford University Press, 2000.

Ainsworth, Mary D. Salter. *Infancy in Uganda: Infant Care and the Growth of Love.* Baltimore: Johns Hopkins University Press, 1967.

Alexander, Franz G., and Sheldon T. Selesnick. *The History of Psychiatry: An Evaluation of Psychiatric Thought and Practice from Prehistoric Times to the Present.* Northvale, N.J.: James Aronson, 1995 (original 1966).

Alvarez, Walter C. *Nervousness, Indigestion, and Pain.* New York: Collier Books, 1962.

Ameisen, Olivier. *The End of My Addiction.* New York: Farrar, Straus and Giroux, 2009.

Andreasen, Nancy C. *The Broken Brain: The Biological Revolution in Psychiatry.* New York: Harper and Row, 1984.

Arieti, Silvano. *The Parnas: A Scene from the Holocaust.* Philadelphia: Paul Dry Books, 2000.

Arikha, Noga. *Passions and Tempers: A History of the Humours.* New York: Ecco, 2007.

Attwell, Khleber Chapman. *100 Questions and Answers About Anxiety.* Jones and Bartlett, 2006.

Auden, W. H. *The Age of Anxiety.* New York: Random House, 1946.

Augustine, *Confessions.* New York: Dover Editions, 2002.

Backus, William. *The Good News About Worry: Applying Biblical Truth to Problems of Anxiety and Fear.* Minneapolis: Bethany House, 1991.

Baenninger, Alex, Joseph Alberto Costa e Silva, Ian Hindmarch, Hans-Juergen Moeller, and Karl Rickels. *Good Chemistry: The Life and Legacy of Valium Inventor Leo Sternbach.* New York: McGraw-Hill, 2004.

Ballard, Chris. *The Art of a Beautiful Game: The Thinking Fan's Tour of the NBA.* New York: Simon and Schuster, 2009.

Balthasar, Hans Urs von. *The Christian and Anxiety.* San Francisco: Ignatius Press, 2000.

Barber, Charles. *Comfortably Numb: How Psychiatry Is Medicating a Nation.* New York: Pantheon, 2008.

Barbu, Zevedei. *Problems of Historical Psychology.* New York: Grove Press, 1960.

Barlow, David. *Anxiety and Its Disorders.* 2nd ed. Guilford Press, 2002.

Barlow, David, and Michelle G. Craske. *Mastery of Your Anxiety and Panic.* 3rd ed. Graywind Publications, 2000.

Barnes, Julian. *Nothing to Be Frightened Of.* New York: Alfred A. Knopf, 2008.

Barondes, Samuel H. *Better Than Prozac: Creating the Next Generation of Psychiatric Drugs.* Oxford University Press, 2003.

———. *Molecules and Mental Illness.* Delhi, India: Indo American Books, 2007.

Bassett, Lucinda. *From Panic to Power: Proven Techniques to Calm Your Anxieties, Conquer Your Fears, and Put You in Control of Your Life.* Quill, 1995.

Bate, Walter Jackson. *Samuel Johnson.* Harcourt, Brace, 1977.

Battie, William. *A Treatise on Madness.* Brunner/Mazel, 1969.

Baumer, Franklin L. *Religion and the Rise of Skepticism.* Harcourt, Brace, 1960.

Beard, George Miller. *American Nervousness, Its Causes and Consequences.* New York: G. P. Putnam's Sons, 1881.

———. *A Practical Treatise on Nervous Exhaustion (Neurasthenia), Its Symptoms, Nature, Sequences, and Treatment.* New York: William Wood, 1880.

Beatty, Jack. *Age of Betrayal: The Triumph of Money in America, 1865–1990.* New York: Alfred A. Knopf, 2007.

Beck, Aaron T. *Depression: Causes and Treatment.* Philadelphia: University of Pennsylvania Press, 1967.

Beck, Aaron T., and Gary Emery. *Anxiety Disorders and Phobias: A Cognitive Perspective.* New York: Basic Books, 1985.

Beck, Aaron T., and Arthur Freeman. *Cognitive Therapy of Personality Disorders.* New York: Guilford Press, 1990.

Becker, Dana. *One Nation Under Stress: The Trouble with Stress as an Idea.* Oxford University Press, 2013.

Becker, Ernest. *The Denial of Death.* Free Press, 1973.

Beilock, Sian. *Choke: What the Secrets of the Brain Reveal About Success and Failure at Work and at Play.* Free Press, 2010.

Berger, Peter L., Brigitte Berger, and Hansfried Kellner. *The Homeless Mind: Modernization and Consciousness.* New York: Random House, 1973.

Berrios, German E. *The History of Mental Symptoms: Descriptive Psychopathology Since the Nineteenth Century.* Cambridge University Press, 1996.

Bertin, Celia. *Marie Bonaparte: A Life.* New Haven, Conn.: Yale University Press, 1982.

Bettelheim, Bruno. *Freud and Man's Soul.* New York: Vintage Books, 1982.

Blanchard, Robert J., Caroline Blanchard, Guy Griebel, and David Nutt. *Handbook of Anxiety and Fear.* Academic Press/Elsevier, 2008.

Blum, Deborah. *Love at Goon Park: Harry Harlow and the Science of Affection.* New York: Basic Books, 2002.

Blythe, Jamie. *Fear Is No Longer My Reality: How I Overcame Panic and Social Anxiety Disorder—and You Can Too.* With Jenna Glatzer. McGraw-Hill, 2005.

Borch-Jacobsen, Mikkel. *Making Minds and Madness: From Hysteria to Depression.* Cambridge University Press, 2009.

Bourke, Joanna. *Fear: A Cultural History.* Virago, 2005.

Bourne, Edmund, and Lorna Garano. *Coping with Anxiety: 10 Simple Ways to Relieve Fear, Anxiety, and Worry.* New Harbinger, 2003.

Bowlby, John. *Charles Darwin: A New Life.* New York: W. W. Norton, 1990.

———. *A Secure Base.* London: Routledge, 1988.

———. *Separation: Anxiety and Anger.* New York: Basic Books, 1973.

Braund, Susanna, and Glenn W. Most, eds. *Ancient Anger: Perspectives from Homer to Galen.* Cambridge University Press, 2003.

Breger, Louis. *A Dream of Undying Fame: How Freud Betrayed His Mentor and Invented Psychoanalysis.* New York: Basic Books, 2009.

———. *Freud: Darkness in the Midst of Vision.* New York: John Wiley and Sons, 2000.

Breggin, Peter R. *Medication Madness: A Psychiatrist Exposes the Dangers of Mood-Altering Medications.* New York: St. Martin's Press, 2008.

———. *Talking Back to Prozac: What Doctors Aren't Telling You About Today's Most Controversial Drug.* New York: St. Martin's Press, 1994.

Bremner, J. Douglas. *Does Stress Damage the Brain? Understanding Trauma-Related Disorders from a Mind–Body Perspective.* New York: W. W. Norton, 2002.

Bretall, Robert. *A Kierkegaard Anthology.* Princeton, N.J.: Princeton University Press, 1936.

Briggs, Rex. *Transforming Anxiety, Transcending Shame.* Health Communications, 1999.

Browne, Janet. *Charles Darwin: The Power of Place.* Princeton, N.J.: Princeton University Press, 2002.

———. *Charles Darwin: Voyaging.* Princeton, N.J.: Princeton University Press, 1995.

Bruner, Jerome. *Acts of Meaning.* Cambridge, Mass.: Harvard University Press, 1990.

Burgess, Thomas H. *The Physiology or Mechanism of Blushing, Illustrative of the Influence of Mental Emotion on the Capillary Circulation, with a General View of the Sympathies.* John Churchill, 1839.

Burijon, Barry N. *Biological Bases of Clinical Anxiety.* New York: W. W. Norton, 2007.

Burns, David D. *When Panic Attacks: The New, Drug-Free Anxiety Therapy That Can Change Your Life.* Morgan Road Books, 2006.

Burton, Robert. *The Anatomy of Melancholy.* New York Review of Books, 2001.

Cannon, Walter B. *Bodily Changes in Pain, Hunger, Fear and Rage.* New York: Harper Torchbooks, 1963 (original edition 1915).

Cantor, Norman F. *The Civilization of the Middle Ages.* New York: HarperCollins, 1993.

Caplan, Paula J. *They Say You're Crazy: How the World's Most Powerful Psychiatrists Decide Who's Normal.* Da Capo Press, 1995.

Capps, Donald. *Social Phobia: Alleviating Anxiety in an Age of Self-Promotion.* St. Louis: Chalice Press, 1999.

Carlat, Daniel. *Unhinged: The Trouble with Psychiatry—a Doctor's Revelations About a Profession in Crisis.* Free Press, 2010.

Carlstedt, Roland A. *Critical Moments During Competition: A Mind-Body Model of Sports Performance When It Counts the Most.* Psychology Press, 2004.

Carter, Rita. *Mapping the Mind.* University of California Press, 1998.

Cassidy, Jude, and Phillip R. Shaver. *Handbook of Attachment: Theory, Research, and Clinical Applications.* 2nd ed. Guilford Press, 2008.

Cassirer, Ernst. *An Essay on Man.* New Haven, Conn.: Yale University Press, 1944.

Chansky, Tamar E. *Freeing Yourself from Anxiety.* Da Capo, 2012.

Charney, Dennis S., and Eric J. Nestler. *Neurobiology of Mental Illness.* 3rd ed. Oxford University Press, 2009.

Cheyne, George. *The English Malady (1733).* Tavistock/Routledge, 1991.

Clark, Taylor. *Nerve: Poise Under Pressure, Serenity Under Stress, and the Brave New Science of Fear and Cool.* Boston: Little, Brown, 2011.

Coleman, Penny. *Flashback: Posttraumatic Stress Disorder, Suicide, and the Lessons of War.* Beacon Press, 2006.

Coles, Robert. *The Mind's Fate: A Psychiatrist Looks at His Profession.* Back Bay Books, 1975.

——. *Walker Percy: An American Searcher.* Boston: Little, Brown, 1978.

Collins, Randall. *Violence: A Micro-sociological Theory.* Princeton, N.J.: Princeton University Press, 2008.

Colp, Ralph, Jr. *To Be an Invalid: The Illness of Charles Darwin.* Chicago: University of Chicago Press, 1977.

Conley, Dalton. *Elsewhere, U.S.A: How We Got from the Company Man, Family Dinners, and the Affluent Society to the Home Office, BlackBerry Moms, and Economic Anxiety.* New York: Pantheon, 2009.

Contosta, David R. *Rebel Giants: The Revolutionary Lives of Abraham Lincoln and Charles Darwin.* Amherst, N.Y.: Prometheus Books, 2008.

Coolidge, Frederick L., and Thomas Wynn. *The Rise of Homo Sapiens: The Evolution of Modern Thinking.* Chichester, U.K.: Wiley-Blackwell, 2009.

Cozolino, Louis. *The Neuroscience of Psychotherapy: Building and Rebuilding the Human Brain.* New York: W. W. Norton, 2002.

Crick, Francis. *The Astonishing Hypothesis: The Scientific Search for the Soul.* New York: Touchstone, 1994.

Cuordileone, Kyle A. *Manhood and American Political Culture in the Cold War.* New York: Routledge, 2005.

Cushman, Philip. *Constructing the Self, Constructing America: A Cultural History of Psychotherapy.* Addison-Wesley, 1995.

Damasio, Antonio. *Descartes' Error: Emotion, Reason, and the Human Brain.* Grosset/Putnam, 1994.

——. *The Feeling of What Happens: Body and Emotion in the Making of Consciousness.* Harcourt, 1999.

——. *Looking for Spinoza: Joy, Sorrow, and the Feeling Brain.* New York: Harcourt, 2003.

Darwin, Charles. *The Autobiography of Charles Darwin, 1809–1882.* New York: Classic Books International, 2009.

——. *The Expression of the Emotions in Man and Animals.* BiblioBazaar (originally published 1872), 2007.

Davenport-Hines, Richard. *The Pursuit of Oblivion: A Global History of Narcotics.* New York: W. W. Norton, 2001.

Davey, Graham C. L., ed. *Phobias: A Handbook of Theory, Research and Treatment.* Chichester, U.K.: Wiley, 1997.

Davey, Graham C. L., and Adrian Wells, eds. *Worry and Its Psychological Disorders.* Wiley, 2006.

Davidson, Jonathan, and Henry Dreher. *The Anxiety Book: Developing Strength in the Face of Fear.* Riverhead Books, 2003.

Davidson, Richard J., and Sharon Begley. *The Emotional Life of Your Brain.* Hudson Street Press, 2012.

Davis, Lennard J. *Obsession: A History.* Chicago: University of Chicago Press, 2008.

Davison, Gerald D., and John M. Neale. *Abnormal Psychology.* 5th ed. John Wiley and Sons, 1990.

Dayhoff, Signe A. *Diagonally-Parked in a Parallel Universe: Working Through Social Anxiety.* Effectiveness-Plus Publications, 2000.

de Botton, Alain. *Status Anxiety.* New York: Pantheon Books, 2004.

DeGrandpre, Richard. *The Cult of Pharmacology: How America Became the World's Most Troubled Drug Culture.* Durham, N.C.: Duke University Press, 2006.

Descartes, René. *Discourse on Method and Meditations.* Library of Liberal Arts, 1960.

Desmond, Adrian, and James Moore. *Darwin: The Life of a Tormented Evolutionist.* New York: W. W. Norton, 1991.

Dessoir, Max, and Donald Fisher. *Outlines of the History of Psychology.* New York: Macmillan, 1912.

Dillon, Brian. *The Hypochondriacs: Nine Tormented Lives.* New York: Faber and Faber, 2010.

Doctor, Ronald M., and Ada P. Kahn. *The Encyclopedia of Phobias, Fears, and Anxieties.* Facts on File, 1989.

Dodds, E. R. *The Greeks and the Irrational.* Berkeley: University of California Press, 1951.

Doi, Takeo. *The Anatomy of Dependence.* Kodansha, 1971.

Dollard, John. *Victory over Fear.* Reynal and Hitchcock, 1942.

Dollard, John, and Neal A. Miller. *Personality and Psychotherapy: An Analysis in Terms of Learning, Thinking, and Culture.* McGraw-Hill, 1950.

Dozois, David J. A., and Keith S. Dobson. *The Prevention of Anxiety and Depression: Theory, Research, and Practice.* American Psychological Association, 2004.

Drinka, George Frederick. *The Birth of Neurosis: Myth, Malady, and the Victorians.* New York: Simon & Schuster, 1984.

Drummond, Edward H. *Overcoming Anxiety Without Tranquilizers.* Dutton, 1997.

Dukakis, Kitty, and Larry Tye. *Shock: The Healing Power of Electroconvulsive Therapy.* Avery, 2006.

Dumont, Raeann. *The Sky Is Falling: Understanding and Coping with Phobias, Panic, and Obsessive-Compulsive Disorders.* New York: W. W. Norton, 1996.

Eghigian, Greg. *From Madness to Mental Health: Psychiatric Disorder and Its Treatment in Western Civilization.* New Brunswick, N.J.: Rutgers University Press, 2010.

Elie, Paul. *The Life You Save May Be Your Own: An American Pilgrimage.* New York: Farrar, Straus and Giroux, 2003.

Ellenberger, Henri F. *The Discovery of the Unconscious: The History and Evolution of Dynamic Psychiatry.* New York: Basic Books, 1970.

Elliott, Carl, and Tod Chambers. *Prozac as a Way of Life.* Chapel Hill: University of North Carolina Press, 2004.

Ellman, Richard. *Yeats: The Man and the Masks.* New York: Macmillan, 1948.

Engel, Jonathan. *American Therapy: The Rise of Psychotherapy in the United States.* Gotham Books, 2008.

Epictetus. *Discourses and Enchiridion.* New York: Walter J. Black, 1944.

Erikson, Erik H. *Childhood and Society.* New York: W. W. Norton, 1950.

Esposito, Janet. *In the Spotlight: Overcome Your Fear of Public Speaking and Performance.* Strong Books, 2000.

Eysenck, H. J., and S. Rachman. *The Causes and Cures of Neurosis.* San Diego: Robert R. Knapp, 1965.

Fann, William E., Ismet Karacan, Alex D. Pokorny, and Robert L. Williams, eds. *Phenomenology and Treatment of Anxiety.* Spectrum Publications, 1979.

Farnbach, Rod, and Eversley Farnbach. *Overcoming Performance Anxiety.* Simon and Schuster Australia, 2001.

Fisher, Paul. *House of Wits: An Intimate Portrait of the James Family.* New York: Henry Holt, 2008.

Ford, Emily. *What You Must Think of Me: A Firsthand Account of One Teenager's Experience with Social Anxiety Disorder.* With Michael R. Liebowitz and Linda Wasmer Andrews. Oxford University Press, 2007.

Forrester, John. *Dispatches from the Freud Wars: Psychoanalysis and Its Passions.* Cambridge, Mass.: Harvard University Press, 1997.

———. *Truth Games: Lies, Money, and Psychoanalysis.* Cambridge, Mass.: Harvard University Press, 1997.

Foxman, Paul. *Dancing with Fear: Overcoming Anxiety in a World of Stress and Uncertainty.* Jason Aronson, 1997.

———. *The Worried Child: Recognizing Anxiety in Children and Helping Them Heal.* Hunter House, 2004.

Frankl, Viktor E. *The Doctor and the Soul: From Psychotherapy to Logotherapy.* New York: Vintage Books, 1986.

———. *Man's Search for Meaning.* New York: Washington Square Press, 1985 (copyright 1959).

Frattaroli, Elio. *Healing the Soul in the Age of the Brain: Why Medication Isn't Enough.* Penguin, 2001.

Freeman, Daniel, and Jason Freeman. *Anxiety: A Very Short Introduction.* Oxford University Press, 2012.

Freud, Sigmund. *The Basic Writings of Sigmund Freud.* Modern Library, 1995.

———. *Beyond the Pleasure Principle.* New York: W. W. Norton, 1961.

———. *Character and Culture.* Collier Books, 1963.

———. *Civilization and Its Discontents.* New York: W. W. Norton, 1961.

———. *The Complete Letters of Sigmund Freud to Wilhelm Fliess, 1887–1904.* Translated and edited by Jeffrey Moussaieff Masson. Cambridge, Mass.: Harvard University Press, 1985.

———. *Five Lectures on Psycho-Analysis.* New York: W. W. Norton, 1989.

———. *The History of the Psycho-Analytic Movement and the Origin and Development of Psychoanalysis.* New York: W. W. Norton, 1990.

———. *The Interpretation of Dreams.* London: Hogarth Press, 1953.

———. *The Problem of Anxiety.* Psychoanalytic Quarterly Press, 1936.

———. *Three Essays on the Theory of Sexuality.* New York: Basic Books, 2000.

———. *Totem and Taboo: Some Points of Agreement Between the Mental Lives of Savages and Neurotics.* Routledge and Kegan Paul, 1950.

Friedman, Steven, ed. *Cultural Issues in the Treatment of Anxiety.* Guilford Press, 1997.

Frink, H. W., and James J. Putnam. *Morbid Fears and Compulsions: Their Psychology and Psychoanalytic Treatment.* Moffat, Yard, 1918.

Fromm, Erich. *Escape from Freedom.* New York: Owl Books, 1969.

———. *Man for Himself: An Inquiry into the Psychology of Ethics.* New York: Henry Holt, 1947.

Furedi, Frank. *Therapy Culture: Cultivating Vulnerability in an Uncertain Age.* London: Routledge, 2004.

Furer, Patricia, John R. Walker, and Murray B. Stein. *Treating Health Anxiety and Fear of Death: A Practitioner's Guide.* New York: Springer, 2007.

Gabriel, Richard A. *No More Heroes: Madness and Psychiatry in War.* Hill and Wang, 1987.

Galdston, Iago, ed. *Historic Derivations of Modern Psychiatry.* New York: McGraw-Hill, 1967.

Gamwell, Lynn, and Nancy Tomes. *Madness in America: Cultural and Medical Perceptions of Mental Illness Before 1914.* Ithaca, N.Y.: Cornell University Press, 1995.

Gandhi, Mohandas K. *An Autobiography: The Story of My Experiments with Truth.* Beacon Press, 1993.

Gardner, Daniel. *The Science of Fear.* Dutton, 2008.

Garff, Joakim. *Søren Kierkegaard: A Biography.* Princeton, N.J.: Princeton University Press, 2005.

Gay, Peter. *Freud: A Life for Our Time.* New York: W. W. Norton, 1988.

Gazzaniga, Michael S. *Nature's Mind: The Biological Roots of Thinking, Emotions, Sexuality, Language, and Intelligence.* New York: Basic Books, 1992.

Gershon, Michael D. *The Second Brain: The Scientific Basis of Gut Instinct and a Groundbreaking New Understanding of Nervous Disorders of the Stomach and Intestine.* New York: HarperCollins, 1998.

Gerzon, Robert. *Finding Serenity in the Age of Anxiety.* New York: Macmillan, 1997.

Gewirtz, Jacob, ed. *Attachment and Dependency.* V. H. Winston and Sons, 1972.

Ghinassi, Cheryl Winning. *Anxiety.* Greenwood, 2010.

Gifford, Frank. *Gifford on Courage.* With Charles Mangel. M. Evans, 1976.

Gijswijt-Hofstra, Marijke, and Roy Porter. *Cultures of Neurasthenia: From Beard to the First World War.* Rodopi, 2001.

Glantz, Kalman, and John K. Pearce. *Exiles from Eden: Psychotherapy from an Evolutionary Perspective.* New York: W. W. Norton, 1989.

Glatzer, Jenna, ed. *Conquering Panic and Anxiety Disorders: Success Stories, Strategies, and Other Good News.* Hunter House, 2002.

Gleick, James. *Faster: The Acceleration of Just About Everything.* New York: Vintage Books, 1999.

Glenmullen, Joseph. *The Antidepressant Solution: The Only Step-by-Step Guide to Safely Overcoming Antidepressant Withdrawal, Dependence, and "Addiction."* New York: Free Press, 2005.

Goldstein, Kurt. *Human Nature in the Light of Psychopathology.* 1940. New York: Schocken Books, 1963.

Goldstein, Michael J., and James O. Palmer. *The Experience of Anxiety: A Casebook.* New York: Oxford University Press, 1963.

Goodwin, Donald W. *Anxiety.* Oxford University Press, 1986.

———. *Phobia: The Facts.* Oxford University Press, 1983.

Gordon, James S. *Unstuck: Your Guide to the Seven-Stage Journey Out of Depression.* New York: Penguin, 2008.

Gorman, Jack, ed. *Fear and Anxiety: The Benefits of Translational Research.* Washington, D.C.: American Psychiatric Publishing, 2004.

Gosling, F. G. *Before Freud: Neurasthenia and the American Medical Community, 1870–1910.* University of Illinois Press, 1987.

Gould, James L. *Ethology: The Mechanisms and Evolution of Behavior.* New York: W. W. Norton, 1982.

Goulding, Regina A., and Richard C. Schwarz. *The Mosaic Mind: Empowering the Tormented Selves of Child Abuse Survivors.* New York: W. W. Norton, 1995.

Gray, Jeffrey A., and Neil McNaughton. *The Neuropsychology of Anxiety.* 2nd ed. Oxford: Oxford University Press, 2000.

Greenberg, Gary. *The Book of Woe: The "DSM" and the Unmaking of Psychiatry.* Blue Rider Press, 2012.

———. *Manufacturing Depression: The Secret History of a Modern Disease.* New York: Simon and Schuster, 2010.

Greist, John H., James W. Jefferson, and Isaac M. Marks. *Anxiety and Its Treatment.* New York: Warner Books, 1986.

Grinker, Roy R., and John P. Spiegel. *Men Under Stress.* Philadelphia: Blakiston, 1945.

Grob, Gerald N. *Mental Illness and American Society, 1875–1940.* Princeton, N.J.: Princeton University Press, 1983.

Grosskurth, Phyllis. *Melanie Klein: Her World and Her Work.* New York: Alfred A. Knopf, 1986.

Hallowell, Edward M. *Worry: Hope and Help for a Common Condition.* New York: Random House, 1997.

Handly, Robert. *Anxiety and Panic Attacks: Their Cause and Cure.* With Pauline Neff. Fawcett Crest, 1985.

Hanford, A. Chester. *Problems in Municipal Government.* A. W. Shaw, 1926.

Harrington, Anne. *The Cure Within: A History of Mind-Body Medicine.* New York: W. W. Norton, 2008.

Hart, Archibald D. *The Anxiety Cure.* New York: Thomas Nelson, 2001.

Harvard Medical School. *The Sensitive Gut.* New York: Fireside Books, 2000.

Hayes, Steven C. *Get Out of Your Mind and into Your Life: The New Acceptance and Commitment Therapy.* New Harbinger, 2005.

Hayes, Steven C., Kirk D. Strosahl, and Kelly G. Wilson. *Acceptance and Commitment Therapy: An Experiential Approach to Behavior Change.* Guilford Press, 1999.

Healy, David. *The Antidepressant Era.* Cambridge, Mass.: Harvard University Press, 1997.

———. *The Creation of Psychopharmacology.* Cambridge, Mass.: Harvard University Press, 2002.

———. *Let Them Eat Prozac.* James Lorimer, 2003.

Heimberg, Richard G., Cynthia L. Turk, and Douglas S. Mennin, eds. *Generalized Anxiety Disorder: Advances in Research and Practice.* Guilford Press, 2004.

Herman, Judith Lewis. *Trauma and Recovery.* New York: Basic Books, 1992.

Heston, Leonard L. *Mending Minds: A Guide to the New Psychiatry of Depression, Anxiety, and Other Serious Mental Disorders.* W. H. Freeman, 1992.

Hobson, J. Allan, and Jonathan A. Leonard. *Out of Its Mind: Psychiatry in Crisis.* Cambridge, Mass.: Perseus Books, 2002.

Hoch, Paul, and Joseph Zubin, eds. *Anxiety.* New York: Grune and Stratton, 1950.

Hofstadter, Richard. *The Age of Reform.* New York: Vintage, 1955.

———. *The American Political Tradition.* New York: Alfred A. Knopf, 1948.

Hollander, Eric, and Daphne Simeon. *Concise Guide to Anxiety Disorders.* American Psychiatric Publishing, 2003.

Hollister, Leo. *Clinical Use of Psychotherapeutic Drugs.* Charles C. Thomas, 1973.

Holmes, Jeremy. *The Search for the Secure Base: Attachment Theory and Psychotherapy.* Routledge, 2001.

Horney, Karen. *Neurosis and Human Growth: The Struggle Toward Self-Realization.* New York: W. W. Norton, 1950.

———. *The Neurotic Personality of Our Time.* New York: W. W. Norton, 1937.

———. *New Ways in Psychoanalysis.* New York: W. W. Norton, 1939.

———. *Our Inner Conflicts.* New York: W. W. Norton, 1945.

———. *Self-Analysis.* New York: W. W. Norton, 1942.

Horstmann, Judith. *Brave New Brain: How Neuroscience, Brain-Machine Interfaces, Psychopharmacology, Epigenetics, the Internet, and Our Own Minds Are Stimulating and Enhancing the Future of Mental Power.* John Wiley and Sons, 2010.

Horwitz, Allan V., and Jerome C. Wakefield. *All We Have to Fear: Psychiatry's Transformation of Natural Anxieties into Mental Disorders.* New York: Oxford University Press, 2012.

———. *The Loss of Sadness: How Psychiatry Transformed Normal Sorrow into Depressive Disorder.* New York: Oxford University Press, 2007.

Huizinga, Johann. *The Waning of the Middle Ages.* 1924. Mineola, N.Y.: Dover Books, 1999.

Hunt, Joseph McVicker, ed. *Personality and the Behavior Disorders: A Handbook Based on Experimental and Clinical Research.* Ronald Press, 1944.

Hunt, Morton. *The Story of Psychology.* New York: Doubleday, 1993.

Hunter, Richard, and Ida Macalpine. *Three Hundred Years of Psychiatry, 1535–1860.* Carlisle Publishing, 1982.

Hustvedt, Siri. *The Shaking Woman; or, A History of My Nerves.* New York: Henry Holt, 2010.

Issroff, Judith, ed. *Donald Winnicott and John Bowlby: Personal and Professional Perspectives.* H. Karnac, 2005.

Izard, Carroll E. *Human Emotions.* Plenum, 1977.

Jackson, Stanley W. *Melancholia and Depression: From Hippocratic Times to Modern Times.* New Haven, Conn.: Yale University Press, 1986.

Jacobson, Edmund. *You Must Relax: A Practical Method for Reducing the Strain of Living.* 1934. Whittsley House, 1942.

James, Oliver. *The Selfish Capitalist.* Vermillion, 2008.

James, William. *Principles of Psychology.* New York: Henry Holt, 1890.

———. *The Varieties of Religious Experience.* Longmans, Green, 1902.

Jamison, Kay Redfield. *An Unquiet Mind: A Memoir of Moods and Madness.* New York: Vintage, 1995.

Janis, Irving L. *Air War and Emotional Stress: Psychological Studies of Bombing and Civilian Defense.* New York: McGraw-Hill, 1951.

Jaspers, Karl. *General Psychopathology.* Vol. 1. Baltimore: Johns Hopkins University Press, 1997.

Jaynes, Julian. *The Origins of Consciousness in the Breakdown of the Bicameral Mind.* New York: Mariner Books, 1990 (original copyright 1976).

Johnson, Haynes. *The Age of Anxiety: From McCarthyism to Terrorism.* Harcourt, 2005.

Jones, Edgar, and Simon Wessely. *Shell Shock to PTSD: Military Psychiatry from 1900 to the Gulf War.* Psychology Press, 2005.

Jordan, Jeanne, and Julie Pederson. *The Panic Diaries: The Frightful, Sometimes Hilarious Truth About Panic Attacks.* Octopus Publishing Group, 2004.

Kagan, Jerome. *An Argument for Mind.* New Haven, Conn.: Yale University Press, 2006.

———. *Galen's Prophecy: Temperament in Human Nature.* New York: Basic Books, 1994.

———. *Psychology's Ghosts: The Crisis in the Profession and the Way Back.* New Haven, Conn.: Yale University Press, 2012.

———. *Unstable Ideas: Temperament, Cognition, and Self.* Cambridge, Mass.: Harvard University Press, 1989.

———. *What Is Emotion?* New Haven, Conn.: Yale University Press, 2007.

Kagan, Jerome, and Nancy Snidman. *The Long Shadow of Temperament.* Cambridge, Mass.: Harvard University Press, 2004.

Kahn, Jeffrey P. *Angst: The Origins of Anxiety and Depression.* Oxford University Press, 2012.

Kardiner, Abram. *The Individual and His Society: The Psychodynamics of Primitive Social Organization.* New York: Columbia University Press, 1939.

Karen, Robert. *Becoming Attached: First Relationships and How They Shape Our Capacity to Love.* Oxford University Press, 1994.

Karp, David A. *Is It Me or My Meds? Living with Antidepressants.* Cambridge, Mass.: Harvard University Press, 2006.

Kasper, Siegfried, Johan A. den Boer, and J. M. Ad Sitsen, eds. *Handbook of Depression and Anxiety.* 2nd ed. Marcel Dekker, 2003.

Kassirer, Jerome P. *On the Take: How Medicine's Complicity with Big Business Can Endanger Your Health.* Oxford University Press, 2005.

Kaster, Robert A. *Emotion, Restraint, and Community in Ancient Rome.* Oxford University Press, 2005.

Kendall, Joshua. *American Obsessives: The Compulsive Energy That Built a Nation.* New York: Grand Central Publishing, 2013.

Kierkegaard, Søren. *The Concept of Anxiety: A Simple Psychologically Orienting Deliberation on the Dogmatic Issue of Hereditary Sin.* Princeton, N.J.: Princeton University Press, 1980.

―――. *Fear and Trembling.* New York: Penguin Books, 1985.

Kirk, Stuart A., and Herb Kutchins. *The Selling of "DSM": The Rhetoric of Science in Psychiatry.* Transaction Publishers, 1992.

Kirsch, Irving. *The Emperor's New Drugs: Exploding the Antidepressant Myth.* New York: Basic Books, 2010.

Klausner, Samuel Z., ed. *Why Man Takes Chances: Studies in Stress-Seeking.* New York: Doubleday Anchor, 1968.

Kleinman, Arthur. *Rethinking Psychiatry: From Cultural Category to Personal Experience.* New York: Free Press, 1988.

Kleinman, Arthur, and Byron Good, eds. *Culture and Depression: Studies in the Anthropology and Cross-Cultural Psychiatry of Affect and Disorder.* Berkeley: University of California Press, 1985.

Kline, Nathan S. *From Sad to Glad: Kline on Depression.* New York: Putnam, 1974.

Kramer, Peter. *Freud: Inventor of the Modern Mind.* Atlas Books/HarperCollins, 2006.

―――. *Listening to Prozac.* Viking, 1993.

Kuijsten, Marcel, ed. *Reflections on the Dawn of Consciousness: Julian Jaynes's Bicameral Mind Theory Revisited.* Julian Jaynes Society, 2006.

Kurzweil, Edith. *The Freudians: A Comparative Perspective.* New Haven, Conn.: Yale University Press, 1989.

Kutchins, Herb, and Stuart A. Kirk. *Making Us Crazy: "DSM"; The Psychiatric Bible and the Creation of Mental Disorders.* New York: Free Press, 1997.

Lane, Christopher. *Shyness: How Normal Behavior Became a Sickness.* New Haven, Conn.: Yale University Press, 2007.

Lasch, Christopher. *The Culture of Narcissism: American Life in an Age of Diminishing Expectations.* New York: Warner Books, 1979.

Last, Cynthia, ed. *Anxiety Across the Lifespan: A Developmental Perspective.* New York: Springer, 1993.

Lazarus, Richard S. *Stress and Emotion: A New Synthesis.* Springer, 1999.

Lazarus, Richard S., and Bernice Lazarus. *Passion and Reason: Making Sense of Our Emotions.* Oxford University Press, 1994.

Leach, John. *Survival Psychology.* Palgrave Macmillan, 1994.

LeDoux, Joseph. *The Emotional Brain: The Mysterious Underpinnings of Emotional Life.* New York: Simon and Schuster, 1996.

LeGoff, Jacques. *Medieval Civilization.* Cambridge, Mass.: Basil Blackwell, 1988 (translated from French edition of 1964).

Levy, David. *Maternal Overprotection.* New York: Columbia University Press, 1943.

Lewis, Marc. *Memoirs of an Addicted Brain: A Neuroscientist Examines His Former Life on Drugs.* Public Affairs, 2012.

Lewis, Nolan. *A Short History of Psychiatric Achievement.* New York: W. W. Norton, 1941.

Lifton, Robert Jay. *The Protean Self: Human Resilience in an Age of Fragmentation.* New York: Basic Books, 1993.

Linton, Ralph, ed. *The Science of Man in the World Crisis.* New York: Oxford University Press, 1945.

Lloyd, G. E. R., ed. *Hippocratic Writings.* London: Penguin Books, 1983.

Lowrie, Walter. *A Short Life of Kierkegaard.* Princeton, N.J.: Princeton University Press, 1942.

Luhrmann, T. M. *Of Two Minds: An Anthropologist Looks at American Psychiatry.* New York: Vintage Books, 2000.

Lutz, Tom. *American Nervousness, 1903: An Anecdotal History.* Ithaca, N.Y.: Cornell University Press, 1991.

MacArthur, John. *Anxiety Attacked: Applying Scripture to the Cares of the Soul.* Victor Books, 1993.

———. *Anxious for Nothing: God's Cure for the Cares of Your Soul.* Colorado Springs, Colo.: Cook Communications Ministries, 2006.

MacDonald, Michael. *Mystical Bedlam: Madness, Anxiety, and Healing in Seventeenth-Century England.* Cambridge University Press, 1981.

Makari, George. *Revolution in Mind: The Creation of Psychoanalysis.* New York: Harper-Collins, 2008.

Malone, John C. *Psychology: Pythagoras to Present.* MIT Press, 2009.

Manchester, William. *Goodbye, Darkness: A Memoir of the Pacific War.* Back Bay Books, 2002.

Mannheim, Karl. *Man and Society in an Age of Reconstruction.* Harcourt, Brace, 1940.

Manning, Martha. *Undercurrents: A Life Beneath the Surface.* New York: Harper-Collins, 1994.

Markel, Howard. *An Anatomy of Addiction: Sigmund Freud, William Halsted, and the Miracle Drug Cocaine.* New York: Pantheon, 2011.

Marks, Isaac M. *Fears, Phobias, and Rituals: Panic, Anxiety, and Their Disorders.* Oxford University Press, 1987.

Markway, Barbara G., Cheryl N. Carmin, C. Alec Pollard, and Teresa Flynn. *Dying of Embarrassment: Help for Social Anxiety and Phobia.* Oakland, Calif.: New Harbinger Publications, 1992.

Markway, Barbara G., and Gregory P. Markway. *Painfully Shy: How to Overcome Social Anxiety and Reclaim Your Life.* New York: St. Martin's Press, 2001.

Marmor, Judd, and Sherwyn M. Woods, eds. *The Interface Between the Psychodynamic and Behavioral Therapies.* New York: Plenum Medical, 1980.

Marshall, John R. *Social Phobia.* New York: Basic Books, 1994.

Maudsley, Henry. *The Pathology of Mind.* D. Appleton, 1860.

Mavissakalian, Matig, and David H. Barlow, eds. *Phobia: Psychological and Pharmacological Treatment.* New York: New York University Press, 1981.

May, Rollo. *The Discovery of Being.* New York: W. W. Norton, 1983.

———. *Love and Will.* New York: W. W. Norton, 1969.

———. *Man's Search for Himself.* New York: W. W. Norton, 1953.

———. *The Meaning of Anxiety.* Rev. ed. New York: W. W. Norton, 1977.

———. *Psychology and the Human Dilemma.* New York: W. W. Norton, 1979.

McEwen, Bruce. *The End of Stress as We Know It.* Washington, D.C.: Joseph Henry Press, 2002.

McGlynn, Thomas J., and Harry L. Metcalf, eds. *Diagnosis and Treatment of Anxiety Disorders: A Physician's Handbook.* American Psychiatric Publishing, 1992.

McKay, Dean, Jonathan S. Abramowitz, Steven Taylor, and Gordon J. G. Asmundson. *Current Perspectives on the Anxiety Disorders: Implications for "DSM-V" and Beyond.* New York: Springer, 2009.

McLean, Peter D., and Sheila R. Woody. *Anxiety Disorder in Adults: An Evidence-Based Approach to Psychological Treatment.* Oxford University Press, 2001.

Menninger, Karl. *The Human Mind.* 3rd ed. New York: Alfred A. Knopf, 1946.

———. *Man Against Himself.* Harcourt, Brace, 1938.

———. *Whatever Became of Sin?* Hawthorn Books, 1973.

Messer, Stanley B., Louis Sass, and Robert Woolfolk. *Hermeneutics and Psychological Theory: Interpretive Perspectives on Personality, Psychotherapy, and Psychopathology.* New Brunswick, N.J.: Rutgers University Press, 1988.

Micale, Mark S. *Hysterical Men: The Hidden History of Male Nervous Illness.* Cambridge, Mass.: Harvard University Press, 2008.

Millon, Theodore. *Masters of the Mind: Exploring the Story of Mental Illness from Ancient Times to the New Millennium.* Hoboken, N.J.: Wiley, 2004.

Mohr, Jay. *Gasping for Airtime: Two Years in the Trenches of "Saturday Night Live."* New York: Hyperion, 2005.

Morita, Shoma. *Morita Therapy and the True Nature of Anxiety-Based Disorders.* Albany: State University of New York Press, 1998.

Morris, Colin. *The Discovery of the Individual, 1050–1200.* Toronto: University of Toronto Press, 1972.

Mumford, Lewis. *The Condition of Man.* Harcourt, Brace, 1944.

Murphy, Gardner. *Historical Introduction to Modern Psychology.* Harcourt, Brace, 1949.

Newman, Paul. *A History of Terror: Fear and Dread Through the Ages.* Sutton Publishing, 2000.

Niebuhr, Reinhold. *The Nature and Destiny of Man.* 2 vols. New York: Scribner, 1941–43.

Northfield, Wilfrid. *Conquest of Nerves: The Inspiring Record of a Personal Triumph over Neurasthenia.* London: Fenland Press, 1933.

Opler, Marvin K. *Culture, Psychiatry, and Human Values: The Methods and Values of a Social Psychiatry.* Charles C. Thomas Publisher, 1956.

Oppenheim, Janet. *"Shattered Nerves": Doctors, Patients, and Depression in Victorian England.* Oxford University Press, 1991.

Parkes, Henry Bamford. *Gods and Men: The Origins of Western Culture.* New York: Alfred A. Knopf, 1959.

Pearson, Patricia. *A Brief History of Anxiety.* Bloomsbury, 2008.

Percy, Walker. *Lancelot.* New York: Farrar, Straus and Giroux, 1977.

———. *The Last Gentleman.* New York: Farrar, Straus and Giroux, 1966.

———. *Lost in the Cosmos: The Last Self-Help Book.* New York: Farrar, Straus and Giroux, 1983.

———. *The Message in the Bottle: How Queer Man Is, How Queer Language Is, and What One Has to Do with the Other.* New York: Farrar, Straus and Giroux, 1975.

———. *The Moviegoer.* New York: Alfred A. Knopf, 1961.

———. *The Second Coming.* New York: Farrar, Straus and Giroux, 1980.

———. *Signposts in a Strange Land.* Picador, 1991.

———. *The Thanatos Syndrome.* New York: Farrar, Straus and Giroux, 1987.

Peurifoy, Reneau. *Anxiety, Phobias, and Panic: A Step-by-Step Program for Regaining Control of Your Life.* New York: Warner Books, 1988.

Pfister, Oscar. *Christianity and Fear: A Study in the History and in the Psychology and Hygiene of Religion.* Unwin Brothers, 1948.

Phillips, Bob. *Overcoming Anxiety and Depression: Practical Tools to Help You Deal with Negative Emotions.* Harvest House, 2007.

Pinero, Jose M. Lopez. *Historical Origins of the Concept of Neurosis.* Cambridge University Press, 1983.

Pinker, Steven. *How the Mind Works.* New York: W. W. Norton, 1997.

Pirenne, Henri. *Medieval Cities.* Princeton, N.J.: Princeton University Press, 1925.

Pollino, Sandra M. *Flying Fear Free: 7 Steps to Relieving Air Travel Anxiety.* New Horizon Press, 2012.

Porter, Roy. *Madness: A Brief History.* New York: Oxford University Press, 2002.

Pressman, Jack D. *Last Resort: Psychosurgery and the Limits of Medicine.* Cambridge University Press, 1998.

Prinz, Jesse J. *Gut Reactions: A Perceptual Theory of Emotion.* Oxford University Press, 2004.

Prochnik, George. *Putnam Camp: Sigmund Freud, James Jackson Putnam, and the Purpose of American Psychology.* Other Press, 2006.

Quammen, David. *The Reluctant Mr. Darwin.* New York: W. W. Norton Books, 2006.

Quinlan, Kieran. *Walker Percy: The Last Catholic Novelist.* Baton Rouge: Louisiana State University Press, 1996.

Quinodoz, Jean-Michel. *The Taming of Solitude: Separation Anxiety in Psychoanalysis.* London: Routledge, 1993.

Rachman, Stanley. *Anxiety.* East Sussex, U.K.: Psychology Press, 1998.

———. *Phobias: Their Nature and Control.* Springfield, Ill.: Charles C. Thomas Publisher, 1968.

Rachman, Stanley, and Padmal de Silva. *Panic Disorder: The Facts.* 2nd ed. New York: Oxford University Press, 2004.

Radden, Jennifer, ed. *The Nature of Melancholy: From Aristotle to Kristeva.* New York: Oxford University Press, 2000.

Radin, Paul. *Primitive Man as Philosopher.* New York: Dover Publications, 1957.

Rank, Otto. *The Trauma of Birth.* New York: Dover Editions, 1993 (original edition 1929).

Rapee, Ronald M. *Overcoming Shyness and Social Phobia.* Rowman and Littlefield, 1998.

Raskin, Marjorie. *The Anxiety Expert: A Psychiatrist's Story of Panic.* AuthorHouse, 2004.

Reich, Wilhelm. *The Mass Psychology of Fascism.* New York: Farrar, Straus and Giroux, 1970.

Reiser, Morton F. *Mind, Brain, Body: Toward a Convergence of Psychoanalysis and Neurobiology.* New York: Basic Books, 1984.

Restak, Richard. *Poe's Heart and the Mountain Climber: Exploring the Effects of Anxiety on Our Brains and Our Culture.* Harmony Books, 2004.

Richardson, Robert D. *William James: In the Maelstrom of American Modernism.* Boston: Houghton Mifflin, 2006.

Riesman, David. *Abundance for What?* Garden City, N.Y.: Doubleday, 1964.

———. *Individualism Reconsidered.* New York: Free Press, 1954.

———. *The Lonely Crowd.* New Haven, Conn.: Yale University Press, 1961.

Roazen, Paul. *Freud and His Followers.* New York: Da Capo Press, 1992.

Robin, Corey. *Fear: The History of a Political Idea.* Oxford: Oxford University Press, 2004.

Roccatagliata, Giuseppe. *A History of Ancient Psychiatry.* New York: Greenwood Press, 1986.

Roche Laboratories. *Aspects of Anxiety.* J. B. Lippincott, 1965.

Rorty, Amelie Oskenberg, ed. *Explaining Emotions.* Berkeley: University of California Press, 1980.

Rosenberg, Charles E., and Janet Golden, eds. *Framing Disease: Studies in Cultural History.* New Brunswick, N.J.: Rutgers University Press, 1997.

Rousseau, G. S., and Roy Porter, eds. *The Ferment of Knowledge: Studies in the Historiography of Eighteenth-Century Science.* Cambridge University Press, 1980.

Rycroft, Charles. *Anxiety and Neurosis.* Middlesex, U.K.: Penguin Books, 1968.

Rygh, Jayne L., and William G. Sanderson. *Treating Generalized Anxiety Disorder: Evidence-Based Strategies, Tools, and Techniques.* Guilford Press, 2004.

Salecl, Renata. *On Anxiety.* London: Routledge, 2004.

Samway, Patrick. *Walker Percy: A Life.* Loyola Press, 1999.

Sapolsky, Robert M. *Monkeyluv and Other Essays on Our Lives as Animals.* New York: Scribner, 2005.

———. *Why Zebras Don't Get Ulcers.* New York: Henry Holt, 2004.

Sarason, Irwin, and Charles Spielberger, eds. *Stress and Anxiety.* Vols. 2, 4, and 5. Washington, D.C.: Hemisphere Publishing, 1975–78.

Satel, Sally, and Scott O. Lilienfeld. *Brainwashed: How We Are Seduced by Mindless Neuroscience.* New York: Basic Books, 2013.

Saul, Helen. *Phobias: Fighting the Fear.* New York: Arcade, 2002.

Schlesinger, Arthur M., Jr. *The Cycles of American History.* Boston: Houghton Mifflin, 1986.

———. *The Vital Center: The Politics of Freedom.* Riverhead Press, 1949.

Schneier, Franklin, and Lawrence Welkowitz. *The Hidden Face of Shyness: Understanding and Overcoming Social Anxiety.* New York: Avon Books, 1996.

Schreber, Daniel Paul. *Memoirs of My Nervous Illness.* New York Review of Books, 2000.

Schuster, David G. *Neurasthenic Nation: America's Search for Health, Happiness, and Comfort, 1869–1920.* New Brunswick, N.J.: Rutgers University Press, 2011.

Schwartz, Barry. *The Paradox of Choice: Why More Is Less.* HarperPerennial, 2004.

Seeley, Karen M. *Therapy After Terror: 9/11, Psychotherapy, and Mental Health.* Cambridge University Press, 2008.

Selye, Hans. *The Physiology and Pathology of Exposure to Stress: A Treatise Based on the Concepts of the General Adaptation Syndrome and the Diseases of Adaptation.* Acta, 1950.

————. *The Stress of Life.* New York: McGraw-Hill, 1956.

————. *Stress Without Distress.* Signet, 1974.

Shapiro, David. *Neurotic Styles.* New York: Basic Books, 1965.

Sharpe, Katherine. *Coming of Age on Zoloft: How Antidepressants Cheered Us Up, Let Us Down, and Changed Who We Are.* HarperPerennial, 2012.

Shawn, Allan. *Wish I Could Be There: Notes from a Phobic Life.* Viking, 2007.

Shay, Jonathan. *Achilles in Vietnam: Combat Trauma and the Undoing of Character.* New York: Scribner, 1994.

Sheehan, David V. *The Anxiety Disease.* New York: Bantam Books, 1983.

Shephard, Ben. *War of Nerves: Soldiers and Psychiatrists in the Twentieth Century.* Cambridge, Mass.: Harvard University Press, 2001.

Shinder, Jason, ed. *Tales from the Couch: Writers on Therapy.* New York: William Morrow, 2000.

Shorter, Edward. *Before Prozac: The Troubled History of Mood Disorders in Psychiatry.* New York: Oxford University Press, 2009.

————. *A History of Psychiatry: From the Age of the Asylum to the Age of Prozac.* New York: Wiley, 1997.

————. *How Everyone Became Depressed: The Rise and Fall of the Nervous Breakdown.* Oxford University Press, 2013.

Shute, Clarence. *The Psychology of Aristotle: An Analysis of the Living Being.* New York: Russell and Russell, 1964.

Simon, Bennett. *Mind and Madness in Ancient Greece: The Classical Roots of Modern Psychiatry.* Ithaca, N.Y.: Cornell University Press, 1978.

Simon, Linda. *Genuine Reality: A Life of William James.* Harcourt, Brace, 1997.

Slater, Lauren. *Prozac Diary.* New York: Random House, 1998.

Smail, Daniel Lord. *On Deep History and the Brain.* Berkeley: University of California Press, 2008.

Smith, Daniel. *Monkey Mind: A Memoir of Anxiety.* New York: Simon & Schuster, 2012.

Smith, Mickey C. *Small Comfort: A History of the Minor Tranquilizers.* Praeger, 1985.

Smoller, Jordan, *The Other Side of Normal: How Biology Is Providing the Clues to Unlock the Secrets of Normal and Abnormal Behavior.* New York: William Morrow, 2012.

Snell, Bruno. *The Discovery of Mind in Greek Philosophy and Literature.* New York: Dover Publications, 1982 (first published 1953).

Solomon, Andrew. *The Noonday Demon: An Atlas of Depression.* New York: Scribner, 2001.

Solomon, Robert. *What Is an Emotion? Classic and Contemporary Readings.* New York: Oxford University Press, 1984.

Spielberger, Charles D., ed. *Anxiety: Current Trends in Theory and Research.* Vol. 1. Academic Press, 1972.

———, ed. *Anxiety and Behavior.* Academic Press, 1966.

———. *Understanding Stress and Anxiety.* New York: Harper and Row, 1979.

Spielberger, Charles D., and Rogelio Diaz-Guerrero, eds. *Cross-Cultural Anxiety.* Vol. 3. Hemisphere Publishing, 1986.

Spinoza, Baruch. *Ethics: Treatise on the Emendation of the Intellect.* Hackett Publishing, 1992.

Stein, Dan J. *Clinical Manual of Anxiety Disorders.* Washington, D.C.: American Psychiatric Publishing, 2004.

Stein, Dan J., and Eric Hollander. *Anxiety Disorders Comorbid with Depression: Social Anxiety Disorder, Post-traumatic Stress Disorder, Generalized Anxiety Disorder and Obsessive Compulsive Disorder.* Martin Dunitz, 2002.

———. *Textbook of Anxiety Disorders.* Washington, D.C.: American Psychiatric Publishing, 2002.

Stein, Murray B., and John R. Walker. *Triumph over Shyness: Conquering Shyness and Social Anxiety.* McGraw-Hill, 2002.

Stekel, W. *Conditions of Nervous Anxiety and Their Treatment.* New York: Dodd, Mead, 1923.

Stepansky, Paul E. *Psychoanalysis at the Margins.* New York: Other Press, 2009.

Stone, Michael. *Healing the Mind: A History of Psychiatry from Antiquity to the Present.* New York: W. W. Norton, 1997.

Stoodley, Bartlett H. *The Concepts of Sigmund Freud.* Glencoe, Ill.: Free Press, 1959.

Strupp, Hans H., Leonard M. Horowitz, and Michael J. Lambert, eds. *Measuring Patient Changes in Mood, Anxiety, and Personality Disorders.* American Psychological Association, 1997.

Sullivan, Paul. *Clutch: Why Some People Excel Under Pressure and Others Don't.* New York: Penguin Books, 2010.

Sulloway, Frank. *Freud, Biologist of the Mind.* Cambridge, Mass.: Harvard University Press, 1979.

Summers, Christina Hoff, and Sally Satel. *One Nation Under Therapy: How the Helping Culture Is Eroding Self-Reliance.* New York: St. Martin's Press, 2005.

Symonds, Percival M. *The Dynamics of Human Adjustment.* New York: Apple-Century-Crofts, 1946.

Szasz, Thomas S. *The Myth of Mental Illness.* New York: HarperPerennial, 1974.

Tallis, Raymond. *The Kingdom of Infinite Space: A Portrait of Your Head.* New Haven, Conn.: Yale University Press, 2008.

Tanielian, Terri, and Lisa H. Jaycox, eds. *Invisible Wounds of War: Psychological and Cognitive Injuries, Their Consequences, and Services to Assist Recovery.* RAND, 2008.

Taylor Manor Hospital, *Discoveries in Biological Psychiatry.* Lippincott, 1970.

Taylor, Steven, ed. *Anxiety Sensitivity: Theory, Research, and Treatment of the Fear of Anxiety.* Mahwah, New Jersey: Lawrence Erlbaum Associates, 1999.

Thomson, Keith. *The Young Charles Darwin.* New Haven, Conn: Yale University Press, 2009.

Tillich, Paul. *The Courage to Be.* New Haven, Conn.: Yale University Press, 1952.

———. *A Theology of Culture.* Oxford University Press, 1959.

Tolson, Jay, ed. *The Correspondence of Shelby Foote and Walker Percy.* New York: W. W. Norton, 1997.

————. *Pilgrim in the Ruins: A Life of Walker Percy.* New York: Simon & Schuster, 1992.

Tone, Andrea. *The Age of Anxiety: A History of America's Turbulent Affair with Tranquilizers.* New York: Basic Books, 2009.

Torrey, E. Fuller, and Judy Miller. *The Invisible Plague: The Rise of Mental Illness from 1750 to the Present.* New Brunswick, N.J.: Rutgers University Press, 2001.

Tseng, Wen-Shing. *Clinician's Guide to Cultural Psychiatry.* Academic Press, 2003.

Tuan, Yi-Fu. *Landscapes of Fear.* New York: Pantheon Books, 1979.

Twenge, Jean M. *Generation Me: Why Today's Young Americans Are More Confident, Assertive, Entitled—and More Miserable Than Ever Before.* New York: Free Press, 2006.

Valenstein, Elliot S. *Blaming the Brain: The Truth About Drugs and Mental Health.* New York: Free Press, 1998.

van den Berg, J. H. *The Changing Nature of Man: Introduction to Historical Psychology.* New York: W. W. Norton, 1961.

Vasey, Michael M., and Mark R. Dadds, eds. *The Developmental Psychopathology of Anxiety.* Oxford University Press, 2001.

Wain, Martin. *Freud's Answer: The Social Origins of Our Psychoanalytic Century.* Ivan R. Dee, 1998.

Wallin, David. *Attachment in Psychotherapy.* New York: Guilford Press, 2007.

Watt, Margo, and Sherry Stewart. *Overcoming the Fear of Fear: How to Reduce Anxiety Sensitivity.* Oakland, Calif.: New Harbinger, 2008.

Watters, Ethan. *Crazy Like Us: The Globalization of the American Psyche.* New York: Free Press, 2010.

Weatherhead, Leslie D. *Prescription for Anxiety: How You Can Overcome Fear and Despair.* Pierce and Washabaugh, 1956.

Weekes, Claire. *Hope and Help for Your Nerves.* Signet, 1969.

Wehrenberg, Margaret, and Steven Prinz. *The Anxious Brain: The Neurological Basis of Anxiety Disorders and How to Effectively Treat Them.* New York: W. W. Norton, 2007.

Wellman, Lee. *My Quarter-Life Crisis: How an Anxiety Disorder Knocked Me Down, and How I Got Back Up.* Tuckett Publishing, 2006.

Wender, Paul H., and Donald F. Klein. *Mind, Mood, and Medicine: A Guide to the New Biopsychiatry.* New York: Farrar, Straus and Giroux, 1981.

Wexler, Bruce E. *Brain and Culture: Neurobiology, Ideology, and Social Change.* Cambridge, Mass.: MIT Press, 2006.

Whitaker, Robert. *Anatomy of an Epidemic: Magic Bullets, Psychiatric Drugs, and the Astonishing Rise of Mental Illness in America.* New York: Crown, 2010.

Wilkinson, Richard, and Kate Pickett. *The Spirit Level: Why Greater Equality Makes Societies Stronger.* London: Bloomsbury, 2010.

Winik, Jay. *The Great Upheaval: America and the Birth of the Modern World, 1788–1800.* New York: HarperCollins, 2007.

Wolf, Stewart, and Harold Wolff. *Human Gastric Function: An Experimental Study of Man and His Stomach.* New York: Oxford University Press, 1943.

Wolfe, Barry E. *Understanding and Treating Anxiety Disorders.* American Psychological Association, 2005.

Wood, Gordon. *The Radicalism of the American Revolution.* New York: Random House, 1991.

Wullschlager, Jackie. *Hans Christian Andersen: The Life of a Storyteller.* New York: Penguin Books, 2000.

Wurtzel, Elizabeth. *Prozac Nation.* Houghton Mifflin, 1994.

Yapko, Michael D. *Depression Is Contagious: How the Most Common Mood Disorder Is Spreading Around the World and How to Stop It.* New York: Free Press, 2009.

Young, Allan. *The Harmony of Illusions: Inventing Post-traumatic Stress Disorder.* Princeton, N.J.: Princeton University Press, 1995.

Young-Bruehl, Elisabeth. *Anna Freud.* 2nd ed. New Haven, Conn.: Yale University Press, 2008.

Zane, Manuel D., and Harry Milt. *Your Phobia: Understanding Your Fears Through Contextual Therapy.* American Psychiatric Press, 1984.

Zeman, Adam. *A Portrait of the Brain.* New Haven, Conn.: Yale University Press, 2008.

Zilboorg, Gregory. *A History of Medical Psychology.* New York: W. W. Norton, 1941.

Zolli, Andrew, and Ann Marie Healy. *Resilience: Why Things Bounce Back.* New York: Free Press, 2012.

# Index

A NOTE ON THE TYPE

This book was set in a modern adaptation of a type designed by the first William Caslon (1692–1766). The Caslon face, an artistic, easily read type, has enjoyed more than two centuries of popularity in the United States. It is of interest to note that the first copies of the Declaration of Independence and the first paper currency distributed to the citizens of the newborn nation were printed in this typeface.


Typeset by Scribe,
Philadelphia, Pennsylvania